STATUTES

European Community Legislation

Second Edition (revised and updated by D G Cracknell
LLB, of the Middle Temple, Barrister)

SERIES EDITOR: D G CRACKNELL
EDITOR: ROBERT M MACLEAN
LLB (Hons), Dip LP, LLM, PhD, Solicitor

OLD BAILEY PRESS

OLD BAILEY PRESS
200 Greyhound Road, London W14 9RY

First published 1994
Second edition 1997
Reprinted 1998

© Old Bailey Press Ltd 1997

All Old Bailey Press publications enjoy copyright protection and the copyright belongs to the Old Bailey Press Ltd

All rights reserved. No part of this publication may be reproduced or transmitted in any form or by any means, electronic, mechanical, photocopying, recording or otherwise, or stored in any retrieval system of any nature without either the written permission of the copyright holder, application for which should be made to the Old Bailey Press Ltd, or a licence permitting restricted copying in the United Kingdom issued by the Copyright Licensing Agency.

Any person who infringes the above in relation to this publication may be liable to criminal prosecution and civil claims for damages.

ISBN 1 85836 085 4

British Library Cataloguing-in-Publication.

A CIP Catalogue record for this book is available from the British Library.

Printed and bound in Great Britain.

CONTENTS

Preface	v
Alphabetical Table of Treaties, Statutes, etc	vii

Treaties, etc

Treaty Establishing the European Coal and Steel Community	1–18
Treaty Establishing the European Community	19–210
Protocol on the Statute of the Court of Justice of the European Communities	160–174
Protocol on the Statute of the European System of Central Banks and of the European Central Bank	174–197
Protocol on the Excessive Deficit Procedure	198–199
Protocol on the Convergence Criteria Referred to in Article 109j of the Treaty Establishing the European Community	199–200
Protocol on the Transition to the Third Stage of Economic and Monetary Union	200–201
Protocol on Certain Provisions Relating to the United Kingdom of Great Britain and Northern Ireland	201–203
Protocol on Social Policy (and Agreement Annexed)	203–208
Protocol on Economic and Social Cohesion	208–210
Treaty Establishing a Single Council and a Single Commission of the European Communities	211–221
Protocol on the Privileges and Immunities of the European Communities	214–221
Luxembourg Accords	222–224

Contents

Act Concerning the Election of the Representatives of the European Parliament by Direct Universal Suffrage	225–229
Fundamental Rights: Joint Declaration by the European Parliament, the Council and the Commission	230
Council Decision Laying Down the Procedures for the Exercise of Implementing Powers Conferred on the Commission	231–235
Council Decision Establishing a Court of First Instance of the European Communities	236–240
Treaty on European Union	241–263
Agreement on the European Economic Area	264–311
Council Decision Concerning the Name to Be Given to the Council Following the Entry into Force of the Treaty on European Union	312
Decision of the European Parliament on the Regulations and General Conditions Governing the Performance of the Ombudsman's Duties	313–320
Council Decision on the Taking of Decisions by a Qualified Majority of the Council	321
Council Decision on the System of the European Communities' Own Resources	322–331
Council Decision Determining the Order in Which the Office of President of the Council Shall Be Held	332–333
Commission Memorandum on Applying Article 171 of the EC Treaty	334–337

United Kingdom Statutes

European Communities Act 1972	338–350
European Parliamentary Elections Act 1978	351–358
European Communities (Amendment) Act 1986	359–360
European Communities (Amendment) Act 1993	361–362
European Parliamentary Elections Act 1993	363–365
European Economic Area Act 1993	366–369

Appendix

Draft Treaty of Amsterdam	373–451
Index	453–455

PREFACE

AS the law of the European Union has become increasingly complex, it is now more important than ever to be able to refer to a source of the basic constitutional documents of the organisation. The goal of this book is to set down the primary treaties and decisions of constitutional importance to the functioning of the European Union, together with the most significant UK statutes which regulate the relationship between the European Union and the United Kingdom.

The EC Treaty, as amended most recently by the Treaty on European Union and the Treaty of Accession for Austria, Finland and Sweden, is set out along with protocols originally agreed and those added by the Treaty on European Union. In addition, the TEU itself is reproduced along with the Agreement on the European Economic Area.

Council Decisions have, especially recently, played an increasingly important role in the constitutional legal order of the EU/EC. Decisions relating to the taking of Decisions by a qualified majority of the Council and determining the order in which the office of President of the Council shall be held have been added in this edition. Also included are the Decision of the European Parliament on the performance of the Ombudsman's duties and the Commission memorandum on applying Article 171 of the EC Treaty.

Six United Kingdom statutes are also included, starting from the European Communities Act 1972 which remains the principal link between the United Kingdom and the EU/EC. Amending legislation has been added directly to the text of the original statute contained in this book and only later statutes with significant residual sections have been included to avoid repetition of material.

This book contains materials available as at 1 July 1997, and all measures contained herein are presently in force. However, the legally-binding Treaty texts set out in the draft Treaty of Amsterdam are included in the Appendix. Subject to final editing and harmonisation of the texts, it is expected that this Treaty will be signed at Amsterdam in October 1997.

ALPHABETICAL TABLE OF TREATIES, STATUTES, ETC

Act Concerning the Election of the Representatives of the European Parliament by Direct Universal Suffrage 225–229
    Article 1   *225*
    Article 2   *225–226*
    Article 3   *226*
    Article 4   *226*
    Article 5   *226–227*
    Article 7   *227*
    Article 8   *227*
    Article 9   *227–228*
    Article 10   *228*
    Article 11   *228*
    Article 12   *228–229*
    Article 13   *229*
    Article 14   *229*
    Article 15   *229*
    Article 16   *229*

Agreement on the European Economic Area 264–311
    Article 1   *266*
    Article 2   *266–267*
    Article 3   *267*
    Article 4   *267*
    Article 5   *267*
    Article 6   *267–268*
    Article 7   *268*
    Article 8   *268*
    Article 9   *269*
    Article 10   *269*
    Article 11   *269*
    Article 12   *269*
    Article 13   *269*
    Article 14   *270*
    Article 15   *270*

Agreement on the European Economic Area (*contd.*)
    Article 16   *270*
    Article 17   *270*
    Article 18   *270–271*
    Article 19   *271*
    Article 20   *271*
    Article 21   *271–272*
    Article 22   *272*
    Article 23   *272*
    Article 24   *272*
    Article 25   *272–273*
    Article 26   *273*
    Article 27   *273*
    Article 28   *273–274*
    Article 29   *274*
    Article 30   *274*
    Article 31   *275*
    Article 32   *275*
    Article 33   *275*
    Article 34   *275–276*
    Article 35   *276*
    Article 36   *276*
    Article 37   *276–277*
    Article 38   *277*
    Article 39   *277*
    Article 40   *277*
    Article 41   *277*
    Article 42   *277*
    Article 43   *278*
    Article 44   *278*
    Article 45   *278–279*
    Article 46   *279*
    Article 47   *279*
    Article 48   *279–280*
    Article 49   *280*

Alphabetical Table of Treaties, Statutes, etc

Agreement on the European Economic Area (contd.)
Article 50	280
Article 51	280
Article 52	281
Article 53	281–282
Article 54	282
Article 55	282–283
Article 56	283
Article 57	284
Article 58	284
Article 59	284–285
Article 60	285
Article 61	285–286
Article 62	286
Article 63	286
Article 64	286–287
Article 65	287
Article 66	287
Article 67	288
Article 68	288
Article 69	288
Article 70	288
Article 71	289
Article 72	289
Article 73	289
Article 74	289
Article 75	289
Article 76	290
Article 77	290
Article 78	290–291
Article 79	291
Article 80	291
Article 81	292
Article 82	292–293
Article 83	293
Article 84	294
Article 85	294
Article 86	294
Article 87	294
Article 88	294
Article 89	295
Article 90	295
Article 91	295–296
Article 92	296

Agreement on the European Economic Area (contd.)
Article 93	296
Article 94	296–297
Article 95	297
Article 96	297–298
Article 97	298
Article 98	298
Article 99	298–299
Article 100	299
Article 101	299
Article 102	300–301
Article 103	301
Article 104	301
Article 105	301–302
Article 106	302
Article 107	302
Article 108	303
Article 109	303–304
Article 110	304
Article 111	304–305
Article 112	305–306
Article 113	306
Article 114	306–307
Article 115	307
Article 116	307
Article 117	307
Article 118	307–308
Article 119	308
Article 120	308
Article 121	308
Article 122	308–309
Article 123	309
Article 124	309
Article 125	309
Article 126	309–310
Article 127	310
Article 128	310–311
Article 129	311

Commission Memorandum on Applying Article 171 of the EC Treaty   334–337
Council Decision Concerning the Name to Be Given to the Council Following the Entry into Force of the Treaty on European Union   312

Council Decision Determining the Order in
Which the Office of the Council Shall Be
Held   332–333
   Article 1   332–333
   Article 2   333
Council Decision Establishing a Court of
First Instance of the European
Communities   236–240
   Article 1   237
   Article 2   237–238
   Article 3   238
   Article 4   238–239
   Article 10   239
   Article 11   239
   Article 12   239
   Article 13   239
   Article 14   240
Council Decision Laying Down the
Procedures for the Exercise of
Implementing Powers Conferred on the
Commission   231–235
   Article 1   231–232
   Article 2   232–234
   Article 3   234
   Article 4   234–235
   Article 5   235
Council Decision on the System of the
European Communities' Own Resources
322–331
   Article 1   324
   Article 2   324–326
   Article 3   326
   Article 4   327–328
   Article 5   328
   Article 6   328
   Article 7   329
   Article 8   329
   Article 9   329–330
   Article 10   330
   Article 11   330–331
Council Decision on the Taking of Decisions
by a Qualified Majority of the Council
321

Decision of the European Parliament on the
Regulations and General Conditions
Governing the Performance of the
Ombudsman's Duties   313–320

Decision of the European Parliament on the
Regulations and General Conditions
Governing the Performance of the
Ombudsman's Duties (contd.)
   Article 1   315
   Article 2   315–316
   Article 3   316–317
   Article 4   317–318
   Article 5   318
   Article 6   318
   Article 7   318
   Article 8   319
   Article 9   319
   Article 10   319
   Article 13   319
   Article 14   320
   Article 15   320
   Article 17   320

European Communites Act 1972
338–350
   s1   338–339
   s2   340–341
   s3   341–342
   s4   342–343
   s5   343–344
   s6   344–346
   s11   346–347
   Schedule 1, Part I   347–348
   Schedule 1, Part II   348
   Schedule 2   349–350
European Communities (Amendment) Act
1986   359–360
   s3   359
   s4   360
European Communities (Amendment) Act
1993   361–362
   s1   361
   s2   361
   s3   361
   s4   362
   s5   362
   s6   362
   s7   362
European Economic Area Act 1993
366–369

European Economic Area Act 1993 (contd.)
   s2   366–367
   s3   367–368
   s4   368
   s5   368–369
   s6   369
European Parliamentary Elections Act 1978   351–358
   s1   351
   s2   351
   s3   351
   s4   351–352
   s6   352
   s7   352
   s8   353
   s9   353
   Schedule 1   353–358
European Parliamentary Elections Act 1993   363–365
   s2   363–364
   Schedule, Part I   364
   Schedule, Part II   364–365

Fundamental Rights: Joint Declaration by the European Parliament, the Council and the Commission   230

Luxembourg Accords   222–224

Treaty Establishing a Single Council and a Single Commission of the European Communities   211–221
   Article 1   212
   Article 9   212
   Article 24   212–213
   Article 28   213
   Article 30   213
   Article 38   213
   Article 39   213
   Protocol on the Privileges and Immunities of the European Communities   214–221
      Article 1   214
      Article 2   214
      Article 3   215
      Article 4   215

Treaty Establishing a Single Council and a Single Commission of the European Communities, Protocol on the Privileges and Immunities of the European Communities (contd.)
      Article 5   215
      Article 6   215–216
      Article 7   216
      Article 8   216
      Article 9   217
      Article 10   217
      Article 11   217
      Article 12   218
      Article 13   218–219
      Article 14   219
      Article 15   219
      Article 16   219–220
      Article 17   220
      Article 18   220
      Article 19   220
      Article 20   220
      Article 21   220–221
      Article 22   221
      Article 23   221
Treaty Establishing the European Coal and Steel Community   1–18
   Article 1   2
   Article 2   2
   Article 3   2–3
   Article 4   3
   Article 5   3–4
   Article 6   4
   Article 7   4
   Article 57   5
   Article 58   5
   Article 59   5–7
   Article 60   7–8
   Article 61   8–9
   Article 62   9
   Article 63   9–10
   Article 64   10
   Article 65   10–11
   Article 66   12–15
   Article 67   15
   Article 71   16

Treaty Establishing the European Coal and
   Steel Community (*contd.*)
     Article 72   *16*
     Article 73   *16*
     Article 74   *17*
     Article 75   *17*
     Article 97   *17*
     Article 99   *18*
     Article 100 *18*
Treaty Establishing the European
   Community *19–210*
     Article 1   *20*
     Article 2   *20*
     Article 3   *20–21*
     Article 3a *21*
     Article 3b *22*
     Article 4   *22*
     Article 4a *22*
     Article 4b *22–23*
     Article 5   *23*
     Article 6   *23*
     Article 7   *23–24*
     Article 7a *24*
     Article 7b *25*
     Article 7c *25*
     Article 8   *25*
     Article 8a *25*
     Article 8b *26*
     Article 8c *26*
     Article 8d *26*
     Article 8e *26–27*
     Article 9   *27*
     Article 10 *27–28*
     Article 11 *28*
     Article 12 *28*
     Article 13 *28*
     Article 14 *28–29*
     Article 15 *30*
     Article 16 *30*
     Article 17 *30*
     Article 18 *31*
     Article 19 *31–32*
     Article 20 *32*
     Article 21 *32*
     Article 22 *32–33*

Treaty Establishing the European
   Community (*contd.*)
     Article 23 *33*
     Article 24 *33*
     Article 25 *34*
     Article 26 *34*
     Article 27 *35*
     Article 28 *35*
     Article 29 *35*
     Article 30 *35*
     Article 31 *36*
     Article 32 *36*
     Article 33 *36–37*
     Article 34 *38*
     Article 35 *38*
     Article 36 *38*
     Article 37 *38–39*
     Article 38 *39–40*
     Article 39 *40*
     Article 40 *40–41*
     Article 41 *41*
     Article 42 *41*
     Article 43 *42*
     Article 44 *42–44*
     Article 45 *44–45*
     Article 46 *45*
     Article 47 *45*
     Article 48 *46*
     Article 49 *46–47*
     Article 50 *47*
     Article 51 *47*
     Article 52 *47–48*
     Article 53 *48*
     Article 54 *48–49*
     Article 55 *49*
     Article 56 *49–50*
     Article 57 *50*
     Article 58 *50*
     Article 59 *51*
     Article 60 *51*
     Article 61 *51*
     Article 62 *52*
     Article 63 *52*
     Article 64 *52*
     Article 65 *52–53*

Treaty Establishing the European
    Community (*contd.*)
    Article 66   53
    Article 73a   53
    Article 73b   53
    Article 73c   53–54
    Article 73d   54
    Article 73e   54
    Article 73f   54
    Article 73g   55
    Article 74   55
    Article 75   55–56
    Article 76   56
    Article 77   56
    Article 78   56
    Article 79   56–57
    Article 80   57
    Article 81   57–58
    Article 82   58
    Article 83   58
    Article 84   58
    Article 85   58–59
    Article 86   59–60
    Article 87   60
    Article 88   60–61
    Article 89   61
    Article 90   61
    Article 91   62
    Article 92   62–63
    Article 93   63–64
    Article 94   64
    Article 95   64–65
    Article 96   65
    Article 97   65
    Article 98   65
    Article 99   65
    Article 100   66
    Article 100a   66–67
    Article 100b   67
    Article 100c   67–68
    Article 100d   68
    Article 101   68
    Article 102   68–69
    Article 102a   69
    Article 103   69–70

Treaty Establishing the European
    Community (*contd.*)
    Article 103a   70
    Article 104   71
    Article 104a   71
    Article 104b   71
    Article 104c   72–74
    Article 105   74–75
    Article 150a   75
    Article 106   75–76
    Article 107   76
    Article 108   76
    Article 108a   76–77
    Article 109   77–78
    Article 109a   78–79
    Article 109b   79
    Article 109c   79–81
    Article 109d   81
    Article 109e   81–82
    Article 109f   82–84
    Article 109g   84
    Article 109h   84–85
    Article 109i   85
    Article 109j   86–87
    Article 109k   87–88
    Article 109l   88–89
    Article 109m   89
    Article 110   90
    Article 112   90
    Article 113   90–91
    Article 115   91
    Article 117   91–92
    Article 118   92
    Article 118a   92–93
    Article 118b   93
    Article 119   93
    Article 120   93
    Article 121   93
    Article 122   94
    Article 123   94
    Article 124   94
    Article 125   94
    Article 126   95
    Article 127   95–96
    Article 128   96–97

Treaty Establishing the European
Community (*contd.*)
   Article 129   *97–98*
   Article 129a   *98*
   Article 129b   *98*
   Article 129c   *99*
   Article 129d   *99–100*
   Article 130   *100*
   Article 130a   *100–101*
   Article 130b   *101*
   Article 130c   *101*
   Article 130d   *101–102*
   Article 130e   *102*
   Article 130f   *102*
   Article 130g   *103*
   Article 130h   *103*
   Article 130i   *103–104*
   Article 130j   *104*
   Article 130k   *104*
   Article 130l   *104*
   Article 130m   *105*
   Article 130n   *105*
   Article 130o   *105*
   Article 130p   *105*
   Article 130r   *105–106*
   Article 130s   *106–107*
   Article 130t   *107–108*
   Article 130u   *108*
   Article 130v   *108*
   Article 130w   *108–109*
   Article 130x   *109*
   Article 130y   *109*
   Article 131   *109–110*
   Article 132   *110*
   Article 133   *110–111*
   Article 134   *111*
   Article 135   *111*
   Article 136   *111–112*
   Article 136a   *112*
   Article 137   *112*
   Article 138   *112*
   Article 138a   *113*
   Article 138b   *113*
   Article 138c   *113*
   Article 138d   *113*

Treaty Establishing the European
Community (*contd.*)
   Article 138e   *114*
   Article 139   *114–115*
   Article 140   *115*
   Article 141   *115*
   Article 142   *115*
   Article 143   *115*
   Article 144   *115–116*
   Article 145   *116*
   Article 146   *116*
   Article 147   *117*
   Article 148   *117*
   Article 150   *117*
   Article 151   *118*
   Article 152   *118*
   Article 153   *118*
   Article 154   *118*
   Article 155   *118–119*
   Article 156   *119*
   Article 157   *119–120*
   Article 158   *120*
   Article 159   *120–121*
   Article 160   *121*
   Article 161   *121*
   Article 162   *121*
   Article 163   *121*
   Article 164   *122*
   Article 165   *122*
   Article 166   *122*
   Article 167   *122–123*
   Article 168   *123*
   Article 168a   *123–124*
   Article 169   *124*
   Article 170   *124*
   Article 171   *124–125*
   Article 172   *125*
   Article 173   *125–126*
   Article 174   *126*
   Article 175   *126*
   Article 176   *126–127*
   Article 177   *127*
   Article 178   *127*
   Article 179   *127*
   Article 180   *127–128*

Alphabetical Table of Treaties, Statutes, etc

Treaty Establishing the European
  Community (*contd.*)
  Article 181   *128*
  Article 182   *128*
  Article 183   *128*
  Article 184   *129*
  Article 185   *129*
  Article 186   *129*
  Article 187   *129*
  Article 188   *129*
  Article 188a   *129*
  Article 188b   *130–131*
  Article 188c   *131–132*
  Article 189   *132*
  Article 189a   *132–133*
  Article 189b   *133–134*
  Article 189c   *135–136*
  Article 190   *136*
  Article 191   *136*
  Article 192   *136–137*
  Article 193   *137*
  Article 194   *137–138*
  Article 195   *138*
  Article 196   *138*
  Article 197   *138–139*
  Article 198   *139*
  Article 198a   *139–140*
  Article 198b   *140*
  Article 198c   *140*
  Article 198d   *141*
  Article 198e   *141*
  Article 199   *142*
  Article 201   *142*
  Article 201a   *142*
  Article 202   *142–143*
  Article 203   *143–146*
  Article 204   *146*
  Article 205   *147*
  Article 2005a   *147*
  Article 206   *147–148*
  Article 207   *148*
  Article 208   *148*
  Article 209   *149*
  Article 209a   *149*
  Article 210   *149*

Treaty Establishing the European
  Community (*contd.*)
  Article 211   *149–150*
  Article 213   *150*
  Article 214   *150*
  Article 215   *150*
  Article 216   *150*
  Article 217   *151*
  Article 219   *151*
  Article 220   *151*
  Article 221   *151*
  Article 222   *151*
  Article 223   *152*
  Article 224   *152*
  Article 225   *152*
  Article 226   *153*
  Article 227   *153–154*
  Article 228   *154–156*
  Article 228a   *156*
  Article 229   *156*
  Article 230   *156*
  Article 231   *156*
  Article 232   *156–157*
  Article 233   *157*
  Article 234   *157*
  Article 235   *157*
  Article 238   *157*
  Article 239   *158*
  Article 240   *158*
  Article 241   *158*
  Article 242   *158*
  Article 243   *158*
  Article 244   *158*
  Article 245   *159*
  Article 246   *159*
  Article 247   *159*
  Article 248   *159*
  Protocol on Certain Provisions Relating
    to the United Kingdom of Great
    Britain and Northern Ireland
    201–203
  Protocol on Economic and Social
    Cohesion   *208–210*
  Protocol on Social Policy   *203–208*
    Agreement on Social Policy
      204–208

Treaty Establishing the European
Community, Protocol on Social Policy
(contd.)
    Article 1   *205*
    Article 2   *205–206*
    Article 3   *206*
    Article 4   *207*
    Article 5   *207*
    Article 6   *207*
    Article 7   *208*
Protocol on the Convergence Criteria
Referred to in Article 109j of the
Treaty Establishing the European
Community   *199–200*
    Article 1   *199*
    Article 2   *199*
    Article 3   *200*
    Article 4   *200*
    Article 5   *200*
    Article 6   *200*
Protocol on the Excessive Debt
Procedure   *198–199*
    Article 1   *198*
    Article 2   *198*
    Article 3   *198–199*
    Article 4   *199*
Protocol on the Statute of the Court of
Justice of the European
Communities   *160–174*
    Article 1   *160*
    Article 2   *160*
    Article 3   *161*
    Article 4   *161*
    Article 5   *161*
    Article 6   *161–162*
    Article 7   *162*
    Article 8   *162*
    Article 9   *162*
    Article 10   *162*
    Article 11   *162*
    Article 12   *162–163*
    Article 13   *163*
    Article 14   *163*
    Article 15   *163*
    Article 16   *163–164*
    Article 17   *164*

Treaty Establishing the European
Community, Protocol on the Statute of
the Court of Justice of the European
Communities (contd.)
    Article 18   *164–165*
    Article 19   *165*
    Article 20   *165*
    Article 21   *166*
    Article 22   *166*
    Article 23   *166*
    Article 24   *166*
    Article 25   *166*
    Article 26   *166–167*
    Article 27   *167*
    Article 28   *167*
    Article 29   *167*
    Article 30   *167*
    Article 31   *167*
    Article 32   *167*
    Article 33   *167*
    Article 34   *168*
    Article 35   *168*
    Article 36   *168*
    Article 37   *168*
    Article 38   *168–169*
    Article 39   *169*
    Article 40   *169*
    Article 41   *169*
    Article 42   *169*
    Article 43   *170*
    Article 44   *170*
    Article 45   *170*
    Article 46   *170–171*
    Article 47   *171*
    Article 48   *171*
    Article 49   *172*
    Article 50   *172*
    Article 51   *172–173*
    Article 52   *173*
    Article 53   *173*
    Article 54   *173*
    Article 55   *174*
    Article 56   *174*
    Article 57   *174*

Treaty Establishing the European
    Community (contd.)
    Protocol on the Statute of the European
    System of Central Banks and of the
    European Central Bank   174–197
        Article 1   175
        Article 2   175
        Article 3   175–176
        Article 4   176
        Article 5   176–177
        Article 6   177
        Article 7   177
        Article 8   177
        Article 9   178
        Article 10   178–179
        Article 11   179–180
        Article 12   180
        Article 13   181
        Article 14   181
        Article 15   182
        Article 16   182
        Article 17   182
        Article 18   183
        Article 19   183
        Article 20   183–184
        Article 21   184
        Article 22   184
        Article 23   184–185
        Article 24   185
        Article 25   185
        Article 26   185–186
        Article 27   186
        Article 28   186–187
        Article 29   187
        Article 30   187–188
        Article 31   188
        Article 32   189
        Article 33   190
        Article 34   190–191
        Article 35   191
        Article 36   191–192
        Article 37   192
        Article 38   192
        Article 39   192
        Article 40   192

Treaty Establishing the European
    Community, Protocol on the Statute of
    the European System of Central Banks
    and of the European Central Bank
    (contd.)
        Article 41   193
        Article 42   193
        Article 43   193–194
        Article 44   194
        Article 45   194
        Article 46   195
        Article 47   195
        Article 48   196
        Article 49   196
        Article 50   196–197
        Article 51   197
        Article 52   197
        Article 53   197
    Protocol on the Transition to the Third
    Stage of Economic and Monetary
    Union   200–201
Treaty of Amsterdam (draft)   373–451
Treaty on European Union   241–263
    Article A   242
    Article B   242–243
    Article C   243
    Article D   243–244
    Article E   244
    Article F   244–245
    Article J   245
    Article J1   245–246
    Article J2   246
    Article J3   246–247
    Article J4   247–248
    Article J5   248
    Article J6   248–249
    Article J7   249
    Article J8   249–250
    Article J9   250
    Article J10 250
    Article J11 250
    Article K   251
    Article K1   251–252
    Article K2   252
    Article K3   252–253

Treaty on European Union (*contd.*)
    Article K4   *253*
    Article K5   *253*
    Article K6   *253–254*
    Article K7   *254*
    Article K8   *254*
    Article K9   *254*
    Article L   *255*
    Article M   *255*
    Article N   *255–256*
    Article O   *256*
    Article P   *256*
    Article Q   *256*
    Article R   *256–257*
    Article S   *257*

Treaty on European Union (*contd.*)
    Declaration on Asylum   *262*
    Declaration on Nationality of a Member State   *257*
    Declaration on Police Cooperation   *262–263*
    Declaration on the Implementation of Community Law   *258*
    Declaration on the Role of National Parliaments in the European Union   *257*
    Declaration on Voting in the Field of the Common Foreign and Security Policy   *258*
    Declarations on Western European Union   *258–262*

TREATY ESTABLISHING THE EUROPEAN COAL AND STEEL COMMUNITY
(Paris, 18 April 1951)

THE PRESIDENT OF THE FEDERAL REPUBLIC OF GERMANY, HIS ROYAL HIGHNESS THE PRINCE ROYAL OF BELGIUM, THE PRESIDENT OF THE FRENCH REPUBLIC, THE PRESIDENT OF THE ITALIAN REPUBLIC, HER ROYAL HIGHNESS THE GRAND DUCHESS OF LUXEMBOURG, HER MAJESTY THE QUEEN OF THE NETHERLANDS,

CONSIDERING that world peace can be safeguarded only by creative efforts commensurate with the dangers that threaten it,

CONVINCED that the contribution which an organised and vital Europe can make to civilisation is indispensable to the maintenance of peaceful relations,

RECOGNISING that Europe can be built only through practical achievements which will first of all create real solidarity, and through the establishment of common bases for economic development,

ANXIOUS to help, by expanding their basic production to raise the standard of living and further the works of peace,

RESOLVED to substitute for age-old rivalries the merging of their essential interests; to create, by establishing an economic community, the basis for a broader and deeper community among peoples long divided by bloody conflicts; and to lay the foundations of institutions which will give direction to a destiny henceforth shared,

HAVE DECIDED to create a European Coal and Steel Community and to this end have designated as their plenipotentiaries: ...

WHO, having exchanged their Full Powers, found in good and due form, HAVE AGREED as follows:

Article 1

By this Treaty, the High Contracting Parties establish among themselves a EUROPEAN COAL AND STEEL COMMUNITY, founded upon a common market, common objectives and common institutions.

Article 2

The European Coal and Steel Community shall have as its task to contribute, in harmony with the general economy of the Member States and through the establishment of a common market as provided in Article 4, to economic expansion, growth of employment and a rising standard of living in the Member States.

The Community shall progressively bring about conditions which will of themselves ensure the most rational distribution of production at the highest possible level of productivity, while safeguarding continuity of employment and taking care not to provoke fundamental and persistent disturbances in the economies of Member States.

Article 3

The institutions of the Community shall, within the limits of their respective powers, in the common interest:

(a) ensure an orderly supply to the common market, taking into account the needs of third countries;

(b) ensure that all comparably placed consumers in the common market have equal access to the sources of production;

(c) ensure the establishment of the lowest prices under such conditions that these prices do not result in higher prices charged by the same undertakings in other transactions or in a higher general price level at another time, while allowing necessary amortisation and normal return on invested capital;

(d) ensure the maintenance of conditions which will encourage undertakings to expand and improve their production potential and to promote a policy of using natural resources rationally and avoiding their unconsidered exhaustion;

(e) promote improved working conditions and an improved standard of living for the workers in each of the industries for which it is responsible, so as to make possible their harmonisation while the improvement is being maintained;

(f) promote the growth of international trade and ensure that equitable limits are observed in export pricing;

(g) promote the orderly expansion and modernisation of production, and the improvement of quality, with no protection against competing industries that is not justified by improper action on their part or in their favour.

Article 4

The following are recognised as incompatible with the common market for coal and steel and shall accordingly be abolished and prohibited within the Community, as provided in this Treaty:

(a) import and export duties, or charges having equivalent effect, and quantitative restrictions on the movement of products;

(b) measures or practices which discriminate between producers, between purchasers or between consumers, especially in prices and delivery terms or transport rates and conditions, and measures or practices which interfere with the purchaser's free choice of supplier;

(c) subsidies or aids granted by States, or special charges imposed by States, in any form whatsoever;

(d) restrictive practices which tend towards the sharing or exploiting of markets.

Article 5

The Community shall carry out its task in accordance with this Treaty, with a limited measure of intervention.

To this end the Community shall:

- provide guidance and assistance for the parties concerned, by obtaining information, organising consultations and laying down general objectives;
- place financial resources at the disposal of undertakings for their investment and bear part of the cost of readaptation;
- ensure the establishment, maintenance and observance of normal competitive conditions and exert direct influence upon production or upon the market only when circumstances so require;
- publish the reasons for its actions and take the necessary measures to ensure the observance of the rules laid down in this Treaty.

The institutions of the Community shall carry out these activities with a minimum of administrative machinery and in close cooperation with the parties concerned.

Article 6

The Community shall have legal personality.

In international relations, the Community shall enjoy the legal capacity it requires to perform its functions and attain its objectives.

In each of the Member States, the Community shall enjoy the most extensive legal capacity accorded to legal persons constituted in that State; it may, in particular, acquire or dispose of movable and immovable property and may be a party to legal proceedings.

The Community shall be represented by its institutions, each within the limits of its powers.

Article 7

The institutions of the Community shall be:

- a HIGH AUTHORITY (hereinafter referred to as 'the Commission');
- a COMMON ASSEMBLY (hereinafter referred to as 'the European Parliament');
- a SPECIAL COUNCIL OF MINISTERS (hereinafter referred to as 'the Council');
- a COURT OF JUSTICE;
- a COURT OF AUDITORS.

The Commission shall be assisted by a Consultative Committee.

Article 57

In the sphere of production, the Commission shall give preference to the indirect means of action at its disposal, such as:

- cooperation with Governments to regularise or influence general consumption, particularly that of the public services;
- intervention in regard to prices and commercial policy as provided for in this Treaty.

Article 58

1 In the event of a decline in demand, if the Commission considers that the Community is confronted with a period of manifest crisis and that the means of action provided for in Article 57 are not sufficient to deal with this, it shall, after consulting the Consultative Committee and with the assent of the Council, establish a system of production quotas, accompanied to the necessary extent by the measures provided for in Article 74.

If the Commission fails to act, a Member State may bring the matter before the Council, which may, acting unanimously, require the Commission to establish a system of quotas.

2 The Commission shall, on the basis of studies made jointly with undertakings and associations of undertakings, determine their quotas on an equitable basis, taking account of the principles set out in Articles 2, 3 and 4. It may in particular regulate the level of activity of undertakings by appropriate levies on tonnages exceeding a reference level set by a general decision.

The funds thus obtained shall be used to support undertakings whose rate of production has fallen below that envisaged, in order, in particular, to maintain employment in these undertakings as far as possible.

3 The system of quotas shall be ended on a proposal made to the Council by the Commission after consulting the Consultative Committee, or by the Government of a Member State, unless the Council decides otherwise, acting unanimously if the proposal emanates from the Commission or by a simple majority if the proposal emanates from a Government. An announcement on the ending of the quota system shall be made by the Commission.

4 The Commission may impose upon undertakings which do not comply with decisions taken by it under this Article fines not exceeding the value of the tonnages produced in disregard thereof.

Article 59

1 If, after consulting the Consultative Committee, the Commission finds that the Community is confronted with a serious shortage of any or all of the products within its jurisdiction, and that the means of action provided for in Article 57 are not sufficient to deal with this, it shall bring the situation to the attention of the Council and shall, unless the Council, acting unanimously, decides otherwise, propose to it the necessary measures.

If the Commission fails to act, a Member State may bring the matter before the Council, which may, acting unanimously, recognise that the situation in question does in fact exist.

2 The Council shall, acting unanimously on a proposal from and in consultation with the Commission, establish consumption priorities and determine the allocation of the coal and steel resources of the Community to the industries within its jurisdiction, to export and to other sectors of consumption.

On the basis of the consumption priorities thus established, the Commission shall, after consulting the undertakings concerned, draw up the production programmes with which the undertakings shall be required to comply.

3 If the Council does not reach a unanimous decision on the measures referred to in paragraph 2, the Commission shall itself allocate the resources of the Community among the Member States on the basis of consumption and exports, irrespective of the place of production.

Within each of the Member States allocation of the resources assigned by the Commission shall be carried out on the responsibility of the Government, provided that the deliveries scheduled to be supplied to other Member States are not affected and that the Commission is consulted concerning the portions to be allotted to export and to the operation of the coal and steel industries.

If the portion allotted by a Government to export is less than the amount taken as the basis for calculating the total tonnage to be assigned to the Member State concerned, the Commission shall, to the necessary extent, at the next allocation, redivide among the Member States the resources thus made available for consumption.

If the portion allotted by a Government to the operation of the coal and steel industries is similarly less and the result is a decrease in Community production of one of these, the tonnage assigned to the Member State concerned shall, at the next allocation, be reduced by the amount of the decrease in production so caused.

4 In all cases, the Commission shall be responsible for allocating equitably among undertakings the quantities assigned to the industries within its jurisdiction, on the basis of studies made jointly with undertakings and association of undertakings.

5 Should the situation provided for in paragraph 1 of this Article arise, the Commission may, in accordance with Article 57, after consulting the Consultative Committee and with the assent of the Council, decide that

restrictions on export to third countries shall be imposed in all the Member States, or, if the Commission fails to act, the Council may, acting unanimously, so decide on a proposal from a Government.

6 The Commission may end the arrangement made under this Article after consulting the Consultative Committee and the Council. It shall not do so if the Council unanimously dissents.

If the Commission fails to act, the Council may, acting unanimously, itself end the arrangements.

7 The Commission may impose upon undertakings which do not comply with decisions taken under this Article fines not exceeding twice the value of prescribed production or deliveries either not effected or diverted from their proper use.

Article 60

1 Pricing practices contrary to Articles 2, 3 and 4 shall be prohibited, in particular:

- unfair competitive practices, especially purely temporary or purely local price reductions tending towards the acquisition of a monopoly position within the common market;
- discriminatory practices involving, with the common market, the application by a seller of dissimilar conditions to comparable transactions, especially on grounds of the nationality of the buyer.

The Commission may define the practices covered by this prohibition by decisions taken after consulting the Consultative Committee and the Council.

2 For these purposes:

(a) the price lists and conditions of sale applied by undertakings within the common market must be made public to the extent and in the manner prescribed by the Commission after consulting the Consultative Committee. If the Commission finds that an undertaking's choice of point on which it bases its price lists is abnormal and in particular makes it possible to evade the provisions of subparagraph (b), it shall make appropriate recommendations to that undertaking;

(b) the methods of quotation used must not have the effect that prices charged by an undertaking in the common market, when reduced to their equivalent at the point chosen for its price lists, result in:

- increases over the price shown in the price list in question for a comparable transaction; or

- reductions below that price the amount of which exceeds either:
  - the extent enabling the quotation to be aligned on the price list, based on another point which secures the buyer the most advantageous delivered terms; or
  - the limits fixed, by the decision of the Commission after the Consultative Committee has delivered its opinion, for each category of product, with due regard, where appropriate, for the origin and destination of products.

  Such decisions shall be taken when found necessary to avoid disturbances in the whole or any part of the common market or disequilibria resulting from a difference between the methods of quotation used for a product and for materials involved in making it. Such decisions shall not preclude undertakings from aligning their quotations on those of undertakings outside the Community, on condition that the transactions are notified to the Commission, which may, in the event of abuse, restrict or abrogate the right of the undertakings concerned to take advantage of this exception.

Article 61

On the basis of studies made jointly with undertakings and associations of undertakings, in accordance with the first paragraph of Article 46 and the third paragraph of Article 48, and after consulting the Consultative Committee and the Council as to the advisability of so doing and the price level to be so determined, the Commission may, for one or more of the products within its jurisdiction:

(a) fix maximum prices within the common market, if it finds that such a decision is necessary to attain the objectives set out in Article 3, and particularly in paragraph (c) thereof;

(b) fix minimum prices within the common market, if it finds that a manifest crisis exists or is imminent and that such a decision is necessary to attain the objectives set out in Article 3;

(c) after consulting the associations to which the undertakings concerned belong, or the undertakings themselves, fix, by methods appropriate to the nature of the export markets, minimum or maximum export prices, if such an arrangement can be effectively supervised and is necessary both in view of the dangers to the undertakings resulting from the state of the market and in order to secure the acceptance in international economic relations of the objectives set out in Article 3(f); any fixing of minimum prices shall be without prejudice to the measures provided for in the last subparagraph of Article 60(2).

In fixing prices, the Commission shall take into account the need to ensure that the coal and steel industries and the consumer industries remain competitive, in accordance with the principles laid down in Article 3(c).

If in these circumstances the Commission fails to act, the Government of a Member State may bring the matter before the Council, which may, acting unanimously, call upon the Commission to fix such maximum or minimum prices.

Article 62

If the Commission considers this the most appropriate way of preventing coal from being priced at the level of the production costs of the mines which have the highest costs but which it is recognised should be temporarily maintained in service in order that the tasks laid down in Article 3 may be performed, it may, after consulting the Consultative Committee, authorise equalisation payments:

- between undertakings in the same coalfield to which the same price lists apply;
- after consulting the Council, between undertakings in different coalfields.

These equalisation payments may, moreover, be instituted as provided in Article 53.

Article 63

1 If the Commission finds that discrimination is being systematically practised by purchasers, in particular under provisions governing contracts entered into by bodies dependent on a public authority, it shall make appropriate recommendations to the Governments concerned.

2 Where the Commission considers it necessary, it may decide that:

(a) undertakings must frame their conditions of sale in such a way that their customers and commission agents acting on their behalf shall be under an obligation to comply with the rules made by the Commission in application of this Chapter;

(b) undertakings shall be held responsible for infringements of this obligation by their direct agents or by commission agents acting on their behalf.

In the event of an infringement of this obligation by a purchaser, the Commission may restrict or, should the infringement be repeated, temporarily prohibit dealings with that purchaser by Community undertakings. If this is done, the purchaser shall have the right, without prejudice to Article 33, to bring an action before the Court.

3 In addition, the Commission is empowered to make to the Member States concerned any appropriate recommendations to ensure that the rules laid down for the application of Article 60(1) are duly observed by all distributive undertakings and agencies in the coal and steel sectors.

Article 64

The Commission may impose upon undertakings which infringe the provisions of this Chapter or decisions taken thereunder fines not exceeding twice the value of the sales effected in disregard thereof. If the infringement is repeated, the maximum shall be doubled.

Article 65

1 All agreements between undertakings, decisions by associations of undertakings and concerted practices tending directly or indirectly to prevent, restrict or distort normal competition within the common market shall be prohibited, and in particular those tending:

(a) to fix or determine prices;

(b) to restrict or control production, technical development or investments;

(c) to share markets, products, customers or sources of supply.

2 However, the Commission shall authorise specialisation agreements or joint-buying or joint-selling agreements in respect of particular products, if it finds that:

(a) such specialisation or such joint-buying or -selling will make for a substantial improvement in the production or distribution of those products;

(b) the agreement in question is essential in order to achieve these results and is not more restrictive than is necessary for that purpose; and

(c) the agreement is not liable to give the undertakings concerned the power to determine the prices, or to control or restrict the production or marketing, of a substantial part of the products in question within the common market, or to shield them against effective competition from other undertakings within the common market.

If the Commission finds that certain agreements are strictly analogous in nature and effect to those referred to above, having particular regard to the fact that this paragraph applies to distributive undertakings, it shall authorise them also when satisfied that they meet the same requirements.

Authorisations may be granted subject to specified conditions and for limited periods. In such cases the Commission shall renew an authorisation once or several times if it finds that the requirements of subparagraphs (a) to (c) are still met at the time of renewal.

The Commission shall revoke or amend an authorisation if it finds that as a result of a change in circumstances the agreement no longer meets these requirements, or that the actual results of the agreement or of the application thereof are contrary to the requirements for its authorisation.

Decisions granting, renewing, amending, refusing or revoking an authorisation shall be published together with the reasons therefor; the restrictions imposed by the second paragraph of Article 47 shall not apply thereto.

3 The Commission may, as provided in Article 47, obtain any information needed for the application of this Article, either by making a special request to the parties concerned or by means of regulations stating the kinds of agreement, decision or practice which must be communicated to it.

4 Any agreement or decision prohibited by paragraph 1 of this Article shall be automatically void and may not be relied upon before any court or tribunal in the Member States.

The Commission shall have sole jurisdiction, subject to the right to bring actions before the Court, to rule whether any such agreement or decision is compatible with this Article.

5 On any undertaking which has entered into an agreement which is automatically void, or has enforced or attempted to enforce, by arbitration, penalty, boycott or any other means, an agreement or decision which is automatically void or an agreement for which authorisation has been refused or revoked, or has obtained an authorisation by means of information which it knew to be false or misleading, or has engaged in practices prohibited by paragraph 1 of this Article, the Commission may impose fines or periodic penalty payments not exceeding twice the turnover on the products which were the subject of the agreement, decision or practice prohibited by this Article; if, however, the purpose of the agreement, decision or practice is to restrict production, technical development or investment, this maximum may be raised to 10 per cent of the annual turnover of the undertakings in question in the case of fines, and 20 per cent of the daily turnover in the case of periodic penalty payments.

Article 66

1 Any transaction shall require the prior authorisation of the Commission, subject to the provisions of paragraph 3 of this Article, if it has in itself the direct or indirect effect of bringing about within the territories referred to in the first paragraph of Article 79, as a result of action by any person or undertaking or group of persons or undertakings, a concentration between undertakings at least one of which is covered by Article 80, whether the transaction concerns a single product or a number of different products, and whether it is effected by merger, acquisition of shares or parts of the undertaking or assets, loan, contract or any other means of control. For the purpose of applying these provisions, the Commission shall, by regulations made after consulting the Council, define what constitutes control of an undertaking.

2 The Commission shall grant the authorisation referred to in the preceding paragraph if it finds that the proposed transaction will not give to the persons or undertakings concerned the power, in respect of the product or products within its jurisdiction:

- to determine prices, to control or restrict production or distribution or to hinder effective competition in a substantial part of the market for those products; or
- to evade the rules of competition instituted under this Treaty, in particular by establishing an artificially privileged position involving a substantial advantage in access to supplies or markets.

In assessing whether this is so, the Commission shall, in accordance with the principle of non-discrimination laid down in Article 4(b), take account of the size of like undertakings in the Community, to the extent it considers justified in order to avoid or correct disadvantages resulting from unequal competitive conditions.

The Commission may make its authorisation subject to any conditions which it considers appropriate for the purposes of this paragraph.

Before ruling on a transaction concerning undertakings at least one of which is not subject to Article 80, the Commission shall obtain the comments of the Government concerned.

3 The Commission shall exempt from the requirement of prior authorisation such classes of transactions as it finds should, in view of the size of the assets or undertakings concerned, taken in conjunction with the kind of concentration to be effected, be deemed to meet the requirements of paragraph 2. Regulations made to this effect, with the assent of the Council, shall also lay down the conditions governing such exemption.

4 Without prejudice to the application of Article 47 to undertakings within its jurisdiction, the Commission may, either by regulations made after consultation with the Council stating the kind of transaction to be communicated to it or by a special request under these regulations to the parties concerned, obtain from the natural or legal persons who have acquired or regrouped or are intending to acquire or regroup the rights or assets in question any information needed for the application of this Article concerning transactions liable to produce the effect referred to in paragraph 1.

5 If a concentration should occur which the Commission finds has been effected contrary to the provisions of paragraph 1 but which nevertheless meets the requirements of paragraph 2, the Commission shall make its approval of that concentration subject to payment by the persons who have acquired or regrouped the rights or assets in question of the fine provided for in the second of the maximum determined in that subparagraph should it be clear that authorisation ought to have been applied for. If the fine is not paid, the Commission shall take the steps hereinafter provided for in respect of concentrations found to be unlawful.

If a concentration should occur which the Commission finds cannot fulfil the general or specific conditions to which an authorisation under paragraph 2 would be subject, the Commission shall, by means of a reasoned decision, declare the concentration unlawful and, after giving the parties concerned the opportunity to submit their comments, shall order separation of the undertakings or assets improperly concentrated or cessation of joint control, and any other measures which it considers appropriate to return the undertakings or assets in question to independent operation and restore normal conditions of competition. Any person directly concerned may institute proceedings against such decisions, as provided in Article 33. By way of derogation from Article 33, the Court shall have unlimited jurisdiction to assess whether the transaction effected is a concentration within the meaning of paragraph 1 and of regulations made in application thereof. The institution of proceedings shall have suspensory effect. Proceedings may not be instituted until the measures provided for above have been ordered, unless the Commission agrees to the institution of separate proceedings against the decision declaring the transaction unlawful.

The Commission may at any time, unless the third paragraph of Article 39 is applied, take or cause to be taken such interim measures of protection as it may consider necessary to safeguard the interests of competing undertakings and of third parties, and to forestall any step which might hinder the implementation of its decisions. Unless the Court decides otherwise, proceedings shall not have suspensory effect in respect of such interim measures.

The Commission shall allow the parties concerned a reasonable period in which to comply with its decisions, on expiration of which it may impose daily penalty payments not exceeding one tenth of one per cent of the value of the rights or assets in question.

Furthermore, if the parties concerned do not fulfil their obligations, the Commission shall itself take steps to implement its decision; it may in particular suspend the exercise, in undertakings within its jurisdiction, of the rights attached to the assets acquired irregularly, obtain the appointment by the judicial authorities of a receiver of such assets, organise the forced sale of such assets subject to the protection of the legitimate interests of their owners, and annul with respect to natural or legal persons who have acquired the rights or assets in question through the unlawful transaction, the acts, decisions, resolutions or proceedings of the supervisory and managing bodies or undertakings over which control has been obtained irregularly.

The Commission is also empowered to make such recommendations to the Member States concerned as may be necessary to ensure that the measures provided for in the preceding subparagraphs are implemented under their own law.

In the exercise of its powers, the Commission shall take account of the rights of third parties which have been acquired in good faith.

6 The Commission may impose fines not exceeding:

- 3 per cent of the value of the assets acquired or regrouped or to be acquired or regrouped, on natural or legal persons who have evaded the obligations laid down in paragraph 4;
- 10 per cent of the value of the assets acquired or regrouped, on natural or legal persons who have evaded the obligations laid down in paragraph 1; this maximum shall be increased by one twenty-fourth for each month which elapses after the end of the twelfth month following completion of the transaction until the Commission establishes that there has been an infringement;
- 10 per cent of the value of the assets acquired or regrouped or to be acquired or regrouped, on natural or legal persons who have obtained or attempted to obtain authorisation under paragraph 2 by means of false or misleading information;
- 15 per cent of the value of the assets acquired or regrouped, on undertakings within its jurisdiction which have engaged in or been party to transactions contrary to the provisions of this Article.

Persons fined under this paragraph may appeal to the Court as provided in Article 36.

7 If the Commission finds that public or private undertakings which, in law or in fact, hold or acquire in the market for one of the products within its jurisdiction a dominant position shielding them against effective competition in a substantial part of the common market are using that position for purposes contrary to the objectives of this Treaty, it shall make to them such recommen-dations as may be appropriate to prevent the position from being so abused. If these recommendations are not implemented satisfactorily within a reasonable time, the Commission shall, by decisions taken in consultation with the Government concerned, determine the prices and conditions of sale to be applied by the undertaking in question or draw up production or delivery programmes with which it must comply, subject to liability to the penalties provided for in Articles 58, 59 and 64.

Article 67

1 Any action by a Member State which is liable to have appreciable repercussions on conditions of competition in the coal or the steel industry shall be brought to the knowledge of the Commission by the Government concerned.

2 If the action is liable, by substantially increasing differences in production costs otherwise than through changes in productivity, to provoke a serious disequilibrium, the Commission, after consulting the Consultative Committee and the Council, may take the following steps:

If the action taken by that State is having harmful effects on the coal or steel undertakings within the jurisdiction of that State, the Commission may authorise it to grant aid to these undertakings, the amount, conditions and duration of which shall be determined in agreement with the Commission. The same shall apply in the case of any change in wages and working conditions which would have the same effects, even if not resulting from any action by that State.

If the action taken by that State is having harmful effects on the coal or steel undertakings within the jurisdiction of other Member States, the Commission shall make a recommendation to that State with a view to remedying these effects by such measures as that State may consider most compatible with its own economic equilibrium.

3 If the action taken by that State reduces differences in production costs by allowing special benefits to or imposing special charges on the coal or steel undertakings within its jurisdiction in comparison with the other industries in the same country, the Commission is empowered to make the necessary recommendations to that State after consulting the Consultative Committee and the Council.

Article 71

The powers of the Governments of Member States in matters of commercial policy shall not be affected by this Treaty, save as otherwise provided therein.

The powers conferred on the Community by this Treaty in matters of commercial policy towards third countries may not exceed those accorded to Member States under international agreements to which they are parties, subject to the provisions of Article 75.

The Governments of Member States shall afford each other such mutual assistance as is necessary to implement measures recognised by the Commission as being in accordance with this Treaty and with existing international agreements. The Commission is empowered to propose to the Member States concerned the methods by which this mutual assistance may be provided.

Article 72

Minimum rates below which Member States undertake not to lower their customs duties on coal and steel as against third countries, and maximum rates above which they undertake not to raise them, may be fixed by decisions of the Council, acting unanimously on a proposal from the Commission made on the latter's own initiative or at the request of a Member State.

Within the limits so fixed, each Government shall determine its tariffs according to its own national procedure. The Commission may, on its own initiative or at the request of a Member State, deliver an opinion suggesting amendment of the tariffs of that State.

Article 73

The administration of import and export licences for trade with third countries shall be a matter for the Government in whose territory the place of destination for imports or the place of origin for exports is situated.

The Commission is empowered to supervise the administration and verification of these licences with respect to coal and steel. Where necessary it shall, after consulting the Council, make recommendations to Member States to ensure that the arrangements in this connection are not more restrictive than the circumstances governing their adoption or retention require, and to secure the coordination of measures taken under the third paragraph of Article 71 or under Article 74.

Article 74

In the cases set out below, the Commission is empowered to take any measures which is in accordance with this Treaty, and in particular with the objectives set out in Article 3, and to make to Governments any recommendation which is in accordance with the second paragraph of Article 71:

(1) if it is found that countries not members of the Community or undertakings situated in such countries are engaging in dumping or other practices condemned by the Havana Charter;

(2) if a difference between quotations by undertakings outside and by undertakings within the jurisdiction of the Community is due solely to the fact that those of the former are based on conditions of competition contrary to this Treaty;

(3) if one of the products referred to in Article 81 of this Treaty is imported into the territory of one or more Member States in relatively increased quantities and under such conditions that these imports cause or threaten to cause serious injury to production within the common market of like or directly competing products.

However, recommendations for the introduction of quantitative restrictions under subparagraph 2 may be made only with the assent of the Council, and under subparagraph 3 only under the conditions laid down in Article 58.

Article 75

The Member States undertake to keep the Commission informed of proposed commercial agreements or arrangements having similar effect where these relate to coal and steel or to the importation of other raw materials and specialised equipment needed for the production of coal and steel in Member States.

If a proposed agreement or arrangement contains clauses which would hinder the implementation of this Treaty, the Commission shall make the necessary recommendations to the State concerned within ten days of receiving notification of the communication addressed to it; in any other case it may deliver opinions.

Article 97

This Treaty is concluded for a period of fifty years from its entry into force.

Article 99

This Treaty shall be ratified by all the Member States in accordance with their respective constitutional requirements; the instruments of ratification shall be deposited with the Government of the French Republic.

This Treaty shall enter into force on the date of deposit of the instrument of ratification by the last signatory State to take this step.

If all the instruments of ratification have not been deposited within six months of the signature of this Treaty, the Governments of the States which have deposited their instruments shall consult each other on the measures to be taken.

Article 100

This Treaty, drawn up in a single original, shall be deposited in the archives of the Government of the French Republic, which shall transmit a certified copy thereof of each to the Governments of the other signatory States.

IN WITNESS WHEREOF, the undersigned plenipotentiaries have signed this Treaty and affixed thereto their seals.

As amended by the Treaty on European Union, art H(1).

TREATY ESTABLISHING THE EUROPEAN COMMUNITY
(Rome, 25 March 1957)

HIS MAJESTY THE KING OF THE BELGIANS, THE PRESIDENT OF THE FEDERAL REPUBLIC OF GERMANY, THE PRESIDENT OF THE FRENCH REPUBLIC, THE PRESIDENT OF THE ITALIAN REPUBLIC, HER ROYAL HIGHNESS THE GRAND DUCHESS OF LUXEMBOURG, HER MAJESTY THE QUEEN OF THE NETHERLANDS,

DETERMINED to lay the foundations of an ever closer union among the peoples of Europe,

RESOLVED to ensure the economic and social progress of their countries by common action to eliminate the barriers which divide Europe,

AFFIRMING as the essential objective of their efforts the constant improvement of the living and working conditions of their peoples,

RECOGNISING that the removal of existing obstacles calls for concerted action in order to guarantee steady expansion, balanced trade and fair competition,

ANXIOUS to strengthen the unity of their economies and to ensure their harmonious development by reducing the differences existing between the various regions and the backwardness of the less favoured regions,

DESIRING to contribute, by means of a common commercial policy, to the progressive abolition of restrictions on international trade,

INTENDING to confirm the solidarity which binds Europe and the overseas countries and desiring to ensure the development of their prosperity, in accordance with the principles of the Charter of the United Nations,

RESOLVED by thus pooling their resources to preserve and strengthen peace and liberty, and calling upon the other peoples of Europe who share their ideal to join in their efforts,

HAVE DECIDED to create a European Community and to this end have designated as their Plenipotentiaries: ...

WHO, having exchanged their Full Powers, found in good and due form, HAVE AGREED as follows:

Part One

PRINCIPLES

Article 1

By this Treaty, the High Contracting Parties establish among themselves a EUROPEAN COMMUNITY.

Article 2

The Community shall have as its task, by establishing a common market and an economic and monetary union and by implementing the common policies or activities referred to in Articles 3 and 3a, to promote throughout the Community a harmonious and balanced development of economic activities, sustainable and non-inflationary growth respecting the environment, a high degree of convergence of economic performance, a high level of employment and of social protection, the raising of the standard of living and quality of life, and economic and social cohesion and solidarity among Member States.

Article 3

For the purposes set out in Article 2, the activities of the Community shall include, as provided in this Treaty and in accordance with the timetable set out therein:

(a) the elimination, as between Member States, of customs duties and quantitative restrictions on the import and export of goods, and of all other measures having equivalent effect;

(b) a common commercial policy;

(c) an internal market characterised by the abolition, as between Member States, of obstacles to the free movement of goods, persons, services and capital;

(d) measures concerning the entry and movement of persons in the internal market as provided for in Article 100c;

(e) a common policy in the sphere of agriculture and fisheries;

(f) a common policy in the sphere of transport;

(g) a system ensuring that competition in the internal market is not distorted;

(h) the approximation of the laws of Member States to the extent required for the functioning of the common market;

(i) a policy in the social sphere comprising a European Social Fund;

(j) the strengthening of economic and social cohesion;

(k) a policy in the sphere of the environment;

(l) the strengthening of the competitiveness of Community industry;

(m) the promotion of research and technological development;

(n) encouragement for the establishment and development of trans-European networks;

(o) a contribution to the attainment of a high level of health protection;

(p) a contribution to education and training of quality and to the flowering of the cultures of the Member States;

(q) a policy in the sphere of development cooperation;

(r) the association of the overseas countries and territories in order to increase trade and promote jointly economic and social development;

(s) a contribution to the strengthening of consumer protection;

(t) measures in the spheres of energy, civil protection and tourism.

Article 3a

(1) For the purposes set out in Article 2, the activities of the Member States and the Community shall include, as provided in this Treaty and in accordance with the timetable set out therein, the adoption of an economic policy which is based on the close coordination of Member States' economic policies, on the internal market and on the definition of common objectives, and conducted in accordance with the principle of an open market economy with free competition.

(2) Concurrently with the foregoing, and as provided in this Treaty and in accordance with the timetable and the procedures set out therein, these activities shall include the irrevocable fixing of exchange rates leading to the introduction of a single currency, the ECU, and the definition and conduct of a single monetary policy and exchange-rate policy the primary objective of both of which shall be to maintain price stability and, without prejudice to this objective, to support the general economic policies in the Community, in accordance with the principle of an open market economy with free competition.

(3) These activities of the Member States and the Community shall entail compliance with the following guiding principles: stable prices, sound public finances and monetary conditions and a sustainable balance of payments.

Article 3b

The Community shall act within the limits of the powers conferred upon it by this Treaty and of the objectives assigned to it therein.

In areas which do not fall within its exclusive competence, the Community shall take action, in accordance with the principle of subsidiarity, only if and in so far as the objectives of the proposed action cannot be sufficiently achieved by the Member States and can therefore, by reason of the scale or effects of the proposed action, be better achieved by the Community.

Any action by the Community shall not go beyond what is necessary to achieve the objectives of this Treaty.

Article 4

(1) The tasks entrusted to the Community shall be carried out by the following institutions:

- a EUROPEAN PARLIAMENT,
- a COUNCIL,
- a COMMISSION,
- a COURT OF JUSTICE,
- a COURT OF AUDITORS.

Each institution shall act within the limits of the powers conferred upon it by this Treaty.

(2) The Council and the Commission shall be assisted by an Economic and Social Committee and a Committee of the Regions acting in an advisory capacity.

Article 4a

A European System of Central Banks (hereinafter referred to as 'ESCB') and a European Central Bank (hereinafter referred to as 'ECB') shall be established in accordance with the procedures laid down in this Treaty; they shall act within the limits of the powers conferred upon them by this Treaty and by the Statute of the ESCB and of the ECB (hereinafter referred to as 'Statute of the ESCB') annexed thereto.

Article 4b

A European Investment Bank is hereby established, which shall act within the limits of the powers conferred upon it by this Treaty and the Statute annexed thereto.

Article 5

Member States shall take all appropriate measures, whether general or particular, to ensure fulfilment of the obligations arising out of this Treaty or resulting from action taken by the institutions of the Community. They shall facilitate the achievement of the Community's tasks.

They shall abstain from any measure which could jeopardise the attainment of the objectives of this Treaty.

Article 6

Within the scope of application of this Treaty, and without prejudice to any special provisions contained therein, any discrimination on grounds of nationality shall be prohibited.

The Council, acting in accordance with the procedure referred to in Article 189c, may adopt rules designed to prohibit such discrimination.

Article 7

(1) The common market shall be progressively established during a transitional period of twelve years.

This transitional period shall be divided into three stages of four years each; the length of each stage may be altered in accordance with the provisions set out below.

(2) To each stage there shall be assigned a set of actions to be initiated and carried through concurrently.

(3) Transition from the first to the second stage shall be conditional upon a finding that the objectives specifically laid down in this Treaty for the first stage have in fact been attained in substance and that, subject to the exceptions and procedures provided for in this Treaty the obligations have been fulfilled.

This finding shall be made at the end of the fourth year by the Council, acting unanimously on a report from the Commission. A Member State may not, however, prevent unanimity by relying upon the non-fulfilment of its own obligations. Failing unanimity, the first stage shall automatically be extended for one year. At the end of the fifth year, the Council shall make its finding under the same conditions. Failing unanimity, the first stage shall automatically be extended for a further year. At the end of the sixth year, the Council shall make its finding, acting by a qualified majority, on a report from the Commission.

(4) Within one month of the last-mentioned vote any Member State which voted with the minority or, if the required majority was not obtained, any Member State shall be entitled to call upon the Council to appoint an arbitration board whose decision shall be binding upon all Member States and upon the institutions of the Community. The arbitration board shall consist of three members appointed by the Council acting unanimously on a proposal from the Commission.

If the Council has not appointed the members of the arbitration board within one month of being called upon to do so, they shall be appointed by the Court of Justice within a further period of one month.

The arbitration board shall elect its own Chairman.

The board shall make its award within six months of the date of the Council vote referred to in the last subparagraph of paragraph 3.

(5) The second and third stages may not be extended or curtailed except by a decision of the Council, acting unanimously on a proposal from the Commission.

(6) Nothing in the preceding paragraphs shall cause the transitional period to last more than fifteen years after the entry into force of this Treaty.

(7) Save for the exceptions or derogations provided for in this Treaty, the expiry of the transitional period shall constitute the latest date by which all the rules laid down must enter into force and all the measures required for establishing the common market must be implemented.

Article 7a

The Community shall adopt measures with the aim of progressively establishing the internal market over a period expiring on 31 December 1992, in accordance with the provisions of this Article and of Articles 7b, 7c, 28, 57(2), 59, 70(1), 84, 99, 100a and 100b and without prejudice to the other provisions of this Treaty.

The internal market shall comprise an area without internal frontiers in which the free movement of goods, persons, services and capital is ensured in accordance with the provisions of this Treaty.

Article 7b

The Commission shall report to the Council before 31 December 1988 and again before 31 December 1990 on the progress made towards achieving the internal market within the time limit fixed in Article 7a.

The Council, acting by a qualified majority on a proposal from the Commission, shall determine the guidelines and conditions necessary to ensure balanced progress in all the sectors concerned.

Article 7c

When drawing up its proposals with a view to achieving the objectives set out in Article 7a, the Commission shall take into account the extent of the effort that certain economies showing differences in development will have to sustain during the period of establishment of the internal market and it may propose appropriate provisions.

If these provisions take the form of derogations, they must be of temporary nature and must cause the least possible disturbance to the functioning of the common market.

Part Two
CITIZENSHIP OF THE UNION

Article 8

(1) Citizenship of the Union is hereby established. Every person holding the nationality of a Member State shall be a citizen of the Union.

(2) Citizens of the Union shall enjoy the rights conferred by this Treaty and shall be subject to the duties imposed thereby.

Article 8a

(1) Every citizen of the Union shall have the right to move and reside freely within the territory of the Member States, subject to the limitations and conditions laid down in this Treaty and by the measures adopted to give it effect.

(2) The Council may adopt provisions with a view to facilitating the exercise of the rights referred to in paragraph 1; save as otherwise provided in this Treaty, the Council shall act unanimously on a proposal from the Commission and after obtaining the assent of the European Parliament.

Article 8b

(1) Every citizen of the Union residing in a Member State of which he is not a national shall have the right to vote and to stand as a candidate at municipal elections in the Member State in which he resides, under the same conditions as nationals of that State. This right shall be exercised subject to detailed arrangements to be adopted before 31 December 1994 by the Council, acting unanimously on a proposal from the Commission and after consulting the European Parliament; these arrangements may provide for derogations where warranted by problems specific to a Member State.

(2) Without prejudice to Article 138(3) and to the provisions adopted for its implementation, every citizen of the Union residing in a Member State of which he is not a national shall have the right to vote and to stand as a candidate in elections to the European Parliament in the Member State in which he resides, under the same conditions as nationals of that State. This right shall be exercised subject to detailed arrangements to be adopted before 31 December 1993 by the Council, acting unanimously on a proposal from the Commission and after consulting the European Parliament; these arrangements may provide for derogations where warranted by problems specific to a Member State.

Article 8c

Every citizen of the Union shall, in the territory of a third country in which the Member State of which he is a national is not represented, be entitled to protection by the diplomatic or consular authorities of any Member State, on the same conditions as the nationals of that State. Before 31 December 1993, Member States shall establish the necessary rules among themselves and start the international negotiations required to secure this protection.

Article 8d

Every citizen of the Union shall have the right to petition the European Parliament in accordance with Article 138d.

Every citizen of the Union may apply to the Ombudsman established in accordance with Article 138e.

Article 8e

The Commission shall report to the European Parliament, to the Council and to the Economic and Social Committee before 31 December 1993 and then every three years on the application of the provisions of this Part. This report shall take account of the development of the Union. On this basis, and without prejudice to the other provisions of this Treaty, the Council, acting unanimously on a proposal from the Commission and after consulting the European Parliament, may adopt provisions to strengthen or to add to the rights laid down in this Part, which it shall recommend to the Member States for adoption in accordance with their respective constitutional requirements.

Part Three

COMMUNITY POLICIES

TITLE I – FREE MOVEMENT OF GOODS

Article 9

(1) The Community shall be based upon a customs union which shall cover all trade in goods and which shall involve the prohibition between Member States of Customs duties on imports and exports and of all charges having equivalent effect, and the adoption of a common customs tariff in their relations with third countries.

(2) The provisions of Chapter 1, Section 1, and of Chapter 2 of this Title shall apply to products originating in Member States and to products coming from third countries which are in free circulation in Member States.

Article 10

(1) Products coming from a third country shall be considered to be in free circulation in a Member State if the import formalities have been complied with and any customs duties or charges having equivalent effect which are payable have been levied in that Member State, and if they have not benefited from a total or partial drawback of such duties or charges.

(2) The Commission shall, before the end of the first year after the entry into force of this Treaty, determine the methods of administrative cooperation to be adopted for the purpose of applying Article 9(2), taking into account the need to reduce as much as possible formalities imposed on trade.

Before the end of the first year after the entry into force of this Treaty, the Commission shall lay down the provisions applicable, as regards trade between Member States, to goods originating in another Member State in whose manufacture products have been used on which the exporting Member State has not levied the appropriate customs duties or charges having equivalent effect, or which have benefited from a total or partial drawback of such duties or charges.

In adopting these provisions, the Commission shall take into account the rules for the elimination of customs duties within the Community and for the progressive application of the common customs tariff.

Article 11

Member States shall take all appropriate measures to enable Governments to carry out, within the periods of time laid down, the obligations with regard to customs duties which devolve upon them pursuant to this Treaty.

CHAPTER 1 – THE CUSTOMS UNION

Section 1

Elimination of Customs Duties between Member States

Article 12

Member States shall refrain from introducing between themselves any new customs duties on imports or exports or any charges having equivalent effect, and from increasing those which they already apply in their trade with each other.

Article 13

(1) Customs duties on imports in force between Member States shall be progressively abolished by them during the transitional period in accordance with Articles 14 and 15.

(2) Charges having an effect equivalent to customs duties on imports, in force between Member States, shall be progressively abolished by them during the transitional period. The Commission shall determine by means of directives the timetable for such abolition. It shall be guided by the rules contained in Article 14(2) and (3) and by the directives issued by the Council pursuant to Article 14(2).

Article 14

(1) For each product, the basic duty to which the successive reductions shall be applied shall be the duty applied on 1 January 1957.

(2) The timetable for the reductions shall be determined as follows:

(a) during the first stage, the first reduction shall be made one year after the date when this Treaty enters into force; the second reduction, eighteen months later; the third reduction, at the end of the fourth year after the date this Treaty enters into force;

(b) during the second stage, a reduction shall be made eighteen months after that stage begins; a second reduction, eighteen months after the preceding one; a third reduction, one year later;

(c) any remaining reductions shall be made during the third stage; the Council shall, acting by a qualified majority on a proposal from the Commission, determine the timetable therefor by means of directives.

(3) At the time of the first reduction, Member States shall introduce between themselves a duty on each product equal to the basic duty minus 10 per cent.

At the time of each subsequent reduction, each Member State shall reduce its customs duties as a whole in such manner as to lower by 10 per cent its total customs receipts as defined in paragraph 4 and to reduce the duty on each product by at least 5 per cent of the basic duty.

In the case, however, of products on which the duty is still in excess of 30 per cent, each reduction must be at least 10 per cent of the basic duty.

(4) The total customs receipts of each Member State, as referred to in paragraph 3, shall be calculated by multiplying the value of its imports from other Member States during 1956 by the basic duties.

(5) Any special problems raised in applying paragraphs 1 to 4 shall be settled by directives issued by the Council acting by a qualified majority on a proposal from the Commission.

(6) Member States shall report to the Commission on the manner in which effect has been given to the preceding rules for the reduction of duties. They shall endeavour to ensure that the reduction made in the duties on each product shall amount:

– at the end of the first stage, to at least 25 per cent of the basic duty;
– at the end of the second stage, to at least 50 per cent of the basic duty.

If the Commission finds that there is as a risk that the objectives laid down in Article 13, and the percentages laid down in this paragraph, cannot be attained, it shall make all appropriate recommendations to Member States.

(7) The provisions of this Article may be amended by the Council, acting unanimously on a proposal from the Commission and after consulting the European Parliament.

Article 15

(1) Irrespective of the provisions of Article 14, any Member State may, in the course of the transitional period, suspend in whole or in part the collection of duties applied by it to products imported from other Member States. It shall inform the other Member States and the Commission thereof.

(2) The Member States declare their readiness to reduce customs duties against the other Member States more rapidly than is provided for in Article 14 if their general economic situations and the situation of the economic sector concerned so permit.

To this end, the Commission shall make recommendations to the Member States concerned.

Article 16

Member States shall abolish between themselves customs duties on exports and charges having equivalent effect by the end of the first stage at the latest.

Article 17

(1) The provisions of Articles 9 to 15(1) shall also apply to customs duties of a fiscal nature. Such duties shall not, however, be taken into consideration for the purpose of calculating either total customs receipts or the reduction of customs duties as a whole as referred to in Article 14(3) and (4).

Such duties shall, at each reduction, be lowered by not less than 10 per cent of the basic duty. Member States may reduce such duties more rapidly than is provided for in Article 14.

(2) Member States shall, before the end of the first year after the entry into force of this Treaty, inform the Commission of their customs duties of a fiscal nature.

(3) Member States shall retain the right to substitute for these duties an internal tax which complies with the provisions of Article 95.

(4) If the Commission finds that substitution for any customs duty of a fiscal nature meets with serious difficulties in a Member State, it shall authorise that State to retain the duty on condition that it shall abolish it not later than six years after the entry into force of this Treaty. Such authorisation must be applied for before the end of the first year after the entry into force of this Treaty.

Section 2

Setting Up of the Common Customs Tariff

Article 18

The Member States declare their readiness to contribute to the development of international trade and the lowering of barriers to trade by entering into agreements designed, on a basis of reciprocity and mutual advantage, to reduce customs duties below the general level of which they could avail themselves as a result of the establishment of a customs union between them.

Article 19

(1) Subject to the conditions and within the limits provided for hereinafter, duties in the common customs tariff shall be at the level of the arithmetical average of the duties applied in the four customs territories comprised in the Community.

(2) The duties taken as the basis for calculating this average shall be those applied by Member States on 1 January 1957.

In the case of the Italian tariff, however, the duty applied shall be that without the temporary 10 per cent reduction. Furthermore, with respect to items on which the Italian tariff contains a conventional duty, this duty shall be substituted for the duty applied as defined above, provided that it does not exceed the latter by more than 10 per cent. Where the conventional duty exceeds the duty applied as defined above by more than 10 per cent, the latter duty plus 10 per cent shall be taken as the basis for calculating the arithmetical average.

With regard to the tariff headings in List A, the duties shown in that List shall, for the purpose of calculating the arithmetical average, be substituted for the duties applied.

(3) The duties in the common customs tariff shall not exceed:

(a) 3 per cent for products within the tariff headings in List B;

(b) 10 per cent for products within the tariff headings in List C;

(c) 15 per cent for products within the tariff headings in List D;

(d) 25 per cent for products within the tariff headings in List E; where, in respect of such products, the tariff of the Benelux countries contains a duty not exceeding 3 per cent, such duty shall, for the purpose of calculating the arithmetical average, be raised to 12 per cent.

(4) List F prescribes the duties applicable to the products listed therein.

(5) The Lists of tariff headings referred to in this Article and in Article 20 are set out in Annex 1 to this Treaty.

Article 20

The duties applicable to the products in List G shall be determined by negotiation between the Member States. Each Member State may add further products to this List to a value not exceeding 2 per cent of the total value of its imports from third countries in the course of the year 1956.

The Commission shall take all appropriate steps to ensure that such negotiations shall be undertaken before the end of the second year after the entry into force of this Treaty and be concluded before the end of the first stage.

If, for certain products, no agreement can be reached within these periods, the Council shall, on a proposal from the Commission, acting unanimously until the end of the second stage and by a qualified majority thereafter, determine the duties in the common customs tariff.

Article 21

(1) Technical difficulties which may arise in applying Articles 19 and 20 shall be resolved, within two years of the entry into force of this Treaty, by directives issued by the Council acting by a qualified majority on a proposal from the Commission.

(2) Before the end of the first stage, or at latest when the duties are determined, the Council shall, acting by a qualified majority on a proposal from the Commission, decide on any adjustments required in the interests of the internal consistency of the common customs tariff as a result of applying the rules set out in Articles 19 and 20, taking account in particular of the degree of processing undergone by the various goods to which the common tariff applies.

Article 22

The Commission shall, within two years of the entry into force of this Treaty, determine the extent to which the customs duties of a fiscal nature referred to in Article 17(2) shall be taken into account in calculating the arithmetical average provided for in Article 19(1). The Commission shall take account of any protective character which such duties may have.

Within six months of such determination, any Member may request that the procedure provided for in Article 20 should be applied to the product in question, but in this event the percentage limit provided in that Article shall not be applicable to that State.

Article 23

(1) For the purpose of the progressive introduction of the common customs tariff, Member States shall amend their tariffs applicable to third countries as follows:

(a) in the case of tariff headings on which the duties applied in practice on 1 January 1957 do not differ by more than 15 per cent in either direction from the duties in the common customs tariff, the latter duties shall be applied at the end of the fourth year after the entry into force of this Treaty;

(b) in any other case, each Member State shall, as from the same date, apply a duty reducing by 30 per cent the difference between the duty applied in practice on 1 January 1957 and the duty in the common tariff;

(c) at the end of the second stage this difference shall again be reduced by 30 per cent;

(d) in the case of tariff headings for which the duties in the common customs tariff are not yet available at the end of the first stage, each Member State shall, within six months of the Council's action in accordance with Article 20, apply such duties as would result from application of the rules contained in this paragraph.

(2) Where a Member State has been granted an authorisation under Article 17(4), it need not, for as long as that authorisation remains valid, apply the preceding provisions to the tariff headings to which the authorisation applies. When such authorisation expires; the Member State concerned shall apply such duty as would have resulted from application of the rules contained in paragraph 1.

(3) The common customs tariff shall be applied in its entirety by the end of the transitional period at the latest.

Article 24

Member States shall remain free to change their duties more rapidly than is provided for in Article 23 in order to bring them into line with the common customs tariff.

Article 25

(1) If the Commission finds that the production in Member States of particular products contained in Lists B, C and D is insufficient to supply the demands of one of the Member States, and that such supply traditionally depends to a considerable extent on imports from third countries, the Council shall, acting by a qualified majority on a proposal from the commission, grant the Member State concerned tariff quotas at a reduced rate of duty or duty free.

Such quotas may not exceed the limits beyond which the risk might arise of activities being transferred to the detriment of other Member States.

(2) In the case of the products in List E, and of those in List G for which the rates of duty have been determined in accordance with the procedure provided for in the third paragraph of Article 20, the Commission shall, where a change in sources of supply or a shortage of supplies within the Community is such as to entail harmful consequences for the processing industries of a Member State, at the request of that Member State, grant it tariff quotas at a reduced rate of duty or duty free.

Such quotas may not exceed the limits beyond which the risk might arise of activities being transferred to the detriment of other Member States.

(3) In the case of the products listed in Annex 11 to this Treaty, the Commission may authorise any Member State to suspend, in whole or in part, collection of the duties applicable or may grant such Member State tariff quotas at a reduced rate of duty or duty free, provided that no serious disturbance of the market of the products concerned results therefrom.

(4) The Commission shall periodically examine tariff quotas granted pursuant to this Article.

Article 26

The Commission may authorise any Member State encountering special difficulties to postpone the lowering or raising of duties provided for in Article 23 in respect of particular headings in its tariff.

Such authorisation may only be granted for a limited period and in respect of tariff headings which, taken together, represent for such State not more than 5 per cent of the value of its imports from third countries in the course of the latest year for which statistical data are available.

Article 27

Before the end of the first stage, Member States shall, in so far as may be necessary, take steps to approximate their provisions laid down by law, regulation or administrative action in respect of customs matters. To this end, the Commission shall make all appropriate recommendations to Member States.

Article 28

Any autonomous alteration or suspension of duties in the common customs tariff shall be decided by the Council acting by a qualified majority on a proposal from the Commission.

Article 29

In carrying out the tasks entrusted to it under the Section the Commission shall be guided by:

(a) the need to promote trade between Member States and third countries;

(b) developments in conditions of competition within the Community in so far as they lead to an improvement in the competitive capacity of undertakings;

(c) the requirements of the Community as regards the supply of raw materials and semi-finished goods; in this connection the Commission shall take care to avoid distorting conditions of competition between Member States in respect of finished goods;

(d) the need to avoid serious disturbances in the economies of Member States and to ensure rational development of production and an expansion of consumption within the Community.

CHAPTER 2 – ELIMINATION OF QUANTITATIVE RESTRICTIONS BETWEEN MEMBER STATES

Article 30

Quantitative restrictions on imports and all measures having equivalent effect shall, without prejudice to the following provisions, be prohibited between Member States.

Article 31

Member States shall refrain from introducing between themselves any new quantitative restrictions or measures having equivalent effect.

This obligation shall, however, relate only to the degree of liberalisation attained in pursuance of the decisions of the Council of the Organisation for European Economic Cooperation of 14 January 1955. Member States shall supply the Commission, not later than six months after the entry into force of this Treaty, with lists of the products liberalised by them in pursuance of these decisions. These lists shall be consolidated between Member States.

Article 32

In their trade with one another Member States shall refrain from making more restrictive the quotas and measures having equivalent effect existing at the date of the entry into force of this Treaty.

These quotas shall be abolished by the end of the transitional period at the latest. During that period, they shall be progressively abolished in accordance with the following provisions.

Article 33

(1) One year after the entry into force of this Treaty, each Member State shall convert any bilateral quotas open to any other Member States into global quotas open without discrimination to all other Member States.

On the same date, Member States shall increase the aggregate of the global quotas so established in such a manner as to bring about an increase of not less than 20 per cent in their total value as compared with the preceding year. The global quota for each product, however, shall be increased by not less than 10 per cent.

The quotas shall be increased annually in accordance with the same rules and in the same proportions in relation to the preceding year.

The fourth increase shall take place at the end of the fourth year after the entry into force of this Treaty; the fifth, one year after the beginning of the second state.

(2) Where, in the case of a product which has not been liberalised, the global quota does not amount to 3 per cent of the national production of the State concerned, a quota equal to not less than 3 per cent of such national

production shall be introduced not later than one year after the entry into force of this Treaty. This quota shall be raised to 4 per cent at the end of the second year, and to 5 per cent at the end of the third. Thereafter, the Member State concerned shall increase the quota by not less than 15 per cent annually.

Where there is no such national production, the Commission shall take a decision establishing an appropriate quota.

(3) At the end of the tenth year, each quota shall be equal to not less than 20 per cent of the national production.

(4) If the Commission finds by means of a decision that during two successive years the imports of any products have been below the level of the quota opened, this global quota shall not be taken into account in calculating the total value of the global quotas. In such case, the Member State shall abolish quota restrictions on the product concerned.

(5) In the case of quotas representing more than 20 per cent of the national production of the product concerned, the Council may, acting by a qualified majority on a proposal from the Commission, reduce the minimum percentage of 10 per cent laid down in paragraph 1. This alteration shall not, however, affect the obligation to increase the total value of global quotas by 20 per cent annually.

(6) Member States which have exceeded their obligations as regards the degree of liberalisation attained in pursuance of the decisions of the Council of the Organisation for European Economic Cooperation of 14 January 1955 shall be entitled, when calculating the annual total increase of 20 per cent provided for in paragraph 1, to take into account the amount of imports liberalised by autonomous action. Such calculation shall be submitted to the Commission for its prior approval.

(7) The Commission shall issue directives establishing the procedure and timetable in accordance with which Member States shall abolish, as between themselves, any measures in existence when this Treaty enters into force which have an effect equivalent to quotas.

(8) If the Commission finds that the application of the provisions of this Article, and in particular of the provisions concerning percentages, makes it impossible to ensure that the abolition of quotas provided for in the second paragraph of Article 32 is carried out progressively, the Council may, on a proposal from the Commission, acting unanimously during the first stage and by a qualified majority thereafter, amend the procedure laid down in this Article and may, in particular, increase the percentage fixed.

Article 34

(1) Quantitative restrictions on exports, and all measures having equivalent effect, shall be prohibited between Member States.

(2) Member States shall, by the end of the first stage at the latest, abolish all quantitative restrictions on exports and any measures having equivalent effect which are in existence when this Treaty enters into force.

Article 35

The Member States declare their readiness to abolish quantitative restrictions on imports from and exports to other Member States more rapidly than is provided for in the preceding Articles, if their general economic situation and the situation of the economic sector concerned so permit.

To this end, the Commission shall make recommendations to the Member States concerned.

Article 36

The provisions of Articles 30 to 34 shall not preclude prohibitions or restrictions on imports, exports or goods in transit justified on grounds of public morality, public policy or public security; the protection of health and life of humans, animals or plants; the protection of national treasures possessing artistic, historic or archaeological value; or the protection of industrial and commercial property. Such prohibitions or restrictions shall not, however, constitute a means of arbitrary discrimination or a disguised restriction on trade between Member States.

Article 37

(1) Member States shall progressively adjust any State monopolies of a commercial character so as to ensure that when the transitional period has ended no discrimination regarding the conditions under which goods are procured and marketed exists between nationals of Member States.

The provisions of this Article shall apply to any body through which a Member State, in law or in fact, either directly or indirectly supervises, determines or appreciably influences imports or exports between Member States. These provisions shall likewise apply to monopolies delegated by the State to others.

(2) Member States shall refrain from introducing any new measure which is contrary to the principles laid down in paragraph 1 or which restricts the scope of the Articles dealing with the abolition of customs duties and quantitative restrictions between Member States.

(3) The timetable for the measures referred to in paragraph 1 shall be harmonised with the abolition of quantitative restrictions on the same products provided for in Articles 30 to 34.

If a product is subject to a State monopoly of a commercial character in only one or some Member States, the Commission may authorise the other Member States to apply protective measures until the adjustment provided for in paragraph 1 has been effected; the Commission shall determine the conditions and details of such measures.

(4) If a State monopoly of a commercial character has rules which are designed to make it easier to dispose of agricultural products or obtain for them the best return, steps should be taken in applying the rules contained in this Article to ensure equivalent safeguards for the employment and standard of living of the producers concerned, account being taken of the adjustments that will be possible and the specialisation that will be needed with the passage of time.

(5) The obligations on Member States shall be binding only in so far as they are compatible with existing international agreements.

(6) With effect from the first stage the Commission shall make recommendations as to the manner in which and the timetable according to which the adjustment provided for in this Article shall be carried out.

TITLE II – AGRICULTURE

Article 38

(1) The common market shall extend to agriculture and trade in agricultural products. 'Agricultural products' means the products of the soil, of stockfarming and of fisheries and products of first-stage processing directly related to these products.

(2) Save as otherwise provided in Articles 39 to 46, rules laid down for the establishment of the common market shall apply to agricultural products.

(3) The products subject to the provisions of Articles 39 to 46 are listed in Annex II to this Treaty. Within two years of the entry into force of this Treaty, however, the Council shall, acting by a qualified majority on a proposal from the Commission, decide what products are to be added to this list.

(4) The operation and development of the common market for agricultural products must be accompanied by the establishment of a common agricultural policy among the Member States.

Article 39

(1) The objectives of the common agricultural policy shall be:

(a) to increase agricultural productivity by promoting technical progress and by ensuring the rational development of agricultural production and the optimum utilisation of the factors of production, in particular labour;

(b) thus to ensure a fair standard of living for the agricultural community, in particular by increasing the individual earnings of persons engaged in agriculture;

(c) to stabilise markets;

(d) to assure the availability of supplies; and

(e) to ensure that supplies reach consumers at reasonable prices.

(2) In working out the common agricultural policy and the special methods for its application, account shall be taken of:

(a) the particular nature of agricultural activity, which results from the social structure of agriculture and from structural and natural disparities between the various agricultural regions;

(b) the need to effect the appropriate adjustments by degrees;

(c) the fact that in the Member States agriculture constitutes a sector closely linked with the economy as a whole.

Article 40

(1) Member States shall develop the common agricultural policy by degrees during the transitional period and shall bring it into force by the end of that period at the latest.

(2) In order to attain the objectives set out in Article 39 a common organisation of agricultural markets shall be established.

This organisation shall take one of the following forms, depending on the product concerned:

(a) common rules on competition;

(b) compulsory coordination of the various national market organisations;

(c) a European market organisation.

(3) The common organisation established in accordance with paragraph 2 may include all measures required to attain the objectives set out in Article 39, in particular regulation of prices, aids for the production and marketing of the various products, storage and carry-over arrangements and common machinery for stabilising imports or exports.

The common organisation shall be limited to pursuit of the objectives set out in Article 39 and shall exclude any discrimination between producers or consumers within the Community.

Any common price policy shall be based on common criteria and uniform methods of calculation.

(4) In order to enable the common organisation referred to in paragraph 2 to attain its objectives, one or more agricultural guidance and guarantee funds may be set up.

Article 41

To enable the objectives set out in Article 39 to be attained, provision may be made within the framework of the common agricultural policy for measures such as:

(a) an effective coordination of efforts in the spheres of vocational training, of research and of the dissemination of agricultural knowledge; this may include joint financing of projects or institutions;

(b) joint measures to promote consumption of certain products.

Article 42

The provisions of the Chapter relating to rules on competition shall apply to production of and trade in agricultural products only to the extent determined by the Council within the framework of Article 43(2) and (3) and in accordance with the procedure laid down therein, account being taken of the objectives set out in Article 39.

The Council may, in particular, authorise the granting of aid:

(a) for the protection of enterprises handicapped by structural or natural conditions;

(b) within the framework of economic development programmes.

Article 43

(1) In order to evolve the broad lines of a common agricultural policy, the Commission shall, immediately this Treaty enters into force, convene a conference of the Member States with a view to making a comparison of their agricultural policies, in particular by producing a statement of their resources and needs.

(2) Having taken into account the work of the conference provided for in paragraph 1, after consulting the Economic and Social Committee and within two years of the entry into force of this Treaty, the Commission shall submit proposals for working out and implementing the common agricultural policy, including the replacement of the national organisations by one of the forms of common organisation provided for in Article 40(2), and for implementing the measures specified in this Title.

These proposals shall take account of the interdependence of the agricultural matters mentioned in this Title.

The Council shall, on a proposal from the Commission and after consulting the European Parliament, acting unanimously during the first two stages and by a qualified majority thereafter, make regulations, issue directives, or take decisions, without prejudice to any recommendations it may also make.

(3) The Council may, acting by a qualified majority and in accordance with paragraph 2, replace the national market organisation by the common organisation provided for in Article 40(2) if:

(a) the common organisation offers Member States which are opposed to this measure and which have an organisation of their own for the production in question equivalent safeguards for the employment and standard of living of the producers concerned, account being taken of the adjustments that will be possible and the specialisation that will be needed with the passage of time;

(b) such an organisation ensures conditions for trade within the Community similar to those existing in a national market.

(4) If a common organisation for certain raw materials is established before a common organisation exists for the corresponding processed products, such raw materials as are used for processed products intended for export to third countries may be imported from outside the Community.

Article 44

(1) In so far as progressive abolition of customs duties and quantitative restrictions between Member States may result in prices likely to jeopardise

the attainment of the objectives set out in Article 39, each Member State shall, during the transitional period, be entitled to apply to particular products, in a non-discriminatory manner and in substitution for quotas and to such an extent as shall not impede the expansion of the volume of trade provided for in Article 45(2), a system of minimum prices below which imports may be either:

- temporarily suspended or reduced; or
- allowed, but subjected to the condition that they are made at a price higher than the minimum price for the product concerned.

In the latter case the minimum prices shall not include customs duties.

(2) Minimum prices shall neither cause a reduction of the trade existing between Member States when this Treaty enters into force nor form an obstacle to progressive expansion of this trade. Minimum prices shall not be applied so as to form an obstacle to the development of a natural preference between Member States.

(3) As soon as this Treaty enters into force the Council shall, on a proposal from the Commission, determine objective criteria for the establishment of minimum price systems and for the fixing of such prices.

These criteria shall in particular take account of the average national production costs in the Member State applying the minimum price, of the position of the various undertakings concerned in relation to such average production costs, and of the need to promote both the progressive improvement of agricultural practice and the adjustments and specialisation needed within the common market.

The Commission shall further propose a procedure for revising these criteria in order to allow for and speed up technical progress and to approximate prices progressively within the common market.

These criteria and the procedure for revising them shall be determined by the Council acting unanimously within three years of the entry into force of this Treaty.

(4) Until the decision of the Council takes effect, Member States may fix minimum prices on condition that these are communicated beforehand to the Commission and to the other Member States so that they may submit their comments.

Once the Council has taken its decision, Member States shall fix minimum prices on the basis of the criteria determined as above.

The Council may, acting by a qualified majority on a proposal from the

Commission, rectify any decisions taken by Member States which do not conform to the criteria defined above.

(5) If it does not prove possible to determine the said objective criteria for certain products by the beginning of the third stage, the Council may, acting by a qualified majority on a proposal from the Commission, vary the minimum prices applied to these products.

(6) At the end of the transitional period, a table of minimum prices still in force shall be drawn up. The Council shall, acting on a proposal from the Commission and by a majority of nine votes in accordance with the weighting laid down in the first subparagraph of Article 148(2), determine the system to be applied within the framework of the common agricultural policy.

Article 45

(1) Until national market organisations have been replaced by one of the forms of common organisation referred to in Article 40(2), trade in products in respect of which certain Member States:

- have arrangements designed to guarantee national producers a market for their products; and
- are in need of imports,

shall be developed by the conclusion of long-term agreements or contracts between importing and exporting Member States.

These agreements or contracts shall be directed towards the progressive abolition of any discrimination in the application of these arrangements to the various producers within the Community. Such agreements or contracts shall be concluded during the first stage; account shall be taken of the principle of reciprocity.

(2) As regards quantities, these agreements or contracts shall be based on the average volume of trade between Member States in the products concerned during the three years before the entry into force of this Treaty and shall provide for an increase in the volume of trade within the limits of existing requirements, account being taken of traditional patterns of trade.

As regards prices, these agreements or contracts shall enable producers to dispose of the agreed quantities at prices which shall be progressively approximated to those paid to national producers on the domestic market of the purchasing country.

This approximation shall proceed as steadily as possible and shall be completed by the end of the transitional period at the latest.

Prices shall be negotiated between the parties concerned within the framework of directives issued by the Commission for the purpose of implementing the two preceding subparagraphs.

If the first stage is extended, these agreements or contracts shall continue to be carried out in accordance with the conditions applicable at the end of the fourth year after the entry into force of this Treaty, the obligation to increase quantities and to approximate prices being suspended until the transition to the second stage.

Member States shall avail themselves of any opportunity open to them under their legislation, particularly in respect of import policy, to ensure the conclusion and carrying out of these agreements or contracts.

(3) To the extent that Member States require raw materials for the manufacture of products to be exported outside the Community in competition with products of third countries, the above agreements or contracts shall not form an obstacle to the importation of raw materials for this purpose from third countries. This provision shall not, however, apply if the Council unanimously decides to make provision for payments required to compensate for the higher price paid on goods imported for this purpose on the basis of these agreements or contracts in relation to the delivered price of the same goods purchased on the world market.

Article 46

Where in a Member State a product is subject to a national market organisation or to internal rules having equivalent effect which affect the competitive position of similar production in another Member State, a countervailing charge shall be applied by Member States to imports of this product coming from the Member State where such organisation or rules exist, unless the State applies a countervailing charge on export.

The Commission shall fix the amount of these charges at the level required to redress the balance; it may also authorise other measures, the conditions and details of which it shall determine.

Article 47

As to the functions to be performed by the Economic and Social Committee in pursuance of this Title, its agricultural section shall hold itself at the disposal of the Commission to prepare, in accordance with the provisions of Articles 197 and 198, the deliberations of the Committee.

TITLE III – FREE MOVEMENT OF PERSONS, SERVICES AND CAPITAL

CHAPTER 1 – WORKERS

Article 48

(1) Freedom of movement for workers shall be secured within the Community by the end of the transitional period at the latest.

(2) Such freedom of movement shall entail the abolition of any discrimination based on nationality between workers of the Member States as regards employment, remuneration and other conditions of work and employment.

(3) It shall entail the right, subject to limitations justified on grounds of public policy, public security or public health:

(a) to accept offers of employment actually made;

(b) to move freely within the territory of Member States for this purpose;

(c) to stay in a Member State for the purpose of employment in accordance with the provisions governing the employment of nationals of that State laid down by law, regulation or administrative action;

(d) to remain in the territory of a Member State after having been employed in that State, subject to conditions which shall be embodied in implementing regulations to be drawn up by the Commission.

(4) The provisions of this Article shall not apply to employment in the public service.

Article 49

As soon as this Treaty enters into force, the Council shall, acting in accordance with the procedure referred to in Article 189b and after consulting the Economic and Social Committee, issue directives or make regulations setting out the measures required to bring about, by progressive stages, freedom of movement for workers, as defined in Article 48, in particular:

(a) by ensuring close cooperation between national employment services;

(b) by systematically and progressively abolishing those admin-istrative procedures and practices and those qualifying periods in respect of eligibility for available employment, whether resulting from national legislation or from agreements previously concluded between Member States, the maintenance of which would form an obstacle to liberalisation of the movement of workers;

(c) by systematically and progressively abolishing all such qualifying periods and other restrictions provided for either under national legislation or under agreements previously concluded between Member States as imposed on workers of other Member States conditions regarding the free choice of employment other than those imposed on workers of the State concerned;

(d) by setting up appropriate machinery to bring offers of employment into touch with applications for employment and to facilitate the achievement of a balance between supply and demand in the employment market in such a way as to avoid serious threats to the standard of living and level of employment in the various regions and industries.

Article 50

Member States shall, within the framework of a joint programme, encourage the exchange of young workers.

Article 51

The Council shall, acting unanimously on a proposal from the Commission, adopt such measures in the field of social security as are necessary to provide freedom of movement for workers; to this end, it shall make arrangements to secure for migrant workers and their dependants:

(a) aggregation, for the purpose of acquiring and retaining the right to benefit and of calculating the amount of benefit, of all periods taken into account under the laws of the several countries;

(b) payment of benefits to persons resident in the territories of Member States.

CHAPTER 2 – RIGHT OF ESTABLISHMENT

Article 52

Within the framework of the provisions set out below, restrictions on the freedom of establishment of nationals of a Member State in the territory of another Member State shall be abolished by progressive stages in the course of the transitional period. Such progressive abolition shall also apply to restrictions of the setting up of agencies, branches or subsidiaries by nationals of any Member State established in the territory of any Member State.

Freedom of establishment shall include the right to take up and pursue activities as self-employed persons and to set up and manage undertakings, in particular companies or firms within the meaning of the second paragraph of Article 58, under the conditions laid down for its own nationals by the law of the country where such establishment is effected, subject to the provisions of the Chapter relating to capital.

Article 53

Member States shall not introduce any new restrictions on the right of establishment in their territories of nationals of other Member States, save as otherwise provided in this Treaty.

Article 54

(1) Before the end of the first stage, the Council shall, acting unanimously on a proposal from the Commission and after consulting the Economic and Social Committee and the European Parliament, draw up a general programme for the abolition of existing restrictions on freedom of establishment within the Community. The Commission shall submit its proposals to the Council during the first two years of the first stage.

The programme shall set out the general conditions under which freedom of freedom of establishment is to be attained in the case of each type of activity and in particular the stages by which it is to be attained.

(2) In order to implement this general programme or, in the absence of such programme, in order to achieve a stage in attaining freedom of establishment as regards a particular activity, the Council, acting in accordance with the procedure referred to in Article 189b and after consulting the Economic and Social Committee, shall act by means of directives.

(3) The Council and the Commission shall carry out the duties devolving upon them under the preceding provisions, in particular:

> (a) by according, as a general rule, priority treatment to activities where freedom of establishment makes a particularly valuable contribution to the development of production and trade;
>
> (b) by ensuring close cooperation between the competent authorities in the Member States in order to ascertain the particular situation within the Community of the various activities concerned;
>
> (c) by abolishing those administrative procedures and practices, whether resulting from national legislation or from agreements previously

concluded between Member States, the maintenance of which would form an obstacle to freedom of establishment;

(d) by ensuring that workers of one Member State employed in the territory of another Member State may remain in that territory for the purpose of taking up activities therein as self-employed persons, where they satisfy the conditions which they would be required to satisfy if they were entering that State at the time when they intended to take up such activities;

(e) by enabling a national of one Member State to acquire and use land and buildings situated in the territory of another Member State, in so far as this does not conflict with the principles laid down in Article 39(2);

(f) by effecting the progressive abolition of restrictions on freedom of establishment in every branch of activity under consideration, both as regards the conditions for setting up agencies, branches or subsidiaries in the territory of a Member State and as regards the conditions governing the entry of personnel belonging to the main establishment into managerial or supervisory posts in such agencies, branches or subsidiaries;

(g) by coordinating to the necessary extent the safeguards which, for the protection of the interests of members and others, are required by Member States of companies or firms within the meaning of the second paragraph of Article 58 with a view to making such safeguards equivalent throughout the Community;

(h) by satisfying themselves that the conditions of establishment are not distorted by aids granted by Member States.

Article 55

The provisions of this chapter shall not apply, so far as any given Member State is concerned, to activities which in that State are connected, even occasionally, with the existence of official authority.

The Council may, acting by qualified majority on a proposal from the Commission, rule that the provisions of this Chapter shall not apply to certain activities.

Article 56

(1) The provisions of this Chapter and measures taken in pursuance thereof shall not prejudice the applicability of provisions laid down by law, regulation or administrative action providing for special treatment for foreign nationals on grounds of public policy, public security or public health.

(2) Before the end of the transitional period, the Council shall, acting unanimously on a proposal from the Commission and after consulting the European Parliament, issue directives for the coordination of the above-mentioned provisions laid down by law, regulation or administrative action. After the end of the second stage, however, the Council shall, acting in accordance with the procedure referred to in Article 189b, issue directives for the coordination of such provisions as, in each Member State, are a matter for regulation or administrative action.

Article 57

(1) In order to make it easier for persons to take up and pursue activities as self-employed persons, the Council shall, acting in accordance with the procedure referred to in Article 189b, issue directives for the mutual recognition of diplomas, certificates and other evidence of formal qualifications.

(2) For the same purpose, the Council shall, before the end of the transitional period, issue directives for the coordination of the provisions laid down by law, regulation or administrative action in Member States concerning the taking up and pursuit of activities as self-employed persons. The Council, acting unanimously on a proposal from the Commission and after consulting the European Parliament, shall decide on directives the implementation of which involves in at least one Member State amendment of the existing principles laid down by law governing the professions with respect to training and conditions of access for natural persons. In other cases the Council shall act in accordance with the procedure referred to in Article 189b.

(3) In the case of the medical and allied and pharmaceutical professions, the progressive abolition of restrictions shall be dependent upon coordination of the conditions for their exercise in the various Member States.

Article 58

Companies or firms formed in accordance with the law of a Member State and having their registered office, central administration or principal place of business within the Community shall, for the purposes of this chapter, be treated in the same way as natural persons who are nationals of Member States.

'Companies or firms' means companies or firms constituted under civil or commercial law, including cooperative societies, and other legal persons governed by public or private law, save for those which are non-profit making.

CHAPTER 3 – SERVICES

Article 59

Within the framework of the provisions set out below, restrictions on freedom to provide services within the Community shall be progressively abolished during the transitional period in respect of nationals of Member States who are established in a State of the Community other than that of the person for whom the services are intended.

The Council may, acting by a qualified majority on a proposal from the Commission, extend the provisions of this Chapter to nationals of a third country who provide services and who are established within the Community.

Article 60

Services shall be considered to be 'services' within the meaning of this Treaty where they are normally provided for remuneration, in so far as they are not governed by the provisions relating to freedom of movement for goods, capital and persons.

'Services' shall in particular include:

(a) activities of an industrial character;

(b) activities of a commercial character;

(c) activities of craftsmen;

(d) activities of the professions.

Without prejudice to the provisions of the Chapter relating to the right of establishment, the person providing a service may, in order to do so, temporarily pursue his activity in the State where the service is provided, under the same conditions as are imposed by that State on its own nationals.

Article 61

(1) Freedom to provide services in the field of transport shall be governed by the provisions of the Title relating to transport.

(2) The liberalisation of banking and insurance services connected with movements of capital shall be effected in step with the progressive liberalisation of movement of capital.

Article 62

Save as otherwise provided in this Treaty, Member States shall not introduce any new restrictions on the freedom to provide services which has in fact been attained at the date of the entry into force of this Treaty.

Article 63

(1) Before the end of the first stage, the Council shall, acting unanimously on a proposal from the Commission and after consulting the Economic and Social Committee and the European Parliament, draw up a general programme for the abolition of existing restrictions on freedom to provide services within the Community. The Commission shall submit its proposal to the Council during the first two years of the first state.

The programme shall set out the general conditions under which and the stages by which each type of service is to be liberalised.

(2) In order to implement this general programme or, in the absence of such programme, in order to achieve a stage in the liberalisation of a specific service, the Council shall, on a proposal from the Commission and after consulting the Economic and Social Committee and the European Parliament, issue directives, acting unanimously until the end of the first stage and by a qualified majority thereafter.

(3) As regards the proposals and decisions referred to in paragraphs 1 and 2, priority shall as a general rule be given to those services which directly affect production costs or the liberalisation of which helps to promote trade in goods.

Article 64

The Member States declare their readiness to undertake the liberalisation of services beyond the extent required by the directives issued pursuant to Article 63(2), if their general economic situation and the situation of the economic sector concerned so permit.

To this end, the Commission shall make recommendations to the Member States concerned.

Article 65

As long as restrictions on freedom to provide services have not been abolished, each Member State shall apply such restrictions without distinction on grounds of nationality or residence to all persons providing services within the meaning of the first paragraph of Article 59.

Article 66

The provisions of Articles 55 to 58 shall apply to the matters covered by this Chapter.

CHAPTER 4 – CAPITAL AND PAYMENTS

Article 73a

As from 1 January 1994, Articles 67 to 73 shall be replaced by Articles 73b, c, d, e, f and g.

Article 73b

(1) Within the framework of the provisions set out in this Chapter, all restrictions on the movement of capital between Member States and between Member States and third countries shall be prohibited.

(2) Within the framework of the provisions set out in this Chapter, all restrictions on payments between Member States and between Member States and third countries shall be prohibited.

Article 73c

(1) The provisions of Article 73b shall be without prejudice to the application to third countries of any restrictions which exist on 31 December 1993 under national or Community law adopted in respect of the movement of capital to or from third countries involving direct investment – including investment in real estate – establishment, the provision of financial services or the admission of securities to capital markets.

(2) Whilst endeavouring to achieve the objective of free movement of capital between Member States and third countries to the greatest extent possible and without prejudice to the other Chapters of this Treaty, the Council may, acting by a qualified majority on a proposal from the Commission, adopt measures on the movement of capital to or from third countries involving direct investment – including investment in real estate – establishment, the provision of financial services or the admission of securities to capital markets.

Unanimity shall be required for measures under this paragraph which constitute a step back in Community law as regards the liberalisation of the movement of capital to or from third countries.

Article 73d

(1) The provisions of Article 73b shall be without prejudice to the right of Member States:

> (a) to apply the relevant provisions of their tax law which distinguish between taxpayers who are not in the same situation with regard to their place of residence or with regard to the place where their capital is invested;
>
> (b) to take all requisite measures to prevent infringements of national law and regulations, in particular in the field of taxation and the prudential supervision of financial institutions, or to lay down procedures for the declaration of capital movements for purposes of administrative or statistical information, or to take measures which are justified on grounds of public policy or public security.

(2) The provisions of this Chapter shall be without prejudice to the applicability of restrictions on the right of establishment which are compatible with this Treaty.

(3) The measures and procedures referred to in paragraphs 1 and 2 shall not constitute a means of arbitrary discrimination or a disguised restriction on the free movement of capital and payments as defined in Article 73b.

Article 73e

By way of derogation from Article 73b, Member States which, on 31 December 1993, enjoy a derogation on the basis of existing Community law, shall be entitled to maintain, until 31 December 1995 at the latest, restrictions on movements of capital authorised by such derogations as exist on that date.

Article 73f

Where, in exceptional circumstances, movements of capital to or from third countries cause, or threaten to cause, serious difficulties for the operation of economic and monetary union, the Council, acting by a qualified majority on a proposal from the Commission and after consulting the ECB, may take safeguard measures with regard to third countries for a period not exceeding six months if such measures are strictly necessary.

Article 73g

(1) If, in the cases envisaged in Article 228a, action by the Community is deemed necessary, the Council may, in accordance with the procedure provided for in Article 228a, take the necessary urgent measures on the movement of capital and on payments as regards the third countries concerned.

(2) Without prejudice to Article 224 and as long as the Council has not taken measures pursuant to paragraph 1, a Member State may, for serious political reasons and on grounds of urgency, take unilateral measures against a third country with regard to capital movements and payments. The Commission and the other Member States shall be informed of such measures by the date of their entry into force at the latest.

The Council may, acting by a qualified majority on a proposal from the Commission, decide that the Member State concerned shall amend or abolish such measures. The President of the Council shall inform the European Parliament of any such decision taken by the Council.

TITLE IV – TRANSPORT

Article 74

The objectives of this Treaty shall, in matters governed by this Title, be pursued by Member States within the framework of a common transport policy.

Article 75

(1) For the purpose of implementing Article 74, and taking into account the distinctive features of transport, the Council shall, acting in accordance with the procedure referred to in Article 189c and after consulting the Economic and Social Committee, lay down:

(a) common rules applicable to international transport to or from the territory of a Member State or passing across the territory of one or more Member States;

(b) the conditions under which non-resident carriers may operate transport services within a Member State;

(c) measures to improve transport safety;

(d) any other appropriate provisions.

(2) The provisions referred to in (a) and (b) of paragraph 1 shall be laid down during the transitional period.

(3) By way of derogation from the procedure provided for in paragraph 1, where the application of provisions concerning the principles of the regulatory system for transport would be liable to have a serious effect on the standard of living and on employment in certain areas and on the operation of transport facilities, they shall be laid down by the Council acting unanimously on a proposal from the Commission, after consulting the European Parliament and the Economic and Social Committee. In so doing, the Council shall take into account the need for adaptation to the economic development which will result from establishing the common market.

Article 76

Until the provisions referred to in Article 75(1) have been laid down, no Member State may, without the unanimous approval of the Council, make the various provisions governing the subject when this Treaty enters into force less favourable in their direct or indirect effect on carriers of other Member States as compared with carriers who are nationals of that State.

Article 77

Aids shall be compatible with this Treaty if they meet the needs of coordination of transport or if they represent reimbursement for the discharge of certain obligations inherent in the concept of a public service.

Article 78

Any measures taken within the framework of this Treaty in respect of transport rates and conditions shall take account of the economic circumstances of carriers.

Article 79

(1) In the case of transport within the Community, discrimination which takes the form of carriers charging different rates and imposing different conditions for the carriage of the same goods over the same transport links on grounds of the country of origin or of destination of the goods in question, shall be abolished, at the latest, before the end of the second stage.

(2) Paragraph 1 shall not prevent the Council from adopting other measures in pursuance of Article 75(1).

(3) Within two years of the entry into force of this Treaty, the Council shall, acting by a qualified majority on a proposal from the Commission and after consulting the Economic and Social Committee, lay down rules for implementing the provisions of paragraph 1.

The Council may in particular lay down the provisions needed to enable the institution of the Community to secure compliance with the rule laid down in paragraph 1 and to ensure that users benefit from it to the full.

(4) The Commission shall, acting on its own initiative or on application by a Member State, investigate any cases of discrimination falling within paragraph 1 and after consulting any Member State concerned, shall take the necessary decisions within the framework of the rules laid down in accordance with the provisions of paragraph 3.

Article 80

(1) The imposition by a Member State, in respect of transport operations carried out within the Community, of rates and conditions involving any element of support or protection in the interest of one or more particular undertakings or industries shall be prohibited as from the beginning of the second stage, unless authorised by the Commission.

(2) The Commission shall, acting on its own initiative or on application by a Member State, examine the rates and conditions referred to in paragraph 1, taking account in particular of the requirements of an appropriate regional economic policy, the needs of underdeveloped areas and the problems of areas seriously affected by political circumstances on the one hand, and of the effects of such rates and conditions on competition between the different modes of transport on the other.

After consulting each Member State concerned, the Commission shall take the necessary decisions.

(3) The prohibition provided for in paragraph 1 shall not apply to tariffs fixed to meet competition.

Article 81

Charges or dues in respect of the crossing of frontiers which are charged by a carrier in addition to the transport rates shall not exceed a reasonable level after taking the costs actually incurred thereby into account.

Member States shall endeavour to reduce these costs progressively.

The Commission may make recommendations to Member States for the application of this Article.

Article 82

The provisions of this Title shall not form an obstacle to the application of measures taken in the Federal Republic of Germany to the extent that such measures are required in order to compensate for the economic disadvantages caused by the division of Germany to the economy of certain areas of the Federal Republic affected by that division.

Article 83

An Advisory Committee consisting of experts designated by the Governments of Member States, shall be attached to the Commission. The Commission, whenever it considers it desirable, shall consult the Committee on transport matters without prejudice to the powers of the transport section of the Economic and Social Committee.

Article 84

(1) The provisions of this Title shall apply to transport by rail, road and inland waterway.

(2) The Council may, acting by a qualified majority, decide whether, to what extent and by what procedure appropriate provisions may be laid down for sea and air transport.

The procedural provisions of Article 75(1) and (3) shall apply.

TITLE V – COMMON RULES ON COMPETITION, TAXATION AND APPROXIMATION OF LAWS

CHAPTER 1 – RULES ON COMPETITION

Section 1

Rules Applying to Undertakings

Article 85

(1) The following shall be prohibited as incompatible with the common market: all agreements between undertakings, decisions by associations of undertakings and concerted practices which may affect trade between

Member States and which have as their object or effect the prevention, restriction or distortion of competition within the common market, and in particular those which:

(a) directly or indirectly fix purchase or selling prices for any other trading conditions;

(b) limit or control production, markets, technical development, or investment;

(c) share markets or sources of supply;

(d) apply dissimilar conditions to equivalent transactions with other trading parties, thereby placing them at a competitive disadvantage;

(e) make the conclusion of contracts subject to acceptance by the other parties of supplementary obligations which, by their nature or according to commercial usage, have no connection with the subject of such contracts.

(2) Any agreements or decisions prohibited pursuant to this Article shall be automatically void.

(3) The provisions of paragraph 1 may, however, be declared inapplicable in the case of:

– any agreement or category of agreements between undertakings;
– any decision or category of decisions by associations of undertakings;
– any concerted practice or category of concerted practices;

which contributes to improving the production or distribution of goods or to promoting technical or economic progress, while allowing consumers a fair share of the resulting benefit, and which does not:

(a) impose on the undertakings concerned restrictions which are not indispensable to the attainment of these objectives;

(b) afford such undertakings the possibility of eliminating competition in respect of a substantial part of the products in question.

Article 86

Any abuse by one or more undertakings of a dominant position within the common market or in a substantial part of it shall be prohibited as incompatible with the common market in so far as it may affect trade between Member States. Such abuse may, in particular, consist in:

(a) directly or indirectly imposing unfair purchase or selling prices or other unfair trading conditions;

(b) limiting production, markets or technical development to the prejudice of consumers;

(c) applying dissimilar conditions to equivalent transactions with other trading parties, thereby placing them at a competitive disadvantage;

(d) making the conclusion of contracts subject to acceptance by the other parties of supplementary obligations which, by their nature or according to commercial usage, have no connection with the subject of such contracts.

Article 87

(1) Within three years of the entry into force of this Treaty the Council shall, acting unanimously on a proposal from the Commission and after consulting the European Parliament, adopt any appropriate regulations or directives to give effect to the principles set out in Articles 85 and 86.

If such provisions have not been adopted within the period mentioned, they shall be laid down by the Council, acting by a qualified majority on a proposal from the Commission and after consulting the European Parliament.

(2) The regulations or directives referred to in paragraph 1 shall be designed, in particular:

(a) to ensure compliance with the prohibitions laid down in Article 85(1) and in Article 86 by making provisions for fines and periodic penalty payments;

(b) to lay down detailed rules for the application of Article 85(3), taking into account the need to ensure effective supervision on the one hand, and to simplify administration to the greatest possible extent on the other;

(c) to define, if need be, in the various branches of the economy, the scope of the provisions of Articles 85 and 86;

(d) to define the respective functions of the Commission and of the Court of Justice in applying the provisions laid down in this paragraph;

(e) to determine the relationship between national laws and the provisions contained in this Section or adopted pursuant to this Article.

Article 88

Until the entry into force of the provisions adopted in pursuance of Article 87, the authorities in Member States shall rule on the admissibility of agreements, decisions and concerted practices and on abuse of a dominant position in the common market in accordance with the law of their country and with the provisions of Article 85, in particular paragraph 3, and of Article 86.

Article 89

(1) Without prejudice to Article 88, the Commission shall, as soon as it takes up its duties, ensure the application of the principles laid down in Articles 85 and 86. On application by a Member State or on its own initiative, and in cooperation with the competent authorities in the Member States, who shall give it their assistance, the Commission shall investigate cases of suspected infringement of these principles. If it finds that there has been an infringement, it shall propose appropriate measures to bring it to an end.

(2) If the infringement is not brought to an end, the Commission shall record such infringement of the principles in a reasoned decision. The Commission may publish its decision and authorise Member States to take the measures, the conditions and details of which it shall determine, needed to remedy the situation.

Article 90

(1) In the case of public undertakings and undertakings to which Member States grant special or exclusive rights, Member States shall neither enact nor maintain in force any measure contrary to the rules contained in this Treaty, in particular to those rules provided for in Article 6 and Articles 85 to 94.

(2) Undertakings entrusted with the operation of services of general economic interest or having the character of a revenue-producing monopoly shall be subject to the rules contained in this Treaty, in particular to the rules on competition, in so far as the application of such rules does not obstruct the performance, in law or in fact, of the particular tasks assigned to them. The development of trade must not be affected to such an extent as would be contrary to the interests of the Community.

(3) The Commission shall ensure the application of the provisions of this Article and shall, where necessary, address appropriate directives or decisions to Member States.

Section 2

Dumping

Article 91

(1) If, during the transitional period, the Commission, on application by a Member State or by any other interested party, finds that dumping is being practised within the common market, it shall address recommendations to the person or persons with whom such practices originate for the purpose of putting an end to them.

Should the practices continue, the Commission shall authorise the injured Member State to take protective measures, the conditions and details of which the Commission shall determine.

(2) As soon as this Treaty enters into force, products which originate in or are in free circulation in one Member State and which have been exported to another Member State shall, on reimportation, be admitted into the territory of the first-mentioned State free of all customs duties, quantitative restrictions or measures having equivalent effect. The Commission shall lay down appropriate rules for the application of this paragraph.

Section 3

Aids Granted by States

Article 92

(1) Save as otherwise provided in this Treaty, any aid granted by a Member State or through State resources in any form whatsoever which distorts or threatens to distort competition by favouring certain undertakings or the production of certain goods shall, in so far as it affects trade between Member States, be incompatible with the common market.

(2) The following shall be compatible with the common market:

(a) aid having a social character, granted to individual consumers, provided that such aid is granted without discrimination related to the origin of the products concerned;

(b) aid to make good the damage caused by natural disasters or exceptional occurrences;

(c) aid granted to the economy of certain areas of the Federal Republic of Germany affected by the division of Germany, in so far as such aid is required in order to compensate for the economic disadvantages caused by that division.

(3) The following may be considered to be compatible with the common market:

(a) aid to promote the economic development of areas where the standard of living is abnormally low or where there is serious underemployment;

(b) aid to promote the execution of an important project of common European interest or to remedy a serious disturbance in the economy of a Member State;

(c) aid to facilitate the development of certain economic activities or of certain economic areas, where such aid does not adversely affect trading conditions to an extent contrary to the common interest. However, the aids granted to shipbuilding as of 1 January 1957 shall, in so far as they serve only to compensate for the absence of customs protection, be progressively reduced under the same conditions as apply to the elimination of customs duties, subject to the provisions of this Treaty concerning common commercial policy towards third countries;

(d) aid to promote culture and heritage conservation where such aid does not affect trading conditions and competition in the Community to an extent that is contrary to the common interest;

(e) such other categories of aid as may be specified by decision of the Council acting by a qualified majority on a proposal from the Commission.

Article 93

(1) The Commission shall, in cooperation with Member States, keep under constant review all systems of aid existing in those States. It shall propose to the latter any appropriate measures required by the progressive development or by the functioning of the common market.

(2) If, after giving notice to the parties concerned to submit their comments, the Commission finds that aid granted by a State or through State resources is not compatible with the common market having regard to Article 92, or that such aid is being misused, it shall decide that the State concerned shall abolish or alter such aid within a period of time to be determined by the Commission.

If the State concerned does not comply with this decision within the prescribed time, the Commission or any other interested State may, in derogation from the provisions of Article 169 and 170, refer the matter to the Court of Justice direct.

On application by a Member State, the Council, may, acting unanimously, decide that aid which that State is granting or intends to grant shall be considered to be compatible with the common market, in derogation from the provisions of Article 92 or from the regulations provided for in Article 92, if such a decision is justified by exceptional circumstances. If, as regards the aid in question, the Commission has already initiated the procedure provided for in the first subparagraph of this paragraph, the fact that the State concerned has made its application to the Council shall have the effect of suspending that procedure until the Council has made its attitude known.

If, however, the Council has not made its attitude known within three months of the said application being made, the Commission shall give its decision on the case.

(3) The Commission shall be informed, in sufficient time to enable it to submit its comments, of any plans to grant or alter aid. If it considers that any such plan is not compatible with the common market having regard to Article 92, it shall without delay initiate the procedure provided for in paragraph 2. The Member State concerned shall not put its proposed measures into effect until this procedure has resulted in a final decision.

Article 94

The Council, acting by a qualified majority on a proposal from the Commission and after consulting the European Parliament, may make any appropriate regulations for the application of Articles 92 and 93 and may in particular determine the conditions in which Article 93(3) shall apply and the categories of aid exempted from this procedure.

CHAPTER 2 – TAX PROVISIONS

Article 95

No Member State shall impose, directly or indirectly, on the products of other Member States any internal taxation of any kind in excess of that imposed directly or indirectly on similar domestic products.

Furthermore, no Member State shall impose on the products of other Member States any internal taxation of such a nature as to afford indirect protection to other products.

Member States shall, not later than at the beginning of the second stage, repeal or amend any provisions existing when this Treaty enters into force which conflict with the preceding rules.

Article 96

Where products are exported to the territory of any Member State, any repayment of internal taxation shall not exceed the internal taxation imposed on them, whether directly or indirectly.

Article 97

Member States which levy a turnover tax calculated on a cumulative multi-stage tax system may, in the case of internal taxation imposed by them on imported products or of repayments allowed by them on exported products, establish average rates for products or groups of products, provided that there is no infringement of the principles laid down in Articles 95 and 96.

Where the average rates established by a Member State do not conform to these principles, the Commission shall address appropriate directives or decisions to the State concerned.

Article 98

In the case of charges other than turnover taxes, excise duties and other forms of indirect taxation, remissions and repayments in respect of exports to other Member States may not be granted and countervailing charges in respect of imports from Member States may not be imposed unless the measures contemplated have been previously approved for a limited period by the Council acting by a qualified majority on a proposal from the Commission.

Article 99

The Council shall, acting unanimously on a proposal from the Commission and after consulting the European Parliament and the Economic and Social Committee, adopt provisions for the harmonisation of legislation concerning turnover taxes, excise duties and other forms of indirect taxation to the extent that such harmonisation is necessary to ensure the establishment and the functioning of the internal market within the time-limit laid down in Article 7a.

CHAPTER 3 – APPROXIMATION OF LAWS

Article 100

The Council shall, acting unanimously on a proposal from the Committee and after consulting the European Parliament and the Economic and Social Committee, issue directives for the approximation of such laws, regulations or administrative provisions of the Member States as directly affect the establishment or functioning of the common market.

Article 100a

(1) By way of derogation from Article 100 and save where otherwise provided in this Treaty, the following provisions shall apply for the achievement of the objectives set out in Article 7a. The Council shall, acting in accordance with the procedure referred to in Article 189b and after consulting the Economic and Social Committee, adopt the measures for the approximation of the provisions laid down by law, regulation or administrative action in Member States which have as their object the establishment and functioning of the internal market.

(2) Paragraph 1 shall not apply to fiscal provisions, to those relating to the free movement of persons nor to those relating to the rights and interests of employed persons.

(3) The Commission, in its proposals envisaged in paragraph 1 concerning health, safety, environmental protection and consumer protection, will take as a base a high level of protection.

(4) If, after the adoption of a harmonisation measure by the Council acting by a qualified majority, a Member State deems it necessary to apply national provisions on grounds of major needs referred to in Article 36, or relating to protection of the environment or the working environment, it shall notify the Commission of these provisions.

The Commission shall confirm the provisions involved after having verified that they are not a means of arbitrary discrimination or a disguised restriction on trade between Member States.

By way of derogation from the procedure laid down in Articles 169 and 170, the Commission or any Member State may bring the matter directly before the Court of Justice if it considers that another Member State is making improper use of the powers provided for in this Article.

(5) The harmonisation measures referred to above shall, in appropriate cases, include a safeguard clause authorising the Member States to take, for

one or more of the non-economic reasons referred to in Article 36, provisional measures subject to a Community control procedure.

Article 100b

(1) During 1992, the Commission shall, together with each Member State, draw up an inventory of national laws, regulations and administrative provisions which fall under Article 100a and which have not been harmonised pursuant to that Article.

The Council, acting in accordance with the provisions of Article 100a, may decide that the provisions in force in a Member State must be recognised as being equivalent to those applied by another Member State.

(2) The provisions of Article 100a (4) shall apply by analogy.

(3) The Commission shall draw up the inventory referred to in the first subparagraph of paragraph 1 and shall submit appropriate proposals in good time to allow the Council to act before the end of 1992.

Article 100c

(1) The Council, acting unanimously on a proposal from the Commission and after consulting the European Parliament, shall determine the third countries whose nationals must be in possession of a visa when crossing the external borders of the Member States.

(2) However, in the event of an emergency situation in a third country posing a threat of a sudden inflow of nationals from that country into the Community, the Council, acting by a qualified majority on a recommendation from the Commission, may introduce, for a period not exceeding six months, a visa requirement for nationals from the country in question. The visa requirement established under this paragraph may be extended in accordance with the procedure referred to in paragraph 1.

(3) From 1 January 1996, the Council shall adopt the decisions referred to in paragraph 1 by a qualified majority. The Council shall, before that date, acting by a qualified majority on a proposal from the Commission and after consulting the European Parliament, adopt measures relating to a uniform format for visas.

(4) In the areas referred to in this Article, the Commission shall examine any request made by a Member State that it submit a proposal to the Council.

(5) This Article shall be without prejudice to the exercise of the responsibilities incumbent upon the Member States with regard to the maintenance of law and order and the safeguarding of internal security.

(6) This Article shall apply to other areas if so decided pursuant to Article K9 of the provisions of the Treaty on European Union which relate to cooperation in the fields of justice and home affairs, subject to the voting conditions determined at the same time.

(7) The provisions of the conventions in force between the Member States governing areas covered by this Article shall remain in force until their content has been replaced by directives or measures adopted pursuant to this Article.

Article 100d

The Coordinating Committee consisting of senior officials set up by Article K4 of the Treaty on European Union shall contribute, without prejudice to the provisions of Article 151, to the preparation of the proceedings of the Council in the fields referred to in Article 100c.

Article 101

Where the Commission finds that a difference between the provisions laid down by law, regulation or administrative action in Member States is distorting the conditions of competition in the common market and that the resultant distortion needs to be eliminated, it shall consult the Member States concerned.

If such consultation does not result in an agreement eliminating the distortion in question, the Council shall, on a proposal from the Commission, acting unanimously during the first stage and by a qualified majority thereafter, issue the necessary directives. The Commission and the Council may take any other appropriate measures provided for in this Treaty.

Article 102

(1) Where there is reason to fear that the adoption or amendment of a provision laid down by law, regulation or administrative action may cause distortion within the meaning of Article 101, a Member State desiring to proceed therewith shall consult the Commission. After consulting the Member States, the Commission shall recommend to the States concerned such measures as may be appropriate to avoid the distortion in question.

(2) If a State desiring to introduce or amend its own provisions does not comply with the recommendations addressed to it by the Commission, other Member States shall not be required, in pursuance of Article 101, to amend their own provisions in order to eliminate such distortion. If the Member State which has ignored the recommendation of the Commission causes distortion detrimental only to itself, the provisions of Articles 101 shall not apply.

TITLE VI – ECONOMIC AND MONETARY POLICY

CHAPTER 1 – ECONOMIC POLICY

Article 102a

Member States shall conduct their economic policies with a view to contributing to the achievement of the objectives of the Community, as defined in Article 2, and in the context of the broad guidelines referred to in Article 103(2). The Member States and the Community shall act in accordance with the principle of an open market economy with free competition, favouring an efficient allocation of resources, and in compliance with the principles set out in Article 3a.

Article 103

(1) Member States shall regard their economic policies as a matter of common concern and shall coordinate them within the Council, in accordance with the provisions of Article 102a.

(2) The Council shall, acting by a qualified majority on a recommendation from the Commission, formulate a draft for the broad guidelines of the economic policies of the Member States and of the Community, and shall report its findings to the European Council.

The European Council shall, acting on the basis of the report from the Council, discuss a conclusion on the broad guidelines of the economic policies of the Member States and of the Community.

On the basis of this conclusion, the Council shall, acting by a qualified majority, adopt a recommendation setting out these broad guidelines. The Council shall inform the European Parliament of its recommendation.

(3) In order to ensure closer coordination of economic policies and sustained convergence of the economic performance of the Member States, the Council shall, on the basis of reports submitted by the Commission, monitor

economic developments in each of the Member States and in the Community as well as the consistency of economic policies with the broad guidelines referred to in paragraph 2, and regularly carry out an overall assessment.

For the purpose of this multilateral surveillance, Member States shall forward information to the Commission about important measures taken by them in the field of their economic policy and such other information as they deem necessary.

(4) Where it is established, under the procedure referred to in paragraph 3, that the economic policies of a Member State are not consistent with the broad guidelines referred to in paragraph 2 or that they risk jeopardising the proper functioning of economic and monetary union, the Council may, acting by a qualified majority on a recommendation from the Commission, make the necessary recommendations to the Member State concerned. The Council may, acting by a qualified majority on a proposal from the Commission, decide to make its recommendations public.

The President of the Council and the Commission shall report to the European Parliament on the results of multilateral surveillance. The President of the Council may be invited to appear before the competent Committee of the European Parliament if the Council has made its recommendations public.

(5) The Council, acting in accordance with the procedure referred to in Article 189c, may adopt detailed rules for the multilateral surveillance procedure referred to in paragraphs 3 and 4 of this Article.

Article 103a

(1) Without prejudice to any other procedures provided for in this Treaty, the Council may, acting unanimously on a proposal from the Commission, decide upon the measures appropriate to the economic situation, in particular if severe difficulties arise in the supply of certain products.

(2) Where a Member State is in difficulties or is seriously threatened with severe difficulties caused by exceptional occurrences beyond its control, the Council may, acting unanimously on a proposal from the Commission, grant, under certain conditions, Community financial assistance to the Member State concerned. Where the severe difficulties are caused by natural disasters, the Council shall act by qualified majority. The President of the Council shall inform the European Parliament of the decision taken.

Article 104

(1) Overdraft facilities or any other type of credit facility with the ECB or with the central banks of the Member States (hereinafter referred to as 'national central banks') in favour of Community institutions or bodies, central governments, regional, local or other public authorities, other bodies governed by public law, or public undertakings of Member States shall be prohibited, as shall the purchase directly from them by the ECB or national central banks of debt instruments.

(2) Paragraph 1 shall not apply to publicly owned credit institutions which, in the context of the supply of resources by central banks, shall be given the same treatment by national central banks and the ECB as private credit institutions.

Article 104a

(1) Any measure, not based on prudential considerations, establishing privileged access by Community institutions or bodies, central governments, regional, local or other public authorities, other bodies governed by public law, or public undertakings of Member States to financial institutions shall be prohibited.

(2) The Council, acting in accordance with the procedure referred to in Article 189c, shall, before 1 January 1994, specify definitions for the application of the prohibition referred to in paragraph 1.

Article 104b

(1) The Community shall not be liable for or assume the commitments of central governments, regional, local or other public authorities, other bodies governed by public law, or public undertakings of any Member State, without prejudice to mutual financial guarantees for the joint execution of a specific project. A Member State shall not be liable for or assume the commitments of central governments, regional, local or other public authorities, other bodies governed by public law or public undertakings of another Member State, without prejudice to mutual financial guarantees for the joint execution of a specific project.

(2) If necessary, the Council, acting in accordance with the procedure referred to in Article 189c, may specify definitions for the application of the prohibitions referred to in Article 104 and in this Article.

Article 104c

(1) Member States shall avoid excessive government deficits.

(2) The Commission shall monitor the development of the budgetary situation and of the stock of government debt in the Member States with a view to identifying gross errors. In particular it shall examine compliance with budgetary discipline on the basis of the following two criteria:

    (a) whether the ratio of the planned or actual government deficit to gross domestic product exceeds a reference value, unless

    – either the ratio has declined substantially and continuously and reached a level that comes close to the reference value;

    – or, alternatively, the excess over the reference value is only exceptional and temporary and the ratio remains close to the reference value;

    (b) whether the ratio of government debt to gross domestic product exceeds a reference value, unless the ratio is sufficiently diminishing and approaching the reference value at a satisfactory pace.

    The reference values are specified in the Protocol on the excessive deficit procedure annexed to this Treaty.

(3) If a Member State does not fulfil the requirements under one or both of these criteria, the Commission shall prepare a report. The report of the Commission shall also take into account whether the government deficit exceeds government investment expenditure and take into account all other relevant factors, including the medium-term economic and budgetary position of the Member State.

The Commission may also prepare a report if, notwithstanding the fulfilment of the requirements under the criteria, it is of the opinion that there is a risk of an excessive deficit in a Member State.

(4) The Committee provided for in Article 109c shall formulate an opinion on the report of the Commission.

(5) If the Commission considers that an excessive deficit in a Member State exists or may occur, the Commission shall address an opinion to the Council.

(6) The Council shall, acting by a qualified majority on a recommendation from the Commission, and having considered any observations which the Member State concerned may wish to make, decide after an overall assessment whether an excessive deficit exists.

(7) Where the existence of an excessive deficit is decided according to paragraph 6, the Council shall make recommendations to the Member State concerned with a view to bringing that situation to an end within a given

period. Subject to the provisions of paragraph 8, these recommendations shall not be made public.

(8) Where it establishes that there has been no effective action in response to its recommendations within the period laid down, the Council may make its recommendations public.

(9) If a Member State persists in failing to put into practice the recommendations of the Council, the Council may decide to give notice to the Member State to take, within a specified time-limit, measures for the deficit reduction which is judged necessary by the Council in order to remedy the situation.

In such a case, the Council may request the Member State concerned to submit reports in accordance with a specific timetable in order to examine the adjustment efforts of that Member State.

(10) The rights to bring actions provided for in Articles 169 and 170 may not be exercised within the framework of paragraphs 1 to 9 of this Article.

(11) As long as a Member State fails to comply with a decision taken in accordance with paragraph 9, the Council may decide to apply or, as the case may be, intensify one or more of the following measures:

- to require the Member State concerned to publish additional information, to be specified by the Council, before issuing bonds and securities;
- to invite the European Investment Bank to reconsider its lending policy towards the Member State concerned;
- to require the Member States concerned to make a non-interest-bearing deposit of an appropriate size with the Community until the excessive deficit has, in the view of the Council, been corrected;
- to impose fines of an appropriate size.

The President of the Council shall inform the European Parliament of the decisions taken.

(12) The Council shall abrogate some or all of its decisions referred to in paragraphs 6 to 9 and 11 to the extent that the excessive deficit in the Member State concerned has, in the view of the Council, been corrected. If the Council has previously made public recommendations, it shall, as soon as the decision under paragraph 8 has been abrogated, take a public statement that an excessive deficit in the Member State concerned no longer exists.

(13) When taking the decisions referred to in paragraphs 7 to 9, 11 and 12, the Council shall act on a recommendation from the Commission by a

majority of two-thirds of the votes of its members weighted in accordance with Article 148(2), excluding the votes of the representative of the Member State concerned.

(14) Further provisions relating to the implementation of the procedure described in this Article are set out in the Protocol on the excessive deficit procedure annexed to this Treaty.

The Council shall, acting unanimously on a proposal from the Commission and after consulting the European Parliament and the ECB, adopt the appropriate provision which shall then replace the said Protocol.

Subject to the other provisions of this paragraph the Council shall, before 1 January 1994, acting by a qualified majority on a proposal from the Commission and after consulting the European Parliament, lay down detailed rules and definitions for the application of the provisions of the said Protocol.

CHAPTER 2 – MONETARY POLICY

Article 105

(1) The primary objective of the ESCB shall be to maintain price stability. Without prejudice to the objective of price stability, the ESCB shall support the general economic policies in the Community with a view to contributing to the achievement of the objectives of the Community as laid down in Article 2. The ESCB shall act in accordance with the principle of an open market economy with free competition, favouring an efficient allocation of resources, and in compliance with the principles set out in Article 3a.

(2) The basic tasks to be carried out through the ESCB shall be:

- to define and implement the monetary policy of the Community;
- to conduct foreign-exchange operations consistent with the provisions of Article 109;
- to hold and manage the official foreign reserves of the Member States;
- to promote the smooth operation of payment systems.

(3) The third indent of paragraph 2 shall be without prejudice to the holding and management by the governments of Member States of foreign-exchange working balances.

(4) The ECB shall be consulted:

- on any proposed Community act in its fields of competence;

— by national authorities regarding any draft legislative provision in its fields of competence, but within the limits and under the conditions set out by the Council in accordance with the procedure laid down in Article 106(6).

The ECB may submit opinions to the appropriate Community institutions or bodies or to national authorities on matters in its fields of competence.

(5) The ESCB shall contribute to the smooth conduct of policies pursued by the competent authorities relating to the prudential supervision of credit institutions and the stability of the financial system.

(6) The Council may, acting unanimously on a proposal from the Commission and after consulting the ECB and after receiving the assent of the European Parliament, confer upon the ECB specific tasks concerning policies relating to the prudential supervision of credit institutions and other financial institutions with the exception of insurance undertakings.

Article 105a

(1) The ECB shall have the exclusive right to authorise the issue of banknotes within the Community. The ECB and the national central banks may issue such notes. The banknotes issued by the ECB and the national central banks shall be the only such notes to have the status of legal tender within the Community.

(2) Member States may issue coins subject to approval by the ECB of the volume of the issue. The Council may, acting in accordance with the procedure referred to in Article 189c and after consulting the ECB, adopt measures to harmonise the denominations and technical specifications of all coins intended for circulation to the extent necessary to permit their smooth circulation within the Community.

Article 106

(1) The ESCB shall be composed of the ECB and of the national central banks.

(2) The ECB shall have legal personality.

(3) The ESCB shall be governed by the decision-making bodies of the ECB which shall be the Governing Council and the Executive Board.

(4) The Statute of the ESCB is laid down in a Protocol annexed to this Treaty.

(5) Articles 5.1, 5.2, 5.3, 17, 18, 19.1, 22, 23, 24, 26, 32.2, 32.3, 32.4, 32.6, 33.1(a) and 36 of the Statute of the ESCB may be amended by the Council, acting either by a qualified majority on a recommendation from the ECB and after consulting the Commission or unanimously on a proposal from the Commission and after consulting the ECB. In either case, the assent of the European Parliament shall be required.

(6) The Council, acting by a qualified majority either on a proposal from the Commission and after consulting the European Parliament and the ECB or on a recommendation from the ECB and after consulting the European Parliament and the Commission, shall adopt the provisions referred to in Articles 4, 5.4, 19.2, 20, 28.1, 29.2, 30.4 and 34.3 of the Statute of the ESCB.

Article 107

When exercising the powers and carrying out the tasks conferred upon them by this Treaty and the Statute of the ESCB, neither the ECB, nor a national central bank, nor any member of their decision-making bodies shall seek to take instructions from Community institutions or bodies, from any government of a Member State or from any other body. The Community institutions and bodies and the governments of the Member States undertake to respect this principle and not to seek to influence the members of the decision-making bodies of the ECB or of the national central banks in the performance of their tasks.

Article 108

Each Member State shall ensure, at the latest at the date of the establishment of the ESCB, that its national legislation including the statutes of its national central bank is compatible with this Treaty and the Statute of the ESCB.

Article 108a

(1) In order to carry out the tasks entrusted to the ESCB, the ECB shall, in accordance with the provisions of this Treaty and under the conditions laid down in the Statute of the ESCB:

– make regulations to the extent necessary to implement the tasks defined in Article 3.1, first indent, Articles 19.1, 22 and 25.2 of the Statute of the ESCB, and in cases which shall be laid down in the acts of the Council referred to in Article 106(6);

- take decisions necessary for carrying out the tasks entrusted to the ESCB under this Treaty and the Statute of the ESCB;
- make recommendations and deliver opinions.

(2) A regulation shall have general application. It shall be binding in its entirety and directly applicable in all Member States.

Recommendations and opinions shall have no binding force.

A decision shall be binding in its entirety upon those to whom it is addressed.

Articles 190 to 192 shall apply to regulations and decisions adopted by the ECB.

The ECB may decide to publish its decisions, recommendations and opinions.

(3) Within the limits and under the conditions adopted by the Council under the procedure laid down in Article 106(6), the ECB shall be entitled to impose fines of periodic penalty payments on undertakings for failure to comply with obligations under its regulations and decisions.

Article 109

(1) By way of derogation from Article 228, the Council may, acting unanimously on a recommendation from the ECB or from the Commission, and after consulting the ECB in an endeavour to reach a consensus consistent with the objective of price stability, after consulting the European Parliament, in accordance with the procedure in paragraph 3 for determining the arrangements, conclude formal agreements on an exchange-rate system for the ECU in relation to non-Community currencies.

The Council may, acting by a qualified majority on a recommendation from the ECB or from the Commission, and after consulting the ECB in an endeavour to reach a consensus consistent with the objective of price stability, adopt, adjust or abandon the central rates of the ECU within the exchange rate system. The President of the Council shall inform the European Parliament of the adoption, adjustment or abandonment of the ECU central rates.

(2) In the absence of an exchange-rate system in relation to one or more non-Community currencies as referred to in paragraph 1, the Council, acting by a qualified majority either on a recommendation from the Commission and after consulting the ECB or on a recommendation from the ECB, may

formulate general orientations for exchange-rate policy in relation to these currencies.

These general orientations shall be without prejudice to the primary objective of the ESCB to maintain price stability.

(3) By way of derogation from Article 228, where agreements concerned monetary or foreign-exchange regime matters need to be negotiated by the Community with one or more States or international organisations, the Council, acting by a qualified majority on a recommendation from the Commission and after consulting the ECB, shall decide the arrangements for the negotiation and for the conclusion of such agreements.

These arrangements shall ensure that the Community expresses a single position. The Commission shall be fully associated with the negotiations.

Agreements concluded in accordance with this paragraph shall be binding on the institutions of the Community, on the ECB and on Member States.

(4) Subject to paragraph 1, the Council shall, on a proposal from the Commission and after consulting the ECB, acting by a qualified majority decide on the position of the Community at international level as regards issues of particular relevance to economic and monetary union and, acting unanimously, decide its representation in compliance with the allocation of powers laid down in Articles 103 and 105.

(5) Without prejudice to Community competence and Community agreements as regards economic and monetary union, Member States may negotiate in international bodies and conclude international agreements.

CHAPTER 3 – INSTITUTIONAL PROVISIONS

Article 109a

(1) The Governing Council of the ECB shall comprise the members of the Executive Board of the ECB and the Governors of the national central banks.

(2) (a) The Executive Board shall comprise the President, the Vice-President and four other members.

(b) The President, the Vice-President and the other members of the Executive Board shall be appointed from among persons of recognised standing and professional experience in monetary or banking matters by common accord of the governments of the Member States at the level of Heads of State or Government, on a recommendation from the Council, after it has consulted the European Parliament and the Governing Council of the ECB.

Their term of office shall be eight years and shall not be renewable.

Only nationals of Member States may be members of the Executive Board.

Article 109b

(1) The President of the Council and a member of the Commission may participate without having the right to vote, in meetings of the Governing Council of the ECB.

The President of the Council may submit a motion for deliberation to the Governing Council of the ECB.

(2) The President of the ECB shall be invited to participate in Council meetings when the Council is discussing matters relating to the objectives and tasks of the ESCB.

(3) The ECB shall address an annual report on the activities of the ESCB and on the monetary policy of both the previous and current year to the European Parliament, the Council and the Commission, and also to the European Council.

The President of the ECB shall present this report to the Council and to the European Parliament, which may hold a general debate on that basis.

The President of the ECB and the other members of the Executive Board may, at the request of the European Parliament or on their own initiative, be heard by the competent Committees of the European Parliament.

Article 109c

(1) In order to promote coordination of the policies of Member States to the full extent needed for the functioning of the internal market, a Monetary Committee with advisory status is hereby set up.

It shall have the following tasks:

- to keep under review the monetary and financial situations of the Member States and of the Community and the general payments system of the Member States and to report regularly thereon to the Council and to the Commission;
- to deliver opinions at the request of the Council or of the Commission, or on its own initiative for submission to those institutions;

- without prejudice to Article 151, to contribute to the preparation of the work of the Council referred to in Articles 73f, 73g, 103(2), (3), (4) and (5), 103a, 104a, 104b, 104c, 109e(2), 109f(6), 109h, 109i, 109j(2) and 109k(1);
- to examine, at least once a year, the situation regarding the movement of capital and the freedom of payments, as they result from the application of this Treaty and of measures adopted by the Council; the examination shall cover all measures relating to capital movements and payments; the Committee shall report to the Commission and to the Council on the outcome of this examination.

The Member States and the Commission shall each appoint two members of the Monetary Committee.

(2) At the start of the third stage, an Economic and Financial Committee shall be set up. The Monetary Committee provided for in paragraph 1 shall be dissolved.

The Economic and Financial Committee shall have the following tasks:

- to deliver opinions at the request of the Council or of the Commission, or on its own initiative for submission to those institutions;
- to keep under review the economic and financial situation of the Member States and of the Community and to report regularly thereon to the Council and the Commission, in particular on financial relations with third countries and international institutions;
- without prejudice to Article 151, to contribute to the preparation of the work of the Council referred to in Articles 73f, 73g, 103(2), (3), (4) and (5), 103a, 104a, 104b, 104c, 105(6), 105a(2), 106(5) and (6), 109, 109h, 109i(2) and (3), 109k(2), 109l(4) and (5), and to carry out other advisory and preparatory tasks assigned to it by the Council;
- to examine, at least once a year, the situation regarding the movement of capital and the freedom of payments, as they result from the application of this Treaty and of measures adopted by the Council; the examination shall cover all measures relating to capital movements and payments; the Committee shall report to the Commission and to the Council on the outcome of this examination.

The Member States, the Commission and the ECB shall each appoint no more than two members of the Committee.

(3) The Council shall, acting by a qualified majority on a proposal from the Commission and after consulting the ECB and the Committee referred to in this Article, lay down detailed provisions concerning the composition of the Economic and Financial Committee. The President of the Council shall inform the European Parliament at such a decision.

(4) In addition to the tasks set out in paragraph 2, if and as long as there are Member States with a derogation as referred to in Article 109k and 109l, the Committee shall keep under review the monetary and financial situation and the general payments system of those Member States and report regularly thereon to the Council and to the Commission.

Article 109d

For matters within the scope of Articles 103(4), 104c with the exception of paragraphs 14, 109, 109j, 109k and 109l(4) and (5), the Council or a Member State may request the Commission to make a recommendation or a proposal, as appropriate. The Commission shall examine this request and submit its conclusions to the Council without delay.

CHAPTER 4 – TRANSITIONAL PROVISIONS

Article 109e

(1) The second stage for achieving economic and monetary union shall begin on 1 January 1994.

(2) Before that date

(a) each Member State shall:
- adopt, where necessary, appropriate measures to comply with the prohibitions laid down in Article 73b, without prejudice to Article 73e, and in Articles 104 and 104a(1);

- adopt, if necessary, with a view to permitting the assessment provided for in subparagraph (b), multiannual programmes intended to ensure the lasting convergence necessary for the achievement of economic and monetary union, in particular with regard to price stability and sound public finances;

(b) the Council shall, on the basis of a report from the Commission, assess the progress made with regard to economic and monetary convergence, in particular with regard to price stability and sound public finances, and the progress made with the implementation of Community law concerning the internal market.

(3) The provisions of Articles 104, 104a(1), 104b(1) and 104c with the exception of paragraphs 1, 9, 11 and 14 shall apply from the beginning of the second stage.

The provisions of Articles 103a(2), 104c(1), (9) and (11), 105, 105a, 107,

109, 109a, 109b and 109c(2) and (4) shall apply from the beginning of the third stage.

(4) In the second stage, Member States shall endeavour to avoid excessive government deficits.

(5) During the second stage, each Member State shall, as appropriate, start the process leading to the independence of its central bank, in accordance with Article 108.

Article 109f

(1) At the start of the second stage, a European Monetary Institute (hereinafter referred to as 'EMI') shall be established and take up its duties; it shall have legal personality and be directed and managed by a Council, consisting of a President and the Governors of the national central banks, one of whom shall be Vice-President.

The President shall be appointed by common accord of the governments of the Member States at the level of Heads of State or Government, on a recommendation from, as the case may be, the Committee of Governors of the central banks of the Member States (hereinafter referred to as 'Committee of Governors') or the Council of the EMI, and after consulting the European Parliament and the Council. The President shall be selected from among persons of recognised standing and professional experience in monetary or banking matters. Only nationals of Member States may be President of the EMI. The Council of the EMI shall appoint the Vice-President.

The Statute of the EMI is laid down in a Protocol annexed to this Treaty.

The Committee of Governors shall be dissolved at the start of the second stage.

(2) The EMI shall:

- strengthen cooperation between the national central banks;
- strengthen the coordination of the monetary policies of the Member States, with the aim of ensuring price stability;
- monitor the functioning of the European Monetary System;
- hold consultations concerning issues falling within the competence of the national central banks and affecting the stability of financial institutions and markets;
- take over the tasks of the European Monetary Cooperation Fund, which shall be dissolved; the modalities of dissolution are laid down in the Statute of the EMI;

- facilitate the use of the ECU and oversee its development, including the smooth functioning of the ECU clearing system.

(3) For the preparation of the third stage, the EMI shall:
- prepare the instruments and the procedures necessary for carrying out a single monetary policy in the third stage;
- promote the harmonisation, where necessary, of the rules and practices governing the collection, compilation and distribution of statistics in the areas within its field of competence;
- prepare the rules for operations to be undertaken by the national central banks within the framework of the ESCB;
- promote the efficiency of cross-border payments;
- supervise the technical preparation of ECU banknotes.

At the latest by 31 December 1996, the EMI shall specify the regulatory, organisational and logistical framework necessary for the ESCB to perform its tasks in the third stage. This framework shall be submitted for decision to the ECB at the date of its establishment.

(4) The EMI, acting by a majority of third-thirds of the members of its Council, may:
- formulate opinions or recommendations on the overall orientation of monetary policy and exchange-rate policy as well as on related measures introduced in each Member State;
- submit opinions or recommendations to governments and to the Council on policies which might affect the internal or external monetary situation in the Community and, in particular, the functioning of the European Monetary System;
- make recommendations to the monetary authorities of the Member States concerning the conduct of their monetary policy.

(5) The EMI, acting unanimously, may decide to publish its opinions and its recommendations.

(6) The EMI shall be consulted by the Council regarding any proposed Community act within its field of competence.

Within the limits and under the conditions set out by the Council, acting by a qualified majority on a proposal from the Commission and after consulting the European Parliament and the EMI, the EMI shall be consulted by the authorities of the Member States on any draft legislative provision within its field of competence.

(7) The Council may, acting unanimously on a proposal from the

Commission and after consulting the European Parliament and the EMI, confer upon the EMI other tasks for the preparation of the third stage.

(8) Where this Treaty provides for a consultative role for the ECB, references to the ECB shall be read as referring to the EMI before the establishment of the ECB.

Where this Treaty provides for a consultative role for the EMI, references to the EMI shall be read, before 1 January 1994, as referring to the Committee of Governors.

(9) During the second stage, the term 'ECB' used in Articles 173, 175, 176, 177, 180 and 215 shall be read as referring to the EMI.

Article 109g

The currency composition of the ECU basket shall not be changed.

From the start of the third stage, the value of the ECU shall be irrevocably fixed in accordance with Article 109(4).

Article 109h

(1) Where a Member State is in difficulties or is seriously threatened with difficulties as regards its balance of payments either as a result of an overall disequilibrium in its balance of payments, or as a result of the type of currency at its disposal, and where such difficulties are liable in particular to jeopardise the functioning of the common market or the progressive implementation of the common commercial policy, the Commission shall immediately investigate the position of the State in question and the action which, making use of all the means at its disposal, that State has taken or may take in accordance with the provisions of this Treaty. The Commission shall state what measure it recommends the State concerned to take.

If the action taken by a Member State and the measures suggested by the Commission do not prove sufficient to overcome the difficulties which have arisen or which threaten, the Commission shall, after consulting the Committee referred to in Article 109c, recommend to the Council the granting of mutual assistance and appropriate methods therefor.

The Commission shall keep the Council regularly informed of the situation and of how it is developing.

(2) The Council, acting by a qualified majority, shall grant such mutual assistance; it shall adopt directives or decisions laying down the conditions and details of such assistance, which may take such forms as:

(a) a concerted approach to or within any other international organisations to which Member States may have recourse;

(b) measures needed to avoid deflection of trade where the State which is in difficulties maintains or re-introduces quantitative restrictions against third countries;

(c) the granting of limited credits by other Member States, subject to their agreement.

(3) If the mutual assistance recommended by the Commission is not granted by the Council or if the mutual assistance granted and the measures taken are insufficient, the Commission shall authorise the State which is in difficulties to take protective measures, the conditions and details of which the Commission shall determine.

Such authorisation may be revoked and such conditions and details may be changed by the Council acting by a qualified majority.

(4) Subject to Article 109k(6), this Article shall cease to apply for the beginning of the third stage.

Article 109i

(1) Where a sudden crisis in the balance of payments occurs and a decision within the meaning of Article 109h(2) is not immediately taken, the Member State concerned may, as a precaution, take the necessary protective measures. Such measures must cause the least possible disturbance in the functioning of the common market and must not be wider in scope than is strictly necessary to remedy the sudden difficulties which have arisen.

(2) The Commission and the other Member States shall be informed of such protective measures not later than when they enter into force. The Commission may recommend to the Council the granting of mutual assistance under Article 109h.

(3) After the Commission has delivered an opinion and the Committee referred to in Article 109c has been consulted, the Council may, acting by a qualified majority, decide that the State concerned shall amend, suspend or abolish the protective measures referred to above.

(4) Subject to Article 108k(6), this Article shall cease to apply from the beginning of the third stage.

Article 109j

(1) The Commission and the EMI shall report to the Council on the progress made in the fulfilment by the Member States of their obligations regarding the achievement of economic and monetary union.

These reports shall include an examination of the compatibility between each Member State's national legislation, including the statutes of its national central bank, and Articles 107 and 108 of this Treaty and the Statute of the ESCB. The reports shall also examine the achievement of a high degree of sustainable convergence by reference to the fulfilments by each Member State of the following criteria:

- the achievement of a high degree of price stability; this will be apparent from a rate of inflation which is close to that of, at most, the three best performing Member States in terms of price stability;
- the sustainability of the government financial position; this will be apparent from having achieved a government budgetary position without a deficit that is excessive as determined in accordance with Article 104c(6);
- the observance of the normal fluctuation margins provided for by the exchange-rate mechanism of the European Monetary System, for at least two years, without devaluing against the currency of any other Member State;
- the durability of convergence achieved by the Member State and of its participation in the exchange-rate mechanism of the European Monetary System being reflected in the long-term interest-rate levels.

The four criteria mentioned in this paragraph and the relevant periods over which they are to be respected are developed further in a Protocol annexed to this Treaty.

The reports of the Commission and the EMI shall also take account of the development of the ECU, the results of the integration of markets, the situation and development of the balances of payments on current account and an examination of the development of unit labour costs and other price indices.

(2) On the basis of these reports, the Council, acting by a qualified majority on a recommendation from the Commission, shall assess:

- for each Member State, whether it fulfils the necessary conditions for the adoption of a single currency;
- whether a majority of the Member States fulfil the necessary conditions for the adoption of a single currency,

and recommend its findings to the Council, meeting in the composition of the Heads of State or Government. The European Parliament shall be consulted and forward its opinion to the Council, meeting in the composition of the Heads of State or of Government.

(3) Taking due account of the reports referred to in paragraph 1 and the opinion of the European Parliament referred to in paragraph 2, the Council, meeting in the composition of Heads of State or of Government, shall, acting by a qualified majority, not later than 31 December 1996:

- decide, on the basis of the recommendations of the Council referred to in paragraph 2, whether a majority of the Member States fulfil the necessary conditions for the adoption of a single currency;
- decide whether it is appropriate for the Community to enter the third stage,

and if so

- set the date for the beginning of the third stage.

(4) If by the end of 1997 the date for the beginning of the third stage has not been set, the third stage shall start on 1 January 1999. Before 1 July 1998, the Council, meeting in the position of Heads of State or of Government, after a repetition of the procedure provided for in paragraphs 1 and 2, with the exception of the second indent of paragraph 2, taking into account the reports referred to in paragraph 1 and the opinion of the European Parliament, shall, acting by a qualified majority and on the basis of the recommendations of the Council referred to in paragraph 2, confirm which Member States fulfil the necessary conditions for the adoption of a single currency.

Article 109k

(1) If the decision has been taken to set the date in accordance with Article 109(3), the Council shall, on the basis of its recommendations referred to in Article 109j(2), acting by a qualified majority on a recommendation from the Commission, decide whether any, if so which, Member States shall have a derogation as defined in paragraph 3 of this Article. Such Member States shall in this Treaty be referred to as 'Member States with a derogation'.

If the Council has confirmed which Member States fulfil the necessary conditions for the adoption of a single currency, in accordance with Article 109j(4), those Member States which do not fulfil the conditions shall have a derogation as defined in paragraph 3 of this Article. Such Member States shall in this Treaty be referred to as 'Member States with a derogation'.

(2) At least once every two years, or at the request of a Member State with a derogation, the Commission and the ECB shall report to the Council in accordance with the procedure laid down in Article 109j(1). After consulting the European Parliament and after discussion in the Council, meeting in the composition of the Heads of State or of Government, the Council shall, acting by a qualified majority on a proposal from the Commission, decide which Member States with a derogation fulfil the necessary conditions on the basis of the criteria set out in Article 109j(1), and abrogate derogations of the Member States concerned.

(3) A derogation referred to in paragraph 1 shall entail that the following Articles do not apply to the Member State concerned: Articles 104c(9) and (11), 105(1), (2), (3) and (5), 105a, 108a, 109 and 109a(2)(b). The exclusion of such a Member State and its national central bank from rights and obligations within the ESCB is laid down in Chapter IX of the Statute of the ESCB.

(4) In Articles 105(1), (2) and (3), 105a, 108a, 109 and 109a(2)(b), 'Member States' shall be read as 'Member States without a derogation'.

(5) The voting rights of Member States with a derogation shall be suspended for the Council decisions referred to in the Articles of this Treaty mentioned in paragraph 3. In that case, by way of derogation from Articles 148 and 189a(1), a qualified majority shall be defined as two-thirds of the votes of the representatives of the Member States without a derogation weighted in accordance with Article 148(2), and unanimity of those Member States shall be required for an act requiring unanimity.

(6) Articles 109h and 109i shall continue to apply to a Member State with a derogation.

Article 109l

(1) Immediately after the decision on the date for the beginning of the third stage has been taken in accordance with Article 109j(3), or, as the case may be, immediately after 1 July 1998:

- the Council shall adopt the provisions referred to in Article 106(6);
- the governments of the Member States without a derogation shall appoint, in accordance with the procedure set out in Article 50 of the Statute of the ESCB, the President, the Vice-President and the other members of the Executive Board of the ECB.

If there are Member States with a derogation, the number of members of the Executive Board may be smaller than provided for in Article 11.1 of the Statute of the ESCB, but in no circumstances shall it be less than four.

As soon as the Executive Board is appointed, the ESCB and the ECB shall be established and shall prepare for their full operation as described in this Treaty and the Statute of the ESCB. The full exercise of their powers shall start from the first day of the third stage.

(2) As soon as the ECB is established, it shall, if necessary, take over tasks of the EMI. The EMI shall go into liquidation upon the establishment of the ECB; the modalities of liquidation are laid down in the Statute of the EMI.

(3) If and as long as there are Member States with a derogation, and without prejudice to Article 106(3) of this Treaty, the General Council of the ECB referred to in Article 45 of the Statute of the ESCB shall be constituted as a third decision-making body of the ECB.

(4) At the starting date of the third stage, the Council shall, acting with the unanimity of the Member States without a derogation, on a proposal from the Commission and after consulting the ECB, adopt the conversion rates at which their currencies shall be irrevocably fixed and at which irrevocably fixed rate the ECU shall be substituted for these currencies, and the ECU will become a currency in its own right. This measure shall by itself not modify the external value of the ECU. The Council shall, acting according to the same procedure, also take the other measures necessary for the rapid introduction of the ECU as the single currency of those Member States.

(5) If it is decided, according to the procedure set out in Article 109k(2), to abrogate a derogation, the Council shall, acting with the unanimity of the Member States without a derogation and the Member State concerned, on a proposal from the Commission and after consulting the ECB, adopt the rate at which the ECU shall be substituted for the currency of the Member State concerned, and take the other measures necessary for the introduction of the ECU as the single currency in the Member State concerned.

Article 109m

(1) Until the beginning of the third stage, each Member State shall treat its exchange-rate policy as a matter of common interest. In so doing, Member States shall take account of the experience acquired in cooperation within the framework of the European Monetary System (EMS) and in developing the ECU, and shall respect existing powers in this field.

(2) From the beginning of the third stage and for as long as a Member State has a derogation, paragraph I shall apply by analogy to the exchange-rate policy of that Member State.

TITLE VII – COMMON COMMERCIAL POLICY

Article 110

By establishing a customs union between themselves Member States aim to contribute, in the common interest, to the harmonious development of world trade, the progressive abolition of restrictions on international trade and the lowering of customs barriers.

The common commercial policy shall take into account the favourable effect which the abolition of customs duties between Member States may have on the increase in the competitive strength of undertakings in those States.

Article 112

(1) Without prejudice to obligations undertaken by them within the framework of other international organisations, Member States shall, before the end of the transitional period, progressively harmonise the systems whereby they grant aid for exports to third countries, to the extent necessary to ensure that competition between undertakings of the Community is not distorted.

On a proposal from the Commission, the Council shall, acting unanimously until the end of the second stage and by a qualified majority thereafter, issue any directives needed for this purpose.

(2) The preceding provisions shall not apply to such drawback of customs duties or charges having equivalent effect nor to such repayment of indirect taxation including turnover taxes, excise duties and other indirect taxes as is allowed when goods are exported from a Member State to a third country, in so far as such drawback or repayment does not exceed the amount imposed, directly or indirectly, on the products exported.

Article 113

(1) The common commercial policy shall be based on uniform principles, particularly in regard to changes in tariff rates, the conclusion of tariff and trade agreements, the achievement of uniformity in measures of liberalisation, export policy and measures to protect trade such as those to be taken in the event of dumping or subsidies.

(2) The Commission shall submit proposals to the Council for implementing the common commercial policy.

(3) Where agreements with one or more States or international

organisations need to be negotiated, the Commission shall make recommendations to the Council, which shall authorise the Commission to open the necessary negotiations.

The Commission shall conduct these negotiations in consultation with a special committee appointed by the Council to assist the Commission in this task and within the framework of such directives as the Council may issue to it.

The relevant provisions of Article 228 shall apply.

(4) In exercising the powers conferred upon it by this Article, the Council shall act by a qualified majority.

Article 115

In order to ensure that the execution of measures of commercial policy taken in accordance with this Treaty by any Member State is not obstructed by deflection of trade, or where differences between such measures lead to economic difficulties in one or more Member States, the Commission shall recommend the methods for the requisite cooperation between Member States. Failing this, the Commission may authorise Member States to take the necessary protective measures, the conditions and details of which it shall determine.

In case of urgency, Member States shall request authorisation to take the necessary measures themselves from the Commission, which shall take a decision as soon as possible; the Member States concerned shall then notify the measures to the other Member States. The Commission may decide at any time that the Member States concerned shall amend or abolish the measures in question.

In the selection of such measures, priority shall be given to those which cause the least disturbance to the functioning of the common market.

TITLE VII – SOCIAL POLICY, EDUCATION, VOCATIONAL TRAINING AND YOUTH

CHAPTER 1 – SOCIAL PROVISIONS

Article 117

Member States agree upon the need to promote improved working conditions and an improved standard of living for workers, so as to make possible their harmonisation while the improvement is being maintained.

They believe that such a development will ensue not only from the functioning of the common market, which will favour the harmonisation of social systems, but also from the procedures provided for in this Treaty and from the approximation of provisions laid down by law, regulation or administrative action.

Article 118

Without prejudice to the other provisions of this Treaty and in conformity with its general objectives, the Commission shall have the task of promoting close cooperation between Member States in the social field, particularly in matters relating to:

- employment
- labour law and working conditions;
- basic and advanced vocational training;
- social security;
- prevention of occupational accidents and diseases;
- occupational hygiene;
- the right of association, and collective bargaining between employers and workers.

To this end, the Commission shall act in close contact with Member States by making studies, delivering opinions and arranging consultations both on problems arising at national level and on those of concern to international organisations.

Before delivering the opinions provided for in this Article, the Commission shall consult the Economic and Social Committee.

Article 118a

(1) Member States shall pay particular attention to encouraging improvements, especially in the working environment, as regards the health and safety of workers, and shall set as their objective the harmonisation of conditions in this area, while maintaining the improvements made.

(2) In order to help achieve the objective laid down in the first paragraph, the Council, acting in accordance with the procedure referred to in Article 189c and after consulting the Economic and Social Committee, shall adopt by means of directives, minimum requirements for gradual implementation, having regard to the conditions and technical rules obtaining in each of the Member States.

Such directives shall avoid imposing administrative, financial and legal constraints in a way which would hold back the creation and development of small and medium-sized undertakings.

(3) The provisions adopted pursuant to this Article shall not prevent any Member State from maintaining or introducing more stringent measures for the protection of working conditions compatible with this Treaty.

Article 118b

The Commission shall endeavour to develop the dialogue between management and labour at European level which could, if the two sides consider it desirable, lead to relations based on agreement.

Article 119

Each Member State shall during the first stage ensure and subsequently maintain the application of the principle that men and women should receive equal pay for equal work.

For the purpose of this Article, 'pay' means the ordinary basic or minimum wage or salary and any other consideration, whether in cash or in kind, which the worker receives, directly or indirectly, in respect of his employment from his employer.

Equal pay without discrimination based on sex means:

(a) that pay for the same work at piece rates shall be calculated on the basis of the same unit of measurement;

(b) that pay for work at time rates shall be the same for the same job.

Article 120

Member States shall endeavour to maintain the existing equivalence between paid holiday schemes.

Article 121

The Council may, acting unanimously and after consulting the Economic and Social Committee, assign to the Commission tasks in connection with the implementation of common measures, particularly as regards social security for the migrant workers referred to in Articles 48 to 51.

Article 122

The Commission shall include a separate chapter on social developments within the Community in its annual report to the European Parliament.

The European Parliament may invite the Commission to draw up reports on any particular problems concerning social conditions.

CHAPTER 2 – THE EUROPEAN SOCIAL FUND

Article 123

In order to improve employment opportunities for workers in the internal market and to contribute thereby to raising the standard of living, a European Social Fund is hereby established in accordance with the provisions set out below; it shall aim to render the employment of workers easier and to increase their geographical and occupational mobility within the Community, and to facilitate their adaptation to industrial changes and to changes in production systems, in particular through vocational training and retraining.

Article 124

The Fund shall be administered by the Commission.

The Commission shall be assisted in this task by a Committee presided over by a member of the Commission and composed of representatives of Governments, trade unions and employers' organisations.

Article 125

The Council, acting in accordance with the procedure referred to in Article 189c and after consulting the Economic and Social Committee, shall adopt implementing decisions relating to the European Social Fund.

CHAPTER 3 – EDUCATION, VOCATIONAL TRAINING AND YOUTH

Article 126

(1) The Community shall contribute to the development of quality education by encouraging cooperation between Member States and, if necessary, by supporting and supplementing their action, while fully respecting the responsibility of the Member States for the content of teaching and the organisation of education systems and their cultural and linguistic diversity.

(2) Community action shall be aimed at:

- developing the European dimension in education, particularly through the teaching and dissemination of the languages of the Member States:
- encouraging mobility of students and teachers, inter alia, by encouraging the academic recognition of diplomas and periods of study;
- promoting cooperation between educational establishments;
- developing exchanges of information and experience on issues common to the education systems of the Member States;
- encouraging the development of youth exchanges and of exchanges of socio-educational instructors;
- encouraging the development of distance education.

(3) The Community and the Member States shall foster cooperation with third countries and the competent international organisations in the field of education, in particular the Council of Europe.

(4) In order to contribute to the achievement of the objectives referred to in this Article, the Council:

- acting in accordance with the procedure referred to in Article 189b, after consulting the Economic and Social Committee and the Committee of the Regions, shall adopt incentive measures, excluding any harmonisation of the laws and regulations of the Member States;
- acting by a qualified majority on a proposal from the Commission, shall adopt recommendations.

Article 127

(1) The Community shall implement a vocational training policy which

shall support and supplement the action of the Member States, while fully respecting the responsibility of the Member States for the content and organisation of vocational training.

(2) Community action shall aim to:

- facilitate adaptation to industrial changes, in particular through vocational training and retraining;
- improve initial and continuing vocational training in order to facilitate vocational integration and re-integration into the labour market;
- facilitate access to vocational training and encourage mobility of instructors and trainees and particularly young people;
- stimulate cooperation on training between educational or training establishments and firms;
- develop exchanges of information and experience on issues common to the training systems of the Member States.

(3) The Community and the Member States shall foster cooperation with third countries and the competent international organisations in the sphere of vocational training.

(4) The Council, acting in accordance with the procedure referred to in Article 189c and after consulting the Economic and Social Committee, shall adopt measures to contribute to the achievement of the objectives referred to in this Article, excluding any harmonisation of the laws and regulations of the Member States.

TITLE IX – CULTURE

Article 128

(1) The Community shall contribute to the flowering of the cultures of the Member States, while respecting their national and regional diversity and at the same time bringing the common cultural heritage to the fore.

(2) Action by the Community shall be aimed at encouraging cooperation between Member States and, if necessary, supporting and supplementing their action in the following areas:

- improvement of the knowledge and dissemination of the culture and history of the European peoples;
- conservation and safeguarding of cultural heritage of European significance;
- non-commercial cultural exchanges;

– artistic and literary creation, including in the audio-visual sector.

(3) The Community and the Member States shall foster cooperation with third countries and the competent international organisations in the sphere of culture, in particular the Council of Europe.

(4) The Community shall take cultural aspects into account in its action under other provisions of this Treaty.

(5) In order to contribute to the achievement of the objectives referred to in this Article, the Council:

- acting in accordance with the procedure referred to in Article 189b and after consulting the Committee of the Regions, shall adopt incentive measures, excluding any harmonisation of the laws and regulations of the Member States. The Council shall act unanimously throughout the procedures referred to in Article 189b;
- acting unanimously on a proposal from the Commission, shall adopt recommendations.

TITLE X – PUBLIC HEALTH

Article 129

(1) The Community shall contribute towards ensuring a high level of human health protection by encouraging cooperation between the Member States and, if necessary, lending support to their action. Community action shall be directed towards the prevention of diseases, in particular the major health scourges, including drug dependence, by promoting research into their causes and their transmission, as well as health information and education.

Health protection requirements shall form a constituent part of the Community's other policies.

(2) Member States shall, in liaison with the Commission, coordinate among themselves their policies and programmes in the areas referred to in paragraph 1. The Commission may, in close contact with the Member States, take any useful initiative to promote such coordination.

(3) The Community and the Member States shall foster cooperation with third countries and the competent international organisations in the sphere of public health.

(4) In order to contribute to the achievement of the objectives referred to in this Article, the Council:

- acting in accordance with the procedure referred to in Article 189b, after consulting the Economic and Social Committee and the Committee of the Regions, shall adopt incentive measures, excluding any harmonisation of the laws and regulations of the Member States;
- acting by a qualified majority on a proposal from the Commission, shall adopt recommendations.

TITLE XI – CONSUMER PROTECTION

Article 129a

(1) The Community shall contribute to the attainment of a high level of consumer protection through:

(a) measures adopted pursuant to Article 100a in the context of the completion of the internal market;

(b) specific action which supports and supplements the policy pursued by the Member States to protect the health, safety and economic interests of consumers and to provide adequate information to consumers.

(2) The Council, acting in accordance with the procedure referred to in Article 189b and after consulting the Economic and Social Committee, shall adopt the specific action referred to in paragraph 1(b).

(3) Action adopted pursuant to paragraph 2 shall not prevent any Member State from maintaining or introducing more stringent protection measures. Such measures must be compatible with this Treaty. The Commission shall be notified of them.

TITLE XII – TRANS-EUROPEAN NETWORKS

Article 129b

(1) To help achieve the objectives referred to in Articles 7a and 130a and to enable citizens of the Union, economic operators and regional and local communities to derive full benefit from the setting up of an area without internal frontiers, the Community shall contribute to the establishment and development of trans-European networks in the areas of transport, telecommunications and energy infrastructures.

(2) Within the framework of a system of open and competitive markets, action by the Community shall aim at promoting the interconnection and interoperability of national networks as well as access to such networks. It shall take account in particular of the need to link island, landlocked and peripheral regions with the central regions of the Community.

Article 129c

(1) In order to achieve the objectives referred to in Article 129b, the Community:

- shall establish a series of guidelines covering the objectives, priorities and broad lines of measures envisaged in the sphere of trans-European networks; these guidelines shall identify projects of common interest;
- shall implement any measures that may prove necessary to ensure the interoperability of their networks, in particular in the field of technical standardisation;
- may support the financial efforts made by the Member States for projects of common interest financed by Member States, which are identified in the framework of the guidelines referred to in the first indent, particularly through feasibility studies, loan guarantees or interest-rate subsidies; the Community may also contribute, through the Cohesion Fund to be set up no later than 31 December 1993 pursuant to Article 130d, to the financing of specific projects in Member States in the transport infrastructure.

The Community's activities shall take into account the potential economic viability of the projects.

(2) Member States shall, in liaison with the Commission, coordinate among themselves the policies pursued at national level which may have a significant impact on the achievement of the objectives referred to in Article 129b. The Commission may, in close cooperation with the Member States, take any useful initiative to promote such coordination.

(3) The Community may decide to cooperate with third countries to promote projects of mutual interest and to ensure the interoperability of networks.

Article 129d

The guidelines referred to in Article 129c(1) shall be adopted by the Council, acting in accordance with the procedure referred to in Article 189b and after consulting the Economic and Social Committee and the Committee of the Regions.

Guidelines and projects of common interest which relate to the territory of a Member State shall require the approval of the Member State concerned.

The Council, acting in accordance with the procedure referred to in Article 189c and after consulting the Economic and Social Committee and the

Committee of the Regions, shall adopt the other measures provided for in Article 129c(1).

TITLE XIII – INDUSTRY

Article 130

(1) The Community and the Member States shall ensure that the conditions necessary for the competitiveness of the Community's industry exist.

For that purpose, in accordance with a system of open and competitive markets, their action shall be aimed at:

- speeding up the adjustment of industry to structural changes;
- encouraging an environment favourable to initiative and to the development of undertakings throughout the Community, particularly small and medium-sized undertakings;
- encouraging an environment favourable to cooperation between undertakings;
- fostering better exploitation of the industrial potential of policies of innovation, research and technological development.

(2) The Member States shall consult each other in liaison with the Commission and, where necessary, shall coordinate their action. The Commission may take any useful initiative to promote such coordination.

(3) The Community shall contribute to the achievement of the objectives set out in paragraph 1 through the policies and activities it pursues under other provisions of this Treaty. The Council, acting unanimously on a proposal from the Commission, after consulting the European Parliament and the Economic and Social Committee, may decide on specific measures in support of action taken in the Member States to achieve the objectives set out in paragraph 1.

This Title shall not provide a basis for the introduction by the Community of any measure which could lead to a distortion of competition.

TITLE XIV – ECONOMIC AND SOCIAL COHESION

Article 130a

In order to promote its overall harmonious development, the Community shall develop and pursue its actions leading to the strengthening of its economic and social cohesion.

In particular, the Community shall aim at reducing disparities between the levels of development of the various regions and the backwardness of the least favoured regions, including rural areas.

Article 130b

Member States shall conduct their economic policies and shall coordinate them in such a way as, in addition, to attain the objectives set out in Article 130a. The formulation and implementation of the Community's policies and actions and the implementation of the internal market shall take into account the objectives set out in Article 130a and shall contribute to their achievement. The Community shall also support the achievement of these objectives by the action it takes through the structural Funds (European Agricultural Guidance and Guarantee Fund – Guidance Section; European Social Fund; European Regional Development Fund), the European Investment Bank and the other existing financial instruments.

The Commission shall submit a report to the European Parliament, the Council, the Economic and Social Committee and the Committee of the Regions every three years on the progress made towards achieving economic and social cohesion and on the manner in which the various means provided for in this Article have contributed to it. This report shall, if necessary, be accompanied by appropriate proposals.

If specific actions prove necessary outside the Funds and without prejudice to the measures decided upon within the framework of the other Community policies, such actions may be adopted by the Council acting unanimously on a proposal from the Commission and after consulting the European Parliament, the Economic and Social Committee and the Committee of the Regions.

Article 130c

The European Regional Development Fund is intended to help to redress the main regional imbalance in the Community through participation in the development and structural adjustment of regions whose development is lagging behind and in the conversion of declining industrial regions.

Article 130d

Without prejudice to Article 130e, the Council, acting unanimously on a proposal from the Commission and after obtaining the assent of the European Parliament and consulting the Economic and Social Committee and the Committee of the Regions, shall define the tasks, priority objectives and the organisation of the structural Funds, which may involve grouping the Funds. The Council, acting by the same procedure, shall also define the general rules applicable to them and the provisions necessary to ensure their effectiveness and the coordination of the Funds with one another and with the other existing financial instruments.

The Council, acting in accordance with the same procedure, shall before 31 December 1993 set up a Cohesion Fund to provide a financial contribution to projects in the fields of environment and trans-European networks in the area of transport infrastructure.

Article 130e

Implementing decisions relating to the European Regional Development Fund shall be taken by the Council, acting in accordance with the procedure referred to in Article 189c and after consulting the Economic and Social Committee and the Committee of the Regions.

With regard to the European Agricultural Guidance and Guarantee Fund, Guidance Section, and the European Social Fund, Articles 43 and 125 respectively shall continue to apply.

TITLE XV – RESEARCH AND TECHNOLOGICAL DEVELOPMENT

Article 130f

(1) The Community shall have the objective of strengthening the scientific and technological bases of Community industry and encouraging it to become more competitive at international level, while promoting all the research activities deemed necessary by virtue of other Chapters of this Treaty.

(2) For this purpose the Community shall, throughout the Community, encourage undertakings, including small and medium-sized undertakings, research centres and universities in their research and technological development activities of high quality; it shall support their efforts to cooperate with one another, aiming, notably, at enabling undertakings to exploit the internal market potential to the full, in particular through the opening up of national public contracts, the definition of common standards and the removal of legal and fiscal obstacles to that cooperation.

(3) All Community activities under this Treaty in the area of research and technological development, including demonstration projects, shall be decided on and implemented in accordance with the provisions of this Title.

Article 130g

In pursuing these objectives, the Community shall carry out the following activities, complementing the activities carried out in the Member States:

(a) implementation of research, technological development and demonstration programmes, by promoting cooperation with and between undertakings, research centres and universities;

(b) promotion of cooperation in the field of Community research, technological development and demonstration with third countries and international organisations;

(c) dissemination and optimisation of the results of activities in Community research, technological development and demonstration;

(d) stimulation of the training and mobility of researchers in the Community.

Article 130h

(1) The Community and the Member States shall coordinate their research and technological development activities so as to ensure that national policies and Community policy are mutually consistent.

(2) In close cooperation with the Member States, the Commission may take any useful initiative to promote the coordination referred to in paragraph 1.

Article 130i

(1) A multiannual framework programme, setting out all the activities of the Community, shall be adopted by the Council, acting in accordance with the procedure referred to in Article 189b after consulting the Economic and Social Committee. The Council shall act unanimously throughout the procedures referred to in Article 189b.

The framework programme shall:

- establish the scientific and technological objectives to be achieved by the activities provided for in Article 130g and fix the relevant priorities;
- indicate the broad lines of such activities;
- fix the maximum overall amount and the detailed rules for Community financial participation in the framework programme and the respective shares in each of the activities provided for.

(2) The framework programme shall be adapted or supplemented as the situation changes.

(3) The framework programme shall be implemented through specific programmes developed within each activity. Each specific programme shall define the detailed rules for implementing it, fix its duration and provide for the means deemed necessary. The sum of the amounts deemed necessary, fixed in the specific programmes, may not exceed the overall maximum amount fixed for the framework programme and each activity.

(4) The Council, acting by a qualified majority on a proposal from the Commission and after consulting the European Parliament and the Economic and Social Committee, shall adopt the specific programmes.

Article 130j

For the implementation of the multiannual framework programme the Council shall:

- determine the rules for the participation of undertakings, research centres and universities;
- lay down the rules governing the dissemination of research results.

Article 130k

In implementing the multiannual framework programme, supplementary programmes may be decided on involving the participation of certain Member States only, which shall finance them subject to possible Community participation.

The Council shall adopt the rules applicable to supplementary programmes, particularly as regards the dissemination of knowledge and access by other Member States.

Article 130l

In implementing the multiannual framework programme the Community may make provision, in agreement with the Member States concerned, for participation in research and development programmes undertaken by several Member States, including participation in the structures created for the execution of those programmes.

Article 130m

In implementing the multiannual framework programme the Community may make provision for cooperation in Community research, technological development and demonstration with third countries or international organisations.

The detailed arrangements for such cooperation may be the subject of agreements between the Community and the third parties concerned, which shall be negotiated and concluded in accordance with Article 228.

Article 130n

The Community may set up joint undertakings or any other structure necessary for the efficient execution of Community research, technological development and demonstration programmes.

Article 130o

The Council, acting unanimously on a proposal from the Commission and after consulting the European Parliament and the Economic and Social Committee, shall adopt the provisions referred to in Article 130n.

The Council, acting in accordance with the procedure referred to in Article 189c and after consulting the Economic and Social Committee, shall adopt the provisions referred to in Articles 130j to 130l. Adoption of the supplementary programmes shall require the agreement of the Member States concerned.

Article 130p

At the beginning of each year the Commission shall send a report to the European Parliament and the Council. The report shall include information on research and technological development activities and the dissemination of results during the previous year, and the work programme for the current year.

TITLE XVI – ENVIRONMENT

Article 130r

(1) Community policy on the environment shall contribute to pursuit of the following objectives:

- preserving, protecting and improving the quality of the environment;
- protecting human health;
- prudent and rational utilisation of natural resources;
- promoting measures at international level to deal with regional or worldwide environmental problems.

(2) Community policy on the environment shall aim at a high level of protection taking into account the diversity of situations in the various regions of the Community. It shall be based on the precautionary principle and on the principles that preventative action should be taken, that environmental damage should as a priority be rectified at source and that the polluter should pay. Environmental protection requirements must be integrated into the definition and implementation of other Community policies.

In this context, harmonisation measures answering these requirements shall include, where appropriate, a safeguard clause allowing Member States to take provisional measures, for non-economic environmental reasons, subject to a Community inspection procedure.

(3) In preparing its policy on the environment, the Community shall take account of:

- available scientific and technical data;
- environmental conditions in the various regions of the Community;
- the potential benefits and costs of action or lack of action;
- the economic and social development of the Community as a whole and the balanced development of its regions.

(4) Within their respective spheres of competence, the Community and the Member States shall cooperate with third countries and with the competent international organisations.

The arrangements for Community cooperation may be the subject of agreements between the Community and the third parties concerned, which shall be negotiated and concluded in accordance with Article 228.

The previous subparagraph shall be without prejudice to Member States' competence to negotiate in international bodies and to conclude international agreements.

Article 130s

(1) The Council, acting in accordance with the procedure referred to in Article 189c and after consulting the Economic and Social Committee, shall

decide what action is to be taken by the Community in order to achieve the objectives referred to in Article 130r.

(2) By way of derogation from the decision-making procedure provided for in paragraph 1 and without prejudice to Article 100a, the Council, acting unanimously on a proposal from the Commission and after consulting the European Parliament and the Economic and Social Committee, shall adopt:

- provisions primarily of a fiscal nature;
- measures concerning town and country planning, land use with the exception of waste management and measures of a general nature, and management of water resources;
- measures significantly affecting the Member State's choice between different energy sources and the general structure of its energy supply.

The Council may, under the conditions laid down in the preceding subparagraph, define those matters referred to in this paragraph on which decisions are to be taken by a qualified majority.

(3) In other areas, general action programmes setting out priority objectives to be attained shall be adopted by the Council, acting in accordance with the procedure referred to in Article 189b and after consulting the Economic and Social Committee.

The Council, acting under the terms of paragraph 1 or paragraph 2 according to the case, shall adopt the measures necessary for the implementation of these programmes.

(4) Without prejudice to certain measures of a Community nature, the Member States shall finance and implement the environment policy.

(5) Without prejudice to the principle that the polluter should pay, if a measure based on the provisions of paragraph 1 involves costs deemed disproportionate for the public authorities of a Member State, the Council shall, in the act adopting that measure, lay down appropriate provisions in the form of:

- temporary derogations, and/or
- financial support from the Cohesion Fund to be set up no later than 31 December 1993 pursuant to Article 130d.

Article 130t

The protective measures adopted pursuant to Article 130s shall not prevent any Member State from maintaining or introducing more stringent protective measures. Such measures must be compatible with this Treaty. They shall be notified to the Commission.

TITLE XVII – DEVELOPMENT COOPERATION

Article 130u

(1) Community policy in the sphere of development cooperation, which shall be complementary to the policies pursued by the Member States, shall foster:

- the sustainable economic and social development of the developing countries, and more particularly the most disadvantaged among them;
- the smooth and gradual integration of the developing countries into the world economy;
- the campaign against poverty in the developing countries.

(2) Community policy in this area shall contribute to the general objective of developing and consolidating democracy and the rule of law, and to that of respecting human rights and fundamental freedoms.

(3) The Community and the Member States shall comply with the commitments and take account of the objectives they have approved in the context of the United Nations and other competent international organisations.

Article 130v

The Community shall take account of the objectives referred to in Article 130u in the policies that it implements which are likely to affect developing countries.

Article 130w

(1) Without prejudice to the other provisions of this Treaty the Council, acting in accordance with the procedure referred to in Article 189c, shall adopt the measures necessary to further the objectives referred to in Article 130u. Such measures may take the form of multiannual programmes.

(2) The European Investment Bank shall contribute, under the terms laid down in its Statute, to the implementation of the measures referred to in paragraph 1.

(3) The provisions of this Article shall not affect cooperation with the African, Caribbean and Pacific countries in the framework of the ACP-EEC Convention.

Article 130x

(1) The Community and the Member States shall coordinate their policies on development cooperation and shall consult each other on their aid programmes, including in international organisations and during international conferences. They may undertake joint action. Member States shall contribute if necessary to the implementation of Community aid programmes.

(2) The Commission may take any useful initiative to promote the coordination referred to in paragraph 1.

Article 130y

Within their respective spheres of competence, the Community and the Member States shall cooperate with third countries and with the competent international organisations. The arrangements for Community cooperation may be the subject of agreements between the Community and the third parties concerned, which shall be negotiated and concluded in accordance with Article 228.

The previous paragraph shall be without prejudice to Member States' competence to negotiate in international bodies and to conclude international agreements.

Part Four

ASSOCIATION OF THE OVERSEAS COUNTRIES AND TERRITORIES

Article 131

The Member States agree to associate with the Community the non-European countries and territories which have special relations with Belgium, Denmark, France, Italy, Netherlands and the United Kingdom. These countries and territories (hereinafter called the 'countries and territories') are listed in Annex IV to this Treaty.

The purpose of association shall be to promote the economic and social development of the countries and territories and to establish close economic relations between them and the Community as a whole.

In accordance with the principles set out in the Preamble to this Treaty, association shall serve primarily to further the interests and prosperity of the inhabitants of these countries and territories in order to lead them to the economic, social and cultural development to which they aspire.

Article 132

Association shall have the following objectives:

(1) Member States shall apply to their trade with the countries and territories the same treatment as they accord each other pursuant to this Treaty.

(2) Each country or territory shall apply to its trade with Member States and with the other countries and territories the same treatment as that which it applies to the European State with which it has special relations.

(3) The Member States shall contribute to the investments required for the progressive development of these countries and territories.

(4) For investments financed by the Community, participation in tenders and supplies shall be open on equal terms to all natural and legal persons who are nationals of a Member State or of one of the countries and territories.

(5) In relations between Member States and the countries and territories the right of establishment of nationals and companies or firms shall be regulated in accordance with the provisions and procedures laid down in the Chapter relating to the right of establishment and on a nondiscriminatory basis, subject to any special provisions laid down pursuant to Article 136.

Article 133

(1) Customs duties on imports into the Member States of goods originating in the countries and territories shall be completely abolished in conformity with the progressive abolition of customs duties between Member States in accordance with the provisions of this Treaty.

(2) Customs duties on imports into each country or territory from Member States or from the other countries or territories shall be progressively abolished in accordance with the provisions of Articles 12, 13, 14, 15 and 17.

(3) The countries and territories may, however, levy customs duties which meet the needs of their development and industrialisation or produce revenue for their budgets.

The duties referred to in the preceding subparagraph shall nevertheless be progressively reduced to the level of those imposed on imports of products from the Member State with which each country or territory has special relations. The percentages and the timetable of the reductions provided for under this Treaty shall apply to the difference between the duty imposed on a product coming from the Member State which has special relations with the country or territory concerned and the duty imposed on the same product coming from within the Community on entry into the importing country or territory.

(4) Paragraph 2 shall not apply to countries and territories which, by reason of the particular international obligations by which they are bound, already apply a non-discriminatory customs tariff when this Treaty enters into force.

(5) The introduction of or any change in customs duties imposed on goods imported into the countries and territories shall not, either in law or in fact, give rise to any direct or indirect discrimination between imports from the various Member States.

Article 134

If the level of the duties applicable to goods from a third country on entry into a country or territory is liable, when the provisions of Article 133(1) have been applied, to cause deflections of trade to the detriment of any Member State, the latter may request the Commission to propose to the other Member States the measures needed to remedy the situation.

Article 135

Subject to the provisions relating to public health, public security or public policy, freedom of movement within Member States for workers from the countries and territories, and within the countries and territories for workers from Member States, shall be governed by agreements to be concluded subsequently with the unanimous approval of Member States.

Article 136

For an initial period of five years after the entry into force of this Treaty, the details of and procedure for the association of the countries and territories with the Community shall be determined by an Implementing Convention annexed to this Treaty.

Before the Convention referred to in the preceding paragraph expires, the Council shall, acting unanimously, lay down provisions for a further period, on the basis of the experience acquired and of the principles set out in this Treaty.

Article 136a

The provisions of Articles 131 to 136 shall apply to Greenland, subject to the specific provisions for Greenland set out in the Protocol on special arrangements for Greenland, annexed to this Treaty.

Part Five

INSTITUTIONS OF THE COMMUNITY

TITLE I – PROVISIONS GOVERNING THE INSTITUTIONS

CHAPTER 1 – THE INSTITUTIONS

Section 1

The European Parliament

Article 137

The European Parliament, which shall consist of representatives of the peoples of the States brought together in the Community, shall exercise the powers conferred upon it by this Treaty.

Article 138

(3) The European Parliament shall draw up proposals for elections by direct universal suffrage in accordance with a uniform procedure in all Member States.

The Council shall, acting unanimously after obtaining the assent of the European Parliament, which shall act by a majority of its component members, lay down the appropriate provisions, which it shall recommend to Member States for adoption in accordance with their respective constitutional requirements.

Article 138a

Political parties at European level are important as a factor for integration within the Union. They contribute to forming a European awareness and to expressing the political will of the citizens of the Union.

Article 138b

In so far as provided in this Treaty, the European Parliament shall participate in the process leading up to the adoption of Community acts by exercising its powers under the procedures laid down in Articles 189b and 189c and by giving its assent or delivering advisory opinions.

The European Parliament may, acting by a majority of its members, request the Commission to submit any appropriate proposal on matters on which it considers that a Community act is required for the purpose of implementing this Treaty.

Article 138c

In the course of its duties, the European Parliament may, at the request of a quarter of its members, set up a temporary Committee of Inquiry to investigate, without prejudice to the powers conferred by this Treaty on other institutions or bodies, alleged contraventions or maladministration in the implementation of Community law, except where the alleged facts are being examined before a court and while the case is still subject to legal proceedings.

The temporary Committee of Inquiry shall cease to exist on the submission of its report.

The detailed provisions governing the exercise of the right of inquiry shall be determined by common accord of the European Parliament, the Council and the Commission.

Article 138d

Any citizen of the Union, and any natural or legal person residing or having his registered office in a Member State, shall have the right to address, individually or in association with other citizens or persons, a petition to the European Parliament on a matter which comes within the Community's fields of activity and which affects him directly.

Article 138e

(1) The European Parliament shall appoint an Ombudsman empowered to receive complaints from any citizen of the Union or any natural or legal person residing or having his registered office in a Member State concerning instances of maladministration in the activities of the Community institutions or bodies, with the exception of the Court of Justice and the Court of First Instance acting in their judicial role.

In accordance with his duties, the Ombudsman shall conduct inquiries for which he finds grounds, either on his own initiative or on the basis of complaints submitted to him direct or through a member of the European Parliament, except where the alleged facts are or have been the subject of legal proceedings. Where the Ombudsman establishes an instance of maladministration, he shall refer the matter to the institution concerned, which shall have a period of three months in which to inform him of its views. The Ombudsman shall then forward a report to the European Parliament and the institution concerned. The person lodging the complaint shall be informed of the outcome of such inquiries.

The Ombudsman shall submit an annual report to the European Parliament on the outcome of his inquiries.

(2) The Ombudsman shall be appointed after each election of the European Parliament for the duration of its term of office. The Ombudsman shall be eligible for reappointment.

The Ombudsman may be dismissed by the Court of Justice at the request of the European Parliament if he no longer fulfils the conditions required for the performance of his duties or if he is guilty of serious misconduct.

(3) The Ombudsman shall be completely independent in the performance of his duties. In the performance of those duties he shall neither seek nor take instructions from any body.

The Ombudsman may not, during his term of office, engage in any other occupation, whether gainful or not.

(4) The European Parliament shall, after seeking an opinion from the Commission and with the approval of the Council acting by a qualified majority, lay down the regulations and general conditions governing the performance of the Ombudsman's duties.

Article 139

The European Parliament shall hold an annual session. It shall meet, without requiring to be convened, on the second Tuesday in March.

The European Parliament may meet in extraordinary session at the request of a majority of its members or at the request of the Council or of the Commission.

Article 140

The European Parliament shall elect its President and its officers from among its members.

Members of the Commission may attend all meetings and shall, at their request, be heard on behalf of the Commission.

The Commission shall reply orally or in writing to questions put to it by the European Parliament or by its members.

The Council shall be heard by the European Parliament in accordance with the conditions laid down by the Council in its rules of procedure.

Article 141

Save as otherwise provided in this Treaty, the European Parliament shall act by an absolute majority of the votes cast.

The rules of procedure shall determine the quorum.

Article 142

The European Parliament shall adopt its rules of procedure, acting by a majority of its members.

The proceedings of the European Parliament shall be published in the manner laid down in its rules of procedure.

Article 143

The European Parliament shall discuss in open session the annual general report submitted to it by the Commission.

Article 144

If a motion of censure on the activities of the Commission is tabled before it, the European Parliament shall not vote thereon until at least three days after the motion has been tabled and only by open vote.

If the motion of censure is carried by a two-thirds majority of the votes cast, representing a majority of the members of the European Parliament, the members of the Commission shall resign as a body. They shall continue to deal with current business until they are replaced in accordance with Article 158. In this case, the term of office of the members of the Commission appointed to replace them shall expire on the date on which the term of office of the members of the Commission obliged to resign as a body would have expired.

Section 2

The Council

Article 145

To ensure that the objectives set out in this Treaty are attained, the Council shall, in accordance with the provisions of this Treaty:

- ensure coordination of the general economic policies of the Member States;
- have power to take decisions;
- confer on the Commission, in the acts which the Council adopts, powers for the implementation of the rules which the Council lays down. The Council may impose certain requirements in respect of the exercise of these powers. The Council may also reserve the right, in specific cases, to exercise directly implementing powers itself. The procedures referred to above must be consonant with principles and rules to be laid down in advance by the Council, acting unanimously on a proposal from the Commission and after obtaining the Opinion of the European Parliament.

Article 146

The Council shall consist of a representative of each Member State at ministerial level, authorised to commit the government of that Member State.

The office of President shall be held in turn by each Member State in the Council for a term of six months in the order decided by the Council acting unanimously.

Article 147

The Council shall meet when convened by its President on his own initiative or at the request of one of its members or of the Commission.

Article 148

(1) Save as otherwise provided in this Treaty, the Council shall act by a majority of its members.

(2) Where the Council is required to act by a qualified majority, the votes of its members shall be weighted as follows:

Belgium	5
Denmark	3
Germany	10
Greece	5
Spain	8
France	10
Ireland	3
Italy	10
Luxembourg	2
Netherlands	5
Austria	4
Portugal	5
Finland	3
Sweden	4
United Kingdom	10

For their adoption, acts of the Council shall require at least:
- sixty-two votes in favour where this Treaty requires them to be adopted on a proposal from the Commission;
- sixty-two votes in favour, cast by at least ten members, in other cases.

(3) Abstentions by members present in person or represented shall not prevent the adoption by the Council of acts which require unanimity.

Article 150

Where a vote is taken, any member of the Council may also act on behalf of not more than one other member.

Article 151

(1) A committee consisting of the Permanent Representatives of the Member States shall be responsible for preparing the work of the Council and for carrying out the tasks assigned to it by the Council.

(2) The Council shall be assisted by a General Secretariat, under the direction of a Secretary-General. The Secretary-General shall be appointed by the Council acting unanimously.

The Council shall decide on the organisation of the General Secretariat.

(3) The Council shall adopt its rules of procedure.

Article 152

The Council may request the Commission to undertake any studies which the Council considers desirable for the attainment of the common objectives, and to submit to it any appropriate proposals.

Article 153

The Council shall, after receiving an opinion from the Commission, determine the rules governing the committees provided for in this Treaty.

Article 154

The Council shall, acting by a qualified majority, determine the salaries, allowances and pensions of the President and members of the Commission, and of the President, Judges, Advocates-General and Registrar of the Court of Justice. It shall also, again by a qualified majority, determine any payment to be made instead of remuneration.

Section 3

The Commission

Article 155

In order to ensure the proper functioning and development of the common market, the Commission shall:

- ensure that the provisions of this Treaty and the measures taken by the institutions pursuant thereto are applied;

- formulate recommendations or deliver opinions on matters dealt with in this Treaty, if it expressly so provides or if the Commission considers it necessary;
- have its own power of decision and participate in the shaping of measures taken by the Council and by the European Parliament in the manner provided for in this Treaty;
- exercise the powers conferred on it by the Council for the implementation of the rules laid down by the latter.

Article 156

The Commission shall publish annually, not later than one month before the opening of the session of the European Parliament, a general report on the activities of the Community.

Article 157

(1) The Commission shall consist of 20 members, who shall be chosen on the grounds of their general competence and whose independence is beyond doubt.

The number of members of the Commission may be altered by the Council, acting unanimously.

Only nationals of Member States may be members of the Commission.

The Commission must include at least one national of each of the Member States, but may not include more than two members having the nationality of the same State.

(2) The members of the Commission shall, in the general interest of the Community, be completely independent in the performance of their duties. In the performance of these duties, they shall neither seek nor take instructions from any government or from any other body. They shall refrain from any action incompatible with their duties. Each Member State undertakes to respect this principle and not to seek to influence the members of the Commission in the performance of their tasks.

The members of the Commission may not, during their term of office, engage in any other occupation, whether gainful or not. When entering upon their duties they shall give a solemn undertaking that, both during and after their term of office, they will respect the obligations arising therefrom and in particular their duty to behave with integrity and discretion as regards the acceptance, after they have ceased to hold office, of certain appointments or benefits. In the event of any breach of these obligations, the Court of Justice may, on application by the Council or the Commission, rule that the member concerned be, according to the circumstances, either compulsorily retired in accordance with Article 160 or deprived of his right to a pension or other benefits in its stead.

Article 158

(1) The members of the Commission shall be appointed, in accordance with the procedure referred to in paragraph 2, for a period of five years, subject, if need be, to Article 144.

Their term of office shall be renewable.

(2) The governments of the Member States shall nominate by common accord, after consulting the European Parliament, the person they intend to appoint as President of the Commission.

The governments of the Member States shall, in consultation with the nominee for President, nominate the other persons whom they intend to appoint as members of the Commission.

The President and the other members of the Commission thus nominated shall be subject as a body to a vote of approval by the European Parliament. After approval by the European Parliament, the President and the other members of the Commission shall be appointed by common accord of the governments of the Member States.

(3) Paragraphs 1 and 2 shall be applied for the first time to the President and the other members of the Commission whose term of office begins on 7 January 1995.

The President and the other members of the Commission whose term of office begins on 7 January 1993 shall be appointed by common accord of the governments of the Member States. Their term of office shall expire on 6 January 1995.

Article 159

Apart from normal replacement, or death, the duties of a member of the Commission shall end when he resigns or is compulsorily retired.

The vacancy thus caused shall be filled for the remainder of the member's term of office by a new member appointed by common accord of the governments of the Member States. The Council may, acting unanimously, decide that such a vacancy need not be filled.

In the event of resignation, compulsory retirement or death, the President shall be replaced for the remainder of his term of office.

The procedure laid down in Article 158(2) shall be applicable for the replacement of the President.

Save in the case of compulsory retirement under Article 160, members of the Commission shall remain in office until they have been replaced.

Article 160

If any member of the Commission no longer fulfils the conditions required for the performance of his duties or if he has been guilty of serious misconduct, the Court of Justice may, on application by the Council or the Commission, compulsorily retire him.

Article 161

The Commission may appoint a Vice-President or two Vice-Presidents from among its members.

Article 162

(1) The Council and the Commission shall consult each other and shall settle by common accord their methods of cooperation.

(2) The Commission shall adopt its rules of procedure so as to ensure that both it and its departments operate in accordance with the provisions of this Treaty. It shall ensure that these rules are published.

Article 163

The Commission shall act by a majority of the number of members provided for in Article 157.

A meeting of the Commission shall be valid only if the number of members laid down in its rules of procedure is present.

Section 4

The Court of Justice

Article 164

The Court of Justice shall ensure that in the interpretation and application of this Treaty the law is observed.

Article 165

The Court of Justice shall consist of 15 Judges.

The Court of Justice shall sit in plenary session. It may, however, form chambers, each consisting of three, five or seven Judges, either to undertake certain preparatory inquiries or to adjudicate on particular categories of cases in accordance with rules laid down for these purposes.

The Court of Justice shall sit in plenary session when a Member State or a Community institution that is a party to the proceedings so requests.

Should the Court of Justice so request, the Council may, acting unanimously, increase the number of Judges and make the necessary adjustments to the second and third paragraphs of this Article and to the second paragraph of Article 167.

Article 166

The Court of Justice shall be assisted by eight Advocates-General. However, a ninth Advocate-General shall be appointed as from the date of accession until 6 October 2000.

It shall be the duty of the Advocate-General, acting with complete impartiality and independence, to make, in open court, reasoned submissions on cases brought before the Court of Justice, in order to assist the Court in the performance of the task assigned to it in Article 164.

Should the Court of Justice so request, the Council may, acting unanimously, increase the number of Advocates-General and make the necessary adjustments to the third paragraph of Article 167.

Article 167

The Judges and Advocates-General shall be chosen from persons whose independence is beyond doubt and who possess the qualifications required for appointment to the highest judicial offices in their respective countries or who are jurisconsults of recognised competence; they shall be appointed by common accord of the Government of the Member States for a term of six years.

Every three years there shall be a partial replacement of the Judges. Eight and seven Judges shall be replaced alternately.

Every three years there shall be a partial replacement of the Advocates-General. Four Advocates-General shall be replaced on each occasion.

Retiring Judges and Advocates-General shall be eligible for reappointment.

The Judges shall elect the President of the Court of Justice from among their number for a term of three years. He may be re-elected.

Article 168

The Court of Justice shall appoint its Registrar and lay down the rules governing his service.

Article 168a

(1) A Court of First Instance shall be attached to the Court of Justice with jurisdiction to hear and determine at first instance, subject to a right of appeal to the Court of Justice on points of law only and in accordance with the conditions laid down by the Statute, certain classes of action or proceeding defined in accordance with the conditions laid down in paragraph 2. The Court of First Instance shall not be competent to hear and determine questions referred for a preliminary ruling under Article 177.

(2) At the request of the Court of Justice and after consulting the European Parliament and the Commission, the Council, acting unanimously, shall determine the classes of action or proceeding referred to in paragraph 1 and the composition of the Court of First Instance and shall adopt the necessary adjustments and additional provisions to the Statute of the Court of Justice. Unless the Council decides otherwise the provisions of this Treaty relating to the Court of Justice, in particular the provisions of the Protocol on the Statute of the Court of Justice, shall apply to the Court of First Instance.

(3) The members of the Court of First Instance shall be chosen from persons whose independence is beyond doubt and who possess the ability required for appointment to judicial office; they shall be appointed by common accord

of the governments of the Member States for a term of six years. The membership shall be partially renewed every three years. Retiring members shall be eligible for reappointment.

(4) The Court of First Instance shall establish its rules of procedure in agreement with the Court of Justice. Those rules shall require the unanimous approval of the Council.

Article 169

If the Commission considers that a Member State has failed to fulfil an obligation under this Treaty, it shall deliver a reasoned opinion on the matter after giving the State concerned the opportunity to submit its observations.

If the State concerned does not comply with the opinion within the period laid down by the Commission, the latter may bring the matter before the Court of Justice.

Article 170

A Member State which considers that another Member State has failed to fulfil an obligation under this Treaty may bring the matter before the Court of Justice.

Before a Member State brings an action against another Member State for an alleged infringement of an obligation under this Treaty, it shall bring the matter before the Commission.

The Commission shall deliver a reasoned opinion after each of the States concerned has been given the opportunity to submit its own case and its observations on the other party's case both orally and in writing.

If the Commission has not delivered an opinion within three months of the date on which the matter was brought before it, the absence of such opinion shall not prevent the matter from being brought before the Court of Justice.

Article 171

(1) If the Court of Justice finds that a Member State has failed to fulfil an obligation under this Treaty, the State shall be required to take the necessary measures to comply with the judgment of the Court of Justice.

(2) If the Commission considers that the Member State concerned has not taken such measures it shall, after giving that State the opportunity to

submit its observations, issue a reasoned opinion specifying the points on which the Member State concerned has not complied with the judgment of the Court of Justice.

If the Member State concerned fails to take the necessary measures to comply with the Court's judgment within the time-limit laid down by the Commission, the latter may bring the case before the Court of Justice. In so doing it shall specify the amount of the lump sum or penalty payment to be paid by the Member State concerned which it considers appropriate in the circumstances.

If the Court of Justice finds that the Member State concerned has not complied with its judgment it may impose a lump sum or penalty payment on it.

This procedure shall be without prejudice to Article 170.

Article 172

Regulations adopted jointly by the European Parliament and the Council, and by the Council, pursuant to the provisions of this Treaty, may give the Court of Justice unlimited jurisdiction with regard to the penalties provided for in such regulations.

Article 173

The Court of Justice shall review the legality of acts adopted jointly by the European Parliament and the Council, of acts of the Council, of the Commission and of the ECB, other than recommendations and opinions, and of acts of the European Parliament intended to produce legal effects vis-à-vis third parties.

It shall for this purpose have jurisdiction in actions brought by a Member State, the Council or the Commission on grounds of lack of competence, infringement of an essential procedural requirement, infringement of this Treaty or of any rule of law relating to its application, or misuse of powers.

The Court shall have jurisdiction under the same conditions in actions brought by the European Parliament and by the ECB for the purpose of protecting their prerogatives.

Any natural or legal person may, under the same conditions, institute proceedings against a decision addressed to that person or against a decision which, although in the form of a regulation or a decision addressed to another person, is of direct and individual concern to the former.

The proceedings provided for in this Article shall be instituted within two months of the publication of the measure, or of its notification to the plaintiff, or, in the absence thereof, of the day on which it came to the knowledge of the latter as the case may be.

Article 174

If the action is well founded, the Court of Justice shall declare the act concerned to be void.

In the case of a regulation, however, the Court of Justice shall, if it considers this necessary, state which of the effects of the regulation which it has declared void shall be considered as definitive.

Article 175

Should the European Parliament, the Council or the Commission, in infringement of this Treaty, fail to act, the Member States and the other institutions of the Community may bring an action before the Court of Justice to have the infringement established.

The action shall be admissible only if the institution concerned has first been called upon to act. If, within two months of being so called upon, the institution concerned has not defined its position, the action may be brought within a further period of two months.

Any natural or legal person may, under the conditions laid down in the preceding paragraphs, complain to the Court of Justice that an institution of the Community has failed to address to that person any act other than a recommendation or an opinion.

The Court of Justice shall have jurisdiction, under the same conditions, in actions or proceedings brought by the ECB in the areas falling within the latter's field of competence and in actions or proceedings brought against the latter.

Article 176

The institution or institutions whose act has been declared void or whose failure to act has been declared contrary to this Treaty shall be required to take the necessary measures to comply with the judgment of the Court of Justice.

This obligation shall not affect any obligation which may result from the application of the second paragraph of Article 215.

This Article shall also apply to the ECB.

Article 177

The Court of Justice shall have jurisdiction to give preliminary rulings concerning:

(a) the interpretation of this Treaty;

(b) the validity and interpretation of acts of the institutions of the Community and of the ECB;

(c) the interpretation of the statutes of bodies established by an act of the Council, where those statutes so provide.

Where such a question is raised before any court or tribunal of a Member State, that court or tribunal may, if it considers that a decision on the question is necessary to enable it to give judgment, request the Court of Justice to give a ruling thereon.

Where any such question is raised in a case pending before a court or tribunal of a Member State against whose decisions there is no judicial remedy under national law, that court or tribunal shall bring the matter before the Court of Justice.

Article 178

The Court of Justice shall have jurisdiction in disputes relating to compensation for damage provided for in the second paragraph of Article 215.

Article 179

The Court of Justice shall have jurisdiction in any dispute between the Community and its servants within the limits and under the conditions laid down in the Staff Regulations or the Conditions of Employment.

Article 180

The Court of Justice shall, within the limits hereinafter laid down, have jurisdiction in disputes concerning:

(a) the fulfilment by Member States of obligations under the Statute of the European Investment Bank. In this connection, the Board of Directors of the Bank shall enjoy the powers conferred upon the Commission by Article 169;

(b) measures adopted by the Board of Governors of the European Investment Bank. In this connection, any Member State, the Commission or the Board of Directors of the Bank may institute proceedings under the conditions laid down in Article 173;

(c) measures adopted by the Board of Directors of the European Investment Bank. Proceedings against such measures may be instituted only by Member States or by the Commission, under the conditions laid down in Article 173, and solely on the grounds of non-compliance with the procedure provided for in Article 21(2), (5), (6) and (7) of the Statute of the Bank;

(d) the fulfilment by national central banks of obligations under this Treaty and the Statute of the ESCB. In this connection the powers of the Council of the ECB in respect of national central banks shall be the same as those conferred upon the Commission in respect of Member States by Article 169. If the Court of Justice finds that a national central bank has failed to fulfil an obligation under this Treaty, that bank shall be required to take the necessary measures to comply with the judgment of the Court of Justice.

Article 181

The Court of Justice shall have jurisdiction to give judgment pursuant to any arbitration clause contained in a contract concluded by or on behalf of the Community, whether that contract be governed by public or private law.

Article 182

The Court of Justice shall have jurisdiction in any dispute between Member States which relates to the subject matter of this Treaty if the dispute is submitted to it under a special agreement between the parties.

Article 183

Save where jurisdiction is conferred on the Court of Justice by this Treaty, disputes to which the Community is a party shall not on that ground be excluded from the jurisdiction of the courts or tribunals of the Member States.

Article 184

Notwithstanding the expiry of the period laid down in the fifth paragraph of Article 173, any party may, in proceedings in which a regulation adopted jointly by the European Parliament and the Council, or a regulation of the Council, of the Commission, or of the ECB is at issue, plead the grounds specified in the second paragraph of Article 173 in order to invoke before the Court of Justice the inapplicability of that regulation.

Article 185

Actions brought before the Court of Justice shall not have suspensory effect. The Court of Justice may, however, if it considers that circumstances so require, order that application of the contested act be suspended.

Article 186

The Court of Justice may in any cases before it prescribe any necessary interim measures.

Article 187

The judgments of the Court of Justice shall be enforceable under the conditions laid down in Article 192.

Article 188

The Statute of the Court of Justice is laid down in a separate Protocol.

The Council may, acting unanimously at the request of the Court of Justice and after consulting the Commission and the European Parliament, amend the provisions of Title III of the Statute.

Section 5

The Court of Auditors

Article 188a

The Court of Auditors shall carry out the audit.

Article 188b

(1) The Court of Auditors shall consist of 15 members.

(2) The members of the Court of Auditors shall be chosen from among persons who belong or have belonged in their respective countries to external audit bodies or who are especially qualified for this office. Their independence must be beyond doubt.

(3) The members of the Court of Auditors shall be appointed for a term of six years by the Council, acting unanimously after consulting the European Parliament.

However, when the first appointments are made, four members of the Court of Auditors, chosen by lot, shall be appointed for a term of office of four years only.

The members of the Court of Auditors shall be eligible for reappointment.

They shall elect the President of the Court of Auditors from among their number for a term of three years.

The President may be re-elected.

(4) The members of the Court of Auditors shall, in the general interest of the Community, be completely independent in the performance of their duties.

In the performance of these duties, they shall neither seek nor take instructions from any government or from any other body. They shall refrain from any action incompatible with their duties.

(5) The members of the Court of Auditors may not, during their term of office, engage in any other occupation, whether gainful or not. When entering upon their duties they shall give a solemn undertaking that, both during and after their term of office, they will respect the obligations arising therefrom and in particular their duty to behave with integrity and discretion as regards the acceptance, after they have ceased to hold office, of certain appointments or benefits.

(6) Apart from normal replacement, or death, the duties of a member of the Court of Auditors shall end when he resigns, or is compulsorily retired by a ruling of the Court of Justice pursuant to paragraph 7.

The vacancy thus caused shall be filled for the remainder of the member's term of office.

Save in the case of compulsory retirement, members of the Court of Auditors shall remain in office until they have been replaced.

(7) A member of the Court of Auditors may be deprived of his office or of his right to a pension or other benefits in its stead only if the Court of Justice, at the request of the Court of Auditors, finds that he no longer fulfils the requisite conditions or meets the obligations arising from his office.

(8) The Council, acting by a qualified majority, shall determine the conditions of employment of the President and the members of the Court of Auditors and in particular their salaries, allowances and pensions. It shall also, by the same majority, determine any payment to be made instead of remuneration.

(9) The provisions of the Protocol on the Privileges and Immunities of the European Communities applicable to the Judges of the Court of Justice shall also apply to the members of the Court of Auditors.

Article 188c

(1) The Court of Auditors shall examine the accounts of all revenue and expenditure of the Community. It shall also examine the accounts of all revenue and expenditure of all bodies set up by the Community in so far as the relevant constituent instrument does not preclude such examination.

The Court of Auditors shall provide the European Parliament and the Council with a statement of assurance as to the reliability of the accounts and the legality and regularity of the underlying transactions.

(2) The Court of Auditors shall examine whether all revenue has been received and all expenditure incurred in a lawful and regular manner and whether the financial management has been sound.

The audit of revenue shall be carried out on the basis both of the amounts established as due and the amounts actually paid to the Community.

The audit of expenditure shall be carried out on the basis both of commitments undertaken and payments made.

These audits may be carried out before the closure of accounts for the financial year in question.

(3) The audit shall be based on records and, if necessary, performed on the spot in the other institutions of the Community and in the Member States. In the Member States the audit shall be carried out in liaison with the national audit bodies or, if these do not have the necessary powers, with the competent national departments. These bodies or departments shall inform the Court of Auditors whether they intend to take part in the audit.

The other institutions of the Community and the national audit bodies or, if these do not have the necessary powers, the competent national departments, shall forward to the Court of Auditors, at its request, any document or information necessary to carry out its task.

(4) The Court of Auditors shall draw up an annual report after the close of each financial year. It shall be forwarded to the other institutions of the Community and shall be published, together with the replies of these institutions to the observations of the Court of Auditors, in the Official Journal of the European Communities.

The Court of Auditors may also, at any time, submit observations, particularly in the form of special reports, on specific questions and deliver opinions at the request of one of the other institutions of the Community.

It shall adopt its annual reports, special reports or opinions by a majority of its members.

It shall assist the European Parliament and the Council in exercising their powers of control over the implementation of the budget.

CHAPTER 2 – PROVISIONS COMMON TO SEVERAL INSTITUTIONS

Article 189

In order to carry out their task and in accordance with the provisions of this Treaty, the European Parliament acting jointly with the Council, the Council and the Commission shall make regulations and issue directives, take decisions, make recommendations or deliver opinions.

A regulation shall have general application. It shall be binding in its entirety and directly applicable in all Member States.

A directive shall be binding, as to the result to be achieved, upon each Member State to which it is addressed, but shall leave to the national authorities the choice of form and methods.

A decision shall be binding in its entirety upon those to whom it is addressed.

Recommendations and opinions shall have no binding force.

Article 189a

(1) Where, in pursuance of this Treaty, the Council acts on a proposal from

the Commission, unanimity shall be required for an act constituting an amendment to that proposal, subject to Article 189b(4) and (5).

(2) As long as the Council has not acted, the Commission may alter its proposal at any time during the procedures leading to the adoption of a Community act.

Article 189b

(1) Where reference is made in this Treaty to this Article for the adoption of an act, the following procedure shall apply.

(2) The Commission shall submit a proposal to the European Parliament and the Council.

The Council, acting by a qualified majority after obtaining the opinion of the European Parliament, shall adopt a common position. The common position shall be communicated to the European Parliament. The Council shall inform the European Parliament fully of the reasons which led it to adopt its common position. The Commission shall inform the European Parliament fully of its position.

If, within three months of such communication, the European Parliament:

(a) approves the common position, the Council shall definitively adopt the act in question in accordance with the common position;

(b) has not taken a decision, the Council shall adopt the act in question in accordance with its common position;

(c) indicates, by an absolute majority of its component members, that it intends to reject the common position, it shall immediately inform the Council. The Council may convene a meeting of the Conciliation Committee referred to in paragraph 4 to explain further its position. The European Parliament shall thereafter either confirm, by an absolute majority of its component members, its rejection of the common position, in which event the proposed act shall be deemed not to have been adopted, or propose amendments in accordance with subparagraph (d) of this paragraph;

(d) proposes amendments to the common position by an absolute majority of its component members, the amended test shall be forwarded to the Council and to the Commission, which shall deliver an opinion on those amendments.

(3) If, within three months of the matter being referred to it, the Council, acting by a qualified majority, approves all the amendments of the European Parliament, it shall amend its common position accordingly and adopt the

act in question; however, the Council shall act unanimously on the amendments on which the Commission has delivered a negative opinion. If the Council does not approve the act in question, the President of the Council, in agreement with the President of the European Parliament, shall forthwith convene a meeting of the Conciliation Committee.

(4) The Conciliation Committee, which shall be composed of the members of the Council or their representatives and an equal number of representatives of the European Parliament, shall have the task of reaching agreement on a joint text, by a qualified majority of the members of the Council or their representatives and by a majority of the representatives of the European Parliament. The Commission shall take part in the Conciliation Committee's proceedings and shall take all the necessary initiatives with a view to reconciling the positions of the European Parliament and the Council.

(5) If, within six weeks of its being convened, the Conciliation Committee approves a joint text, the European Parliament, acting by an absolute majority of the votes cast, and the Council, acting by a qualified majority, shall have a period of six weeks from that approval in which to adopt the act in question in accordance with the joint text. If one of the two institutions fails to approve the proposed act, it shall be deemed not to have been adopted.

(6) Where the Conciliation Committee does not approve a joint text, the proposed act shall be deemed not to have been adopted unless the Council, acting by a qualified majority within six weeks of expiry of the period granted to the Conciliation Committee, confirms the common position to which it agreed before the conciliation procedure was initiated, possibly with amendments proposed by the European Parliament. In this case, the act in question shall be finally adopted unless the European Parliament, within six weeks of the date of confirmation by the Council, rejects the text by an absolute majority of its component members, in which case the proposed act shall be deemed not to have been adopted.

(7) The periods of three months and six weeks referred to in this Article may be extended by a maximum of one month and two weeks respectively by common accord of the European Parliament and the Council. The period of three months referred to in paragraph 2 shall be automatically extended by two months where paragraph 2(c) applies.

(8) The scope of the procedure under this Article may be widened, in accordance with the procedure provided for in Article N(2) of the Treaty on European Union, on the basis of a report to be submitted to the Council by the Commission by 1996 at the latest.

Article 189c

Where reference is made in this Treaty to this Article for the adoption of an act, the following procedure shall apply:

(a) The Council, acting by a qualified majority on a proposal from the Commission and after obtaining the opinion of the European Parliament, shall adopt a common position.

(b) The Council's common position shall be communicated to the European Parliament. The Council and the Commission shall inform the European Parliament fully of the reasons which led the Council to adopt its common position and also of the Commission's position.

If, within three months of such communication, the European Parliament approves this common position or has not taken a decision within that period, the Council shall definitively adopt the act in question in accordance with the common position.

(c) The European Parliament may, within the period of three months referred to in subparagraph (b), by an absolute majority of its component members, propose amendments to the Council's common position. The European Parliament may also, by the same majority, reject the Council's common position. The result of the proceedings shall be transmitted to the Council and the Commission.

If the European Parliament has rejected the Council's common position, unanimity shall be required for the Council to act on a second reading.

(d) The Commission shall, within a period of one month, re-examine the proposal on the basis of which the Council adopted its common position, by taking into account the amendments proposed by the European Parliament.

The Commission shall forward to the Council, at the same time as its re-examined proposal, the amendments of the European Parliament which it has not accepted, and shall express its opinion on them. The Council may adopt these amendments unanimously.

(e) The Council, acting by a qualified majority, shall adopt the proposal as re-examined by the Commission.

Unanimity shall be required for the Council to amend the proposal as re-examined by the Commission.

(f) In the cases referred to in subparagraphs (c), (d) and (e), the Council shall be required to act within a period of three months. If no decision is taken within this period, the Commission proposal shall be deemed not to have been adopted.

(g) The periods referred to in subparagraphs (b) and (f) may be extended by a maximum of one month by common accord between the Council and the European Parliament.

Article 190

Regulations, directives and decisions adopted jointly by the European Parliament and the Council, and such acts adopted by the Council or the Commission, shall state the reasons on which they are based and shall refer to any proposals or opinions which were required to be obtained pursuant to this Treaty.

Article 191

(1) Regulations, directives and decisions adopted in accordance with the procedure referred to in Article 189b shall be signed by the President of the European Parliament and by the President of the Council and published in the Official Journal of the European Communities. They shall enter into force on the date specified in them or, in the absence thereof, on the 20th day following that of their publication.

(2) Regulations of the Council and of the Commission, as well as directives of those institutions which are addressed to all Member States, shall be published in the Official Journal of the European Communities. They shall enter into force on the date specified in them or, in the absence thereof, on the 20th day following that of their publication.

(3) Other directives, and decisions, shall be notified to those to whom they are addressed and shall take effect upon such notification.

Article 192

Decisions of the Council or of the Commission which impose a pecuniary obligation on persons other than States shall be enforceable.

Enforcement shall be governed by the rules of civil procedure in force in the State in the territory of which it is carried out. The order for its enforcement shall be appended to the decision, without other formality than verification of the authenticity of the decision, by the national authority which the Government of each Member State shall designate for this purpose and shall make known to the Commission and to the Court of Justice.

When these formalities have been completed on application by the party concerned, the latter may proceed to enforcement in accordance with the national law, by bringing the matter directly before the competent authority.

Enforcement may be suspended only by a decision of the Court of Justice. However, the courts of the country concerned shall have jurisdiction over complaints that enforcement is being carried out in an irregular manner.

CHAPTER 3 – THE ECONOMIC AND SOCIAL COMMITTEE

Article 193

An Economic and Social Committee is hereby established. It shall have advisory status.

The Committee shall consist of representatives of the various categories of economic and social activity, in particular, representatives of producers, farmers, carriers, workers, dealers, craftsmen, professional occupations and representatives of the general public.

Article 194

The number of members of the Economic and Social Committee shall be as follows:

Belgium	12
Denmark	9
Germany	24
Greece	12
Spain	21
France	24
Ireland	9
Italy	24
Luxembourg	6
Netherlands	12
Austria	12
Portugal	12
Finland	9
Sweden	12
United Kingdom	24

The members of the Committee shall be appointed by the Council, acting unanimously, for four years. Their appointments shall be renewable.

The members of the Committee may not be bound by any mandatory instructions. They shall be completely independent in the performance of their duties, in the general interest of the Community.

The Council, acting by a qualified majority, shall determine the allowances of members of the Committee.

Article 195

(1) For the appointment of the members of the Committee, each Member State shall provide the Council with a list containing twice as many candidates as there are seats allotted to its nationals.

The composition of the Committee shall take account of the need to ensure adequate representation of the various categories of economic and social activity.

(2) The Council shall consult the Commission. It may obtain the opinion of European bodies which are representative of the various economic and social sectors to which the activities of the Community are of concern.

Article 196

The Committee shall elect its chairman and officers from among its members for a term of two years.

It shall adopt its rules of procedure.

The Committee shall be convened by its chairman at the request of the Council or of the Commission. It may also meet on its own initiative.

Article 197

The Committee shall include specialised sections for the principal fields covered by this Treaty.

In particular, it shall contain an agricultural section and a transport section, which are the subject of special provisions in the Titles relating to agriculture and transport.

These specialised sections shall operate within the general terms of reference of the Committee. They may not be consulted independently of the Committee.

Sub-committees may also be established within the Committee to prepare, on specific questions or in specified fields, draft opinions to be submitted to the Committee for its consideration.

The rules of procedure shall lay down the methods of composition and the terms of reference of the specialised sections and of the sub-committees.

Article 198

The Committee must be consulted by the Council or by the Commission where this Treaty so provides. The Committee may be consulted by these institutions in all cases in which they consider it appropriate. It may issue an opinion on its own initiative in cases in which it considers such action appropriate.

The Council or the Commission shall, if it considers it necessary, set the Committee, for the submission of its opinion, a time-limit which may not be less than one month from the date on which the chairman receives notification to this effect. Upon expiry of the time-limit, the absence of an opinion shall not prevent further action.

The opinion of the Committee and that of the specialised section, together with a record of the proceedings, shall be forwarded to the Council and to the Commission.

CHAPTER 4 – THE COMMITTEE OF THE REGIONS

Article 198a

A Committee consisting of representatives of regional and local bodies, hereinafter referred to as 'the Committee of the Regions', is hereby established with advisory status.

The number of members of the Committee of the Regions shall be as follows:

Belgium	12
Denmark	9
Germany	24
Greece	12
Spain	21
France	24
Ireland	9
Italy	24
Luxembourg	6

Netherlands	12
Austria	12
Portugal	12
Finland	9
Sweden	12
United Kingdom	24

The members of the Committee and an equal number of alternate members shall be appointed for four years by the Council acting unanimously on proposals from the respective Member States.

Their term of office shall be renewable.

The members of the Committee may not be bound by any mandatory instructions. They shall be completely independent in the performance of their duties, in the general interest of the Community.

Article 198b

The Committee of the Regions shall elect its chairman and officers from among its members for a term of two years.

It shall adopt its rules of procedure and shall submit them for approval to the Council, acting unanimously.

The Committee shall be convened by its chairman at the request of the Council or of the Commission. It may also meet on its own initiative.

Article 198c

The Committee of the Regions shall be consulted by the Council or by the Commission where this Treaty so provides and in all other cases in which one of these two institutions considers it appropriate.

The Council or the Commission shall, if it considers it necessary, set the Committee, for the submission of its opinion, a time-limit which may not be less than one month from the date on which the chairman receives notification to this effect. Upon expiry of the time-limit, the absence of an opinion shall not prevent further action.

Where the Economic and Social Committee is consulted pursuant to Article 198, the Committee of the Regions shall be informed by the Council or the Commission of the request for an opinion. Where it considers that specific regional interests are involved, the Committee of the Regions may issue an opinion on the matter.

It may issue an opinion on its own initiative in cases in which it considers such action appropriate.

The opinion of the Committee, together with a record of the proceedings, shall be forwarded to the Council and to the Commission.

CHAPTER 5 – EUROPEAN INVESTMENT BANK

Article 198d

The European Investment Bank shall have legal personality.

The members of the European Investment Bank shall be the Member States.

The Statute of the European Investment Bank is laid down in a Protocol annexed to this Treaty.

Article 198e

The task of the European Investment Bank shall be to contribute, by having recourse to the capital market and utilising its own resources, to the balanced and steady development of the common market in the interest of the Community. For this purpose the Bank shall, operating on a non-profit-making basis, grant loans and give guarantees which facilitate the financing of the following projects in all sectors of the economy:

(a) projects for developing less-developed regions;

(b) projects for modernising or converting undertakings or for developing fresh activities called for by the progressive establishment of the common market, where these projects are of such a size or nature that they cannot be entirely financed by the various means available in the individual Member States;

(c) projects of common interest to several Member States which are of such a size or nature that they cannot be entirely financed by the various means available in the individual Member States.

In carrying out its task, the Bank shall facilitate the financing of investment programmes in conjunction with assistance from the structural Funds and other Community financial instruments.

TITLE II – FINANCIAL PROVISIONS

Article 199

All items of revenue and expenditure of the Community, including those relating to the European Social Fund, shall be included in estimates to be drawn up for each financial year and shall be shown in the budget.

Administrative expenditure occasioned for the institutions by the provisions of the Treaty on European Union relating to common foreign and security policy and to cooperation in the fields of justice and home affairs shall be charged to the budget. The operational expenditure occasioned by the implementation of the said provision may, under the conditions referred to therein, be charged to the budget.

The revenue and expenditure shown in the budget shall be in balance.

Article 201

Without prejudice to other revenue, the budget shall be financed wholly from own resources.

The Council, acting unanimously on a proposal from the Commission and after consulting the European Parliament, shall lay down provisions relating to the system of own resources of the Community, which it shall recommend to the Member States for adoption in accordance with their respective constitutional requirements.

Article 201a

With a view to maintaining budgetary discipline, the Commission shall not make any proposal for a Community act, or alter its proposals, or adopt any implementing measure which is likely to have appreciable implications for the budget, without providing the assurance that that proposal or that measure is capable of being financed within the limit of the Community's own resources arising under provisions laid down by the Council pursuant to Article 201.

Article 202

The expenditure shown in the budget shall be authorised for one financial year, unless the regulations made pursuant to Article 209 provide otherwise.

In accordance with conditions to be laid down pursuant to Article 209, any appropriations, other than those relating to staff expenditure, that are unexpended at the end of the financial year may be carried forward to the next financial year only.

Appropriations shall be classified under different chapters grouping items of expenditure according to their nature or purpose and subdivided, as far as may be necessary, in accordance with the regulations made pursuant to Article 209.

The expenditure of the European Parliament, the Council, the Commission and the Court of Justice shall be set out in separate parts of the budget, without prejudice to special arrangements for certain common items of expenditure.

Article 203

(1) The financial year shall run from 1 January to 31 December.

(2) Each institution of the Community shall, before 1 July, draw up estimates of its expenditure. The Commission shall consolidate these estimates in a preliminary draft budget. It shall attach thereto an opinion which may contain different estimates.

The preliminary draft budget shall contain an estimate of revenue and an estimate of expenditure.

(3) The Commission shall place the preliminary draft budget before the Council not later than 1 September of the year preceding that in which the budget is to be implemented.

The Council shall consult the Commission and, where appropriate, the other institutions concerned whenever it intends to depart from the preliminary draft budget.

The Council shall, acting by a qualified majority, establish the draft budget and forward it to the European Parliament.

(4) The draft budget shall be placed before the European Parliament not later than 5 October of the year preceding that in which the budget is to be implemented.

The European Parliament shall have the right to amend the draft budget, acting by a majority of its members and to propose to the Council, acting by an absolute majority of the votes cast, modifications to the draft budget relating to expenditure necessary resulting from this Treaty or from acts adopted in accordance therewith.

If, within forty-five days of the draft budget being placed before it, the European Parliament has given its approval, the budget shall stand as finally adopted. If within this period the European Parliament has not amended the draft budget nor proposed any modifications thereto, the budget shall be deemed to be finally adopted.

If within this period the European Parliament has adopted amendments or proposed modifications, the draft budget together with the amendments or proposed modifications shall be forwarded to the Council.

(5) After discussing the draft budget with the commission and, where appropriate, with the other institutions concerned, the Council shall act under the following conditions:

(a) The Council may, acting by a qualified majority, modify any of the amendments adopted by the European Parliament;

(b) With regard to the proposed modifications:

- where a modification proposed by the European Parliament does not have the effect of increasing the total amount of the expenditure of an institution, owing in particular to the fact that the increase in expenditure which it would involve would be expressly compensated by one or more proposed modifications correspondingly reducing expenditure, the Council may, acting by a qualified majority, reject the proposed modification. In the absence of a decision to reject it, the proposed modification shall stand as accepted;

- where a modification proposed by the European Parliament has the effect of increasing the total amount of the expenditure of an institution, the Council may, acting by a qualified majority, accept this proposed modification. In the absence of a decision to accept it, the proposed modification shall stand as rejected;

- where, in pursuance of one of the two preceding sub-paragraphs, the Council has rejected a proposed modification, it may, acting by a qualified majority, either retain the amount shown in the draft budget or fix another amount.

The draft budget shall be modified on the basis of the proposed modifications accepted by the Council.

If within fifteen days of the draft budget being placed before it, the Council has not modified any of the amendments adopted by the European Parliament and if the modifications proposed by the latter have been accepted, the budget shall be deemed to be finally adopted. The Council shall inform the European Parliament that it has not modified any of the amendments and that the proposed modifications have been accepted.

If within this period the Council has modified one or more of the amendments adopted by the European Parliament or if the modifications proposed by the latter have been rejected or modified, the modified draft budget shall again be forwarded to the European Parliament. The Council shall inform the European Parliament of the results of its deliberations.

(6) Within fifteen days of the draft budget being placed before it, the European Parliament, which shall have been notified of the action taken on its proposed modifications, may, acting by a majority of its members and three-fifths of the votes cast, amend or reject the modifications to its amendments made by the Council and shall adopt the budget accordingly. If within this period the European Parliament has not acted, the budget shall be deemed to be finally adopted.

(7) When the procedure provided for in this Article has been completed, the President of the European Parliament shall declare that the budget has been finally adopted.

(8) However, the European Parliament, acting by a majority of its members and two-thirds of the votes cast, may if there are important reasons reject the draft budget and ask for a new draft to be submitted to it.

(9) A maximum rate of increase in relation to the expenditure of the same type to be incurred during the current year shall be fixed annually for the total expenditure other than that necessarily resulting from this Treaty or from acts adopted in accordance therewith.

The Commission shall, after consulting the Economic Policy Committee, declare what this maximum rate is as it results from:

- the trend in terms of volume, of the gross national product within the community;
- the average variation in the budgets of the Member States; and
- the trend of the cost of living during the preceding financial year. The maximum rate shall be communicated, before 1 May, to all the institutions of the Community. The latter shall be required to conform to this during the budgetary procedure, subject to the provisions of the fourth and fifth subparagraphs of this paragraph.

If, in respect of expenditure other than that necessarily resulting from this Treaty or from acts adopted in accordance therewith, the actual rate of increase in the draft budget established by the Council is over half of the maximum rate, the European Parliament may, exercising its right of amendment, further increase the total amount of that expenditure to a limit not exceeding half the maximum rate.

Where the European Parliament, the Council or the Commission consider that the activities of the Communities require that the rate determined according to the procedure laid down in this paragraph should be exceeded, another rate may be fixed by agreement between the Council, acting by a qualified majority, and the European Parliament, acting by a majority of its members and three-fifths of the votes cast.

(10) Each institution shall exercise the powers conferred upon it by this Article, with due regard for the provisions of the Treaty and for acts adopted in accordance therewith, in particular those relating to the Communities' own resources and to the balance between revenue and expenditure.

Article 204

If, at the beginning of a financial year, the budget has not yet been voted, a sum equivalent to not more than one twelfth of the budget appropriations for the preceding financial year may be spent each month in respect of any chapter or other subdivision of the budget in accordance with the provisions of the regulations made pursuant to Article 209; this arrangement shall not, however, have the effect of placing at the disposal of the Commission appropriations in excess of one twelfth of those provided for in the draft budget in course of preparation.

The Council may, acting by a qualified majority, provided that the other conditions laid down in the first subparagraph are observed, authorise expenditure in excess of one twelfth.

If the decision relates to expenditure which does not necessarily result from this Treaty or from acts adopted in accordance therewith, the Council shall forward it immediately to the European Parliament; within thirty days the European Parliament, acting by a majority of its members and three-fifths of the votes cast, may adopt a different decision on the expenditure in excess of the one-twelfth referred to in the first subparagraph. This part of the decision of the Council shall be suspended until the European Parliament has taken its decision. If within the period the European Parliament has not taken a decision which differs from the decision of the Council, the latter shall be deemed to be finally adopted.

The decisions referred to in the second and third subparagraphs shall lay down the necessary measures relating to resources to ensure application of this Article.

Article 205

The Commission shall implement the budget, in accordance with the provisions of the regulations made pursuant to Article 209, on its own responsibility and within the limits of the appropriations, having regard to the principles of sound financial management.

The regulations shall lay down detailed rules for each institution concerning its part in effecting its own expenditure.

Within the budget, the Commission may, subject to the limits and conditions laid down in the regulations made pursuant to Article 209, transfer appropriations from one chapter to another or from one subdivision to another.

Article 205a

The Commission shall submit annually to the Council and to the European Parliament the accounts of the preceding financial year relating to the implementation of the budget. The Commission shall also forward to them a financial statement of the assets and liabilities of the Community.

Article 206

(1) The European Parliament, acting on a recommendation from the Council which shall act by a qualified majority, shall give a discharge to the Commission in respect of the implementation of the budget.

To this end, the Council and the European Parliament in turn shall examine the accounts and the financial statement referred to in Article 205a, the annual report by the Court of Auditors together with the replies of the institutions under audit to the observations of the Court of Auditors, and any relevant special reports by the Court of Auditors.

(2) Before giving a discharge to the Commission, or for any other purpose in connection with the exercise of its powers over the implementation of the budget, the European Parliament may ask to hear the Commission give evidence with regard to the execution of expenditure or the operation of financial control systems.

The Commission shall submit any necessary information to the European Parliament at the latter's request.

(3) The Commission shall take all appropriate steps to act on the observations in the decisions giving discharge and on other observations by

the European Parliament relating to the execution of expenditure, as well as on comments accompanying the recommendations on discharge adopted by the Council.

At the request of the European Parliament or the Council, the Commission shall report on the measures taken in the light of these observations and comments and in particular on the instructions given to the departments which are responsible for the imple-mentation of the budget. These reports shall also be forwarded to the Court of Auditors.

Article 207

The budget shall be drawn up in the unit of account determined in accordance with the provisions of the regulations made pursuant to Article 209. The financial contributions provided for in Article 200(1) shall be placed at the disposal of the Community by the Member States in their national currencies.

The available balances of these contributions shall be deposited with the Treasuries of Member States or with bodies designated by them. While on deposit, such funds shall retain the value corresponding to the parity, at the date of deposit, in relation to the unit of account referred to in the first paragraph.

The balances may be invested on terms to be agreed between the Commission and the Member State concerned.

The regulations made pursuant to Article 209 shall lay down the technical conditions under which financial operations relating to the European Social Fund shall be carried out.

Article 208

The Commission may, provided it notifies the competent authorities of the Member States concerned, transfer into the currency of one of the Member States its holdings in the currency of another Member State, to the extent necessary to enable them to be used for purposes which come within the scope of this Treasury. The Commission shall as far as possible avoid making such transfers if it possesses cash or liquid assets in the currencies which it needs.

The Commission shall deal with each Member State through the authority designated by the State concerned. In carrying out financial operations the Commission shall employ the services of the bank of issue of the Member State concerned or of any other financial institution approved by that State.

Article 209

The Council, acting unanimously on a proposal from the Commission and after consulting the European Parliament and obtaining the opinion of the Court of Auditors, shall:

(a) make Financial Regulations specifying in particular the procedure to be adopted for establishing and implementing the budget and for presenting and auditing accounts;

(b) determine the methods and procedure whereby the budget revenue provided under the arrangements relating to the Community's own resources shall be made available to the Commission, and determine the measures to be applied, if need be, to meet cash requirements;

(c) lay down rules concerning the responsibility of financial controllers, authorising officers and accounting officers, and concerning appropriate arrangements for inspection.

Article 209a

Member States shall take the same measures to counter fraud affecting the financial interests of the Community as they take to counter fraud affecting their own financial interests.

Without prejudice to other provisions of this Treaty, Member States shall coordinate their action aimed at protecting the financial interests of the Community against fraud. To this end they shall organise with the help of the Commission, close and regular cooperation between the competent departments of their administration.

Part Six

GENERAL AND FINAL PROVISIONS

Article 210

The Community shall have legal personality.

Article 211

In each of the Member States, the Community shall enjoy the most extensive legal capacity accorded to legal persons under their laws; it may, in particular, acquire or dispose of movable and immovable property and may be a party to legal proceedings. To this end, the Community shall be represented by the Commission.

Article 213

The Commission may, within the limits and under the conditions laid down by the Council in accordance with the provisions of this Treaty, collect any information and carry out any checks required for the performance of the tasks entrusted to it.

Article 214

The members of the institutions of the Community, the members of committees, and the officials and other servants of the Community shall be required, even after their duties have ceased, not to disclose information of the kind covered by the obligation of professional secrecy, in particular information about undertakings, their business relations or their cost components.

Article 215

The contractual liability of the Community shall be governed by the law applicable to the contract in question.

In the case of non-contractual liability, the Community shall, in accordance with the general principles common to the laws of the Member States, make good any damage caused by its institutions or by its servants in the performance of their duties.

The preceding paragraph shall apply under the same conditions to damage caused by the ECB or by its servants in the performance of their duties.

The personal liability of its servants towards the Community shall be governed by the provisions laid down in their Staff Regulations or in the Conditions of Employment applicable to them.

Article 216

The seat of the institutions of the Community shall be determined by common accord of the Governments of the Member States.

Article 217

The rules governing the languages of the institutions of the Community shall, without prejudice to the provisions contained in the rules of procedure of the Court of Justice, be determined by the Council, acting unanimously.

Article 219

Member States undertake not to submit a dispute concerning the interpretation or application of this Treaty to any method of settlement other than those provided for therein.

Article 220

Member States shall, so far as is necessary, enter into negotiations with each other with a view to securing for the benefit of their nationals:

- the protection of persons and the enjoyment and protection of rights under the same conditions as those accorded by each State to its own nationals;
- the abolition of double taxation within the Community;
- the mutual recognition of companies or firms within the meaning of the second paragraph of Article 58, the retention of legal personality in the event of transfer of their seat from one country to another, and the possibility of mergers between companies or firms governed by the laws of different countries;
- the simplification of formalities governing the reciprocal recognition and enforcement of judgments of courts or tribunals and of arbitration awards.

Article 221

Within three years of the entry into force of this Treaty, Member States shall accord nationals of the other Member States the same treatment as their own nationals as regards participation in the capital of companies or firms within the meaning of Article 58, without prejudice to the application of the other provisions of this Treaty.

Article 222

This Treaty shall in no way prejudice the rules in Member States governing the system of property ownership.

Article 223

(1) The provisions of this Treaty shall not preclude the application of the following rules:

(a) No Member States shall be obliged to supply information the disclosure of which it considers contrary to the essential interests of its security;

(b) Any Member State may take such measures as it considers necessary for the protection of the essential interests of its security which are connected with the production of or trade in arms, munitions and war material: such measures shall not adversely affect the conditions of competition in the common market regarding products which are not intended for specifically military purposes.

(2) During the first year after the entry into force of this Treaty, the Council shall, acting unanimously, draw up a list of products to which the provisions of paragraph 1(b) shall apply.

(3) The Council may, acting unanimously on a proposal from the Commission, make changes in this list.

Article 224

Member States shall consult each other with a view to taking together the steps needed to prevent the functioning of the common market being affected by measures which a Member State may be called upon to take in the event of serious internal disturbances affecting the maintenance of law and order, in the event of war or serious international tension constituting a threat of war, or in order to carry out obligations it has accepted for the purpose of maintaining peace and international security.

Article 225

If measures taken in the circumstances referred to in Articles 223 and 224 have the effect of distorting the conditions of competition in the common market, the Commission shall, together with the State concerned, examine how these measures can be adjusted to the rules laid down in this Treaty.

By way of derogation from the procedure laid down in Articles 169 and 170, the Commission or any Member State may bring the matter directly before the Court of Justice if it considers that another Member State is making improper use of the powers provided for in Articles 223 and 224. The Court of Justice shall give its ruling in camera.

Article 226

(1) If, during the transitional period, difficulties arise which are serious and liable to persist in any sector of the economy or which could bring about serious deterioration in the economic situation of a given area, a Member State may apply for authorisation to take protective measures in order to rectify the situation and adjust the sector concerned to the economy of the common market.

(2) On application by the State concerned, the Commission shall, by emergency procedure, determine without delay the protective measures which it considers necessary, specifying the circumstances and the manner in which they are to be put into effect.

(3) The measures authorised under paragraph 2 may involve derogations from the rules of this Treaty, to such an extent and for such periods as are strictly necessary in order to attain the objectives referred to in paragraph 1. Priority shall be given to such measures as will disturb the functioning of the common market.

Article 227

(1) This Treaty shall apply to the Kingdom of Belgium, the Kingdom of Denmark, the Federal Republic of Germany, the Hellenic Republic, the Kingdom of Spain, the French Republic, Ireland, the Italian Republic, the Grand Duchy of Luxembourg, the Kingdom of the Netherlands, the Republic of Austria, the Portuguese Republic, the Republic of Finland, the Kingdom of Sweden and the United Kingdom of Great Britain and Northern Ireland.

(2) With regard to the French overseas departments, the general and particular provisions of this Treaty relating to:

- the free movement of goods;
- agriculture, save for Article 40(4);
- the liberalisation of services;
- the rules on competition;
- the protective measures provided for in Articles 109h, 109i and 226;
- the institutions,

shall apply as soon as this Treaty enters into force.

The conditions under which the other provisions of this Treaty are to apply shall be determined, within two years of the entry into force of this Treaty, by decisions of the Council, acting unanimously on a proposal from the Commission.

The institutions of the Community will, within the framework of the procedures provided for in this Treaty, in particular Article 226, take care that the economic and social development of these areas is made possible.

(3) The special arrangements for association set out in Part Four of this Treaty shall apply to the overseas countries and territories listed in Annex IV to this Treaty.

This Treaty shall not apply to those overseas countries and territories having special relations with the United Kingdom of Great Britain and Northern Ireland which are not included in the aforementioned list.

(4) The provisions of this Treaty shall apply to the European territories for whose external relations a Member State is responsible.

(5) Notwithstanding the preceding paragraphs:

(a) This Treaty shall not apply to the Faroe Islands.

(b) This Treaty shall not apply to the Sovereign Base Areas of the United Kingdom of Great Britain and Northern Ireland in Cyprus.

(c) This Treaty shall apply to the Channel Islands and the Isle of Man only to the extent necessary to ensure the imple-mentation of the arrangements for those islands set out in the Treaty concerning the accession of new Member States to the European Community and to the European Atomic Energy Community signed on 22 January 1972.

(d) This Treaty shall not apply to the Åland islands. The Government of Finland may, however, give notice, by a declaration deposited when ratifying this Treaty with the Government of the Italian Republic, that the Treaty shall apply to the Åland islands in accordance with the provisions set out in Protocol No 2 to the Act concerning the accession of the Republic of Austria, the Republic of Finland and the Kingdom of Sweden to the European Union. The Government of the Italian Republic shall transmit a certified copy of any such declaration to the Member States.

Article 228

(1) Where this Treaty provides for the conclusion of agreements between the Community and one or more States or international organisations, the Commission shall make recommendations to the Council, which shall authorise the Commission to open the necessary negotiations. The Commission shall conduct these negotiations in consultation with special committees appointed by the Council to assist it in this task and within the framework of such directives as the Council may issue to it.

In exercising the powers conferred upon it by this paragraph, the Council shall act by a qualified majority, except in the cases provided for in the second sentence of paragraph 2, for which it shall act unanimously.

(2) Subject to the powers vested in the Commission in this field, the agreements shall be concluded by the Council, acting by a qualified majority on a proposal from the Commission. The Council shall act unanimously when the agreement covers a field for which unanimity is required for the adoption of internal rules, and for the agreements referred to in Article 238.

(3) The Council shall conclude agreements after consulting the European Parliament, except for the agreements referred to in Article 113(3), including cases where the agreement covers a field for which the procedure referred to in Article 189b or that referred to in Article 189c is required for the adoption of internal rules. The European Parliament shall deliver its opinion within a time-limit which the Council may lay down according to the urgency of the matter. In the absence of an opinion within that time-limit, the Council may act.

By way of derogation from the previous subparagraph, agreements referred to in Article 238, other agreements establishing a specific institutional framework by organising cooperation procedures, agreements having important budgetary implications for the Community and agreements entailing amendment of an act adopted under the procedure referred to in Article 189b, shall be concluded after the assent of the European Parliament has been obtained.

The Council and the European Parliament may, in an urgent situation, agree upon a time-limit for the assent.

(4) When concluding an agreement, the Council may, by way of derogation from paragraph 2, authorise the Commission to approve modifications on behalf of the Community where the agreement provides for them to be adopted by a simplified procedure or by a body set up by the agreement; it may attach specific conditions to such authorisation.

(5) When the Council envisages concluding an agreement which calls for amendments to this Treaty, the amendments must first be adopted in accordance with the procedure laid down in Article N of the Treaty on European Union.

(6) The Council, the Commission or a Member State may obtain the opinion of the Court of Justice as to whether an agreement envisaged is compatible with the provisions of this Treaty. Where the opinion of the Court of Justice is adverse, the agreement may enter into force only in accordance with Article N of the Treaty on European Union.

(7) Agreements concluded under the conditions set out in this Article shall be binding on the institutions of the Community and on Member States.

Article 228a

Where it is provided, in a common position or in a joint action adopted according to the provisions of the Treaty on European Union relating to the common foreign and security policy, for an action by the Community to interrupt or to reduce, in part or completely, economic relations with one or more third countries, the Council shall take the necessary urgent measures.

The Council shall act by a qualified majority on a proposal from the Commission.

Article 229

It shall be for the Commission to ensure the maintenance of all appropriate relations with the organs of the United Nations, of its specialised agencies and of the General Agreement on Tariffs and Trade.

The Commission shall also maintain such relations as are appropriate with all international organisations.

Article 230

The Community shall establish all appropriate forms of cooperation with the Council of Europe.

Article 231

The Community shall establish close cooperation with the Organisation for Economic Cooperation and Development, the details of which shall be determined by common accord.

Article 232

(1) The provisions of this Treaty shall not affect the provisions of the Treaty establishing the European Coal and Steel Community, in particular as regards the rights and obligations of Member States, the powers of the institutions of that Community and the rules laid down by that Treaty for the functioning of the common market in coal and steel.

(2) The provisions of this Treaty shall not derogate from those of the Treaty establishing the European Atomic Energy Community.

Article 233

The provisions of this Treaty shall not preclude the existence or completion of regional unions between Belgium and Luxembourg, or between Belgium, Luxembourg and the Netherlands, to the extent that the objectives of these regional unions are not attained by application of this Treaty.

Article 234

The rights and obligations arising from agreements concluded before the entry into force of this Treaty between one or more Member States on the one hand, and one or more third countries on the other, shall not be affected by the provisions of this Treaty.

To the extent that such agreements are not compatible with this Treaty, the Member State or States concerned shall take all appropriate steps to eliminate the incompatibilities established. Member States shall, where necessary, assist each other to this end and shall, where appropriate, adopt a common attitude.

In applying the agreements referred to in the first paragraph, Member States shall take into account the fact that the advantages accorded under this Treaty by each Member State form an integral part of the establishment of the Community and are thereby inseparably linked with the creation of common institutions, the conferring of powers upon them and the granting of the same advantages by all the other Member States.

Article 235

If action by the Community should prove necessary to attain, in the course of the operation of the common market, one of the objectives of the Community and this Treaty has not provided the necessary powers, the Council shall, acting unanimously on a proposal from the Commission and after consulting the European Parliament, take the appropriate measures.

Article 238

The Community may conclude with one or more States or international organisations agreements establishing an association involving reciprocal rights and obligations, common action and special procedures.

Article 239

The Protocols annexed to this Treaty by common accord of the Member States shall form an integral part thereof.

Article 240

This Treaty is concluded for an unlimited period.

SETTING UP OF THE INSTITUTIONS

Article 241

The Council shall meet within one month of the entry into force of this Treaty.

Article 242

The Council shall, within three months of its first meeting, take all appropriate measures to constitute the Economic and Social Committee.

Article 243

The European Parliament shall meet within two months of the first meeting of the Council, having been convened by the President of the Council, in order to elect its officers and draw up its rules of procedure. Pending the election of its officers, the oldest member shall take the chair.

Article 244

The Court of Justice shall take up its duties as soon as its members have been appointed. Its first President shall be appointed for three years in the same manner as its members.

The Court of Justice shall adopt its rules of procedure within three months of taking up its duties.

No matter may be brought before the Court of Justice until its rules of procedure have been published. The time within which an action must be brought shall run only from the date of this publication.

Upon his appointment, the President of the Court of Justice shall exercise the powers conferred upon him by this Treaty.

Article 245

The Commission shall take up its duties and assume the responsibilities conferred upon it by this Treaty as soon as its members have been appointed.

Upon taking up its duties, the Commission shall undertake the studies and arrange the contacts needed for making an overall survey of the economic situation of the Community.

Article 246

(1) The first financial year shall run from the date on which this Treaty enters into force until 31 December following. Should this Treaty, however, enter into force during the second half of the year, the first financial year shall run until 31 December of the following year.

(2) Until the budget for the first financial year has been established, Member States shall make the Community interest-free advances which shall be deducted from their financial contributions to the implementation of the budget.

(3) Until the Staff Regulations of officials and the Conditions of Employment of other servants of the Community provided for in Article 212 have been laid down, each institution shall recruit the Staff it needs and to this end conclude contracts of limited duration.

Each institution shall examine together with the Council any question concerning the number, remuneration and distribution of posts.

FINAL PROVISIONS

Article 247

This Treaty shall be ratified by the High Contracting Parties in accordance with their respective constitutional requirements. The instruments of ratification shall be deposited with the Government of the Italian Republic.

This Treaty shall enter into force on the first day of the month following the deposit of the instrument of ratification by the last signatory State to take this step. If, however, such deposit is made less than fifteen days before the beginning of the following month, this Treaty shall not enter into force until the first day of the second month after the date of such deposit.

Article 248

This Treaty, drawn up in a single original in the Dutch, French, German and Italian languages, all four texts being equally authentic, shall be deposited in the archives of the Government of the Italian Republic, which shall transmit a certified copy to each of the Governments of the other signatory States.

IN WITNESS WHEREOF, the undersigned Plenipotentiaries have signed this Treaty.

PROTOCOLS

PROTOCOL ON THE STATUTE OF THE COURT OF JUSTICE OF THE EUROPEAN COMMUNITIES

The High Contracting Parties to the Treaty establishing the European Economic Community:

Desiring to lay down the Statute of the Court provided for in Article 188 of this Treaty,

Have designated ... their Plenipotentiaries for this purpose: ...

Who, having exchanged their Full Powers, found in good and due form,

Have agreed upon the following provisions, which shall be annexed to the Treaty establishing the European Economic Community.

Article 1

The Court established by Article 4 of this Treaty shall be constituted and shall function in accordance with the provisions of this Treaty and of this Statute.

TITLE I – JUDGES AND ADVOCATES-GENERAL

Article 2

Before taking up his duties each Judge shall, in open court, take an oath to perform his duties impartially and conscientiously and to preserve the secrecy of the deliberations of the Court.

Article 3

The Judge shall be immune from legal proceedings. After they have ceased to hold office, they shall continue to enjoy immunity in respect of acts performed by them in their official capacity, including words spoken or written.

The Court, sitting in plenary session, may waive the immunity.

Where immunity has been waived and criminal proceedings are instituted against a Judge, he shall be tried, in any of the Member States, only by the Court competent to judge the members of the highest national judiciary.

Article 4

The Judges may not hold any political or administrative office.

They may not engage in any occupation, whether gainful or not, unless exemption is exceptionally granted by the Council.

When taking up their duties, they shall give a solemn undertaking that, both during and after their term of office, they will respect the obligations arising therefrom, in particular the duty to behave with integrity and discretion as regards the acceptance, after they have ceased to hold office, of certain appointments or benefits.

Any doubt on this point shall be settled by decision of the Court.

Article 5

Apart from normal replacement, or death, the duties of a Judge shall end when he resigns.

Where a Judge resigns, his letter of resignation shall be addressed to the President of the Court for transmission to the President of the Council. Upon this notification a vacancy shall arise on the bench.

Save where Article 6 applies, a Judge shall continue to hold office until his successor takes up his duties.

Article 6

A Judge may be deprived of his office or of his right to a pension or other benefits in its stead only if, in the unanimous opinion of the Judges and Advocates-General of the Court, he no longer fulfils the requisite conditions or meets the obligations arising from his office. The Judge concerned shall not take part in any such deliberations.

The Registrar of the Court shall communicate the decision of the Court to the President of the European Parliament and to the President of the Commission and shall notify it to the President of the Council.

In the case of a decision depriving a Judge of his office, a vacancy shall arise on the bench upon this latter notification.

Article 7

A Judge who is to replace a member of the Court whose term of office has not expired shall be appointed for the remainder of his predecessor's term.

Article 8

The provisions of Articles 2 to 7 shall apply to the Advocates-General.

TITLE II – ORGANISATION

Article 9

The Registrar shall take an oath before the Court to perform his duties impartially and conscientiously and to preserve the secrecy of the deliberations of the Court.

Article 10

The Court shall arrange for replacement of the Registrar on occasions when he is prevented from attending the Court.

Article 11

Officials and other servants shall be attached to the Court to enable it to function. They shall be responsible to the Registrar under the authority of the President.

Article 12

On a proposal from the Court, the Council may, acting unanimously, provide for the appointment of Assistant Rapporteurs and lay down the rules governing their service. The Assistant Rapporteurs may be required, under conditions laid down in the rules of procedure, to participate in preparatory inquiries in cases pending before the Court and to cooperate with the Judge who acts as Rapporteur.

The Assistant Rapporteurs shall be chosen from persons whose independence is beyond doubt and who possess the necessary legal qualifications; they shall be appointed by the Council. They shall take an oath before the Court to perform their duties impartially and conscientiously and to preserve the secrecy of the deliberations of the Court.

Article 13

The Judges, the Advocates-General and the Registrar shall be required to reside at the place where the Court has its seat.

Article 14

The Court shall remain permanently in session. The duration of the judicial vacations shall be determined by the Court with due regard to the needs of its business.

Article 15

Decisions of the Court shall be valid only when an uneven number of its members is sitting in the deliberations. Decisions of the full Court shall be valid if nine members are sitting. Decisions of the Chambers consisting of three or five Judges shall be valid only if three Judges are sitting. Decisions of the Chambers consisting of seven Judges shall be valid only if five Judges are sitting. In the event of one of the Judges of a Chamber being prevented from attending, a Judge of another Chamber may be called upon to sit in accordance with conditions laid down in the rules of procedure.

Article 16

No Judge or Advocate-General may take part in the disposal of any case in which he has previously taken part as agent or adviser or has acted for one of the parties, or on which he has been called upon to pronounce as a member of a court or tribunal, of a commission of inquiry or in any other capacity.

If, for some special reason, any Judge or Advocate-General considers that he should not take part in the judgment or examination of a particular case, he shall so inform the President. If, for some special reason, the President considers that any Judge or Advocate-General should not sit or make submissions in a particular case, he shall notify him accordingly.

Any difficulty arising as to the application of this Article shall be settled by decision of the Court.

A party may not apply for a change in the composition of the Court or of one of its Chambers on the grounds of either the nationality of a Judge or the absence from the Court or from the Chamber of a Judge of the nationality of that party.

TITLE III – PROCEDURE

Article 17

The States and the institutions of the Community shall be represented before the Court by an agent appointed for each case; the agent may be assisted by an adviser or by a lawyer entitled to practise before a court of a Member State.

Other parties must be represented by a lawyer entitled to practise before a court of a Member State.

Such agents, advisers and lawyers shall, when they appear before the Court, enjoy the rights and immunities necessary to the independent exercise of their duties, under conditions laid down in the rules of procedure.

As regards such advisers and lawyers who appear before it, the Court shall have the powers normally accorded to courts of law, under conditions laid down in the rules of procedure.

University teachers being nationals of a Member State whose law accords them a right of audience shall have the same rights before the Court as are accorded by this Article to lawyers entitled to practise before a court of a Member State.

Article 18

The procedure before the Court shall consist of two parts: written and oral.

The written procedure shall consist of the communication to the parties and to the institutions of the Community whose decisions are in dispute of applications, statements of case, defences and observations, and of replies, if any, as well as of all papers and documents in support or of certified copies of them.

Communications shall be made by the Registrar in the order and within the time laid down in the rules of procedure.

The oral procedure shall consist of the reading of the report presented by a Judge acting as Rapporteur, the hearing by the Court of agents, advisers and lawyers entitled to practise before a court of a Member State and of the submissions of the Advocate-General, as well as the hearing, if any, of witnesses and experts.

Article 19

A case shall be brought before the Court by a written application addressed to the Registrar. The application shall contain the applicant's name and permanent address and the description of the signatory, the name of the party against whom the application is made, the subject matter of the dispute, the submissions and a brief statement of the grounds on which the application is based.

The application shall be accompanied, where appropriate, by the measure the annulment of which is sought or, in the circumstances referred to in Article 175 of this Treaty, by documentary evidence of the date on which an institution was, in accordance with that Article, requested to act. If the documents are not submitted with the application, the Registrar shall ask the party concerned to produce them within a reasonable period, but in that event the rights of the party shall not lapse even if such documents are produced after the time limit for bringing proceedings.

Article 20

In the cases governed by Article 177 of this Treaty, the decision of the court or tribunal of a Member State which suspends its proceedings and refers a case to the Court shall be notified to the Court by the court or tribunal concerned. The decision shall then be notified by the Registrar of the Court to the parties, to the Member States and to the Commission, and also to the Council if the act the validity or interpretation of which is in dispute originates from the Council.

Within two months of this notification, the parties, the Member States, the Commission and, where appropriate, the Council, shall be entitled to submit statements of case or written observations to the Court.

Article 21

The Court may require the parties to produce all documents and to supply all information which the Court considers desirable. Formal note shall be taken of any refusal.

The Court may also require the Member States and institutions not being parties to the case to supply all information which the Court considers necessary for the proceedings.

Article 22

The Court may at any time entrust any individual, body, authority, committee or other organisation it chooses with the task of giving an expert opinion.

Article 23

Witnesses may be heard under conditions laid down in the rules of procedure.

Article 24

With respect to defaulting witnesses the Court shall have the powers generally granted to courts and tribunals and may impose pecuniary penalties under conditions laid down in the rules of procedure.

Article 25

Witnesses and experts may be heard on oath taken in the form laid down in the rules of procedure or in the manner laid down by the law of the country of the witness or expert.

Article 26

The Court may order that a witness or expert be heard by the judicial authority of his place of permanent residence.

The order shall be sent for implementation to the competent judicial authority under conditions laid down in the rules of procedure. The documents drawn up in compliance with the letters rogatory shall be returned to the Court under the same conditions.

The Court shall defray the expenses, without prejudice to the right to charge them, where appropriate, to the parties.

Article 27

A Member State shall treat any violation of an oath by a witness or expert in the same manner as if the offence had been committed before one of its courts with jurisdiction in civil proceedings. At the instance of the Court, the Member State concerned shall prosecute the offender before its competent court.

Article 28

The hearing in court shall be public, unless the Court, of its own motion or on application by the parties, decides otherwise for serious reasons.

Article 29

During the hearings the Court may examine the experts, the witnesses and the parties themselves. The latter, however, may address the Court only through their representatives.

Article 30

Minutes shall be made of each hearing and signed by the President and the Registrar.

Article 31

The case list shall be established by the President.

Article 32

The deliberations of the Court shall be and shall remain secret.

Article 33

Judgments shall state the reasons on which they are based. They shall contain the names of the Judges who took part in the deliberations.

Article 34

Judgments shall be signed by the President and the Registrar. They shall be read in open court.

Article 35

The Court shall adjudicate upon costs.

Article 36

The President of the Court may, by way of summary procedure, which may, in so far as necessary, differ from some of the rules contained in this Statute and which shall be laid down in the rules of procedure, adjudicate upon applications to suspend execution, as provided for in Article 185 of this Treaty, or to prescribe interim measures in pursuance of Article 186, or to suspend enforcement in accordance with the last paragraph of Article 192.

Should the President be prevented from attending, his place shall be taken by another Judge under conditions laid down in the rules of procedure.

The ruling of the President or of the Judge replacing him shall be provisional and shall in no way prejudice the decision of the Court on the substance of the case.

Article 37

Member States and institutions of the Community may intervene in cases before the Court.

The same right shall be open to any other person establishing an interest in the result of any case submitted to the Court, save in cases between Member States, between institutions of the Community or between Member States and institutions of the Community.

Submissions made in an application to intervene shall be limited to supporting the submissions of one of the parties.

Article 38

Where the defending party, after having been duly summoned, fails to file written submissions in defence, judgment shall be given against that party by default. An objection may be lodged against the judgment within one month of it being notified. The objection shall not have the effect of staying enforcement of the judgment by default unless the Court decides otherwise.

Article 39

Member States, institutions of the Community and any other natural or legal persons may, in cases and under conditions to be determined by the rules of procedure, institute third-party proceedings to contest a judgment rendered without their being heard, where the judgment is prejudicial to their rights.

Article 40

If the meaning or scope of a judgment is in doubt, the Court shall construe it on application by any party or any institution of the Community establishing an interest therein.

Article 41

An application for revision of a judgment may be made to the Court only on discovery of a fact which is of such a nature as to be a decisive factor, and which, when the judgment was given, was unknown to the Court and to the party claiming the revision.

The revision shall be opened by a judgment of the Court expressly recording the existence of a new fact, recognising that it is of such a character as to lay the case open to revision and declaring the application admissible on this ground.

No application for revision may be made after the lapse of ten years from the date of the judgment.

Article 42

Periods of grace based on considerations of distance shall be determined by the rules of procedure.

No right shall be prejudiced in consequence of the expiry of a time limit if the party concerned proves the existence of unforeseeable circumstances or a force majeure.

Article 43

Proceedings against the Community in matters arising from non-contractual liability shall be barred after a period of five years from the occurrence of the event giving rise thereto. The period of limitation shall be interrupted if proceedings are instituted before the Court or if prior to such proceedings an application is made by the aggrieved party to the relevant institution of the Community. In the latter event the proceedings must be instituted within the period of two months provided for in Article 173; the provisions of the second paragraph of Article 175 shall apply where appropriate.

TITLE IV – THE COURT OF FIRST INSTANCE OF THE EUROPEAN COMMUNITIES

Article 44

Articles 2 to 8, and 13 to 16 of this Statute shall apply to the Court of First Instance and its members. The oath referred to in Article 2 shall be taken before the Court of Justice and the decision referred to in Articles 3, 4 and 6 shall be adopted by that Court after hearing the Court of First Instance.

Article 45

The Court of First Instance shall appoint its Registrar and lay down the rules governing his service. Articles 9, 10 and 13 of this Statute shall apply to the Registrar of the Court of First Instance mutatis mutandis.

The President of the Court of Justice and the President of the Court of First Instance shall determine, by common accord, the conditions under which officials and other servants attached to the Court of Justice shall render their services to the Court of First Instance to enable it to function. Certain officials or other servants shall be responsible to the Registrar of the Court of First Instance under the authority of the President of the Court of First Instance.

Article 46

The procedure before the Court of First Instance shall be governed by Title III of this Statute, with the exception of Article 20.

Such further and more detailed provisions as may be necessary shall be laid down in the Rules of Procedure established in accordance with Article 168a(4) of this Treaty.

Notwithstanding the fourth paragraph of Article 18 of this Statute, the Advocate-General may make his reasoned submissions in writing.

Article 47

Where an application or other procedural document addressed to the Court of First Instance is lodged by mistake with the Registrar of the Court of Justice it shall be transmitted immediately by that Registrar to the Registrar of the Court of First Instance; likewise, where an application or other procedural document addressed to the Court of Justice is lodged by mistake with the Registrar of the Court of First Instance, it shall be transmitted immediately by that Registrar to the Registrar of the Court of Justice.

Where the Court of First Instance finds that it does not have jurisdiction to hear and determine an action in respect of which the Court of Justice has jurisdiction, it shall refer the action to the Court of Justice; likewise, where the Court of Justice finds that an action falls within the jurisdiction of the Court of First Instance, it shall refer that action to the Court of First Instance, whereupon that Court may not decline jurisdiction.

Where the Court of Justice and the Court of First Instance are seised of cases in which the same relief is sought, the same issue of interpretation is raised or the validity of the same act is called in question, the Court of First Instance may, after hearing the parties, stay the proceedings before it until such time as the Court of Justice shall have delivered judgment. Where applications are made for the same act to be declared void, the Court of First Instance may also decline jurisdiction in order that the Court of Justice may rule on such applications. In the cases referred to in this subparagraph, the Court of Justice may also decide to stay the proceedings before it; in the event, the proceedings before the Court of First Instance shall continue.

Article 48

Final decisions of the Court of First Instance, decisions disposing of the substantive issues in part only or disposing of a procedural issue concerning a plea of lack of competence of inadmissibility, shall be notified by the Registrar of the Court of First Instance to all parties as well as all Member States and the Community institutions even if they did not intervene in the case before the Court of First Instance.

Article 49

An appeal may be brought before the Court of Justice, within two months of the notification of the decision appealed against, against final decisions of the Court of First Instance and decisions of that Court disposing of the substantive issues in part only or disposing of a procedural issue concerning a plea of lack of competence or inadmissibility.

Such an appeal may be brought by any party which has been unsuccessful, in whole or in part, in its submissions. However, interveners other than the Member States and the Community institutions may bring such an appeal only where the decision of the Court of First Instance directly affects them.

With the exception of cases relating to disputes between the Community and its servants, an appeal may also be brought by Member States and Community institutions which did not intervene in the proceedings before the Court of First Instance. Such Member States and institutions shall be in the same position as Member States or institutions which intervened at first instance.

Article 50

Any person whose application to intervene has been dismissed by the Court of First Instance may appeal to the Court of Justice within two weeks of the notification of the decision dismissing the application.

The parties to the proceedings may appeal to the Court of Justice against any decision of the Court of First Instance made pursuant to Article 185 or 186 or the fourth paragraph of Article 192 of this Treaty within two months from their notification.

The appeal referred to in the first two paragraphs of this Article shall be heard and determined under the procedure referred to in Article 36 of this Statute.

Article 51

An appeal to the Court of Justice shall be limited to points of law. It shall lie on the grounds of lack of competence of the Court of First Instance, a breach of procedure before it which adversely affects the interests of the appellant as well as the infringement of Community law by the Court of First Instance.

No appeal shall lie regarding only the amount of the costs or the party ordered to pay them.

Article 52

Where an appeal is brought against a decision of the Court of First Instance, the procedure before the Court of Justice shall consist of a written part and an oral part. In accordance with conditions laid down in the Rules of Procedure the Court of Justice, having heard the Advocate-General and the parties, may dispense with the oral procedure.

Article 53

Without prejudice to Articles 185 and 186 of this Treaty, an appeal shall not have suspensory effect.

By way of derogation from Article 44 of the Treaty, decisions of the Court of First Instance declaring a general decision or general recommendation to be void shall take effect only as from the date of expiry of the period referred to in the first paragraph of Article 49 of this Statute, or if an appeal shall have been brought within that period, as from the date of dismissal of the appeal, without prejudice, however, to the right of a party to apply to the Court of Justice pursuant to the second and third paragraphs of Article 39 of the Treaty, for the suspension of the effects of the act which has been declared void or for the prescription of any other interim measure.

Article 54

If the appeal is well founded, the Court of Justice shall quash the decision of the Court of First Instance. It may itself give final judgment in the matter, where the state of the proceedings so permits, or refer the case back to the Court of First Instance for judgment.

Where a case is referred back to the Court of First Instance, this Court shall be bound by the decision of the Court of Justice on points of law.

When an appeal brought by a Member State or a Community institution, which did not intervene in the proceedings before the Court of First Instance, is well founded the Court of Justice may, if it considers this necessary, state which of the effects of the decision of the Court of First Instance which has been quashed shall be considered as definitive in respect of the parties to the litigation.

Article 55

The rules of procedure of the Court provided for in Article 188 of this Treaty shall contain, apart from the provisions contemplated by this Statute, any other provisions necessary for applying and, where required, supplementing it.

Article 56

The Council may, acting unanimously, make such further adjustments to the provisions of this Statute as may be required by reason of measures taken by the Council in accordance with the last paragraph of Article 165 of this Treaty.

Article 57

Immediately after the oath has been taken, the President of the Council shall proceed to choose by lot the Judges and the Advocates-General whose terms of office are to expire at the end of the first three years in accordance with the second and third paragraphs of Article 167 of this Treaty.

In witness whereof, the undersigned Plenipotentiaries have signed this Protocol.

Done at Brussels this 17 April 1957.

PROTOCOL ON THE STATUTE OF THE EUROPEAN SYSTEM OF CENTRAL BANKS AND OF THE EUROPEAN CENTRAL BANK

The High Contracting Parties,

DESIRING to lay down the Statute of the European System of Central Banks and of the European Central Bank provided for in Article 4a of the Treaty establishing the European Community,

HAVE AGREED upon the following provisions, which shall be annexed to the Treaty establishing the European Community:

CHAPTER I

CONSTITUTION OF THE ESCB

Article 1

The European System of Central Banks

1.1 The European System of Central Banks (ESCB) and the European Central Bank (ECB) shall be established in accordance with Article 4a of this Treaty; they shall perform their tasks and carry on their activities in accordance with the provisions of this Treaty and of this Statute.

1.2 In accordance with Article 106(1) of this Treaty, the ESCB shall be composed of the ECB and of the central banks of the Member States ('national central banks'). The Institut Monétaire Luxembourgeois will be the central bank of Luxembourg.

CHAPTER II

OBJECTIVES AND TASKS OF THE ESCB

Article 2

Objectives

In accordance with Article 105(1) of this Treaty, the primary objective of the ESCB shall be to maintain price stability. Without prejudice to the objective of price stability, it shall support the general economic policies in the Community with a view to contributing to the achievement of the objectives of the Community as laid down in Article 2 of this Treaty. The ESCB shall act in accordance with the principle of an open market economy in free competition, favouring an efficient allocation of resources, and in compliance with the principles set out in Article 3a of this Treaty.

Article 3

Tasks

3.1 In accordance with Article 105(2) of this Treaty, the basic tasks to be carried out through the ESCB shall be:

- to define and implement the monetary policy of the Community;
- to conduct foreign-exchange operations consistent with the provisions of Article 109 of this Treaty;

- to hold and manage the official foreign reserves of the Member States;
- to promote the smooth operation of payment systems.

3.2 In accordance with Article 105(3) of this Treaty, the third indent of Article 3.1 shall be without prejudice to the holding and management by the governments of Member States of foreign-exchange working balances.

3.3 In accordance with Article 105(5) of this Treaty, the ESCB shall contribute to the smooth conduct of policies pursued by the competent authorities relating to the prudential supervision of credit institutions and the stability of the financial system.

Article 4

Advisory functions

In accordance with Article 105(4) of this Treaty:

(a) the ECB shall be consulted:

- on any proposed Community act in its fields of competence;
- by national authorities regarding any draft legislative provision in its fields of competence, but within the limits and under the conditions set out by the Council in accordance with the procedure laid down in Article 42;

(b) the ECB may submit opinions to the appropriate Community institutions or bodies or to national authorities on matters in its fields of competence.

Article 5

Collection of statistical information

5.1 In order to undertake the tasks of the ESCB, the ECB, assisted by the national central banks, shall collect the necessary statistical information either from the competent national authorities or directly from economic agents. For these purposes it shall cooperate with the Community institutions or bodies and with the competent authorities of the Member States or third countries and with international organisations.

5.2 The national central banks shall carry out, to the extent possible, the tasks described in Article 5.1.

5.3 The ECB shall contribute to the harmonisation, where necessary, of the rules and practices governing the collection, compilation and distribution of statistics in the areas within its fields of competence.

5.4 The Council, in accordance with the procedure laid down in Article 42, shall define the natural and legal persons subject to reporting requirements, the confidentiality regime and the appropriate provisions for enforcement.

Article 6

International cooperation

6.1 In the field of international cooperation involving the tasks entrusted to the ESCB, the ECB shall decide how the ESCB shall be represented.

6.2 The ECB and, subject to its approval, the national central banks may participate in international monetary institutions.

6.3 Articles 6.1 and 6.2 shall be without prejudice to Article 109(4) of this Treaty.

CHAPTER III

ORGANISATION OF THE ESCB

Article 7

Independence

In accordance with Article 107 of this Treaty, when exercising the powers and carrying out the tasks and duties conferred upon them by this Treaty and this Statute, neither the ECB, nor a national central bank, nor any member of their decision-making bodies shall seek or take instructions from Community institutions or bodies, from any government of a Member State or from any other body. The Community institutions and bodies and the governments of the Member States undertake to respect this principle and not to seek to influence the members of the decision-making bodies of the ECB or of the national central banks in the performance of their tasks.

Article 8

General principle

The ESCB shall be governed by the decision-making bodies of the ECB.

Article 9

The European Central Bank

9.1 The ECB which, in accordance with Article 106(2) of this Treaty, shall have legal personality, shall enjoy in each of the Member States the most extensive legal capacity accorded to legal persons under its law; it may, in particular, acquire or dispose of movable and immovable property and may be a party to legal proceedings.

9.2 The ECB shall ensure that the tasks conferred upon the ESCB under Article 105(2), (3) and (5) of this Treaty are implemented either by its own activities pursuant to this Statute or through the national central banks pursuant to Articles 12.1 and 14.

9.3 In accordance with Article 106(3) of this Treaty, the decision-making bodies of the ECB shall be the Governing Council and the Executive Board.

Article 10

The Governing Council

10.1 In accordance with Article 109a(1) of this Treaty, the Governing Council shall comprise the members of the Executive Board of the ECB and the Governors of the national central banks.

10.2 Subject to Article 10.3, only members of the Governing Council present in person shall have the right to vote. By way of derogation from this rule, the Rules of Procedure referred to in Article 12.3 may lay down that members of the Governing Council may cast their vote by means of teleconferencing. These rules shall also provide that a member of the Governing Council who is prevented from voting for a prolonged period may appoint an alternate as a member of the Governing Council.

Subject to Articles 10.3 and 11.3, each member of the Governing Council shall have one vote. Save as otherwise provided for in this Statute, the Governing Council shall act by a simple majority. In the event of a tie, the President shall have the casting vote.

In order for the Governing Council to vote, there shall be a quorum of two-thirds of the members. If the quorum is not met, the President may convene an extraordinary meeting at which decisions may be taken without regard to the quorum.

10.3 For any decisions to be taken under Articles 28, 29, 30, 32, 33 and 51, the votes in the Governing Council shall be weighted according to the national central banks' shares in the subscribed capital of the ECB. The weights of the votes of the members of the Executive Board shall be zero. A decision requiring a qualified majority shall be adopted if the votes cast in favour represent at least two-thirds of the subscribed capital of the ECB and represent at least half of the shareholders. If a Governor is unable to be present, he may nominate an alternate to cast his weighted vote.

10.4 The proceedings of the meetings shall be confidential. The Governing Council may decide to make the outcome of its deliberations public.

10.5 The Governing Council shall meet at least 10 times a year.

Article 11

The Executive Board

11.1 In accordance with Article 109a(2)(a) of this Treaty, the Executive Board shall comprise the President, the Vice-President and four other members.

The members shall perform their duties on a full-time basis. No member shall engage in any occupation, whether gainful or not, unless exemption is exceptionally granted by the Governing Council.

11.2 In accordance with Article 109a(2)(b) of this Treaty, the President, the Vice-President and the other Members of the Executive Board shall be appointed from among persons of recognised standing and professional experience in monetary or banking matters by common accord of the governments of the Member States at the level of the Heads of State or Government, on a recommendation from the Council after it has consulted the European Parliament and the Governing Council.

Their term of office shall be eight years and shall not be renewable.

Only nationals of Member States may be members of the Executive Board.

11.3 The terms and conditions of employment of the members of the Executive Board, in particular their salaries, pensions and other social security benefits shall be the subject of contracts with the ECB and shall be fixed by the Governing Council on a proposal from a Committee comprising three members appointed by the Governing Council and three members appointed by the Council. The members of the Executive Board shall not have the right to vote on matters referred to in this paragraph.

11.4 If a member of the Executive Board no longer fulfils the conditions required for the performance of his duties or if he has been guilty of serious misconduct, the Court of Justice may, on application by the Governing Council or the Executive Board, compulsorily retire him.

11.5 Each member of the Executive Board present in person shall have the right to vote and shall have, for that purpose, one vote. Save as otherwise provided, the Executive Board shall act by a simple majority of the votes cast. In the event of a tie, the President shall have the casting vote. The voting arrangements shall be specified in the Rules of Procedure referred to in Article 12.3.

11.6 The Executive Board shall be responsible for the current business of the ECB.

11.7 Any vacancy on the Executive Board shall be filled by the appointment of a new member in accordance with Article 11.2.

Article 12

Responsibilities of the decision-making bodies

12.1 The Governing Council shall adopt the guidelines and make the decisions necessary to ensure the performance of the tasks entrusted to the ESCB under this Treaty and this Statute. The Governing Council shall formulate the monetary policy of the Community including, as appropriate, decisions relating to intermediate monetary objectives, key interest rates and the supply of reserves in the ESCB, and shall establish the necessary guidelines for their implementation.

The Executive Board shall implement monetary policy in accordance with the guidelines and decisions laid down by the Governing Council. In doing so the Executive Board shall give the necessary instructions to national central banks. In addition the Executive Board may have certain powers delegated to it where the Governing Council so decides.

To the extent deemed possible and appropriate and without prejudice to the provisions of this Article, the ECB shall have recourse to the national central banks to carry out operations which form part of the tasks of the ESCB.

12.2 The Executive Board shall have responsibility for the preparation of meetings of the Governing Council.

12.3 The Governing Council shall adopt Rules of Procedure which determine the internal organisation of the ECB and its decision-making bodies.

12.4 The Governing Council shall exercise the advisory functions referred to in Article 4.

12.5 The Governing Council shall take the decisions referred to in Article 6.

Article 13

The President

13.1 The President or, in his absence, the Vice-President shall chair the Governing Council and the Executive Board of the ECB.

13.2 Without prejudice to Article 39, the President or his nominee shall represent the ECB externally.

Article 14

National central banks

14.1 In accordance with Article 108 of this Treaty, each Member State shall ensure, at the latest at the date of the establishment of the ESCB, that its national legislation, including the statutes of its national central bank, is compatible with this Treaty and this Statute.

14.2 The statutes of the national central banks shall, in particular, provide that the term of office of a Governor of a national central bank shall be no less than five years.

A Governor may be relieved from office only if he no longer fulfils the conditions required for the performance of his duties or if he has been guilty of serious misconduct. A decision to this effect may be referred to the Court of Justice by the Governor concerned or the Governing Council on grounds of infringement of this Treaty or of any rule of law relating to its application. Such proceedings shall be instituted within two months of the publication of the decision or of its notification to the plaintiff or, in the absence thereof, of the day on which it came to the knowledge of the latter, as the case may be.

14.3 The national central banks are an integral part of the ESCB and shall act in accordance with the guidelines and instructions of the ECB. The Governing Council shall take the necessary steps to ensure compliance with the guidelines and instructions of the ECB, and shall require that any necessary information be given to it.

14.4 National central banks may perform functions other than those specified in this Statute unless the Governing Council finds, by a majority of two thirds of the votes cast, that these interfere with the objectives and tasks of the ESCB. Such functions shall be performed on the responsibility and liability of national central banks and shall not be regarded as being part of the functions of the ESCB.

Article 15

Reporting commitments

15.1 The ECB shall draw up and publish reports on the activities of the ESCB at least quarterly.

15.2 A consolidated financial statement of the ESCB shall be published each week.

15.3 In accordance with Article 109b(3) of this Treaty, the ECB shall address an annual report on the activities of the ESCB and on the monetary policy of both the previous and the current year to the European Parliament, the Council and the Commission, and also to the European Council.

15.4 The reports and statements referred to in this Article shall be made available to interested parties free of charge.

Article 16

Banknotes

In accordance with Article 105a(1) of this Treaty, the Governing Council shall have the exclusive right to authorise the issue of banknotes within the Community. The ECB and the national central banks may issue such notes. The banknotes issued by the ECB and the national central banks shall be the only such notes to have the status of legal tender within the Community.

The ECB shall respect as far as possible existing practices regarding the issue and design of banknotes.

CHAPTER IV

MONETARY FUNCTIONS AND OPERATIONS OF THE ESCB

Article 17

Accounts with the ECB and the national central banks

In order to conduct their operations, the ECB and the national central bank may open accounts for credit institutions, public entities and other market participants and accept assets, including book-entry securities, as collateral.

Article 18

Open market and credit operations

18.1 In order to achieve the objectives of the ESCB and to carry out its tasks, the ECB and the national central banks may:

- operate in the financial markets by buying and selling outright (spot and forward) or under repurchase agreement and by lending or borrowing claims and marketable instruments, whether in Community or in non-Community currencies, as well as precious metals;
- conduct credit operations with credit institutions and other market participants, with lending being based on adequate collateral.

18.2 The ECB shall establish general principles for open market and credit operations carried out by itself or the national central banks, including for the announcement of conditions under which they stand ready to enter into such transactions.

Article 19

Minimum reserves

19.1 Subject to Article 2, the ECB may require credit institutions established in Member States to hold minimum reserves on accounts with the ECB and national central banks in pursuance of monetary policy objectives. Regulations concerning the calculation and determination of the required minimum reserves may be established by the Governing Council. In cases of non-compliance the ECB shall be entitled to levy penalty interests and to impose other sanctions with comparable effect.

19.2 For the application of this Article, the Council shall, in accordance with the procedure laid down in Article 42, define the basis for minimum reserves and the maximum permissible ratios between those reserves and their basis, as well as the appropriate sanctions in cases of non-compliance.

Article 20

Other instruments of monetary control

The Governing Council may, by a majority of two thirds of the votes cast, decide upon the use of such other operational methods of monetary control as it sees fit, respecting Article 2.

The Council shall, in accordance with the procedure laid down in Article 42, define the scope of such methods if they impose obligations on third parties.

Article 21

Operations with public entities

21.1 In accordance with Article 104 of this Treaty, overdrafts or any other type of credit facility with the ECB or with the national central banks in favour of Community institutions or bodies, central governments, regional, local or other public authorities, other bodies governed by public law, or public undertakings of Member States, shall be prohibited, as shall the purchase directly from them by the ECB or national central banks of debt instruments.

21.2 The ECB and national central banks may act as fiscal agents for the entities referred to in Article 21.1.

21.3 The provisions of this Article shall not apply to publicly-owned credit institutions which, in the context of the supply of reserves by central banks, shall be given the same treatment by national central banks and the ECB as private credit institutions.

Article 22

Clearing and payment systems

The ECB and national central banks may provide facilities, and the ECB may make regulations, to ensure efficient and sound clearing and payment systems within the Community and with other countries.

Article 23

External operations

The ECB and national central banks may:

- establish relations with central banks and financial institutions in other countries and, where appropriate, with international organisations;
- acquire and sell spot and forward all types of foreign exchange assets and precious metals; the term 'foreign exchange asset' shall include securities and all other assets in the currency of any country or units of account and in whatever form held;

- hold and manage the assets referred to in this Article;
- conduct all types of banking transactions in relations with third countries and international organisations, including borrowing and lending operations.

Article 24

Other operations

In addition to operations arising from their tasks, the ECB and national central banks may enter into operations for their administrative purposes or for their staff.

CHAPTER V

PRUDENTIAL SUPERVISION

Article 25

Prudential supervision

25.1 The ECB may offer advice to and be consulted by the Council, the Commission and the competent authorities of the Member States on the scope and implementation of Community legislation relating to the prudential supervision of credit institutions and to the stability of the financial system.

25.2 In accordance with any decision of the Council under Article 105(6) of this Treaty, the ECB may perform specific tasks concerning policies relating to the prudential supervision of credit institutions and other financial institutions with the exception of insurance undertakings.

CHAPTER VI

FINANCIAL PROVISIONS OF THE ESCB

Article 26

Financial accounts

26.1 The financial year of the ECB and national central banks shall begin on the first day of January and end on the last day of December.

26.2 The annual accounts of the ECB shall be drawn up by the Executive Board, in accordance with the principles established by the Governing

Council. The accounts shall be approved by the Governing Council and shall thereafter be published.

26.3 For analytical and operational purposes, the Executive Board shall draw up a consolidated balance sheet of the ESCB, comprising those assets and liabilities of the national central banks that fall within the ESCB.

26.4 For the application of this Article, the Governing Council shall establish the necessary rules for standardising the accounting and reporting of operations undertaken by the national central banks.

Article 27

Auditing

27.1 The accounts of the ECB and national central banks shall be audited by independent external auditors recommended by the Governing Council and approved by the Council. The auditors shall have full power to examine all books and accounts of the ECB and national central banks and obtain full information about their transactions.

27.2 The provisions of Article 188c of this Treaty shall only apply to an examination of the operational efficiency of the management of the ECB.

Article 28

Capital of the ECB

28.1 The capital of the ECB, which shall become operational upon its establishment, shall be ECU 5,000 million. The capital may be increased by such amounts as may be decided by the Governing Council acting by the qualified majority provided for in Article 10.3, within the limits and under the conditions set by the Council under the procedure laid down in Article 42.

28.2 The national central banks shall be the sole subscribers to and holders of the capital of the ECB. The subscription of capital shall be according to the key established in accordance with Article 29.

28.3 The Governing Council, acting by the qualified majority provided for in Article 10.3, shall determine the extent to which and the form in which the capital shall be paid up.

28.4 Subject to Article 28.5, the shares of the national central banks in the subscribed capital of the ECB may not be transferred, pledged or attached.

28.5 If the key referred to in Article 29 is adjusted, the national central banks shall transfer among themselves capital shares to the extent necessary to ensure that the distribution of capital shares corresponds to the adjusted key. The Governing Council shall determine the terms and conditions of such transfers.

Article 29

Key for capital subscription

29.1 When in accordance with the procedure referred to in Article 109l(1) of this Treaty the ESCB and the ECB have been established, the key for subscription of the ECB's capital shall be established. Each national central bank shall be assigned a weighting in this key which shall be equal to the sum of:
- 50% of the share of its respective Member State in the population of the Community in the penultimate year preceding the establishment of the ESCB;
- 50% of the share of its respective Member State in the gross domestic product at market prices of the Community as recorded in the last five years preceding the penultimate year before the establishment of the ESCB;

The percentages shall be rounded up to the nearest multiple of 0.05 percentage points.

29.2 The statistical data to be used for the application of this Article shall be provided by the Commission in accordance with the rules adopted by the Council under the procedure provided for in Article 42.

29.3 The weightings assigned to the national central banks shall be adjusted every five years after the establishment of the ESCB by analogy with the provisions laid down in Article 29.1. The adjusted key shall apply with effect from the first day of the following year.

29.4 The Governing Council shall take all other measures necessary for the application of this Article.

Article 30

Transfer of foreign reserve assets to the ECB

30.1 Without prejudice to Article 28, the ECB shall be provided by the national central banks with foreign reserve assets, other than Member

States' currencies, ECUs, IMF reserve positions and SDRs, up to an amount equivalent to ECU 50,000 million. The Governing Council shall decide upon the proportion to be called up by the ECB following its establishment and the amounts called up at later dates. The ECB shall have the full right to hold and manage the foreign reserves that are transferred to it and to use them for the purposes set out in this Statute.

30.2 The contributions of each national central bank shall be fixed in proportion to its share in the subscribed capital of the ECB.

30.3 Each national central bank shall be credited by the ECB with a claim equivalent to its contribution. The Governing Council shall determine the denomination and remuneration of such claims.

30.4 Further calls of foreign reserve assets beyond the limit set in Article 30.1 may be effected by the ECB, in accordance with Article 30.2, within the limits and under the conditions set by the Council in accordance with the procedure laid down in Article 42.

30.5 The ECB may hold and manage IMF reserve positions and SDRs and provide for the pooling of such assets.

30.6 The Governing Council shall take all other measures necessary for the application of this Article.

Article 31

Foreign reserve assets held by national central banks

31.1 The national central banks shall be allowed to perform transactions in fulfilment of their obligations towards international organisations in accordance with Article 23.

31.2 All other operations in foreign reserve assets remaining with the national central banks after the transfers referred to in Article 30, and Member States' transactions with their foreign exchange working balances shall, above a certain limit to be established within the framework of Article 31.3, be subject to approval by the ECB in order to ensure consistency with the exchange rate and monetary policies of the Community.

31.3 The Governing Council shall issue guidelines with a view to facilitating such operations.

Article 32

Allocation of monetary income of national central banks

32.1 The income accruing to the national central banks in the performance of the ESCB's monetary policy function (hereinafter referred to as 'monetary income') shall be allocated at the end of each financial year in accordance with the provisions of this Article.

32.2 Subject to Article 32.3, the amount of each national central bank's monetary income shall be equal to its annual income derived from its assets held against notes in circulation and deposit liabilities to credit institutions. These assets shall be earmarked by national central banks in accordance with guidelines to be established by the Governing Council.

32.3 If, after the start of the third stage, the balance sheet structures of the national central banks do not, in the judgment of the Governing Council, permit the application of Article 32.3, the Governing Council, acting by a qualified majority, may decide that, by way of derogation from Article 32.3, monetary income shall be measured according to an alternative method for a period of not more than five years.

32.4 The amount of each national central bank's monetary income shall be reduced by an amount equivalent to any interest paid by that central bank on its deposit liabilities to credit institutions in accordance with Article 19.

The Governing Council may decide that national central banks shall be indemnified against costs incurred in connection with the issue of banknotes or in exceptional circumstances for specific losses arising from monetary policy operations undertaken for the ESCB. Indemnification shall be in a form deemed appropriate in the judgment of the Governing Council; these amounts may be offset against the national central banks' monetary income.

32.5 The sum of the national central banks' monetary income shall be allocated to the national central banks in proportion to their paid-up shares in the capital of the ECB, subject to any decision taken by the Governing Council pursuant to Article 33.2.

32.6 The clearing and settlement of the balances arising from the allocation of monetary income shall be carried out by the ECB in accordance with guidelines established by the Governing Council.

32.7 The Governing Council shall take all other measures necessary for the application of this Article.

Article 33

Allocation of net profits and losses of the ECB

33.1 The net profit of the ECB shall be transferred in the following order:

(a) an amount to be determined by the Governing Council, which may not exceed 20% of the net profit, shall be transferred to the general reserve fund subject to a limit equal to 100% of the capital;

(b) the remaining net profit shall be distributed to the shareholders of the ECB in proportion to their paid-up shares.

33.2 In the event of a loss incurred by the ECB, the shortfall may be offset against the general reserve fund of the ECB and, if necessary, following a decision by the Governing Council, against the monetary income of the relevant financial year in proportion and up to the amounts allocated to the national central banks in accordance with Article 32.5.

CHAPTER VII

GENERAL PROVISIONS

Article 34

Legal acts

34.1 In accordance with Article 108a of this Treaty, the ECB shall:

- make regulations to the extent necessary to implement the tasks defined in Article 3.1, first indent, Articles 19.1, 22 or 25.2 and in cases which shall be laid down in the acts of the Council referred to in Article 42;
- take decisions necessary for carrying out the tasks entrusted to the ESCB under this Treaty and this Statute;
- make recommendations and deliver opinions.

34.2 A regulation shall have general application. It shall be binding in its entirety and directly applicable in all Member States.

Recommendations and opinions shall have no binding force.

A decision shall be binding in its entirety upon those to whom it is addressed.

Articles 190 and 192 of this Treaty shall apply to regulations and decisions adopted by the ECB.

The ECB may decide to publish its decisions, recommendations and opinions.

34.3 Within the limits and under the conditions adopted by the Council under the procedure laid down in Article 42, the ECB shall be entitled to impose fines or periodic penalty payments on undertakings for failure to comply with obligations under its regulations and decisions.

Article 35

Judicial control and related matters

35.1 The acts or omissions of the ECB shall be open to review or interpretation by the Court of Justice in the cases and under the conditions laid down in this Treaty. The ECB may institute proceedings in the cases and under the conditions laid down in this Treaty.

35.2 Disputes between the ECB, on the one hand, and its creditors, debtors or any other person, on the other, shall be decided by the competent national courts, save where jurisdiction has been conferred upon the Court of Justice.

35.3 The ECB shall be subject to the liability regime provided for in Article 215 of this Treaty. The national central banks shall be liable according to their respective national laws.

35.4 The Court of Justice shall have jurisdiction to give judgment pursuant to any arbitration clause contained in a contract concluded by or on behalf of the ECB, whether that contract be governed by public or private law.

35.5 A decision of the ECB to bring an action before the Court of Justice shall be taken by the Governing Council.

35.6 The Court of Justice shall have jurisdiction in disputes concerning the fulfilment by a national central bank of obligations under this Statute. If the ECB considers that a national central bank has failed to fulfil an obligation under this Statute, it shall deliver a reasoned opinion on the matter after giving the national central bank concerned the opportunity to submit its observations. If the national central bank concerned does not comply with the opinion within the period laid down by the ECB, the latter may bring the matter before the Court of Justice.

Article 36

Staff

36.1 The Governing Council, on a proposal from the Executive Board, shall lay down the conditions of employment of the staff of the ECB.

36.2 The Court of Justice shall have jurisdiction in any dispute between the ECB and its servants within the limits and under the conditions laid down in the conditions of employment.

Article 37

Seat

Before the end of 1992, the decision as to where the seat of the ECB will be established shall be taken by common accord of the governments of the Member States at the level of Heads of State or Government.

Article 38

Professional secrecy

38.1 Members of the governing bodies and the staff of the ECB and the national central banks shall be required, even after their duties have ceased, not to disclose information of the kind covered by the obligation of professional secrecy.

38.2 Persons having access to data covered by Community legislation imposing an obligation of secrecy shall be subject to such legislation.

Article 39

Signatories

The ECB shall be legally committed to third parties by the President or by two members of the Executive Board or by the signatures of two members of the staff of the ECB who have been duly authorised by the President to sign on behalf of the ECB.

Article 40

Privileges and immunities

The ECB shall enjoy in the territories of the Member States such privileges and immunities as are necessary for the performance of its tasks, under the conditions laid down in the Protocol on the Privileges and Immunities of the European Communities annexed to the Treaty establishing a Single Council and a Single Commission of the European Communities.

CHAPTER VIII

AMENDMENT OF THE STATUTE AND COMPLEMENTARY LEGISLATION

Article 41

Simplified amendment procedure

41.1 In accordance with Article 106(5) of this Treaty, Articles 5.1, 5.2, 5.3, 17, 18, 19.1, 22, 23, 24, 26, 32.2, 32.3, 32.4, 32.6, 33.1(a) and 36 of this Statute may be amended by the Council, acting either by a qualified majority on a recommendation from the ECB and after consulting the Commission, or unanimously on a proposal from the Commission and after consulting the ECB. In either case the assent of the European Parliament shall be required.

41.2 A recommendation made by the ECB under this Article shall require a unanimous decision by the Governing Council.

Article 42

Complementary legislation

In accordance with Article 106(6) of this Treaty, immediately after the decision on the date for the beginning of the third stage, the Council, acting by a qualified majority either on a proposal from the Commission and after consulting the European Parliament and the ECB or on a recommendation from the ECB and after consulting the European Parliament and the Commission, shall adopt the provisions referred to in Articles 4, 5.4, 19.2, 20, 28.1, 29.2, 30.4 and 34.3 of this Statute.

CHAPTER IX

TRANSITIONAL AND OTHER PROVISIONS FOR THE ESCB

Article 43

General provisions

43.1 A derogation as referred to in Article 109k(1) of this Treaty shall entail that the following Articles of this Statute shall not confer any rights or impose any obligation on the Member State concerned: 3, 6, 9.2, 12.1, 14.3, 16, 18, 19, 20, 22, 23, 26.2, 27, 30, 31, 32, 33, 34, 50 and 52.

43.2 The central banks of Member States with a derogation as specified in

Article 109k(1) of this Treaty shall retain their powers in the field of monetary policy according to national law.

43.3 In accordance with Article 109k(4) of this Treaty, 'Member States' shall be read as 'Member States without a derogation' in the following Articles of this Statute: 3, 11.2, 19, 34.2 and 50.

43.4 'National central banks' shall be read as 'central banks of Member States without a derogation' in the following Articles of this Statute: 9.2, 10.1, 10.3, 12.1, 16, 17, 18, 22, 23, 27, 30, 31, 32, 33.2 and 52.

43.5 'Shareholders' shall be read as 'central banks of Member States without a derogation' in Articles 10.3 and 33.1.

43.6 'Subscribed capital of the ECB' shall be read as 'capital of the ECB subscribed by the central banks of Member States without a derogation' in Articles 10.3 and 30.2.

Article 44

Transitional tasks of the ECB

The ECB shall take over those tasks of the EMI which, because of the derogations of one or more Member States, still have to be performed in the third stage.

The ECB shall give advice in the preparations for the abrogation of the derogations specified in Article 109k of this Treaty.

Article 45

The General Council of the ECB

45.1 Without prejudice to Article 106(3) of this Treaty, the General Council shall be constituted as a third decision-making body of the ECB.

45.2 The General Council shall comprise the President and Vice-President of the ECB and the Governors of the national central banks. The other members of the Executive Board may participate, without having the right to vote, in meetings of the General Council.

45.3 The responsibilities of the General Council are listed in full in Article 47 of this Statute.

Article 46

Rules of procedure of the General Council

46.1 The President or, in his absence, the Vice-President of the ECB shall chair the General Council of the ECB.

46.2 The President of the Council and a member of the Commission may participate, without having the right to vote, in meetings of the General Council.

46.3 The President shall prepare the meetings of the General Council.

46.4 By way of derogation from Article 12.3, the General Council shall adopt its Rules of Procedure.

46.5 The Secretariat of the General Council shall be provided by the ECB.

Article 47

Responsibilities of the General Council

47.1 The General Council shall:

- perform the tasks referred to in Article 44;
- contribute to the advisory functions referred to in Articles 4 and 25.1.

47.2 The General Council shall contribute to:

- the collection of statistical information as referred to in Article 5;
- the reporting activities of the ECB as referred to in Article 15;
- the establishment of the necessary rules for the application of Article 26 as referred to in Article 26.4;
- the taking of all other measures necessary for the application of Article 29 as referred to in Article 29.4;
- the laying down of the conditions of employment of the staff of the ECB as referred to in Article 36.

47.3 The General Council shall contribute to the necessary preparations for irrevocably fixing the exchange rates of the currencies of Member States with a derogation against the currencies, or the single currency, of the Member States without a derogation, as referred to in Article 109l(5) of this Treaty.

47.4 The General Council shall be informed by the President of the ECB of decisions of the Governing Council.

Article 48

Transitional provisions for the capital of the ECB

In accordance with Article 29.1 each national central bank shall be assigned a weighting in the key for subscription of the ECB's capital. By way of derogation from Article 28.3, central banks of Member States with a derogation shall not pay up their subscribed capital unless the General Council, acting by a majority representing at least two-thirds of the subscribed capital of the ECB and at least half of the shareholders, decides that a minimal percentage has to be paid up as a contribution to the operational costs of the ECB.

Article 49

Deferred payment of capital, reserves and provisions of the ECB

49.1 The central bank of a Member State whose derogation has been abrogated shall pay up its subscribed share of the capital of the ECB to the same extent as the central banks of other Member States without a derogation, and shall transfer to the ECB foreign reserve assets in accordance with Article 30.1. The sum to be transferred shall be determined by multiplying the ECU value at current exchange rates of the foreign reserve assets which have already been transferred to the ECB in accordance with Article 30.1, by the ratio between the number of shares subscribed by the national central bank concerned and the number of shares already paid up by the other national central banks.

49.2 In addition to the payment to be made in accordance with Article 49.1, the central bank concerned shall contribute to the reserves of the ECB, to those provisions equivalent to reserves, and to the amount still to be appropriated to the reserves and provisions corresponding to the balance of the profit and loss account as at 31 December of the year prior to the abrogation of the derogation. The sum to be contributed shall be determined by multiplying the amount of the reserves, as defined above and as stated in the approved balance sheet of the ECB, by the ratio between the number of shares subscribed by the central bank concerned and the number of shares already paid up by the other central banks.

Article 50

Initial appointment of the members of the Executive Board

When the Executive Board of the ECB is being established, the President, the Vice-President and the other members of the Executive Board shall be appointed by common accord of the governments of the Member States at the level of Heads of State or Government, on a recommendation from the Council and after consulting the European Parliament and the Council of the EMI. The President of the Executive Board shall be appointed for eight years. By way of derogation from Article 11.2, the Vice-President shall be appointed for four years and the other members of the Executive Board for terms of office of between five and eight years. No term of office shall be renewable. The number of members of the Executive Board may be smaller than provided for in Article 11.1, but in no circumstances shall it be less than four.

Article 51

Derogation from Article 32

51.1 If, after the start of the third stage, the Governing Council decides that the application of Article 32 results in significant changes in national central banks' relative income positions, the amount of income to be allocated pursuant to Article 32 shall be reduced by a uniform percentage which shall not exceed 60% in the first financial year after the start of the third stage and which shall decrease by at least 12 percentage points in each subsequent financial year.

51.2 Article 51.1 shall be applicable for not more than five financial years after the start of the third stage.

Article 52

Exchange of banknotes in Community currencies

Following the irrevocable fixing of exchange rates, the Governing Council shall take the necessary measures to ensure that banknotes denominated in currencies with irrevocably fixed exchange rates are exchanged by the national central banks at their respective par values.

Article 53

Applicability of the transitional provisions

If and as long as there are Member States with a derogation Articles 43 to 48 shall be applicable.

PROTOCOL ON THE EXCESSIVE DEFICIT PROCEDURE

The High Contracting Parties,

DESIRING to lay down the details of the excessive deficit procedure referred to in Article 104c of the Treaty establishing the European Community,

HAVE AGREED upon the following provisions, which shall be annexed to the Treaty establishing the European Community:

Article 1

The reference values referred to in Article 104c(2) of this Treaty are:

(1) 3% for the ratio of the planned or actual government deficit to gross domestic product at market prices:

(2) 60% for the ratio of government debt to gross domestic product at market prices.

Article 2

In Article 104c of this Treaty and in this Protocol:

(1) Government means general government, that is central government, regional or local government and social security funds, to the exclusion of commercial operations, as defined in the European System of Integrated Economic Accounts:

(2) Deficit means net borrowing as defined in the European System of Integrated Economic Accounts;

(3) Investment means gross fixed capital formation as defined in the European System of Integrated Economic Accounts;

(4) Debt means total gross debt at nominal value outstanding at the end of the year and consolidated between and within the sectors of general government as defined in the first indent.

Article 3

In order to ensure the effectiveness of the excessive deficit procedure, the governments of the Member States shall be responsible under this procedure for the deficits of general government as defined in the first indent of Article 2. The Member States shall ensure that national procedures in the budgetary area enable them to meet their obligations in this area deriving from this Treaty. The Member States shall report their planned and actual deficits and the levels of their debt promptly and regularly to the Commission.

Article 4

The statistical data to be used for the application of this Protocol shall be provided by the Commission.

PROTOCOL ON THE CONVERGENCE CRITERIA REFERRED TO IN ARTICLE 109j OF THE TREATY ESTABLISHING THE EUROPEAN COMMUNITY

The High Contracting Parties,

DESIRING to lay down the details of the convergence criteria which shall guide the Community in taking decisions on the passage to the third stage of economic and monetary union, referred to in Article 109j(1) of this Treaty,

HAVE AGREED upon the following provisions, which shall be annexed to the Treaty establishing the European Community:

Article 1

The criterion on price stability referred to in the first indent of Article 109j(1) of the Treaty shall mean that a Member State has a price performance that is sustainable and an average rate of inflation, observed over a period of one year before the examination, that does not exceed by more than 1 1/2 percentage points that of, at most, the three best performing Member States in terms of price stability. Inflation shall be measured by means of the consumer price index on a comparable basis, taking into account differences in national definitions.

Article 2

The criterion on the government budgetary position referred to in the second indent of Article 109j(1) of this Treaty shall mean that at the time of the examination the Member State is not the subject of a Council decision under Article 104c(6) of this Treaty that an excessive deficit exists.

Article 3

The criterion on participation in the exchange-rate mechanism of the European Monetary System referred to in the third indent of Article 109j(1) of this Treaty shall mean that a Member State has respected the normal fluctuation margins provided for by the exchange-rate mechanism of the European Monetary System without severe tensions for at least the last two years before the examination. In particular, the Member State shall not have devalued its currency's bilateral central rate against any other Member State's currency on its own initiative for the same period.

Article 4

The criterion on the convergence of interest rates referred to in the fourth indent of Article 109j(1) of this Treaty shall mean that, observed over a period of one year before the examination, a Member State has had an average nominal long-term interest rate that does not exceed by more than two percentage points that of, at most, the three best performing Member States in terms of price stability. Interest rates shall be measured on the basis of long-term government bonds or comparable securities, taking into account differences in national definitions.

Article 5

The statistical data to be used for the application of this Protocol shall be provided by the Commission.

Article 6

The Council shall, acting unanimously on a proposal from the Commission and after consulting the European Parliament, the EMI or the ECB as the case may be, and the Committee referred to in Article 109c, adopt appropriate provisions to lay down the details of the convergence criteria referred to in Article 109j of this Treaty, which shall then replace this Protocol.

PROTOCOL ON THE TRANSITION TO THE THIRD STAGE OF ECONOMIC AND MONETARY UNION

The High Contracting Parties,

Declare the irreversible character of the Community's movement to the third stage of economic and monetary union by signing the new Treaty provisions on economic and monetary union.

Therefore all Member States shall, whether they fulfil the necessary conditions for the adoption of a single currency or not, respect the will for the Community to enter swiftly into the third stage, and therefore no Member State shall prevent the entering into the third stage.

If by the end of 1997 the date of the beginning of the third stage has not been set, the Member States concerned, the Community institutions and other bodies involved shall expedite all preparatory work during 1998, in order to enable the Community to enter the third stage irrevocably on 1 January 1999 and to enable the ECB and the ESCB to start their full functioning from this date.

This Protocol shall be annexed to the Treaty establishing the European Community.

PROTOCOL ON CERTAIN PROVISIONS RELATING TO THE UNITED KINGDOM OF GREAT BRITAIN AND NORTHERN IRELAND

The High Contracting Parties,

RECOGNISING that the United Kingdom shall not be obliged or committed to move to the third stage of economic and monetary union without a separate decision to do so by its government and Parliament,

NOTING the practice of the government of the United Kingdom to fund its borrowing requirement by the sale of debt to the private sector,

HAVE AGREED the following provisions, which shall be annexed to the Treaty establishing the European Community:

(1) The United Kingdom shall notify the Council whether it intends to move to the third stage, before the Council makes its assessment under Article 109j(2) of this Treaty.

Unless the United Kingdom notifies the Council that it intends to move to the third stage, it shall be under no obligation to do so.

If no date is set for the beginning of the third stage under Article 109j(3) of this Treaty, the United Kingdom may notify its intention to move to the third stage before 1 January 1998.

(2) Paragraphs 3 to 9 shall have effect if the United Kingdom notifies the Council that it does not intend to move to the third stage.

(3) The United Kingdom shall not be included among the majority of Member States which fulfil the necessary conditions referred to in the second indent of Article 109j(2) and the first indent of Article 109j(3) of this Treaty.

(4) The United Kingdom shall retain its powers in the field of monetary policy according to national law.

(5) Articles 3a(2), 104c(1), (9) and (11), 105(1) to (5), 105a, 107, 108, 108a, 109, 109a(1) and (2)(b) and 109l(4) and (5) of this Treaty shall not apply to the United Kingdom. In these provisions references to the Community or the Member States shall not include the United Kingdom and references to national central banks shall not include the Bank of England.

(6) Articles 109e(4) and 109h and i of this Treaty shall continue to apply to the United Kingdom. Articles 109c(4) and 109m shall apply to the United Kingdom as if it had a derogation.

(7) The voting rights of the United Kingdom shall be suspended in respect of acts of the Council referred to in the Articles listed in paragraph 5. For this purpose the weighted votes of the United Kingdom shall be excluded from any calculation of a qualified majority under Article 109k(5) of this Treaty.

The United Kingdom shall also have no right to participate in the appointment of the President, the Vice-President and the other members of the Executive Board of the ECB under Articles 109a(2)(b) and 109l(1) of this Treaty.

(8) Articles 3, 4, 6, 7, 9.2, 10.1, 10.3, 11.2, 12.1, 14, 16, 18 to 20, 22, 23, 26, 27, 30 to 34, 50 and 52 of the Protocol on the Statute of the European System of Central Banks and of the European Central Bank ('the Statute') shall not apply to the United Kingdom.

In those Articles, references to the Community or the Member States shall not include the United Kingdom and references to national central banks or shareholders shall not include the Bank of England.

References in Articles 10.3 and 30.2 of the Statute to 'subscribed capital of the ECB' shall not include capital subscribed by the Bank of England.

(9) Article 109l(3) of this Treaty and Articles 44 to 48 of the Statute shall have effect, whether or not there is any Member State with a derogation, subject to the following amendments:

> (a) References in Article 44 to the tasks of the ECB and the EMI shall include those tasks that still need to be performed in the third stage owing to any decision of the United Kingdom not to move to that stage.

(b) In addition to the tasks referred to in Article 47 the ECB shall also give advice in relation to and contribute to the preparation of any decision of the Council with regard to the United Kingdom taken in accordance with paragraphs 10(a) and 10(c).

(c) The Bank of England shall pay up its subscription to the capital of the ECB as a contribution to its operational costs on the same basis as national central banks of Member States with a derogation.

(10) If the United Kingdom does not move to the third stage, it may change its notification at any time after the beginning of that stage. In that event:

(a) The United Kingdom shall have the right to move to the third stage provided only that it satisfies the necessary conditions. The Council, acting at the request of the United Kingdom and under the conditions and in accordance with the procedure laid down in Article 109k(2) of this Treaty, shall decide whether it fulfils the necessary conditions.

(b) The Bank of England shall pay up its subscribed capital, transfer to the ECB foreign reserve assets and contribute to its reserve on the same basis as the national central bank of a Member State whose derogation has been abrogated.

(c) The Council, acting under the conditions and in accordance with the procedure laid down in Article 109l(5) of this Treaty, shall take all other necessary decisions to enable the United Kingdom to move to the third stage.

If the United Kingdom moves to the third stage pursuant to the provisions of this Protocol, paragraphs 3 to 9 shall cease to have effect.

(11) Notwithstanding Articles 104 and 109e(3) of this Treaty and Article 21.1 of the Statute, the government of the United Kingdom may maintain its 'ways and means' facility with the Bank of England if and so long as the United Kingdom does not move to the third stage.

PROTOCOL ON SOCIAL POLICY

The High Contracting Parties,

NOTING that 11 Member States, that is to say the Kingdom of Belgium, the Kingdom of Denmark, the Federal Republic of Germany, the Hellenic Republic, the Kingdom of Spain, the French Republic, Ireland, the Italian Republic, the Grand Duchy of Luxembourg, the Kingdom of the Netherlands and the Portuguese Republic, wish to continue along the path laid down in the 1989 Social Charter; that they have adopted among themselves an Agreement to this end; that this Agreement is annexed to this Protocol: that this Protocol and the said Agreement are without prejudice to the provisions of this Treaty, particularly those relating to social policy which constitute an integral part of the acquis communautaire:

(1) Agree to authorise those 11 Member States to have recourse to the institutions, procedures and mechanisms of the Treaty for the purposes of taking among themselves and applying as far as they are concerned the acts and decisions required for giving effect to the above mentioned Agreement.

(2) The United Kingdom of Great Britain and Northern Ireland shall not take part in the deliberations and the adoption by the Council of Commission proposals made on the basis of this Protocol and the above mentioned Agreement.

By way of derogation from Article 148(2) of the Treaty, acts of the Council which are made pursuant to this Protocol and which must be adopted by a qualified majority shall be deemed adopted if they have received at least 52 votes in favour. The unanimity of the members of the Council, with the exception of the United Kingdom of Great Britain and Northern Ireland, shall be necessary for acts of the Council which must be adopted unanimously and for those amending the Commission proposal.

Acts adopted by the Council and any financial consequences other than administrative costs entailed for the institutions shall not be applicable to the United Kingdom of Great Britain and Northern Ireland.

(3) This Protocol shall be annexed to the Treaty establishing the European Community.

AGREEMENT ON SOCIAL POLICY CONCLUDED BETWEEN THE MEMBER STATES OF THE EUROPEAN COMMUNITY WITH THE EXCEPTION OF THE UNITED KINGDOM OF GREAT BRITAIN AND NORTHERN IRELAND

The undersigned 11 High Contracting Parties, that is to say the Kingdom of Belgium, the Kingdom of Denmark, the Federal Republic of Germany, the Hellenic Republic, the Kingdom of Spain, the French Republic, Ireland, the Italian Republic, the Grand Duchy of Luxembourg, the Kingdom of the Netherlands and the Portuguese Republic (hereinafter referred to as 'the Member States'),

WISHING to implement the 1989 Social Charter on the basis of the acquis communautaire,

CONSIDERING the Protocol on social policy,

HAVE AGREED as follows:

Article 1

The Community and the Member States shall have as their objectives the promotion of employment, improved living and working conditions, proper social protection, dialogue between management and labour, the development of human resources with a view to lasting high employment and the combating of exclusion. To this end the Community and the Member States shall implement measures which take account of the diverse forms of national practices, in particular in the field of contractual relations, and the need to maintain the competitiveness of the Community economy.

Article 2

(1) With a view to achieving the objectives of Article 1, the Community shall support and complement the activities of the Member States in the following field:

- improvement in particular of the working environment to protect workers' health and safety;
- working conditions:
- the information and consultation of workers;
- equality between men and women with regard to labour market opportunities and treatment at work;
- the integration of persons excluded from the labour market, without prejudice to Article 127 of the Treaty establishing the European Community (hereinafter referred to as 'the Treaty').

(2) To this end, the Council may adopt, by means of directives, minimum requirements for gradual implementation, having regard to the conditions and technical rules obtaining in each of the Member States. Such directives shall avoid imposing administrative, financial and legal constraints in a way which would hold back the creation and development of small and medium-sized undertakings.

The Council shall act in accordance with the procedure referred to in Article 189c of the Treaty after consulting the Economic and Social Committee.

(3) However, the Council shall act unanimously on a proposal from the Commission, after consulting the European Parliament and the Economic and Social Committee, in the following areas:

- social security and social protection of workers;
- protection of workers where their employment contract is terminated;

- representation and collective defence of the interests of workers and employers, including co-determination, subject to paragraph 6;
- conditions of employment for third-country nationals legally residing in Community territory;
- financial contributions for promotion of employment and job-creation, without prejudice to the provisions relating to the Social Fund.

(4) A Member State may entrust management and labour, at their joint request, with the implementation of directives adopted pursuant to paragraphs 2 and 3.

In this case, it shall ensure that, no later than the date on which a directive must be transposed in accordance with Article 189, management and labour have introduced the necessary measures by agreement, the Member State concerned being required to take any necessary measure enabling it at any time to be in a position to guarantee the results imposed by that directive.

(5) The provisions adopted pursuant to this Article shall not prevent any Member State from maintaining or introducing more stringent protective measures compatible with the Treaty.

(6) The provisions of this Article shall not apply to pay, the right of association, the right to strike or the right to impose lock-outs.

Article 3

(1) The Commission shall have the task of promoting the consultation of management and labour at Community level and shall take any relevant measure to facilitate their dialogue by ensuring balanced support for the parties.

(2) To this end, before submitting proposals in the social policy field, the Commission shall consult management and labour on the possible direction of Community action.

(3) If, after such consultation, the Commission considers Community action advisable, it shall consult management and labour on the content of the envisaged proposal. Management and labour shall forward to the Commission an opinion or, where appropriate, a recommendation.

(4) On the occasion of such consultation, management and labour may inform the Commission of their wish to initiate the process provided for in Article 4. The duration of the procedure shall not exceed nine months, unless the management and labour concerned and the Commission decide jointly to extend it.

Article 4

(1) Should management and labour so desire, the dialogue between them at Community level may lead to contractual relations, including agreements.

(2) Agreements concluded at Community level shall be implemented either in accordance with the procedures and practices specific to management and labour and the Member States or, in matters covered by Article 2, at the joint request of the signatory parties, by a Council decision on a proposal from the Commission.

The Council shall act by qualified majority, except where the agreement in question contains one or more provisions relating to one of the areas referred to in Article 2(3), in which case it shall act unanimously.

Article 5

With a view to achieving the objectives of Article 1 and without prejudice to the other provisions of the Treaty, the Commission shall encourage cooperation between the Member States and facilitate the coordination of their action in all social policy fields under this Agreement.

Article 6

(1) Each Member State shall ensure that the principle of equal pay for male and female workers for equal work is applied.

(2) For the purpose of this Article, 'pay' means the ordinary basic or minimum wage or salary and any other consideration, whether in cash or in kind, which the worker receives directly or indirectly, in respect of his employment, from his employer.

Equal pay without discrimination based on sex means:

(a) that pay for the same work at piece rates shall be calculated on the basis of the same unit of measurement;
(b) that pay for work at time rates shall be the same for the same job.

(3) This Article shall not prevent any Member State from maintaining or adopting measures providing for specific advantages in order to make it easier for women to pursue a vocational activity or to prevent or compensate for disadvantages in their professional careers.

Article 7

(1) The Commission shall draw up a report each year on progress in achieving the objectives of Article 1, including the demographic situation in the Community. It shall forward the report to the European Parliament, the Council and the Economic and Social Committee.

(2) The European Parliament may invite the Commission to draw up reports on particular problems concerning the social situation.

DECLARATIONS

(1) Declaration on Article 2(2)

> The 11 High Contracting Parties note that in the discussions on Article 2(2) of the Agreement it was agreed that the Community does not intend, in laying down minimum requirements for the protection of the safety and health of employees, to discriminate in a manner unjustified by the circumstances against employees in small and medium-sized undertakings.

(2) Declaration on Article 4(2)

> The 11 High Contracting Parties declare that the first of the arrangements for application of the agreements between management and labour at Community level – referred to in Article 4(2) – will consist in developing, by collective bargaining according to the rules of each Member State, the content of the agreements, and that consequently this arrangement implies no obligation on the Member States to apply the agreements directly or to work out rules for their transposition, nor any obligation to amend national legislation in force to facilitate their implementation.

PROTOCOL ON ECONOMIC AND SOCIAL COHESION

The High Contracting Parties,

RECALLING that the Union has set itself the objective of promoting economic and social progress, inter alia, through the strengthening of economic and social cohesion,

RECALLING that Article 2 of the Treaty establishing the European Community includes the task of promoting economic and social cohesion and solidarity between Member States and that the strengthening of economic and social cohesion figures among the activities of the Community listed in Article 3,

RECALLING that the provisions of Part Three, Title XIV, on economic and social cohesion as a whole provide the legal basis for consolidating and further developing the Community's action in the field of economic and social cohesion, including the creation of a new fund,

RECALLING that the provisions of Part Three, Title XII on trans-European networks and Title XVI on environment envisage a Cohesion Fund to be set up before 31 December 1993,

STATING their belief that progress towards economic and monetary union will contribute to the economic growth of all Member States,

NOTING that the Community's structural Funds are being doubled in real terms between 1987 and 1993, implying large transfers, especially as a proportion of GDP of the less prosperous Member States,

NOTING that the European Investment Bank is lending large and increasing amounts for the benefit of the poorer regions,

NOTING the desire for greater flexibility in the arrangements for allocations from the structural Funds,

NOTING the desire for modulation of the levels of Community participation in programmes and projects in certain countries,

NOTING the proposal to take greater account of the relative prosperity of Member States in the system of own resources,

REAFFIRM that the promotion of economic and social cohesion is vital to the full development and enduring success of the Community, and underline the importance of the inclusion of economic and social cohesion in Articles 2 and 3 of this Treaty,

REAFFIRM their conviction that the structural Funds should continue to play a considerable part in the achievement of Community objectives in the field of cohesion,

REAFFIRM their conviction that the European Investment Bank should continue to devote the majority of its resources to the promotion of economic and social cohesion, and declare their willingness to review the capital needs of the European Investment Bank as soon as this is necessary for that purpose,

REAFFIRM the need for a thorough evaluation of the operation and effectiveness of the structural Funds in 1992, and the need to review, on that occasion, the appropriate size of these Funds in the light of the tasks of the Community in the area of economic and social cohesion,

AGREE that the Cohesion Fund to be set up before 31 December 1993 will provide Community financial contributions to projects in the field of environment and trans-European networks in Member States with a per capital GNP of less than 90% of the Community average which have a programme leading to the fulfilment of the conditions of economic convergence as set out in Article 104c,

DECLARE their intention of allowing a greater margin of flexibility in allocating financing from the structural Funds to specific needs not covered under the present structural Funds regulations,

DECLARE their willingness to modulate the levels of Community participation in the context of programmes and projects of the structural Funds, with a view to avoiding excessive increases in budgetary expenditure in the less prosperous Member States,

RECOGNISE the need to monitor regularly the progress made towards achieving economic and social cohesion and state their willingness to study all necessary measures in this respect.

DECLARE their intention of taking greater account of the contributive capacity of the individual Member States in the system of own resources, and of examining means of correcting, for the less prosperous Member States, regressive elements existing in the present own resources system,

AGREE to annex this Protocol to the Treaty establishing the European Community.

As amended by the Merger Treaty, Articles 27(1), 28; Financial Provisions Treaty, Articles 12-14; Greenland Treaty, articles 2, 3; Single European Act, Articles 3(1), 6(3), 10, 12, 16(1), (3), (5), (6), 19, 21, 22; Council Decision 88/591 ECSC, EEC, Euratom; Treaty on European Union, Article G(1)-(84), Final Act; Council Decision 95/1/EC, Euratom, ECSC, arts 2, 6, 8–15, 18, 19; Acts of Accession.

TREATY ESTABLISHING A SINGLE COUNCIL AND A SINGLE COMMISSION OF THE EUROPEAN COMMUNITIES
(Brussels, 8 April 1965)

His Majesty the King of the Belgians, the President of the Federal Republic of Germany, the President of the French Republic, the President of the Italian Republic, His Royal Highness the Grand Duke of Luxembourg, Her Majesty the Queen of the Netherlands,

Having regard to Article 96 of the Treaty establishing the European Coal and Steel Community,

Having regard to Article 236 of the Treaty establishing the European Economic Community,

Having regard to Article 204 of the Treaty establishing the European Atomic Energy Community,

RESOLVED to continue along the road to European unity,

RESOLVED to effect the unification of the three Communities,

MINDFUL of the contribution which the creation of single Community institutions represents for such unification,

HAVE DECIDED to create a single Council and a single Commission of the European Communities and to this end have designated as their plenipotentiaries: ...

WHO, having exchanged their Full Powers, found in good and due form,

HAVE AGREED as follows:

CHAPTER I

THE COUNCIL OF THE EUROPEAN COMMUNITIES

Article 1

A Council of the European Communities (hereinafter called the 'Council') is hereby established. The Council shall take the place of the Special Council of Ministers of the European Coal and Steel Community, the Council of the European Economic Community and the Council of the European Atomic Energy Community.

It shall exercise the powers and jurisdiction conferred on those institutions in accordance with the provisions of the Treaties establishing the European Coal and Steel Community, the European Economic Community and the European Atomic Energy Community, and of this Treaty.

CHAPTER II

THE COMMISSION OF THE EUROPEAN COMMUNITIES

Article 9

(1) A Commission of the European Communities (hereinafter called the 'Commission') is hereby established. This Commission shall take the place of the High Authority of the European Coal and Steel Community, the Commission of the European Economic Community and the Commission of the European Atomic Energy Community.

(2) It shall exercise the powers and jurisdiction conferred on those institutions in accordance with the provisions of the Treaties establishing the European Coal and Steel Community, the European Economic Community and the European Atomic Energy Community, and of this Treaty.

CHAPTER IV

OFFICIALS AND OTHER SERVANTS OF THE EUROPEAN COMMUNITIES

Article 24

(1) The officials and the other servants of the European Coal and Steel Community, the European Economic Community and the European Atomic

Energy Community shall, at the date of entry into force of this Treaty, become officials and other servants of the European Communities and form part of the single administration of those Communities.

The Council shall, acting by a qualified majority on a proposal from the Commission and after consulting the other institutions concerned, lay down the Staff Regulations of officials of the European Communities and the Conditions of Employment of other servants of those Communities.

CHAPTER V

GENERAL AND FINAL PROVISIONS

Article 28

The European Communities shall enjoy in the territories of the Member States such privileges and immunities as are necessary for the performance of their tasks, under the conditions laid down in the Protocol annexed to this Treaty. The same shall apply to the European Investment Bank.

Article 30

The provisions of the Treaties establishing the European Economic Community and the European Atomic Energy Community relating to the jurisdiction shall be applicable to the provisions of this Treaty and of the Protocol annexed thereto, with the exception of those which represent amendments to Articles of the Treaty establishing the European Coal and Steel Community, in respect of which the provisions of the Treaty establishing the European Coal and Steel Community shall remain applicable.

Article 38

(1) This Treaty shall be ratified by the High Contracting Parties in accordance with their respective constitutional requirements. The instruments of ratification shall be deposited with the Government of the Italian Republic.

(2) The Treaty shall enter into force on the first day of the month following the deposit of the instrument of ratification by the last signatory State to take this step.

Article 39

This Treaty, drawn up in a single original in the Dutch, French, German and Italian languages, all four texts being equally authentic, shall be deposited in the archives of the Government of the Italian Republic, which shall transmit a certified copy to each of the Governments of the other signatory States.

IN WITNESS WHEREOF, the undersigned Plenipotentiaries have signed this Treaty ...

PROTOCOL ON THE PRIVILEGES AND IMMUNITIES OF THE EUROPEAN COMMUNITIES

The High Contracting Parties,

Considering that, in accordance with Article 28 of the Treaty establishing a Single Council and a Single Commission of the European Communities, these Communities and the European Investment Bank shall enjoy in the territories of the Member States such privileges and immunities as are necessary for the performance of their tasks.

Have agreed upon the following provisions, which shall be annexed to this Treaty:

CHAPTER I

PROPERTY, FUNDS, ASSETS AND OPERATIONS OF THE EUROPEAN COMMUNITIES

Article 1

The premises and buildings of the Communities shall be inviolable. They shall be exempt from search, requisition, confiscation or expropriation. The property and assets of the Communities shall not be the subject of any administrative or legal measure of constraint without the authorisation of the Court of Justice.

Article 2

The archives of the Communities shall be inviolable.

Article 3

The Communities, their assets, revenues and other property shall be exempt from all taxes.

The Governments of the Member States shall, wherever possible, take the appropriate measures to remit or refund the amount of indirect taxes or sales taxes included in the price of movable or immovable property, where the Communities make, for their official use, substantial purchases the price of which includes taxes of this kind. These provisions shall not be applied, however, so as to have the effect of distorting competition within the Communities.

No exemption shall be granted in respect of taxes and dues which amount merely to charges for public utility services.

Article 4

The Communities shall be exempt from all customs duties, prohibitions and restrictions on imports and exports in respect of articles intended for their official use; articles so imported shall not be disposed of, whether or not in return for payment, in the territory of the country into which they have been imported, except under conditions approved by the Government of that country.

The Communities shall also be exempt from any customs duties and any prohibitions and restrictions on imports and exports in respect of their publications.

Article 5

The European Coal and Steel Community may hold currency of any kind and operate accounts in any currency.

CHAPTER II

COMMUNICATIONS AND LAISSEZ-PASSER

Article 6

For their official communications and the transmission of all their documents, the institutions of the Communities shall enjoy in the territory of each Member State the treatment accorded by that State to diplomatic missions.

Official correspondence and other official communications of the institutions of the Communities shall not be subject to censorship.

Article 7

(1) Laissez-passer in a form to be prescribed by the Council, which be recognised as valid travel documents by the authorities of the Member States, may be issued to members and servants of the institutions of the Communities by the Presidents of these institutions. These laissez-passer shall be issued to officials and other servants under conditions laid down in the Staff Regulations of officials and the Conditions of Employment of other servants of the Communities.

The Commission may conclude agreements for these laissez-passer to be recognised as valid travel documents within the territory of third countries.

(2) The provisions of Article 6 of the Protocol on the Privileges and Immunities of the European Coal and Steel Community shall, however, remain applicable to members and servants of the institutions who are at the date of entry into force of this Treaty in possession of the laissez-passer provided for in that Article, until the provisions of paragraph 1 of this Article are applied.

CHAPTER III

MEMBERS OF THE EUROPEAN PARLIAMENT

Article 8

No administrative or other restriction shall be imposed on the free movement of members of the European Parliament travelling to or from the place of meeting of the European Parliament.

Members of the European Parliament shall, in respect of customs and exchange control, be accorded:

(a) by their own Government, the same facilities as those accorded to senior officials travelling abroad on temporary official missions;

(b) by the Governments of other Member States, the same facilities as those accorded to representatives of foreign Governments on temporary official missions.

Article 9

Members of the European Parliament shall not be subject to any form of inquiry, detention or legal proceedings in respect of opinions expressed or votes cast by them in the performance of their duties.

Article 10

During the sessions of the European Parliament, its members shall enjoy:

(a) in the territory of their own State, the immunities accorded to members of their parliament;

(b) in the territory of any other Member State, immunity from any measure of detention and from legal proceedings.

Immunity shall likewise apply to members while they are travelling to and from the place of meeting of the European Parliament.

Immunity cannot be claimed when a member is found in the act of committing an offence and shall not prevent the European Parliament from exercising its right to waive the immunity of one of its members.

CHAPTER IV

REPRESENTATIVES OF MEMBER STATES TAKING PART IN THE WORK OF THE INSTITUTIONS OF THE EUROPEAN COMMUNITIES

Article 11

Representatives of Member States taking part in the work of the institutions of the Communities, their advisers and technical experts shall, in the performance of their duties and during their travel to and from the place of meeting, enjoy the customary privileges, immunities and facilities.

This article shall also apply to members of the advisory bodies of the Communities.

CHAPTER V

OFFICIALS AND OTHER SERVANTS OF THE EUROPEAN COMMUNITIES

Article 12

In the territory of each Member State and whatever their nationality, officials and other servants of the Communities shall:

(a) subject to the provisions of the Treaties relating, on the one hand, to the rules on the liability of officials and other servants towards the Communities and, on the other hand, to the jurisdiction of the Court in disputes between the Communities and their officials and other servants, be immune from legal proceedings in respect of acts performed by them in their official capacity, including their words spoken or written. They shall continue to enjoy this immunity after they have ceased to hold office;

(b) together with their spouses and dependent members of their families, not be subject to immigration restrictions or to formalities for registration of aliens;

(c) in respect of currency or exchange regulations, be accorded the same facilities as are customarily accorded to officials of international organisations;

(d) enjoy the right to import free of duty their furniture and effects at the time of first taking up their post in the country concerned, and the right to re-export free of duty their furniture and effects, on termination of their duties in that country, subject in either case to the conditions considered to be necessary by the Government of the country in which this right is exercised;

(e) have the right to import free of duty a motor car for their personal use, acquired either in the country of their last residence or in the country of which they are nationals on the terms ruling in the home market in that country, and the re-export it free of duty, subject in either case to the conditions considered to be necessary by the Government of the country concerned.

Article 13

Officials and other servants of the Communities shall be liable to a tax for the benefit of the Communities on salaries, wages and emoluments paid to them by the Communities, in accordance with the conditions and procedure laid down by the Council, acting on a proposal from the Commission.

They shall be exempt from national taxes on salaries, wages and emoluments paid by the Communities.

Article 14

In the application of income tax, wealth tax and death duties and in the application of conventions on the avoidance of double taxation concluded between Member States of the Communities, officials and other servants of the Communities who, solely by reason of the performance of their duties in the service of the Communities, establish their residence in the territory of a Member State other than their country of domicile for tax purposes at the time of entering the service of the Communities, shall be considered, both in the country of their actual residence and in the country of domicile in the latter country provided that it is a member of the Communities. This provision shall also apply to a spouse to the extent that the latter is not separately engaged in a gainful occupation, and to children dependent on and in the care of the persons referred to in this Article.

Movable property belonging to persons referred to in the first paragraph and situated in the territory of the country where they are staying shall be exempt from death duties in that country; such property shall, for the assessment of such duty, be considered as being in the country of domicile for tax purposes, subject to the rights of third countries and to the possible application of provisions of international conventions on double taxation.

Any domicile acquired solely by reason of the performance of duties in the service of other international organisations shall not be taken into consideration in applying the provisions of this Article.

Article 15

The Council shall, acting unanimously on a proposal from the Commission, lay down the scheme of social security benefits for officials and other servants of the Communities.

Article 16

The Council shall, acting on a proposal from the Commission and after consulting the other institutions concerned, determine the categories of officials and other servants of the Communities to whom the provisions of Article 12, the second paragraph of Article 13, and Article 14 shall apply, in whole or in part.

The names, grades and addresses of officials and other servants included in such categories shall be communicated periodically to the Governments of the Member States.

CHAPTER VI

PRIVILEGES AND IMMUNITIES OF MISSIONS OF THIRD COUNTRIES ACCREDITED TO THE EUROPEAN COMMUNITIES

Article 17

The Member State in whose territory the Communities have their seat shall accord the customary diplomatic immunities and privileges to missions of third countries accredited to the Communities.

CHAPTER VII

GENERAL PROVISIONS

Article 18

Privileges, immunities and facilities shall be accorded to officials and other servants of the Communities solely in the interest of the Communities.

Each institution of the Communities shall be required to waive the immunity accorded to an official or other servant whatever that institution considers that the waiver of such immunity is not contrary to the interests of the Communities.

Article 19

The institutions of the Communities shall, for the purpose of applying this Protocol, cooperate with the responsible authorities of the Member States concerned.

Article 20

Articles 12 to 15 and Article 18 shall apply to members of the Commission.

Article 21

Articles 12 to 15 and Article 18 shall apply to the Judges, the Advocates-

General, the Registrar and the Assistant Rapporteurs of the Court of Justice, without prejudice to the provisions of Article 3 of the Protocols on the Statute of the Court of Justice concerning immunity from legal proceedings of Judges and Advocates-General.

Article 22

This Protocol shall also apply to the European Investment Bank, to the members of its organs, to its staff and to the representatives of the Member States taking part in its activities, without prejudice to the provisions of the Protocol on the Statute of the Bank.

The European Investment Bank shall in addition be exempt from any form of taxation or imposition of a like nature on the occasion of any increase in its capital and from the various formalities which may be connected therewith in the State where the Bank has its seat. Similarly, its dissolution or liquidation shall not give rise to any imposition. Finally, the activities of the Bank and of its organs carried on in accordance with its Statute shall not be subject to any turnover tax.

Article 23

This Protocol shall also apply to the European Central Bank, to the members of its organs and to its staff, without prejudice to the provisions of the Protocol on the Statute of the European System of Central Banks and the European Central Bank.

The European Central Bank shall, in addition, be exempt from any form of taxation or imposition of a nature on the occasion of any increase in its capital and from the various formalities which may be connected therewith in the State where the Bank has its seat. The activities of the Bank and of its organs carried on in accordance with the Statute of the European System of Central Banks and of the European Central Bank shall not be subject to any turnover tax.

The above provisions shall also apply to the European Monetary Institute. Its dissolution or liquidation shall not give rise to any imposition.

In witness whereof, the undersigned Plenipotentiaries have signed this Protocol ...

As amended by the Budgetary Provisions Treaty, Article 10; Financial Provisions Treaty, Article 27; Single European Act, Article 3(1); Treaty on European Union, Article P(1), Protocol on the Privileges and Immunities of the European Communities.

LUXEMBOURG ACCORDS
(28 and 29 January 1966)

At the extraordinary Council session of 28 and 29 January 1966 the Six reached agreement and the following statements were issued:

(a) Relations between the Commission and the Council.

Close co-operation between the Council and the Commission is essential for the functioning and development of the Community.

In order to improve and strengthen this co-operation at every level, the Council considers the following practical methods of co-operation should be applied, these methods to be adopted by joint agreement, on the basis of Article 162 of the EEC Treaty, without compromising the respective competences and powers of the two Institutions.

(1) Before adopting any particularly important proposal, it is desirable that the Commission should take up the appropriate contacts with the Governments of the Member States, through the Permanent Representatives, without this procedure compromising the right initiative which the Commission derives from the Treaty.

(2) Proposals and any other official acts which the Commission submits to the Council and to the Member States are not to be made public until the recipients have had formal notice of them and are in possession of the texts.

The 'Journal Officiel' (official gazette) should be arranged so as to show clearly which acts are of binding force. The methods to be employed for publishing those texts whose publication is required will be adopted in the context of the current work on the re-organisation of the 'Journal Officiel'.

(3) The credentials of Heads of Missions of non-member states accredited to the Community will be submitted jointly to the President of the Council and to the President of the Commission, meeting together for this purpose.

(4) The Council and the Commission will inform each other rapidly and fully of any approaches relating to fundamental questions made to either institution by the representatives of non-member states.

(5) Within the scope of application of Article 162, the Council and the Commission will consult together on the advisability of, the procedure

for, and the nature of any links which the Commission might establish with international organisations pursuant to Article 229 of the Treaty.

(6) Co-operation between the Council and the Commission on the Community's information policy, which was the subject of the Council's discussions on 24 September 1963, will be strengthened in such a way that the programme of the Joint Information Service will be drawn up and carried out in accordance with procedures which are to be decided upon at a later date, and which may include the establishment of an ad hoc body.

(7) Within the framework of the financial regulations relating to the drawing up and execution of the Communities' budgets, the Council and the Commission will decide on means for more effective control over the commitment and expenditure of Community funds.

(b) Majority voting procedure

(i) Where, in the case of decisions which may be taken by majority vote on a proposal of the Commission, very important interests of one or more partners are at stake, the Members of the Council will endeavour, within a reasonable time, to reach solutions which can be adopted by all the Members of the Council while respecting their mutual interests and those of the Community, in accordance with Article 2 of the Treaty.

(ii) With regard to the preceding paragraph, the French delegation considers that where very important interests are at stake the discussion must be continued until unanimous agreement is reached.

(iii) The six delegations note that there is a divergence of views on what should be done in the event of a failure to reach complete agreement.

(iv) The six delegations nevertheless consider that this divergence does not prevent the Community's work being resumed in accordance with the normal procedure.

The members of the Council agreed that decisions on the following should be by common consent:

(a) The financial regulation for agriculture;

(b) Extensions on the market organisation for fruit and vegetables;

(c) The regulation on the organisation of sugar markets;

(d) The regulation on the organisation of markets for oils and fats;

(e) The fixing of common prices for milk, beef and veal, rice, sugar, olive oil and oil seeds.

Finally the Council drew up the following programme of work;

(1) The draft EEC and Euratom budgets will be approved by written procedure before 15 February 1966.

(2) The EEC Council will meet as soon as possible to settle as a matter of priority the problem of financing the common agricultural policy. Concurrently, discussions will be resumed on the other questions, particularly the trade negotiations in GATT and the problems of adjusting national duties on imports from non-member countries.

(3) The Representatives of the Member States' Government will meet on the day fixed for the next Council meeting and will begin discussions on the composition of the new single Commission and on the election of the President and Vice-Presidents.

They will also agree on the date – in the first half of 1966 – when instruments of ratification of the Treaty on the merger of the institutions are to be deposited, on condition that the required parliamentary ratifications have been obtained and agreement has been reached on the composition and on the presidency and vice-presidency of the Commission.

ACT CONCERNING THE ELECTION OF THE REPRESENTATIVES OF THE EUROPEAN PARLIAMENT BY DIRECT UNIVERSAL SUFFRAGE
(Annexed to Council Decision 76/787/ECSC, EEC, Euratom)

Article 1

The representatives in the European Parliament of the peoples of the States brought together in the Community shall be elected by direct universal suffrage.

Article 2

The number of representatives elected in each Member State shall be as follows:

Belgium	25
Denmark	16
Germany	99
Greece	25
Spain	64
France	87
Ireland	15
Italy	87
Luxembourg	6
Netherlands	31
Austria	21
Portugal	25
Finland	16

Sweden   22
United Kingdom   87

Article 3

(1) Representatives shall be elected for a term of five years.

(2) This five-year period shall begin at the opening of the first session following each election.

It may now be extended or curtailed pursuant to the second subparagraph of Article 10(2).

(3) The term of office of each representative shall begin and end at the same time as the period referred to in paragraph 2.

Article 4

(1) Representatives shall vote on an individual and personal basis. They shall not be bound by any instructions and shall not receive a binding mandate.

(2) Representatives shall enjoy the privileges and immunities applicable to members of the European Parliament by virtue of the Protocol on the Privileges and Immunities of the European Communities annexed to the Treaty establishing a Single Council and a Single Commission of the European Communities.

Article 5

(1) The office of representative in the European Parliament shall be incompatible with that of:

- member of the Government of a Member State;
- member of the Commission of the European Communities;
- Judge, Advocate-General or Registrar of the Court of Justice of the European Communities;
- member of the Court of Auditors of the European Communities;
- member of the Consultative Committee of the European Coal and Steel Community or member of the Economic Community and of the European Atomic Energy Community;
- member of committees or other bodies set up pursuant to the Treaties

establishing the European Coal and Steel Community, the European Economic Community and the European Atomic Energy Community for the purpose of managing the Communities' funds or carrying out a permanent direct administrative task;
- member of the Board of Directors, Management Committee or staff of the European Investment Bank;
- active official or servant of the institutions of the European Communities or of the specialised bodies attached to them.

(2) In addition, each Member State may, in the circumstances provided for in Article 7(2), lay down rules at national level relating to incompatibility.

(3) Representatives in the European Parliament to whom paragraphs 1 and 2 become applicable in the course of the five-year period referred to in Article 3 shall be replaced in accordance with Article 12.

Article 7

(1) Pursuant to Article 21(3) of the Treaty establishing the European Coal and Steel Community, Article 138(3) of the Treaty establishing the European Economic Community and Article 108(3) of the Treaty establishing the European Atomic Energy Community, the European Parliament shall draw up a proposal for a uniform electoral procedure.

(2) Pending the entry into force of a uniform electoral procedure and subject to the other provisions of this Act, the electoral procedure shall be governed in each Member State by its national provisions.

Article 8

No one may vote more than once in any election of representatives to the European Parliament.

Article 9

(1) Elections to the European Parliament shall be held on the date fixed by each Member State; for all Member States this date shall fall within the same period starting on a Thursday morning and ending on the following Sunday.

(2) The counting of votes may not begin until after the close of polling in the Member State whose electors are the last to vote within the period referred to in paragraph 1.

(3) If a Member State adopts a double ballot system for elections to the European Parliament, the first ballot must take place during the period referred to in paragraph 1.

Article 10

(1) The Council, acting unanimously after consulting the European Parliament, shall determine the period referred to in Article 9(1) for the first elections.

(2) Subsequent elections shall take place in the corresponding period in the year of the five-year period referred to in Article 3.

Should it prove impossible to hold the elections in the Community during that period, the Council acting unanimously shall, after consulting the European Council, determine another period which shall be not more than one month before or one month after the period fixed pursuant to the preceding subparagraph.

(3) Without prejudice to Article 22 of the Treaty establishing the European Coal and Steel Community, Article 139 of the Treaty establishing the European Economic Community and Article 109 of the Treaty establishing the European Atomic Energy Community, the European Parliament shall meet, without requiring to be convened, on the first Tuesday after expiry of an interval of one month from the end of the period referred to in Article 9(1).

(4) The powers of the outgoing European Parliament shall cease upon the opening of the first sitting of the new European Parliament.

Article 11

Pending the entry into force of the uniform electoral procedure referred to in Article 7(1), the European Parliament shall verify the credentials of representatives. For this purpose it shall take note of the results declared officially by the Member States and shall rule on any disputes which may arise out of the provisions of this Act other than those arising out of the national provisions to which the Act refers.

Article 12

(1) Pending the entry into force of the uniform electoral procedure referred to in Article 7(1) and subject to the other provisions of this Act, each Member State shall lay down appropriate procedures for filling any seat

which falls vacant during the five-year term of office referred to in Article 3 for the remainder of that period.

(2) Where a seat falls vacant pursuant to national provisions in force in a Member State, the latter shall inform the European Parliament, which shall take note of that fact.

In all other cases, the European Parliament shall establish that there is a vacancy and inform the Member State thereof.

Article 13

Should it appear necessary to adopt measures to implement this Act, the Council, acting unanimously on a proposal from the European Parliament after consulting the Commission, shall adopt such measures after endeavouring to reach agreement with the European Parliament in a conciliation committee consisting of the Council and representatives of the European Parliament.

Article 14

Article 21(1) and (2) of the Treaty establishing the European Coal and Steel Community, Article 138(1) and (2) of the Treaty estab-lishing the European Economic Community and Article 108(1) and (2) of the Treaty establishing the European Atomic Energy Community shall lapse on the date of the sitting held in accordance with Article 10(3) by the first European Parliament elected pursuant to this Act.

Article 15

This Act is drawn up in the Danish, Dutch, English, French, German, Irish and Italian languages, all the texts being equally authentic ...

Article 16

The provisions of this Act shall enter into force on the first day of the month following that during which the last of the notifications referred to in the Decision is received ...

As amended by the Single European Act, Article 3(1); Council Decision 93/81/Euratom, ECSC, EEC of February 1, 1993; Council Decision 95/1/EC, Euratom, ECSC, art 5; Acts of Accession.

FUNDAMENTAL RIGHTS: JOINT DECLARATION BY THE EUROPEAN PARLIAMENT, THE COUNCIL AND THE COMMISSION
(Luxembourg, 5 April 1977)

The European Parliament, the Council and the Commission.

Whereas the Treaties establishing the European Communities are based on the principle of respect for the law;

Whereas, as the Court of Justice has recognised, that law comprises, over and above the rules embodied in the treaties and secondary Community legislation, the general principles of law and in particular the fundamental rights, principles and rights on which the constitutional law of the Member States is based;

Whereas, in particular, all the Member States are Contracting Parties to the European Convention for the Protection of Human Rights and Fundamental Freedoms signed in Rome on 4 November 1950,

Have adopted the following declaration;

(1) The European Parliament, the Council and the Commission stress the prime importance they attach to the protection of fundamental rights, as derived in particular from the constitutions of the Member States and the European Convention for the Protection of Human Rights and Fundamental Freedoms.

(2) In the exercise of their powers and in pursuance of the aims of the European Communities they respect and will continue to respect these rights.

COUNCIL DECISION LAYING DOWN THE PROCEDURES FOR THE EXERCISE OF IMPLEMENTING POWERS CONFERRED ON THE COMMISSION
(87/373/EEC)

The Council of the European Communities,

Having regard to the Treaty establishing the European Economic Community, and in particular Article 145 thereof,

Having regard to the proposal from the Commission,

Having regard to the opinion of the European Parliament,

Whereas, in the acts which it adopts, the Council confers on the Commission powers for the implementation of the rules which the Council lays down; whereas the Council may impose certain requirements in respect of the exercise of these powers; whereas it may also reserve the right, in specific cases, to exercise directly implementing powers itself;

Whereas, in order to improve the efficiency of the Community's decision-making process, the types of procedure to which it may henceforth have recourse should be limited; whereas certain rules governing any new provision introducing procedures for the exercise of implementing powers conferred by the Council on the Commission should therefore be laid down;

Whereas this Decision must not affect procedures for implementing Commission powers contained in acts which predate its entry into force; whereas it must be possible, when amending or extending such acts, to adapt the procedures to conform with those set out in this Decision or to retain the existing procedures,

Has decided as follows:

Article 1

Other than in specific cases where it reserves the right to exercise directly implementing powers itself, the Council shall, in the acts which it adopts, confer on the Commission powers for the implementation of the rules which it lays down. The Council shall specify the essential elements of these powers.

The Council may impose requirements in respect of the exercise of these powers, which must be in conformity with the procedures set out in Articles 2 and 3.

Article 2

Procedure I

The Commission shall be assisted by a committee of an advisory nature composed of the representatives of the Member States and chaired by the representative of the Commission.

The representative of the Commission shall submit to the committee a draft of the measures to be taken. The committee shall deliver its opinion on the draft, within a time limit which the chairman may lay down according to the urgency of the matter, if necessary by taking a vote.

The opinion shall be recorded in the minutes; in addition, each Member State shall have the right to ask to have its position recorded in the minutes.

The Commission shall take the utmost account of the opinion delivered by the committee. It shall inform the committee of the manner in which its opinion has been taken into account.

Procedure II

The Commission shall be assisted by a committee composed of the representatives of the Member States and chaired by the representative of the Commission.

The representative of the Commission shall submit to the committee a draft of the measures to be taken. The committee shall deliver its opinion on the draft within a time limit which the chairman may lay down according to the urgency of the matter. The opinion shall be delivered by the majority laid down in Article 148(2) of the Treaty in the case of decisions which the Council is required to adopt on a proposal from the Commission. The votes of the representatives of the Member States with the committee shall be weighted in the manner set out in that Article. The chairman shall not vote.

The Commission shall adopt measures which shall apply immediately.

However, if these measures are not in accordance with the opinion of the committee, they shall be communicated by the Commission to the Council forthwith. In that event:

Variant (a)

The Commission may defer application of the measures which it has decided for a period of not more than one month from the date of such communication;

The Council, acting by a qualified majority, may take a different decision within the time limit referred to in the previous paragraph.

Variant (b)

The Commission shall defer application of the measures which it has decided for a period to be laid down in each act adopted by the Council, but which may in no case exceed three months from the date of communication.

The Council, acting by a qualified majority, may take a different decision within the time limit referred to in the previous paragraph.

Procedure III

The Commission shall be assisted by a committee composed of the representatives of the Member States and chaired by the representative of the Commission.

The representative of the Commission shall submit to the committee a draft of the measures to be taken. The committee shall deliver its opinion on the draft within a time limit which the chairman may lay down according to the urgency of the matter. The opinion shall be delivered by the majority laid down in Article 148(2) of the Treaty in the case of decisions which the Council is required to adopt on a proposal from the Commission. The votes of the representatives of the Member States within the committee shall be weighted in the manner set out in that Article. The chairman shall not vote.

The Commission shall adopt the measures envisaged if they are in accordance with the opinion of the committee.

If the measures envisaged are not in accordance with the opinion of the committee, or if no opinion is delivered, the Commission shall, without delay, submit to the Council a proposal relating to the measures to be taken. The Council shall act by a qualified majority.

Variant (a)

If, on the expiry of a period to be laid down in each act to be adopted by the Council under this paragraph but which may in no case exceed three months from the date of referral to the Council, the Council has not acted, the proposed measures shall be adopted by the Commission.

Variant (b)

If, on the expiry of a period to be laid down in each act to be adopted by the Council under this paragraph but which may in no case exceed three months from the date of referral to the Council, the Council has not acted, the proposed measures shall be adopted by the Commission, save where the Council has decided against the said measures by a simple majority.

Article 3

The following procedure may be applied where the Council confers on the Commission the power to decide on safeguard measures:

- the Commission shall notify the Council and the Member States of any decision regarding safeguard measures.
- any Member State may refer the Commission's decision to the Council within a time limit to be determined in the act in question.

Variant (a)

The Council, acting by a qualified majority, may take a different decision within a time limit to be determined in the act in question.

Variant (b)

The Council, acting by a qualified majority, may confirm, amend or revoke the decision adopted by the Commission. If the Council has not taken a decision within a time limit to be determined in the act in question, the decision of the Commission is deemed to be revoked.

Article 4

This Decision shall not affect the procedures for the exercise of the powers conferred on the Commission in acts which predate its entry into force.

Where such acts are amended or extended the Council may adapt the procedures laid down by these acts to conform with those set out in Articles 2 and 3 or retain the existing procedures.

Article 5

The Council shall review the procedures provided for in this Decision on the basis of a report submitted by the Commission before 31 December 1990.

COUNCIL DECISION ESTABLISHING A COURT OF FIRST INSTANCE OF THE EUROPEAN COMMUNITIES
(88/591/ECSC, EEC, Euratom)
(Luxembourg, 24 October 1988)

The Council of the European Communities,

Having regard to the Treaty establishing the European Coal and Steel Community, and in particular Article 32d thereof,

Having regard to the Treaty establishing the European Economic Community, and in particular Article 168a thereof,

Having regard to the Treaty establishing the European Atomic Energy Community, and in particular Article 140a thereof,

Having regard to the Protocol on the Statute of the Court of Justice of the European Coal and Steel Community, signed in Paris on 18 April 1951,

Having regard to the Protocol on the Statute of the Court of Justice of the European Economic Community, signed in Brussels on 17 April 1957,

Having regard to the Protocol on the Statute of the Court of Justice of the European Atomic Energy Community, signed in Brussels on 17 April 1957,

Having regard to the Protocol on Privileges and Immunities of the European Communities, signed in Brussels on 8 April 1965,

Having regard to the request of the Court of Justice,

Having regard to the opinion of the Commission,

Having regard to the opinion of the European Parliament,

Whereas Article 32d of the ECSC Treaty, Article 168a of the EEC Treaty and Article 140a of the EAEC Treaty empower the Council to attach to the Court of Justice a Court of First Instance called upon to exercise important judicial functions and whose members are independent beyond doubt and possess the ability required for performing such functions;

Whereas the aforesaid provisions empower the Council to give the Court of First Instance jurisdiction to hear and determine at first instance, in accordance with the conditions laid down by the Statutes, certain classes of action or proceeding brought by natural or legal persons, subject to the right of appeal to the Court of Justice on questions of law alone;

Whereas the Council is to determine, pursuant to the aforesaid provisions, the composition of that court and adopt the necessary adjustments and additional provisions to the Statutes of the Court of Justice;

Whereas, in respect of actions requiring close examination of complex facts, the establishment of a second court will improve the judicial protection of individual interests;

Whereas it is necessary, in order to maintain the quality and effectiveness of judicial review in the Community legal order, to enable the Court to concentrate its activities on its fundamental task of ensuring uniform interpretation of Community law;

Whereas it is therefore necessary to make use of the powers granted by Article 32d of the ECSC Treaty, Article 168a of the EEC Treaty and Article 140a of the EAEC Treaty and to transfer to the Court of First Instance jurisdiction to hear and determine at first instance certain classes of action or proceeding which frequently require an examination of complex facts, that is to say actions or proceedings brought by servants of the Communities and also, in so far as the ECSC Treaty is concerned, by undertakings and associations in matters concerning levies, production, prices, restrictive agreements, decisions or practices and concentrations, and so far as the EEC Treaty is concerned, by natural or legal persons in competition matters,

Has decided as follows:

Article 1

A Court, to be called the Court of First Instance of the European Communities, shall be attached to the Court of Justice of the European Communities. Its seat shall be at the Court of Justice.

Article 2

(1) The Court of First Instance shall consist of 15 judges.

(2) The members shall elect the President of the Court of First Instance from among their number for a term of three years. He may be re-elected.

(3) The members of the Court of First Instance may be called upon to perform the task of an Advocate-General.

(a) It shall be the duty of the Advocate-General, acting with complete impartiality and independence, to make, in open court, reasoned submissions on certain cases brought before the Court of First Instance in order to assist the Court of First Instance in the performance of its task.

(b) The criteria for selecting such cases, as well as the procedures for designating the Advocates-General, shall be laid down in the Rules of Procedure of the Court of First Instance.

(c) A member called upon to perform the task of Advocate-General in a case may not take part in the judgment of the case.

(4) The Court of First Instance shall sit in chambers of three or five judges. The composition of the chambers and the assignment of cases to them shall be governed by the Rules of Procedure. In certain cases governed by the Rules of Procedure the Court of First Instance may sit in plenary session.

(5) Article 21 of the Protocol on Privileges and Immunities of the European Communities and Article 6 of the Treaty establishing a Single Council and a Single Commission of the European Communities shall apply to the members of the Court of First Instance and to its Registrar.

Article 3

(1) The Court of First Instance shall exercise at first instance the jurisdiction conferred on the Court of Justice by the Treaties establishing the Communities and by the acts adopted in implementation thereof, however, in respect of actions brought by natural or legal persons pursuant to the second paragraph of Article 33, Article 35 and the first and second paragraphs of Article 40 of the ECSC Treaty and which concern acts relating to the application of Article 74 of the said Treaty and in respect of actions brought by natural or legal persons pursuant to the fourth paragraph of Article 173, the third paragraph of Article 175 and Article 178 of the EC Treaty and relating to measures to protect trade within the meaning of Article 113 of that Treaty in the case of dumping and subsidies, its entry into force shall be fixed at 15 March 1994.

Article 4

Save as hereinafter provided, Articles 34, 36, 39, 44 and 92 of the ECSC Treaty, Articles 172, 174, 176, 184 to 187 and 192 of the EEC Treaty and

Articles 49, 83, 144b, 147, 149, 156 to 159 and 164 of the Euratom Treaty shall apply to the Court of First Instance.

Article 10

The former Articles 45, 46 and 47 of the Protocol on the Statute of the Court of Justice of the European Atomic Energy Community shall become Articles 56, 57, and 58 respectively.

Article 11

The first President of the Court of First Instance shall be appointed for three years in the same manner as its members. However, the Governments of the Member States may, by common accord, decide that the procedure laid down in Article 2(2) shall be applied.

The Court of First Instance shall adopt its Rules of Procedure immediately upon its constitution.

Until the entry into force of the Rules of Procedure of the Court of First Instance, the Rules of Procedure of the Court of Justice shall apply mutatis mutandis.

Article 12

Immediately after all members of the Court of First Instance have taken oath, the President of the Council shall proceed to choose by lot the members of the Court of First Instance whose terms of office are to expire at the end of the first three years in accordance with Article 32d(3) of the ECSC Treaty, Article 168a(3) of the EEC Treaty, and Article 140a(3) of the EAEC Treaty.

Article 13

This Decision shall enter into force on the day following its publication in the *Official Journal of the European Communities*, with the exception of Article 3, which shall enter into force on the date of the publication in the *Official Journal of the European Communities* of the ruling by the President of the Court of Justice that the Court of First Instance has been constituted in accordance with law.

Article 14

Cases referred to in Article 3 of which the Court of Justice is seised on the date on which that Article enters into force but in which the preliminary report provided for in Article 44(1) of the Rules of Procedure of the Court of Justice has not yet been presented shall be referred back to the Court of First Instance ...

As amended by Council Decision 93/350 Euratom, ECSC, EEC; Council Decision 94/149/ECSC, EC; Council Decision 95/1/EC, Euratom, ECSC, art 10.

TREATY ON EUROPEAN UNION
(Maastricht, 7 February 1992)

His Majesty the King of the Belgians, Her Majesty the Queen of Denmark, the President of the Federal Republic of Germany, the President of the Hellenic Republic, His Majesty the King of Spain, the President of the French Republic, the President of Ireland, the President of the Italian Republic, His Royal Highness the Grand Duke of Luxembourg, Her Majesty the Queen of the Netherlands, the President of the Portuguese Republic, Her Majesty the Queen of the United Kingdom of Great Britain and Northern Ireland,

RESOLVED to mark a new stage in the process of European integration undertaken with the establishment of the European Communities,

RECALLING the historic importance of the ending of the division of the European continent and the need to create firm bases for the construction of the future Europe,

CONFIRMING their attachment to the principles of liberty, democracy and respect for human rights and fundamental freedoms and of the rule of law,

DESIRING to deepen the solidarity between their peoples while respecting their history, their culture and their traditions,

DESIRING to enhance further the democratic and efficient functioning of the institutions so as to enable them better to carry out, within a single institutional framework, the tasks entrusted to them,

RESOLVED to achieve the strengthening and the convergence of their economies and to establish an economic and monetary union including, in accordance with the provisions of this Treaty, a single and stable currency,

DETERMINED to promote economic and social progress for their peoples, within the context of the accomplishment of the internal market and of reinforced cohesion and environmental protection, and to implement policies ensuring that advances in economic integration are accompanied by parallel progress in other fields,

RESOLVED to establish a citizenship common to nationals of their countries,

RESOLVED to implement a common foreign and security policy including the eventual framing of a common defence policy, which might in time lead to a common defence, thereby reinforcing the European identity and its independence in order to promote peace, security and progress in Europe and in the world,

REAFFIRMING their objective to facilitate the free movement of persons, while ensuring the safety and security of their peoples, by including provisions on justice and home affairs in this Treaty,

RESOLVED to continue the process of creating an ever closer union among the peoples of Europe, in which decisions are taken as closely as possible to the citizen in accordance with the principle of subsidiarity,

IN VIEW of further steps to be taken in order to advance European integration,

HAVE DECIDED to establish a European Union ...

TITLE I

COMMON PROVISIONS

Article A

By this Treaty, the High Contracting Parties establish among themselves a European Union, hereinafter called 'the Union'.

This Treaty marks a new stage in the process of creating an ever closer union among the peoples of Europe, in which decisions are taken as closely as possible to the citizen.

The Union shall be founded on the European Communities, supplemented by the policies and forms of cooperation established by this Treaty. Its tasks shall be to organise, in a manner demonstrating consistency and solidarity, relations between the Member States and between their peoples.

Article B

The Union shall set itself the following objectives:

- to promote economic and social progress which is balanced and sustainable, in particular through the creation of an area without internal frontiers, through the strengthening of economic and social

cohesion and through the establishment of economic and monetary union, ultimately including a single currency in accordance with the provisions of this Treaty;
- to assert its identity on the international scene, in particular through the implementation of a common foreign and security policy including the eventual framing of a common defence policy, which might in time lead to a common defence;
- to strengthen the protection of the rights and interests of the nationals of its Member States through the introduction of a citizenship of the Union;
- to develop close cooperation on justice and home affairs;
- to maintain in full the acquis communautaire and build on it with a view to considering, through the procedure referred to in Article N(2), to what extent the policies and forms of cooperation introduced by this Treaty may need to be revised with the aim of ensuring the effectiveness of the mechanisms and the institutions of the Community.

The objectives of the Union shall be achieved as provided in this Treaty and in accordance with the conditions and the timetable set out therein while respecting the principle of subsidiarity as defined in Article 3b of the Treaty establishing the European Community.

Article C

The Union shall be served by a single institutional framework which shall ensure the consistency and the continuity of the activities carried out in order to attain its objectives while respecting and building upon the acquis communautaire.

The Union shall in particular ensure the consistency of its external activities as a whole in the context of its external relations, security, economic and development policies. The Council and the Commission shall be responsible for ensuring such consistency. They shall ensure the implementation of these policies, each in accordance with its respective powers.

Article D

The European Council shall provide the Union with the necessary impetus for its development and shall define the general political guidelines thereof.

The European Council shall bring together the Heads of State or

Government of the Member States and the President of the Commission. They shall be assisted by the Ministers for Foreign Affairs of the Member States and by a Member of the Commission. The European Council shall meet at least twice a year, under the chairmanship of the Head of State or Government of the Member State which holds the Presidency of the Council.

The European Council shall submit to the European Parliament a report after each of its meetings and a yearly report on the progress achieved by the Union.

Article E

The European Parliament, the Council, the Commission and the Court of Justice shall exercise their powers under the conditions and for the purposes provided for, on the one hand, by the provisions of the Treaties establishing the European Communities and of the subsequent Treaties and Acts modifying and supplementing them and, on the other hand, by the other provisions of this Treaty.

Article F

(1) The Union shall respect the national identities of its Member States, whose systems of government are founded on the principles of democracy.

(2) The Union shall respect fundamental rights, as guaranteed by the European Convention for the Protection of Human Rights and Fundamental Freedoms signed in Rome on 4 November 1950 and as they result from the constitutional traditions common to the Member States, as general principles of Community law.

(3) The Union shall provide itself with the means necessary to attain its objectives and carry through its policies.

TITLE II

PROVISIONS AMENDING THE TREATY ESTABLISHING THE EUROPEAN ECONOMIC COMMUNITY WITH A VIEW TO ESTABLISHING THE EUROPEAN COMMUNITY ...

TITLE III

PROVISIONS AMENDING THE TREATY ESTABLISHING THE EUROPEAN COAL AND STEEL COMMUNITY ...

TITLE IV

PROVISIONS AMENDING THE TREATY ESTABLISHING THE EUROPEAN ATOMIC ENERGY COMMUNITY ...

TITLE V

PROVISIONS ON A COMMON FOREIGN AND SECURITY POLICY

Article J

A common foreign and security policy is hereby established which shall be governed by the following provisions.

Article J1

(1) The Union and its Member States shall define and implement a common foreign and security policy governed by the provisions of this Title and covering all areas of foreign and security policy.

(2) The objectives of the common foreign and security policy shall be:

- to safeguard the common values, fundamental interests and independence of the Union;
- to strengthen the security of the Union and its Member States in all ways;
- to preserve peace and strengthen international security, in accordance with the principles of the United Nations Charter as well as the principles of the Helsinki Final Act and the objectives of the Press Charter;
- to promote international cooperation;
- to promote and consolidate democracy and the rule of law, and respect for human rights and fundamental freedoms.

(3) The Union shall pursue these objectives:

- by establishing systematic cooperation between Member States in the conduct of policy, in accordance with Article J2;
- by gradually implementing, in accordance with Article J3, joint action in the areas in which the Member States have important interests in common.

(4) The Member States shall support the Union's external and security

policy actively and unreservedly in a spirit of loyalty and mutual solidarity. They shall refrain from any action which is contrary to the interests of the Union or likely to impair its effectiveness as a cohesive force in international relations. The Council shall ensure that these principles are complied with.

Article J2

(1) Member States shall inform and consult one another within the Council on any matter of foreign and security policy of general interest in order to ensure that their combined influence is exerted as effectively as possible by means of concerted and convergent action.

(2) Whenever it deems it necessary, the Council shall define a common position.

Member States shall ensure that their national policies conform to the common positions.

(3) Member States shall coordinate their action in international organisations and at international conferences. They shall uphold the common positions in such forums.

In international organisations and at international conferences where not all the Member States participate, those which do take part shall uphold the common positions.

Article J3

The procedure for adopting joint action in matters covered by the foreign and security policy shall be the following:

(1) The Council shall decide, on the basis of general guidelines from the European Council, that the matter should be subject of joint action.

Whenever the Council decides on the principle of joint action, it shall lay down the specific scope, the Union's general and specific objectives in carrying out such action, if necessary its duration, and the means, procedures and conditions for its implementation.

(2) The Council shall, when adopting the joint action and at any stage during its development, define those matters on which decisions are to be taken by a qualified majority.

Where the Council is required to act by a qualified majority pursuant to the preceding subparagraph, the votes of its members shall be weighted in accordance with Article 148(2) of the Treaty establishing the European

Community, and for their adoption, acts of the Council shall require at least 62 votes in favour, cast by at least ten members.

(3) If there is a change in circumstances having a substantial effect on a question subject to joint action, the Council shall review the principles and objectives of that action and take the necessary decisions. As long as the Council has not acted, the joint action shall stand.

(4) Joint actions shall commit the Member States in the positions they adopt and in the conduct of their activity.

(5) Whenever there is any plan to adopt a national position or take national action pursuant to a joint action, information shall be provided in time to allow, if necessary, for prior consultations within the Council. The obligation to provide prior information shall not apply to measures which are merely a national transposition of Council decisions.

(6) In cases of imperative need arising from changes in the situation and failing a Council decision, Member States may take the necessary measures as a matter of urgency having regard to the general objectives of the joint action. The Member State concerned shall inform the Council immediately of any such measures.

(7) Should there be any major difficulties in implementing a joint action, a Member State shall refer them to the Council which shall discuss them and seek appropriate solutions. Such solutions shall not run counter to the objectives of the joint action or impair its effectiveness.

Article J4

(1) The common foreign and security policy shall include all questions related to the security of the Union, including the eventual framing of a common defence policy, which might in time lead to a common defence.

(2) The Union requests the Western European Union (WEU), which is an integral part of the development of the Union, to elaborate and implement decisions and actions of the Union which have defence implications. The Council shall, in agreement with the institutions of the WEU, adopt the necessary practical arrangements.

(3) Issues having defence implications dealt with under this Article shall not be subject to the procedures set out in Article J3.

(4) The policy of the Union in accordance with this Article shall not prejudice the specific character of the security and defence policy of certain Member States and shall respect the obligations of certain Member States under

the North Atlantic Treaty and be compatible with the common security and defence policy established within that framework.

(5) The provisions of this Article shall not prevent the development of closer cooperation between two or more Member States on bilateral level, in the framework of the WEU and the Atlantic Alliance, provided such cooperation does not run counter to or impede that provided for in this Title.

(6) With a view to furthering the objective of this Treaty, and having in view the date of 1998 in the context of Article XII of the Brussels Treaty, the provisions of this Article may be revised as provided for in Article N(2) on the basis of a report to be presented in 1996 by the Council to the European Council, which shall include an evaluation of the progress made and the experience gained until then.

Article J5

(1) The Presidency shall represent the Union in matters coming within the common foreign and security policy.

(2) The Presidency shall be responsible for the implementation of common measures; in that capacity it shall in principle express the position of the Union in international organisations and international conferences.

(3) In the tasks referred to in paragraphs 1 and 2, the Presidency shall be assisted if need be by the previous and next Member States to hold the Presidency. The Commission shall be fully associated in these tasks.

(4) Without prejudice to Article J2(3) and Article J3(4), Member States represented in international organisations or international conferences where not all the Member States participate shall keep the latter informed of any matter of common interest.

Member States which are also members of the United Nations Security Council will concert and keep the other Member States fully informed. Member States which are permanent members of the Security Council will, in the execution of their functions, ensure the defence of the positions and the interests of the Union, without prejudice to their responsibilities under the provisions of the United Nations Charter.

Article J6

The diplomatic and consular missions of the Member States and the Commission Delegations in third countries and international conferences, and their representations to international organisations, shall cooperate in ensuring that the common positions and common measures adopted by the Council are complied with and implemented.

They shall step up cooperation by exchanging information, carrying out joint assessments and contributing to the implementation of the provisions referred to in Article 8c of the Treaty establishing the European Community.

Article J7

The Presidency shall consult the European Parliament on the main aspects and the basic choices of the common foreign and security policy and shall ensure that the views of the European Parliament are duly taken into consideration. The European Parliament shall be kept regularly informed by the Presidency and the Commission of the development of the Union's foreign and security policy.

The European Parliament may ask questions of the Council or make recommendations to it. It shall hold an annual debate on progress in implementing the common foreign and security policy.

Article J8

(1) The European Council shall define the principles of and general guidelines for the common foreign and security policy.

(2) The Council shall take the decisions necessary for defining and implementing the common foreign and security policy on the basis of the general guidelines adopted by the European Council. It shall ensure the unity, consistency and effectiveness of action by the Union.

The Council shall act unanimously, except for procedural questions and in the case referred to in Article J3(2).

(3) Any Member State or the Commission may refer to the Council any question relating to the common foreign and security policy and may submit proposals to the Council.

(4) In cases requiring a rapid decision, the Presidency, of its own motion, or at the request of the Commission or a Member State, shall convene an extraordinary Council meeting within 48 hours or, in an emergency, within a shorter period.

(5) Without prejudice to Article 151 of the Treaty establishing the European Community, a Political Committee consisting of Political Directors shall monitor the international situation in the areas covered by common foreign and security policy and contribute to the definition of policies by delivering

opinions to the Council at the request of the Council or on its own initiative. It shall also monitor the implementation of agreed policies, without prejudice to the responsibility of the Presidency and the Commission.

Article J9

The Commission shall be fully associated with the work carried out in the common foreign and security policy field.

Article J10

On that occasion of any review of the security provisions under Article J4, the Conference which is convened to that effect shall also examine whether any other amendments need to be made to provisions relating to the common foreign and security policy.

Article J11

(1) The provisions referred to in Articles 137, 138, 139 to 142, 146, 147, 150 to 153, 157 to 163 and 217 of the Treaty establishing the European Community shall apply to the provisions relating to the areas referred to in this Title.

(2) Administrative expenditure which the provisions relating to the areas referred to in this Title entail for the institutions shall be charged to the budget of the European Communities.

The Council may also:

- either decide unanimously that operational expenditure to which the implementation of those provisions give rise is to be charged to the budget of the European Communities; in that event, the budgetary procedure laid down in the Treaty establishing the European Community shall be applicable;
- or determine that such expenditure shall be charged to the Member States, where appropriate in accordance with a scale to be decided.

TITLE VI

PROVISIONS ON COOPERATION IN THE FIELDS OF JUSTICE AND HOME AFFAIRS

Article K

Cooperation in the fields of justice and home affairs shall be governed by the following provisions.

Article K1

For the purposes of achieving the objectives of the Union, in particular the free movement of persons, and without prejudice to the powers of the European Community, Member States shall regard the following areas as matters of common interest:

(1) Asylum policy;

(2) Rules governing the crossing by persons of the external borders of the Member States and the exercise of controls thereon;

(3) Immigration policy and policy regarding nationals of third countries;

> (a) conditions of entry and movement by nationals of third countries on the territory of Member States;
>
> (b) conditions of residence by nationals of third countries on the territory of Member States, including family reunion and access to employment;
>
> (c) combating unauthorised immigration, residence and work by nationals of third countries on the territory of Member States;

(4) Combating drug addiction in so far as this is not covered by (7) to (9);

(5) Combating fraud on an international scale in so far as this is not covered by (7) to (9);

(6) Judicial cooperation in civil matters;

(7) Judicial cooperation in criminal matters;

(8) Customs cooperation;

(9) Police cooperation for the purposes of preventing and combating terrorism, unlawful drug trafficking and other serious forms of international crime, including if necessary certain aspects of customs

cooperation, in connection with the organisation of a Union-wide system for exchanging information within a European Police Office (Europol).

Article K2

(1) The matters referred to in Article K1 shall be dealt with in compliance with the European Convention for the Protection of Human Rights and Fundamental Freedoms of 4 November 1950 and the Convention relating to the Status of Refugees of 28 July 1951 and having regard to the protection afforded by Member States to persons persecuted on political grounds.

(2) This Title shall not affect the exercise of the responsibilities incumbent upon Member States with regard to the maintenance of law and order and the safeguarding of internal security.

Article K3

(1) In the areas referred to in Article K1, Member States shall inform and consult one another within the Council with a view to coordinating their action. To that end, they shall establish collaboration between the relevant departments of their administrations.

(2) The Council may:

- on the initiative of any Member State or of the Commission, in the areas referred to in Article K1(1) to (6);
- on the initiative of any Member State, in the areas referred to in Article K1(7) to (9);

   (a) adopt joint positions and promote, using the appropriate form and procedures, any cooperation contributing to the pursuit of the objectives of the Union;

   (b) adopt joint action in so far as the objectives of the Union can be attained better by joint action than by the Member States acting individually on account of the scale or effects of the action envisaged; it may decide that measures implementing joint action are to be adopted by a qualified majority;

   (c) without prejudice to Article 220 of the Treaty establishing the European Community, draw up conventions which it shall recommend to the Member States for adoption in accordance with their respective constitutional requirements.

Unless otherwise provided by such conventions, measures implementing them shall be adopted within the Council by a majority of two-thirds of the High Contracting Parties.

Such conventions may stipulate that the Court of Justice shall have jurisdiction to interpret their provisions and to rule on any disputes regarding their application, in accordance with such arrangements as they may lay down.

Article K4

A Coordinating Committee shall be set up consisting of senior officials. In addition to its coordinating role, it shall be the task of the Committee to:
- give opinions for the attention of the Council, either at the Council's request or on its own initiative;
- contribute, without prejudice to Article 151 of the Treaty establishing the European Community, to the preparation of the Council's discussions in the areas referred to in Article K1 and, in accordance with the conditions laid down in Article 100d of the Treaty establishing the European Community, in the areas referred to in Article 100c of that Treaty.

(2) The Commission shall be fully associated with the work in the areas referred to in this Title.

(3) The Council shall act unanimously, except on matters of procedure and in cases where Article K3 expressly provides for other voting rules.

Where the Council is required to act by a qualified majority, the votes of its members shall be weighted as laid down in Article 148(2) of the Treaty establishing the European Community, and for their adoption, acts of the Council shall require at least 62 votes in favour, cast by at least ten members.

Article K5

Within international organizations and at international conferences in which they take part, Member States shall defined the common positions adopted under the provisions of this Title.

Article K6

The Presidency and the Commission shall regularly inform the European Parliament of discussions in the areas covered by this Title.

The Presidency shall consult the European Parliament on the principal aspects of activities in the areas referred to in this Title and shall ensure that the views of the European Parliament are duly taken into consideration.

The European Parliament may ask questions of the Council or make recommendations to it. Each Year, it shall hold a debate on the progress made in implementation of the areas referred to in this Title.

Article K7

The provisions of this Title shall not prevent the establishment or developing of closer cooperation between two or more Member States in so far as such cooperation does not conflict with, or impede, that provided for in this Title.

Article K8

(1) The provisions referred to in Articles 137, 138, 139 to 142, 146, 147, 150 to 153, 157 to 163 and 217 of the Treaty establishing the European Community shall apply to the provisions relating to the areas referred to in this Title.

(2) Administrative expenditure which the provisions relating to the areas referred to in this Title entail for the institutions shall be charged to the budget of the European Communities.

The Council may also:

- either decide unanimously that operational expenditure to which the implementation of those provisions gives rise is to be charged to the budget of the European Communities; in that event, the budgetary procedure laid down in the Treaty establishing the European Community shall be applicable;
- or determine that such expenditure shall be charged to the Member States, where appropriate in accordance with a scale to be decided.

Article K9

The Council, acting unanimously on the initiative of the Commission or a Member State, may decide to apply Article 100c of the Treaty establishing the European Community to action in areas referred to in Article K1(1) to (6), and at the same time determine the relevant voting conditions relating to it. It shall recommend the Member States to adopt that decision in accordance with their respective constitutional requirements.

TITLE VII
FINAL PROVISIONS

Article L

The provisions of the Treaty establishing the European Community, the Treaty establishing the European Coal and Steel Community and the Treaty establishing the European Atomic Energy Community concerning the powers of the Court of Justice of the European Communities and the exercise of those powers shall apply only to the following provisions of this Treaty:

(a) provisions amending the Treaty establishing the European Economic Community with a view to establishing the European Community, the Treaty establishing the European Coal and Steel Community and the Treaty establishing the European Atomic Energy Community;

(b) the third subparagraph of Article K3(2)(c);

(c) Articles L to S.

Article M

Subject to the provisions amending the Treaty establishing the European Economic Community with a view to establishing the European Community, the Treaty establishing the European Coal and Steel Community and the Treaty establishing the European Atomic Energy Community, and to these final provisions, nothing in this Treaty shall affect the Treaties establishing the European Communities or the subsequent Treaties and Acts modifying or supplementing them.

Article N

(1) The government of any Member State or the Commission may submit to the Council proposals for the amendment of the Treaties on which the Union is founded.

If the Council, after consulting the European Parliament and, where appropriate, the Commission, delivers an opinion in favour of calling a conference of representatives of the governments of the Member States, the conference shall be convened by the President of the Council for the purpose of determining by common accord the amendments to be made to those Treaties. The European Central Bank shall also be consulted in the case of institutional changes in the monetary area.

The amendments shall enter into force after being ratified by all the Member States in accordance with their respective constitutional requirements.

(2) A conference of representatives of the governments of the Member States shall be convened in 1996 to examine those provisions of this Treaty for which revision is provided, in accordance with the objectives set out in Articles A and B.

Article O

Any European State may apply to become a Member of the Union. It shall address its application to the Council, which shall act unanimously after consulting the Commission and after receiving the assent of the European Parliament, which shall act by an absolute majority of its component members.

The conditions of admission and the adjustments to the Treaties on which the Union is founded which such admissions entails shall be the subject of an agreement between the Member States and the applicant State. This agreement shall be submitted for ratification by all the contracting States in accordance with their respective constitutional requirements.

Article P

(1) Articles 2 to 7 and 10 to 19 of the Treaty establishing a Single Council and a Single Commission of the European Communities, signed in Brussels on 8 April 1965, are hereby repealed.

(2) Article 2, Article 3(2) and Title III of the single European Act signed in Luxembourg on 17 December 1986 and in The Hague on 28 February 1986 are hereby repealed.

Article Q

This Treaty is concluded for an unlimited period.

Article R

(1) This Treaty shall be ratified by the High Contracting Parties in accordance with their respective constitutional requirements. The instruments of ratification shall be deposited with the government of the Italian Republic.

(2) This Treaty shall enter into force on 1 January 1993, provided that all the instruments of ratification have been deposited, or, failing that, on the first day of the month following the deposit of the instrument of ratification by the last signatory State to take this step.

Article S

This Treaty, drawn up in a single original in the Danish, Dutch, English, French, German, Greek, Irish, Italian, Portuguese and Spanish languages, the texts in each of these languages being equally authentic, shall be deposited in the archieves of the government of the Italian Republic, which will transmit a certified copy to each of the governments of other signatory States.

DECLARATION ON NATIONALITY OF A MEMBER STATE

The Conference declares that, wherever in the Treaty establishing the European Community reference is made to nationals of the Member States, the question whether an individual possesses the nationality of a Member State shall be settled solely by reference to the national law of the Member State concerned. Member States may declare, for information, who are to be considered their nationals for Community purposes by way of a declaration lodged with the Presidency and may amend any such declaration when necessary ...

DECLARATION ON THE ROLE OF NATIONAL PARLIAMENTS IN THE EUROPEAN UNION

The Conference considers that it is important to encourage greater involvement of national parliaments in the activities of the European Union.

To this end, the exchange of information between national parliaments and the European Parliament should be stepped up. In this context, the governments of the Member States will ensure, inter alia, that national parliaments receive Commission proposals for legislation in good time for information or possible examination.

Similarly, the Conference considers that it is important for contacts between the national parliaments and the European Parliament to be stepped up, in particular through the granting of appropriate reciprocal facilities and regular meetings between members of Parliament interested in the same issues ...

DECLARATION ON THE IMPLEMENTATION OF COMMUNITY LAW

(1) The Conference stresses that it is central to the coherence and unity of the process of European construction that each Member State should fully and accurately transpose into national law the Community Directives addressed to it within the deadlines laid down therein.

Moreover, the Conference, while recognising that it must be for each Member State to determine how the provisions of Community law can best be enforced in the light of its own particular institutions, legal system and other circumstances, but in any event in compliance with Article 189 of the Treaty establishing the European Community, considers it essential for the proper functioning of the Community that the measures taken by the different Member States should result in Community law being applied with the same effectiveness and rigour as in the application of their national law.

(2) The Conference calls on the Commission to ensure, in exercising its powers under Article 155 of this Treaty, that Member States fulfil their obligations. It asks the Commission to publish periodically a full report for the Member States and the European Parliament ...

DECLARATION ON VOTING IN THE FIELD OF THE COMMON FOREIGN AND SECURITY POLICY

The Conference agrees that, with regard to Council decisions requiring unanimity, Member States will, to the extent possible, avoid preventing a unanimous decision where a qualified majority exists in favour of that decision ...

DECLARATIONS ON WESTERN EUROPEAN UNION

The Conference notes the following declarations:

I DECLARATION by Belgium, Germany, Spain, France, Italy, Luxembourg, the Netherlands, Portugal and the United Kingdom of Great Britain and Northern Ireland, which are members of the Western European Union and also members of the European Union on

THE ROLE OF THE WESTERN EUROPEAN UNION AND ITS RELATIONS WITH THE EUROPEAN UNION AND WITH THE ATLANTIC ALLIANCE

Introduction

(1) WEU Member States agree on the need to develop a genuine European security and defence identity and a greater European responsibility on defence matters. This identity will be pursued through a gradual process involving successive phases. WEU will form an integral part of the process of the development of the European Union and will enhance its contribution to solidarity within the Atlantic Alliance. WEU Member States agree to strengthen the role of WEU, in the longer term perspective of a common defence policy within the European Union which might in time lead to a common defence, compatible with that of the Atlantic Alliance.

(2) WEU will be developed as the defence component of the European Union and as a means to strengthen the European pillar of the Atlantic Alliance. To this end, it will formulate common European defence policy and carry forward its concrete implementation through the further development of its own operational role.

WEU Member States take note of Article J4 relating to the common foreign and security policy of the Treaty on European Union which reads as follows ...

A – WEU's relations with European Union

(3) The objective is to build up WEU in stages as the defence component of the European Union. To this end, WEU is prepared, at the request of the European Union, to elaborate and implement decisions and actions of the Union which have defence implications.

To this end, WEU will take the following measures to develop a close working relationship with the Union:

- as appropriate, synchronisation of the dates and venues of meetings and harmonisation of working methods;
- establishment of close cooperation between the Council and Secretariat-General of WEU on one hand, and the Council of the Union and General Secretariat of the Council on the other;
- consideration of the harmonisation of the sequence and duration of the respective Presidencies;
- arranging for appropriate mobilities so as to ensure that the

Commission of the European Communities is regularly informed and, as appropriate, consulted on WEU activities in accordance with the role of the Commission in the common foreign and security policy as defined in the Treaty on European Union;
- encouragement of closer cooperation between the Parliamentary Assembly of WEU and the European Parliament.

The WEU Council shall, in agreement with the competent bodies of the European Union, adopt the necessary practical arrangements.

B – WEU's relations with the Atlantic Alliance

(4) The objective is to develop WEU as a means to strengthen the European pillar of the Atlantic Alliance. Accordingly WEU is prepared to develop further the close working links between WEU and the Alliance and to strengthen the role, responsibilities and contributions of WEU Member States in the Alliance. This will be undertaken on the basis of the necessary transparency and complementarity between the emerging European security and defence identity and the Alliance. WEU will act in conformity with the positions adopted in the Atlantic Alliance.

- WEU Member States will intensify their coordination on Alliance issues which represent an important common interest with the aim of introducing joint positions agreed in WEU into the process of consultation in the Alliance which will remain the essential forum for consultation among its members and the venue for agreement on policies bearing on the security and defence commitments of Allies under the North Atlantic Treaty.
- Where necessary, dates and venues of meetings will be synchronised and working methods harmonised.
- Close cooperation will be established between the Secretariats-General of WEU and NATO.

C – Operational role of WEU

(5) WEU's operational role will be strengthened by examining and defining appropriate missions, structures and means, covering in particular:

- WEU planning cell;
- closer military cooperation complementary to the Alliance in particular in the fields of logistics, transport, training and strategic surveillance;
- meetings of WEU Chiefs of Defence Staff;
- military units answerable to WEU.

Other proposals will be examined further, including:
- enhanced cooperation in the field of armaments with the aim of creating a European armaments agency;
- development of the WEU Institute into a European Security and Defence Academy.

Arrangements aimed at giving WEU a stronger operational role will be fully compatible with the military dispositions necessary to ensure the collective defence of all Allies.

D – Other measures

(6) As a consequence of the measures set out above, and in order to facilitate the strengthening of WEU's role, the seat of the WEU Council and Secretariat will be transferred to Brussels.

(7) Representation on the WEU Council must be such that the Council is able to exercise its functions continuously in accordance with Article VII of the modified Brussels Treaty. Member States may draw on a double-hatting formula, to be worked out, consisting of their representatives to the Alliance and to the European Union.

(8) WEU notes that, in accordance with the provisions of Article J4(6) concerning the common foreign and security policy of the Treaty on European Union, the Union will decide to review the provisions of this Article with a view to furthering the objective to be set by it in accordance with the procedure defined. The WEU will re-examine the present provisions in 1996. This re-examination will take account of the progress and experience acquired and will extend to relations between WEU and the Atlantic Alliance.

II DECLARATION by Belgium, Germany, Spain, France, Italy, Luxembourg, the Netherlands, Portugal and the United Kingdom of Great Britain and Northern Ireland which are members of the Western European Union:

The Member States of WEU welcome the development of the European security and defence identity. They are determined, taking into account the role of WEU as the defence component of the European Union and as the means to strengthen the European pillar of the Atlantic Alliance, to put the relationship between WEU and the other European States on a new basis for the sake of stability and security in Europe. In this spirit, they propose the following:

States which are members of the European Union are invited to accede to WEU on conditions to be agreed in accordance with Article XI of the modified Brussels Treaty, or to become observers if they so wish. Simultaneously, other European Member States of NATO are invited to become associate members of WEU in a way which will give them the possibility of participating fully in the activities of WEU.

The Member States of WEU assume that treaties and agreements corresponding with the above proposals will be concluded before 31 December 1992.

DECLARATION ON ASYLUM

(1) The Conference agrees that, in the context of the proceedings provided for in Articles K1 and K3 of the provisions on cooperation in the fields of justice and home affairs, the Council will consider as a matter of priority questions concerning Member States' asylum policies, with the aim of adopting, by the beginning of 1993, common action to harmonise aspects of them, in the light of the work programme and timetable contained in the report on asylum drawn up at the request of the European Council meeting in Luxembourg on 28 and 29 June 1991.

(2) In this connection, the Council will also consider, by the end of 1993, on the basis of a report, the possibility of applying Article K9 to such matters.

DECLARATION ON POLICE COOPERATION

(1) The Conference confirms the agreement of the Member States on the objectives underlying the German delegation's proposals at the European Council meeting in Luxembourg on 28 and 29 June 1991.

(2) For the present, the Member States agree to examine as a matter of priority the drafts submitted to them, on the basis of the work programme and timetable agreed upon in the report drawn up at the request of the Luxembourg European Council, and they are willing to envisage the adoption of practical measures in areas such as those suggested by the German delegation, relating to the following functions in the exchange of information and experience:

- support for national criminal investigation and security authorities, in particular in the coordination of investigations and search operations;
- creation of databases;
- central analysis and assessment of information in order to take stock of the situation and identify investigative approaches;

- collection and analysis of national prevention programmes for forwarding to Member States and for drawing up Europe-wide prevention strategies;
- measures relating to further training, research, forensic matters and criminal records departments.

(3) Member States agree to consider on the basis of a report, during 1994 at the latest, whether the scope of such cooperation should be extended.

As amended by Council Decision 95/1/EC, Euratom, ECSC, art 8.

AGREEMENT ON THE EUROPEAN ECONOMIC AREA
(Oporto, 2 May 1992)

Preamble

The European Economic Community, the European Coal and Steel Community, the Kingdom of Belgium, the Kingdom of Denmark, the Federal Republic of Germany, the Hellanic Republic, the Kingdom of Spain, the French Republic, Ireland, the Italian Republic, the Grand Duchy of Luxembourg, the Kingdom of the Netherlands, the Portuguese Republic, the United Kingdom of Great Britain and Northern Ireland,

and

The Republic of Austria, the Republic of Finland, the Republic of Iceland, the Principality of Liechtenstein, the Kingdom of Norway, the Kingdom of Sweden

hereinafter referred to as the CONTRACTING PARTIES;

CONVINCED of the contribution that a European Economic Area will bring to the construction of a Europe based on peace, democracy and human rights;

REAFFIRMING the high priority attached to the privileged relationship between the European Community, its Member States and the EFTA States, which is based on proximity, long-standing common values and European identity;

DETERMINED to contribute, on the basis of market economy, to world-wide trade liberalisation and cooperation, in particular in accordance with the provisions of the General Agreement on Tariffs and Trade and the Convention on the Organisation for Economic Cooperation and Development;

CONSIDERING the objective of establishing a dynamic and homogeneous European Economic Area, based on common rules and equal conditions of competition and providing for the adequate means of enforcement including at the judicial level, and achieved on the basis of equality and reciprocity and of an overall balance of benefits, rights and obligations for the Contracting Parties;

DETERMINED to provide for the fullest possible realisation of the free movement of goods, persons, services and capital within the whole European Economic Area, as well as for strengthened and broadened cooperation in flanking and horizontal policies;

AIMING to promote a harmonious development of the European Economic Area and convinced of the need to contribute through the application of this Agreement to the reduction of economic and social regional disparities;

DESIROUS of contributing to the strengthening of the cooperation between the members of the European Parliament and of the Parliaments of the EFTA States, as well as between the social partners in the European Community and in the EFTA States;

CONVINCED of the important role that individuals will play in the European Economic Area through the exercise of the rights conferred on them by this Agreement and through the judicial defence of these rights;

DETERMINED to preserve, protect and improve the quality of the environment and to ensure a prudent and rational utilisation of natural resources on the basis, in particular, of the principle of sustainable development, as well as the principle that precautionary and preventive action should be taken;

DETERMINED to take, in the further development of rules, a high level of protection concerning health, safety and the environment as a basis;

NOTING the importance of the development of the social dimension, including equal treatment of men and women, in the European Economic Area and wishing to ensure economic and social progress and to promote conditions for full employment, an improved standard of living and improved working conditions within the European Economic Area;

DETERMINED to promote the interests of consumers and to strengthen their position in the market place, aiming at a high level of consumer protection;

ATTACHED to the common objectives of strengthening the scientific and technological basis of European industry and of encouraging it to become more competitive at the international level;

CONSIDERING that the conclusion of this Agreement shall not prejudge in any way the possibility of any EFTA State to accede to the European Communities;

WHEREAS, in full deference to the independence of the courts, the objective of the Contracting Parties is to arrive at, and maintain, a uniform interpretation and application of this Agreement and those provisions of Community legislation which are substantially reproduced in this Agreement and to arrive at an equal treatment of individuals and economic operators as regards the four freedoms and the conditions of competition;

WHEREAS this Agreement does not restrict the decision-making autonomy or the treaty-making power of the Contracting Parties, subject to the provisions of this Agreement and the limitations set by public international law;

HAVE DECIDED to conclude the following Agreement:

PART I

OBJECTIVES AND PRINCIPLES

Article 1

(1) The aim of this Agreement of association is to promote a continuous and balanced strengthening of trade and economic relations between the Contracting Parties with equal conditions of competition, and the respect of the same rules, with a view to creating a homogeneous European Economic Area, hereinafter referred to as the EEA.

(2) In order to attain the objectives set out in paragraph 1, the association shall entail, in accordance with the provisions of this Agreement:

(a) the free movement of goods;

(b) the free movement of persons;

(c) the free movement of services;

(d) the free movement of capital;

(e) the setting up of a system ensuring that competition is not distorted and that the rules thereon are equally respected; as well as

(f) closer cooperation in other fields, such as research and development, the environment, education and social policy.

Article 2

For the purposes of this Agreement:

(a) the term 'Agreement' means the main Agreement, its Protocols and Annexes as well as the acts referred to therein;

(b) the term 'EFTA States' means the Republic of Austria, the Republic of Finland, the Republic of Iceland, the Kingdom of Norway, the Kingdom of Sweden and, under the conditions laid down in Article 1(2) of the Protocol adjusting the Agreement on the European Economic Area, the Principality of Liechtenstein;

(c) the term 'Contracting Parties' means, concerning the Community and the EC Member States, the Community and the EC Member States, or the Community, or the EC Member States. The meaning to be attributed to this expression in each case is to be deduced from the relevant provisions of this Agreement and from the respective competences of the Community and the EC Member States as they follow from the Treaty establishing the European Economic Community and the Treaty establishing the European Coal and Steel Community.

Article 3

The Contracting Parties shall take all appropriate measures, whether general or particular, to ensure fulfilment of the obligations arising out of this Agreement.

They shall abstain from any measure which could jeopardise the attainment of the objectives of this Agreement.

Moreover, they shall facilitate cooperation within the framework of this Agreement.

Article 4

Within the scope of application of this Agreement, and without prejudice to any special provisions contained therein, any discrimination on grounds of nationality shall be prohibited.

Article 5

A Contracting Party may at any time raise a matter of concern at the level of the EEA Joint Committee or the EEA Council according to the modalities laid down in Articles 92(2) and 89(2), respectively.

Article 6

Without prejudice to future developments of case-law, the provisions of this Agreement, in so far as they are identical in substance to corresponding rules of the Treaty establishing the European Economic Community and the

Treaty establishing the European Coal and Steel Community and to acts adopted in application of these two Treaties, shall, in their implementation and application, be interpreted in conformity with the relevant rulings of the Court of Justice of the European Communities given prior to the date of signature of this Agreement.

Article 7

Acts referred to or contained in the Annexes to this Agreement or in decisions of the EEA Joint Committee shall be binding upon the Contracting Parties and be, or be made, part of their internal legal order as follows:

(a) an act corresponding to an EEC regulation shall as such be made part of the internal legal order of the Contracting Parties;

(b) an act corresponding to an EEC directive shall leave to the authorities of the Contracting Parties the choice of form and method of implementation.

PART II

FREE MOVEMENT OF GOODS

CHAPTER 1

BASIC PRINCIPLES

Article 8

(1) Free movement of goods between the Contracting Parties shall be established in conformity with the provisions of this Agreement.

(2) Unless otherwise specified, Articles 10 to 15, 19, 20 and 25 to 27 shall apply only to products originating in the Contracting Parties.

(3) Unless otherwise specified, the provisions of this Agreement shall apply only to:

(a) products falling within Chapters 25 to 97 of the Harmonised Commodity Description and Coding System, excluding the products listed in Protocol 2;

(b) products specified in Protocol 3, subject to the specific arrangements set out in that Protocol.

Article 9

(1) The rules of origin are set out in Protocol 4. They are without prejudice to any international obligations which have been, or may be, subscribed to by the Contracting Parties under the General Agreement on Tariffs and Trade.

(2) With a view to developing the results achieved in this Agreement, the Contracting Parties will continue their efforts in order further to improve and simplify all aspects of rules of origin and to increase cooperation in customs matters.

(3) A first review will take place before the end of 1993. Subsequent reviews will take place at two-yearly intervals. On the basis of these reviews, the Contracting Parties undertake to decide on the appropriate measures to be included in this Agreement.

Article 10

Customs duties on imports and exports, and any charges having equivalent effect, shall be prohibited between the Contracting Parties. Without prejudice to the arrangements set out in Protocol 5, this shall also apply to customs duties of a fiscal nature.

Article 11

Quantitative restrictions on imports and all measures having equivalent effect shall be prohibited between the Contracting Parties.

Article 12

Quantitative restrictions on exports and all measures having equivalent effect shall be prohibited between the Contracting Parties.

Article 13

The provisions of Articles 11 and 12 shall not preclude prohibitions or restrictions on imports, exports or goods in transit justified on grounds of public morality, public policy or public security; the protection of health and life of humans, animals or plants; the protection of national treasures possessing artistic, historic or archaeological value; or the protection of industrial and commercial property. Such prohibitions or restrictions shall not, however, constitute a means of arbitrary discrimination or a disguised restriction on trade between the Contracting Parties.

Article 14

No Contracting Party shall impose, directly or indirectly, on the products of other Contracting Parties any internal taxation of any kind in excess of that imposed directly or indirectly on similar domestic products.

Furthermore, no Contracting Party shall impose on the products of other Contracting Parties any internal taxation of such a nature as to afford indirect protection to other products.

Article 15

Where products are exported to the territory of any Contracting Party, any repayment of internal taxation shall not exceed the internal taxation imposed on them whether directly or indirectly.

Article 16

(1) The Contracting Parties shall ensure that any State monopoly of a commercial character be adjusted so that no discrimination regarding the conditions under which goods are procured and marketed will exist between nationals of EC Member States and EFTA States.

(2) The provisions of this Article shall apply to any body through which the competent authorities of the Contracting Parties, in law or in fact, either directly or indirectly supervise, determine or appreciably influence imports or exports between Contracting Parties. These provisions shall likewise apply to monopolies delegated by the State to others.

CHAPTER 2

AGRICULTURAL AND FISHERY PRODUCTS

Article 17

Annex I contains specific provisions and arrangements concerning veterinary and phytosanitary matters.

Article 18

Without prejudice to the specific arrangements governing trade in agricultural products, the Contracting Parties shall ensure that the arrangements provided for in Articles 17 and 23(a) and (b), as they apply to products other than those covered by Article 8(3), are not compromised by other technical barriers to trade. Article 13 shall apply.

Article 19

(1) The Contracting Parties shall examine any difficulties that might arise in their trade in agricultural products and shall endeavour to seek appropriate solutions.

(2) The Contracting Parties undertake to continue their efforts with a view to achieving progressive liberalisation of agricultural trade.

(3) To this end, the Contracting Parties will carry out, before the end of 1993 and subsequently at two-yearly intervals, reviews of the conditions of trade in agricultural products.

(4) In the light of the results of these reviews, within the framework of their respective agricultural policies and taking into account the results of the Uruguay Round, the Contracting Parties will decide, within the framework of this Agreement, on a preferential, bilateral or multilateral, reciprocal and mutually beneficial basis, on further reductions of any type of barriers to trade in the agricultural sector, including those resulting from State monopolies of a commercial character in the agricultural field.

Article 20

Provisions and arrangements that apply to fish and other marine products are set out in Protocol 9.

CHAPTER 3

COOPERATION IN CUSTOMS-RELATED MATTERS AND TRADE FACILITATION

Article 21

(1) In order to facilitate trade between them, the Contracting Parties shall simplify border controls and formalities. Arrangements for this purpose are set out in Protocol 10.

(2) The Contracting Parties shall assist each other in customs matters in order to ensure that customs legislation is correctly applied. Arrangements for this purpose are set out in Protocol 11.

(3) The Contracting Parties shall strengthen and broaden cooperation with

the aim of simplifying the procedures for trade in goods, in particular in the context of Community programmes, projects and actions aimed at trade facilitation, in accordance with the rules set out in Part VI.

(4) Notwithstanding Article 8(3), this Article shall apply to all products.

Article 22

A Contracting Party which is considering the reduction of the effective level of its duties or charges having equivalent effect applicable to third countries benefiting from most-favoured-nation treatment, or which is considering the suspension of their application, shall, as far as may be practicable, notify the EEA Joint Committee not later than 30 days before such reduction or suspension comes into effect. It shall take note of any representations by other Contracting Parties regarding any distortions which might result therefrom.

CHAPTER 4

OTHER RULES RELATING TO THE FREE MOVEMENT OF GOODS

Article 23

Specific provisions and arrangements are laid down in:

(a) Protocol 12 and Annex II in relation to technical regulations, standards, testing and certification;

(b) Protocol 47 in relation to the abolition of technical barriers to trade in wine;

(c) Annex III in relation to product liability.

They shall apply to all products unless otherwise specified.

Article 24

Annex IV contains specific provisions and arrangements concerning energy.

Article 25

Where compliance with the provisions of Articles 10 and 12 leads to:

(a) re-export towards a third country against which the exporting Contracting Party maintains, for the product concerned, quantitative export restrictions, export duties or measures or charges having equivalent effect; or

(b) a serious shortage, or threat thereof, of a product essential to the exporting Contracting Party;

and where the situations referred to above give rise, or are likely to give rise, to major difficulties for the exporting Contracting Party, that Contracting Party may take appropriate measures in accordance with the procedures set out in Article 113.

Article 26

Anti-dumping measures, countervailing duties and measures against illicit commercial practices attributable to third countries shall not be applied in relations between the Contracting Parties, unless otherwise specified in this Agreement.

CHAPTER 5

COAL AND STEEL PRODUCTS

Article 27

Provisions and arrangements concerning coal and steel products are set out in Protocols 14 and 25.

PART III

FREE MOVEMENT OF PERSONS, SERVICES AND CAPITAL

CHAPTER 1

WORKERS AND SELF-EMPLOYED PERSONS

Article 28

(1) Freedom of movement for workers shall be secured among EC Member States and EFTA States.

(2) Such freedom of movement shall entail the abolition of any discrimination based on nationality between workers of EC Member States and EFTA States as regards employment, remuneration and other conditions of work and employment.

(3) It shall entail the right, subject to limitations justified on grounds of public policy, public security or public health:

(a) to accept offers of employment actually made;

(b) to move freely within the territory of EC Member States and EFTA States for this purpose;

(c) to stay in the territory of an EC Member State or an EFTA State for the purpose of employment in accordance with the provisions governing the employment of nationals of that State laid down by law, regulation or administrative action;

(d) to remain in the territory of an EC Member State or an EFTA State after having been employed there.

(4) The provisions of this Article shall not apply to employment in the public service.

(5) Annex V contains specific provisions on the free movement of workers.

Article 29

In order to provide freedom of movement for workers and self-employed persons, the Contracting Parties shall, in the field of social security, secure, as provided for in Annex VI, for workers and self-employed persons and their dependants, in particular:

(a) aggregation, for the purpose of acquiring and retaining the right to benefit and of calculating the amount of benefit, of all periods taken into account under the laws of the several countries;

(b) payment of benefits to persons resident in the territories of Contracting Parties.

Article 30

In order to make it easier for persons to take up and pursue activities as workers and self-employed persons, the Contracting Parties shall take the necessary measures, as contained in Annex VII, concerning the mutual recognition of diplomas, certificates and other evidence of formal qualifications, and the coordination of the provisions laid down by law, regulation or administrative action in the Contracting Parties concerning the taking up and pursuit of activities by workers and self-employed persons.

CHAPTER 2

RIGHT OF ESTABLISHMENT

Article 31

(1) Within the framework of the provisions of this Agreement, there shall be no restrictions on the freedom of establishment of nationals of an EC Member State or an EFTA State in the territory of any other of these States. This shall also apply to the setting up of agencies, branches or subsidiaries by nationals of any EC Member State or EFTA State established in the territory of any of these States.

Freedom of establishment shall include the right to take up and pursue activities as self-employed persons and to set up and manage undertakings, in particular companies or firms within the meaning of Article 34, second paragraph, under the conditions laid down for its own nationals by the law of the country where such establishment is effected, subject to the provisions of Chapter 4.

(2) Annexes VIII to XI contain specific provisions on the right of establishment.

Article 32

The provisions of this Chapter shall not apply, so far as any given Contracting Party is concerned, to activities which in that Contracting Party are connected, even occasionally, with the exercise of official authority.

Article 33

The provisions of this Chapter and measures taken in pursuance thereof shall not prejudice the applicability of provisions laid down by law, regulation or administrative action providing for special treatment for foreign nationals on grounds of public policy, public security or public health.

Article 34

Companies or firms formed in accordance with the law of an EC Member State or an EFTA State and having their registered office, central administration or principal place of business within the territory of the Contracting Parties shall, for the purposes of this Chapter, be treated in the same way as natural persons who are nationals of EC Member States or EFTA States.

'Companies or firms' means companies or firms constituted under civil or commercial law, including cooperative societies, and other legal persons governed by public or private law, save for those which are non-profit-making.

Article 35

The provisions of Article 30 shall apply to the matters covered by this Chapter.

CHAPTER 3

SERVICES

Article 36

(1) Within the framework of the provisions of this Agreement, there shall be no restrictions on freedom to provide services within the territory of the Contracting Parties in respect of nationals of EC Member States and EFTA States who are established in an EC Member State or an EFTA State other than that of the person for whom the services are intended.

(2) Annexes IX to XI contain specific provisions on the freedom to provide services.

Article 37

Services shall be considered to be 'services' within the meaning of this Agreement where they are normally provided for remuneration, in so far as they are not governed by the provisions relating to freedom of movement for goods, capital and persons.

'Services' shall in particular include:

(a) activities of an industrial character;

(b) activities of a commercial character;

(c) activities of craftsmen;

(d) activities of the professions.

Without prejudice to the provisions of Chapter 2, the person providing a service may, in order to do so, temporarily pursue his activity in the State where the service is provided, under the same conditions as are imposed by that State on its own nationals.

Article 38

Freedom to provide services in the field of transport shall be governed by the provisions of Chapter 6.

Article 39

The provisions of Articles 30 and 32 to 34 shall apply to the matters covered by this Chapter.

CHAPTER 4

CAPITAL

Article 40

Within the framework of the provisions of this Agreement, there shall be no restrictions between the Contracting Parties on the movement of capital belonging to persons resident in EC Member States or EFTA States and no discrimination based on the nationality or on the place of residence of the parties or on the place where such capital is invested. Annex XII contains the provisions necessary to implement this Article.

Article 41

Current payments connected with the movement of goods, persons, services or capital between Contracting Parties within the framework of the provisions of this Agreement shall be free of all restrictions.

Article 42

(1) Where domestic rules governing the capital market and the credit system are applied to the movements of capital liberalised in accordance with the provisions of this Agreement, this shall be done in a non-discriminatory manner.

(2) Loans for the direct or indirect financing of an EC Member State or an EFTA State or its regional or local authorities shall not be issued or placed in other EC Member States or EFTA States unless the States concerned have reached agreement thereon.

Article 43

(1) Where differences between the exchange rules of EC Member States and EFTA States could lead persons resident in one of these States to use the freer transfer facilities within the territory of the Contracting Parties which are provided for in Article 40 in order to evade the rules of one of these States concerning the movement of capital to or from third countries, the Contracting Party concerned may take appropriate measures to overcome these difficulties.

(2) If movements of capital lead to disturbances in the functioning of the capital market in any EC Member State or EFTA State, the Contracting Party concerned may take protective measures in the field of capital movements.

(3) If the competent authorities of a Contracting Party make an alteration in the rate of exchange which seriously distorts conditions of competition, the other Contracting Parties may take, for a strictly limited period, the necessary measures in order to counter the consequences of such alteration.

(4) Where an EC Member State or an EFTA State is in difficulties, or is seriously threatened with difficulties, as regards its balance of payments either as a result of an overall disequilibrium in its balance of payments, or as a result of the type of currency at its disposal, and where such difficulties are liable in particular to jeopardise the functioning of this Agreement, the Contracting Party concerned may take protective measures.

Article 44

The Community, on the one hand, and the EFTA States, on the other, shall apply their internal procedures, as provided for in Protocol 18, to implement the provisions of Article 43.

Article 45

(1) Decisions, opinions and recommendations related to the measures laid down in Article 43 shall be notified to the EEA Joint Committee.

(2) All measures shall be the subject of prior consultations and exchange of information within the EEA Joint Committee.

(3) In the situation referred to in Article 43(2), the Contracting Party concerned may, however, on the grounds of secrecy and urgency take the measures, where this proves necessary, without prior consultations and exchange of information.

(4) In the situation referred to in Article 43(4), where a sudden crisis in the balance of payments occurs and the procedures set out in paragraph 2 cannot be followed, the Contracting Party concerned may, as a precaution, take the necessary protective measures. Such measures must cause the least possible disturbance in the functioning of this Agreement and must not be wider in scope than is strictly necessary to remedy the sudden difficulties which have arisen.

(5) When measures are taken in accordance with paragraphs 3 and 4, notice thereof shall be given at the latest by the date of their entry into force, and the exchange of information and consultations as well as the notifications referred to in paragraph 1 shall take place as soon as possible thereafter.

CHAPTER 5

ECONOMIC AND MONETARY POLICY COOPERATION

Article 46

The Contracting Parties shall exchange views and information concerning the implementation of this Agreement and the impact of the integration on economic activities and on the conduct of economic and monetary policies. Furthermore, they may discuss macroeconomic situations, policies and prospects. This exchange of views and information shall take place on a non-binding basis.

CHAPTER 6

TRANSPORT

Article 47

(1) Articles 48 to 52 shall apply to transport by rail, road and inland waterway.

(2) Annex XIII contains specific provisions on all modes of transport.

Article 48

(1) The provisions of an EC Member State or an EFTA State, relative to transport by rail, road and inland waterway and not covered by Annex XIII, shall not be made less favourable in their direct or indirect effect on carriers of other States as compared with carriers who are nationals of that State.

(2) Any Contracting Party deviating from the principle laid down in

paragraph 1 shall notify the EEA Joint Committee thereof. The other Contracting Parties which do not accept the deviation may take corresponding counter measures.

Article 49

Aid shall be compatible with this Agreement if it meets the needs of coordination of transport or if it represents reimbursement for the discharge of certain obligations inherent in the concept of a public service.

Article 50

(1) In the case of transport within the territory of the Contracting Parties, there shall be no discrimination which takes the form of carriers charging different rates and imposing different conditions for the carriage of the same goods over the same transport links on grounds of the country of origin or of destination of the goods in question.

(2) The competent authority according to Part VII shall, acting on its own initiative or on application by an EC Member State or an EFTA State, investigate any cases of discrimination falling within this Article and take the necessary decisions within the framework of its internal rules.

Article 51

(1) The imposition, in respect of transport operations carried out within the territory of the Contracting Parties, of rates and conditions involving any element of support or protection in the interest of one or more particular undertakings or industries, shall be prohibited unless authorised by the competent authority referred to in Article 50(2).

(2) The competent authority shall, acting on its own initiative or on application by an EC Member State or an EFTA State, examine the rates and conditions referred to in paragraph 1, taking account in particular of the requirements of an appropriate regional economic policy, the needs of underdeveloped areas and the problems of areas seriously affected by political circumstances, on the one hand, and of the effects of such rates and conditions on competition between the different modes of transport, on the other.

The competent authority shall take the necessary decisions within the framework of its internal rules.

(3) The prohibition provided for in paragraph 1 shall not apply to tariffs fixed to meet competition.

Article 52

Charges or dues in respect of the crossing of frontiers which are charged by a carrier in addition to transport rates shall not exceed a reasonable level after taking the costs actually incurred thereby into account. The Contracting Parties shall endeavour to reduce these costs progressively.

PART IV

COMPETITION AND OTHER COMMON RULES

CHAPTER 1

RULES APPLICABLE TO UNDERTAKINGS

Article 53

(1) The following shall be prohibited as incompatible with the functioning of the Agreement: all agreements between undertakings, decisions by associations of undertakings and concerted practices which may affect trade between Contracting Parties and which have as their object or effect the prevention, restriction or distortion of competition within the territory covered by this Agreement, and in particular those which:

(a) directly or indirectly fix purchase or selling prices or any other trading conditions;

(b) limit or control production, markets, technical development, or investment;

(c) share markets or sources of supply;

(d) apply dissimilar conditions to equivalent transactions with other trading parties, thereby placing them at a competitive disadvantage;

(e) make the conclusion of contracts subject to acceptance by the other parties of supplementary obligations which, by their nature or according to commercial usage, have no connection with the subject of such contracts.

(2) Any agreements or decisions prohibited pursuant to this Article shall be automatically void.

(3) The provisions of paragraph 1 may, however, be declared inapplicable in the case of:

— any agreement or category of agreements between undertakings;

— any decision or category of decisions by associations of undertakings;

— any concerted practice or category of concerted practices;

which contributes to improving the production or distribution of goods or to promoting technical or economic progress, while allowing consumers a fair share of the resulting benefit, and which does not:

(a) impose on the undertakings concerned restrictions which are not indispensable to the attainment of these objectives;

(b) afford such undertakings the possibility of eliminating competition in respect of a substantial part of the products in question.

Article 54

Any abuse by one or more undertakings of a dominant position within the territory covered by this Agreement or in a substantial part of it shall be prohibited as incompatible with the functioning of this Agreement in so far as it may affect trade between Contracting Parties.

Such abuse may, in particular, consist in:

(a) directly or indirectly imposing unfair purchase or selling prices or other unfair trading conditions;

(b) limiting production, markets or technical development to the prejudice of consumers;

(c) applying dissimilar conditions to equivalent transactions with other trading parties, thereby placing them at a competitive disadvantage;

(d) making the conclusion of contracts subject to acceptance by the other parties of supplementary obligations which, by their nature or according to commercial usage, have no connection with the subject of such contracts.

Article 55

(1) Without prejudice to the provisions giving effect to Articles 53 and 54 as contained in Protocol 21 and Annex XIV of this Agreement, the EC Commission and the EFTA Surveillance Authority provided for in Article 108(1) shall ensure the application of the principles laid down in Articles 53 and 54.

The competent surveillance authority, as provided for in Article 56, shall investigate cases of suspected infringement of these principles, on its own initiative, or on application by a State within the respective territory or by the other surveillance authority. The competent surveillance authority shall carry out these investigations in cooperation with the competent national authorities in the respective territory and in cooperation with the other surveillance authority, which shall give it its assistance in accordance with its internal rules.

If it finds that there has been an infringement, it shall propose appropriate measures to bring it to an end.

(2) If the infringement is not brought to an end, the competent surveillance authority shall record such infringement of the principles in a reasoned decision.

The competent surveillance authority may publish its decision and authorise States within the respective territory to take the measures, the conditions and details of which it shall determine, needed to remedy the situation. It may also request the other surveillance authority to authorise States within the respective territory to take such measures.

Article 56

(1) Individual cases falling under Article 53 shall be decided upon by the surveillance authorities in accordance with the following provisions:

> (a) individual cases where only trade between EFTA States is affected shall be decided upon by the EFTA Surveillance Authority;
>
> (b) without prejudice to subparagraph (c), the EFTA Surveillance Authority decides, as provided for in the provisions set out in Article 58, Protocol 21 and the rules adopted for its implementation, Protocol 23 and Annex XIV, on cases where the turnover of the undertakings concerned in the territory of the EFTA States equals 33% or more of their turnover in the territory covered by this Agreement;
>
> (c) the EC Commission decides on the other cases as well as on cases under (b) where trade between EC Member States is affected, taking into account the provisions set out in Article 58, Protocol 21, Protocol 23 and Annex XIV.

(2) Individual cases falling under Article 54 shall be decided upon by the surveillance authority in the territory of which a dominant position is found to exist. The rules set out in paragraph 1(b) and (c) shall apply only if dominance exists within the territories of both surveillance authorities.

(3) Individual cases falling under subparagraph (c) of paragraph 1, whose effects on trade between EC Member States or on competition within the Community are not appreciable, shall be decided upon by the EFTA Surveillance Authority.

(4) The terms 'undertaking' and 'turnover' are, for the purposes of this Article, defined in Protocol 22.

Article 57

(1) Concentrations the control of which is provided for in paragraph 2 and which create or strengthen a dominant position as a result of which effective competition would be significantly impeded within the territory covered by this Agreement or a substantial part of it, shall be declared incompatible with this Agreement.

(2) The control of concentrations falling under paragraph 1 shall be carried out by:

(a) the EC Commission in cases falling under Regulation (EEC) No 4064/89 in accordance with that Regulation and in accordance with Protocols 21 and 24 and Annex XIV to this Agreement. The EC Commission shall, subject to the review of the EC Court of Justice, have sole competence to take decisions on these cases;

(b) the EFTA Surveillance Authority in cases not falling under subparagraph (a) where the relevant thresholds set out in Annex XIV are fulfilled in the territory of the EFTA States in accordance with Protocols 21 and 24 and Annex XIV. This is without prejudice to the competence of EC Member States.

Article 58

With a view to developing and maintaining a uniform surveillance throughout the European Economic Area in the field of competition and to promoting a homogeneous implementation, application and interpretation of the provisions of this Agreement to this end, the competent authorities shall cooperate in accordance with the provisions set out in Protocols 23 and 24.

Article 59

(1) In the case of public undertakings and undertakings to which EC Member States or EFTA States grant special or exclusive rights, the Contracting Parties shall ensure that there is neither enacted nor maintained in force any measure contrary to the rules contained in this Agreement, in particular to those rules provided for in Articles 4 and 53 to 63.

(2) Undertakings entrusted with the operation of services of general economic interest or having the character of a revenue-producing monopoly shall be subject to the rules contained in this Agreement, in particular to the rules on competition, in so far as the application of such rules does not obstruct the performance, in law or in fact, of the particular tasks assigned

to them. The development of trade must not be affected to such an extent as would be contrary to the interests of the Contracting Parties.

(3) The EC Commission as well as the EFTA Surveillance Authority shall ensure within their respective competence the application of the provisions of this Article and shall, where necessary, address appropriate measures to the States falling within their respective territory.

Article 60

Annex XIV contains specific provisions giving effect to the principles set out in Articles 53, 54, 57 and 59.

CHAPTER 2

STATE AID

Article 61

(1) Save as otherwise provided in this Agreement, any aid granted by EC Member States, EFTA States or through State resources in any form whatsoever which distorts or threatens to distort competition by favouring certain undertakings or the production of certain goods shall, in so far as it affects trade between Contracting Parties, be incompatible with the functioning of this Agreement.

(2) The following shall be compatible with the functioning of this Agreement:

(a) aid having a social character, granted to individual consumers, provided that such aid is granted without discrimination related to the origin of the products concerned;

(b) aid to make good the damage caused by natural disasters or exceptional occurrences;

(c) aid granted to the economy of certain areas of the Federal Republic of Germany affected by the division of Germany, in so far as such aid is required in order to compensate for the economic disadvantages caused by that division.

(3) The following may be considered to be compatible with the functioning of this Agreement:

(a) aid to promote the economic development of areas where the standard of living is abnormally low or where there is serious under employment;

(b) aid to promote the execution of an important project of common European interest or to remedy a serious disturbance in the economy of an EC Member State or an EFTA State;

(c) aid to facilitate the development of certain economic activities or of certain economic areas, where such aid does not adversely affect trading conditions to an extent contrary to the common interest;

(d) such other categories of aid as may be specified by the EEA Joint Committee in accordance with Part VII.

Article 62

(1) All existing systems of State aid in the territory of the Contracting Parties, as well as any plans to grant or alter State aid, shall be subject to constant review as to their compatibility with Article 61. This review shall be carried out:

(a) as regards the EC Member States, by the EFTA Surveillance Authority according to the rules set out in an agreement between the EFTA States establishing the EFTA Surveillance Authority which is entrusted with the powers and functions laid down in Protocol 26.

(2) With a view to ensuring a uniform surveillance in the field of State aid throughout the territory covered by this Agreement, the EC Commission and the EFTA Surveillance Authority shall cooperate in accordance with the provisions set out in Protocol 27.

Article 63

Annex XV contains specific provisions on State aid.

Article 64

(1) If one of the surveillance authorities considers that the implementation by the other surveillance authority of Articles 61 and 62 of this Agreement and Article 5 of Protocol 14 is not in conformity with the maintenance of equal conditions of competition within the territory covered by this Agreement, exchange of views shall be held within two weeks according to the procedure of Protocol 27, paragraph (f).

If a commonly agreed solution has not been found by the end of this two-week period, the competent authority of the affected Contracting Party may immediately adopt appropriate interim measures in order to remedy the resulting distortion of competition.

Consultations shall then be held in the EEA Joint Committee with a view to finding a commonly acceptable solution.

If within three months the EEA Joint Committee has not been able to find such a solution, and if the practice in question causes, or threatens to cause, distortion of competition affecting trade between the Contracting Parties, the interim measures may be replaced by definitive measures, strictly necessary to offset the effect of such distortion. Priority shall be given to such measures that will least disturb the functioning of the EEA.

(2) The provisions of this Article will also apply to State monopolies, which are established after the date of signature of the Agreement.

CHAPTER 3

OTHER COMMON RULES

Article 65

(1) Annex XVI contains specific provisions and arrangements concerning procurement which, unless otherwise specified, shall apply to all products and to services as specified.

(2) Protocol 28 and Annex XVII contain specific provisions and arrangements concerning intellectual, industrial and commercial property, which, unless otherwise specified, shall apply to all products and services.

PART V

HORIZONTAL PROVISIONS RELEVANT TO THE FOUR FREEDOMS

CHAPTER 1

SOCIAL POLICY

Article 66

The Contracting Parties agree upon the need to promote improved working conditions and an improved standard of living for workers.

Article 67

(1) The Contracting Parties shall pay particular attention to encouraging improvements, especially in the working environment, as regards the health and safety of workers. In order to help achieve this objective, minimum requirements shall be applied for gradual implementation, having regard to the conditions and technical rules obtaining in each of the Contracting Parties. Such minimum requirements shall not prevent any Contracting Party from maintaining or introducing more stringent measures for the protection of working conditions compatible with this Agreement.

(2) Annex XVIII specifies the provisions to be implemented as the minimum requirements referred to in paragraph 1.

Article 68

In the field of labour law, the Contracting Parties shall introduce the measure necessary to ensure the good functioning of this Agreement. These measures are specified in Annex XVIII.

Article 69

(1) Each Contracting Party shall ensure and maintain the application of the principle that men and women should receive equal pay for equal work.

For the purposes of this Article, 'pay' means the ordinary basic or minimum wage or salary and any other consideration, whether in cash or in kind, which the worker receives, directly or indirectly, in respect of his employment from his employer.

Equal pay without discrimination based on sex means:

(a) that pay for the same work at piece rates shall be calculated on the basis of the same unit of measurement;

(b) that pay for work at time rates shall be the same for the same job.

(2) Annex XVIII contains specific provisions for the implementation of paragraph 1.

Article 70

The Contracting Parties shall promote the principle of equal treatment for men and women by implementing the provisions specified in Annex XVIII.

Article 71

The Contracting Parties shall endeavour to promote the dialogue between management and labour at European level.

CHAPTER 2

CONSUMER PROTECTION

Article 72

Annex XIX contains provisions on consumer protection.

CHAPTER 3

ENVIRONMENT

Article 73

(1) Action by the Contracting Parties relating to the environment shall have the following objectives:

(a) to preserve, protect and improve the quality of the environment;
(b) to contribute towards protecting human health;
(c) to ensure a prudent and rational utilisation of natural resources.

(2) Action by the Contracting Parties relating to the environment shall be based on the principles that preventive action should be taken, that environmental damage should as a priority be rectified at source, and that the polluter should pay. Environmental protection requirements shall be a component of the Contracting Parties' other policies.

Article 74

Annex XX contains the specific provisions on protective measures which shall apply pursuant to Article 73.

Article 75

The protective measures referred to in Article 74 shall not prevent any Contracting Party from maintaining or introducing more stringent protective measures compatible with this Agreement.

CHAPTER 4

STATISTICS

Article 76

(1) The Contracting Parties shall ensure the production and dissemination of coherent and comparable statistical information for describing and monitoring all relevant economic, social and environmental aspects of the EEA.

(2) To this end the Contracting Parties shall develop and use harmonised methods, definitions and classifications as well as common programmes and procedures organising statistical work at appropriate administrative levels and duly observing the need for statistical confidentiality.

(3) Annex XXI contains specific provisions on statistics.

(4) Protocol 30 contains specific provisions on the organisation of cooperation in the field of statistics.

CHAPTER 5

COMPANY LAW

Article 77

Annex XXII contains specific provisions on company law.

PART VI

COOPERATION OUTSIDE THE FOUR FREEDOMS

Article 78

The Contracting Parties shall strengthen and broaden cooperation in the framework of the Community's activities in the fields of:

- research and technological development,
- information services,
- the environment,
- education, training and youth,
- social policy,
- consumer protection,
- small and medium-sized enterprises,

- tourism,
- the audio visual sector, and
- civil protection,

in so far as these matters are not regulated under the provisions of other Parts of this Agreement.

Article 79

(1) The Contracting Parties shall strengthen the dialogue between them by all appropriate means, in particular through the procedures provided for in Part VII, with a view to identifying areas and activities where closer cooperation could contribute to the attainment of their common objectives in the fields referred to in Article 78.

(2) They shall, in particular, exchange information and, at the request of a Contracting Party, hold consultations with the EEA Joint Committee in respect of plans or proposals for the establishment or amendment of framework programmes, specific programmes, actions and projects in the fields referred to in Article 78.

(3) Part VII shall apply mutatis mutandis with regard to this Part whenever the latter or Protocol 31 specifically provides therefor.

Article 80

The cooperation provided for in Article 78 shall normally take one of the following forms:

- participation by EFTA States in EC framework programmes, specific programmes, projects or other actions;
- establishment of joint activities in specific areas, which may include concertation or coordination of activities, fusion of existing activities and establishment of ad hoc joint activities;
- the formal and informal exchange or provision of information;
- common efforts to encourage certain activities throughout the territory of the Contracting Parties;
- parallel legislation, where appropriate, of identical or similar content;
- coordination, where this is of mutual interest, of efforts and activities via, or in the context of, international organisations, and of cooperation with third countries.

Article 81

Where cooperation takes the form of participation by EFTA States in the EC framework programme, specific programme, project or other action, the following principles shall apply:

(a) The EFTA States shall have access to all parts of a programme.

(b) The status of the EFTA States in the committees which assist the EC Commission in the management or development of a Community activity to which EFTA States may be contributing financially by virtue of their participation shall take full account of that contribution.

(c) Decisions by the Community, other than those relating to the general budget of the Community, which affect directly or indirectly a framework programme, specific programme, project or other action, in which EFTA States participate by a decision under this Agreement, shall be subject to the provisions of Article 79(3). The terms and conditions of the continued participation in the activity in question may be reviewed by the EEA Joint Committee in accordance with Article 86.

(d) At the project level, institutions, undertakings, organisations and nationals of EFTA States shall have the same rights and obligations in the Community programme or other action in question as those applicable to partner institutions, undertakings, organisations and nationals of EC Member States. The same shall apply mutatis mutandis to participants in exchanges between EC Member States and EFTA States, under the activity in question.

(e) EFTA States, their institutions, undertakings, organisations and nationals shall have the same rights and obligations with regard to dissemination, evaluation and exploitation of results as those applicable to EC Member States, their institutions, undertakings, organisations and nationals.

(f) The Contracting Parties undertake, in accordance with their respective rules and regulations, to facilitate the movement of participants in the programme and other action to the extent necessary.

Article 82

(1) When the cooperation envisaged under the present Part involves a financial participation of the EFTA States, this participation shall take one of the following forms:

(a) The contribution of the EFTA States, arising from their participation in Community activities, shall be calculated proportionally:

– to the commitment appropriations; and

— to the payment appropriations;

entered each year for the Community in the general budget of the Community for each budgetary line corresponding to the activities in question.

The 'proportionality factor' determining the participation of the EFTA States shall be the sum of the ratios between, on the one hand, the gross domestic product at market prices of each of the EFTA States and, on the other hand, the sum of the gross domestic products at market prices of the EC Member States and of that EFTA State. This factor shall be calculated, for each budgetary year, on the basis of the most recent statistical data.

The amount of the contribution of the EFTA States shall be additional, both in commitment appropriations and in payment appropriations, to the amounts entered for the Community in the general budget on each line corresponding to the activities concerned.

The contributions to be paid each year by the EFTA States shall be determined on the basis of the payment appropriations.

Commitments entered into by the Community prior to the entry into force, on the basis of this Agreement, of the participation of the EFTA States in the activities in question — as well as the payments which result from this — shall give rise to no contribution on the part of the EFTA States.

(b) The financial contribution of the EFTA States deriving from their participation in certain projects or other activities shall be based on the principle that each Contracting Party shall cover its own costs, with an appropriate contribution which shall be fixed by the EEA Joint Committee to the Community's overhead costs.

(c) The EEA Joint Committee shall take the necessary decisions concerning the contribution of the Contracting Parties to the costs of the activity in question.

(2) The detailed provisions for the implementation of this Article are set out in Protocol 32.

Article 83

Where cooperation takes the form of an exchange of information between public authorities, the EFTA States shall have the same rights to receive, and obligations to provide, information as EC Member States, subject to the requirements of confidentiality, which shall be fixed by the EEA Joint Committee.

Article 84

Provisions governing cooperation in specific fields are set out in Protocol 31.

Article 85

Unless otherwise provided for in Protocol 31, cooperation already established between the Community and individual EFTA States in the field referred to in Article 78 on the date of entry into force of this Agreement shall thereafter be governed by the relevant provisions of this Part and of Protocol 31.

Article 86

The EEA Joint Committee shall, in accordance with Part VII, take all decisions necessary for the implementation of Articles 78 to 85 and measures derived therefrom, which may include, inter alia, supplementing and amending the provisions of Protocol 31, as well as adopting any transitional arrangements required by way of implementation of Article 85.

Article 87

The Contracting Parties shall take the necessary steps to develop, strengthen or broaden cooperation in the framework of the Community's activities in fields not listed in Article 78, where such cooperation is considered likely to contribute to the attainment of the objectives of this Agreement, or is otherwise deemed by the Contracting Parties to be of mutual interest. Such steps may include the amendment of Article 78 by the addition of new fields to those listed therein.

Article 88

Without prejudice to provisions of other Parts of this Agreement, the provisions of this Part shall not preclude the possibility for any Contracting Party to prepare, adopt and implement measures independently.

PART VII

INSTITUTIONAL PROVISIONS

CHAPTER 1

THE STRUCTURE OF THE ASSOCIATION

SECTION 1

THE EEA COUNCIL

Article 89

(1) An EEA Council is hereby established. It shall, in particular, be responsible for giving the political impetus in the implementation of this Agreement and laying down the general guidelines for the EEA Joint Committee.

To this end, the EEA Council shall assess the overall functioning and the development of the Agreement. It shall take the political decisions leading to amendments of the Agreement.

(2) The Contracting Parties, as to the Community and the EC Member States in their respective fields of competence, may, after having discussed it in the EEA Joint Committee, or directly in exceptionally urgent cases, raise in the EEA Council any issue giving rise to a difficulty.

(3) The EEA Council shall by decision adopt its rules of procedure.

Article 90

(1) The EEA Council shall consist of the members of the Council of the European Communities and members of the EC Commission, and of one member of the Government of each of the EFTA States.

Members of the EEA Council may be represented in accordance with the conditions to be laid down in its rule of procedure.

(2) Decisions by the EEA Council shall be taken by agreement between the Community, on the one hand, and the EFTA States, on the other.

Article 91

(1) The office of President of the EEA Council shall be held alternately, for a period of six months, by a member of the Council of the European Communities and a member of the Government of an EFTA State.

(2) The EEA Council shall be convened twice a year by its President. The EEA Council shall also meet whenever circumstances so require, in accordance with its rules of procedure.

SECTION 2

THE EEA JOINT COMMITTEE

Article 92

(1) An EEA Joint Committee is hereby established. It shall ensure the effective implementation and operation of this Agreement. To this end, it shall carry out exchanges of views and information and take decisions in the cases provided for in this Agreement.

(2) The Contracting Parties, as to the Community and the EC Member States in their respective fields of competence, shall hold consultations in the EEA Joint Committee on any point of relevance to the Agreement giving rise to a difficulty and raised by one of them.

(3) The EEA Joint Committee shall by decision adopt its rules of procedure.

Article 93

(1) The EEA Joint Committee shall consist of representatives of the Contracting Parties.

(2) The EEA Joint Committee shall take decisions by agreement between the Community, on the one hand, and the EFTA States speaking with one voice, on the other.

Article 94

(1) The office of President of the EEA Joint Committee shall be held alternately, for a period of six months, by the representative of the Community, ie the EC Commission, and the representative of one of the EFTA States.

(2) In order to fulfil its functions, the EEA Joint Committee shall meet, in principle, at least once a month. It shall also meet on the initiative of its President or at the request of one of the Contracting Parties in accordance with its rules of procedure.

(3) The EEA Joint Committee may decide to establish any subcommittee or working group to assist it in carrying out its tasks. The EEA Joint

Committee shall in its rules of procedure lay down the composition and mode of operation of such subcommittees and working groups. Their tasks shall be determined by the EEA Joint Committee in each individual case.

(4) The EEA Joint Committee shall issue an annual report on the functioning and the development of this Agreement.

SECTION 3

PARLIAMENTARY COOPERATION

Article 95

(1) An EEA Joint Parliamentary Committee is hereby established. It shall be composed of equal numbers of, on the one hand, members of the European Parliament and, on the other, members of Parliaments of the EFTA States. The total number of members of the Committee is laid down in the Statute in Protocol 36.

(2) The EEA Joint Parliamentary Committee shall alternately hold sessions in the Community and in an EFTA State in accordance with the provisions laid down in Protocol 36.

(3) The EEA Joint Parliamentary Committee shall contribute, through dialogue and debate, to a better understanding between the Community and the EFTA States in the fields covered by this Agreement.

(4) The EEA Joint Parliamentary Committee may express its views in the form of reports or resolutions, as appropriate. It shall, in particular, examine the annual report of the EEA Joint Committee, issued in accordance with Article 94(4), on the functioning and the development of this Agreement.

(5) The President of the EEA Council may appear before the EEA Joint Parliamentary Committee in order to be heard by it.

(6) The EEA Joint Parliamentary Committee shall adopt its rules of procedure.

SECTION 4

COOPERATION BETWEEN ECONOMIC AND SOCIAL PARTNERS

Article 96

(1) Members of the Economic and Social Committee and other bodies representing the social partners in the Community and the corresponding

bodies in the EFTA States shall work to strengthen contacts between them and to cooperate in an organised and regular manner in order to enhance the awareness of the economic and social aspects of the growing interdependence of the economics of the Contracting Parties and of their interests within the context of the EEA.

(2) To this end, an EEA Consultative Committee is hereby established. It shall be composed of equal numbers of, on the one hand, members of the Economic and Social Committee of the Community and, on the other, members of the EFTA Consultative Committee. The EEA Consultative Committee may express its views in the form of reports or resolutions, as appropriate.

(3) The EEA Consultative Committee shall adopt its rules of procedure.

CHAPTER 2

THE DECISION-MAKING PROCEDURE

Article 97

(1) This Agreement does not prejudge the right for each Contracting Party to amend, without prejudice to the principle of non-discrimination and after having informed the other Contracting Parties, its internal legislation in the areas covered by this Agreement:

- if the EEA Joint Committee concludes that the legislation as amended does not affect the good functioning of this Agreement; or
- if the procedures referred to in Article 98 have been completed.

Article 98

The Annexes to this Agreement and Protocols 1 to 7, 9 to 11, 19 to 27, 30 to 32, 37, 39, 41 and 47, as appropriate, may be amended by a decision of the EEA Joint Committee in accordance with Articles 93(2), 99, 100, 102 and 103.

Article 99

(1) As soon as new legislation is being drawn up by the EC Commission in a field which is governed by this Agreement, the EC Commission shall informally seek advice from experts of the EFTA States in the same way as its seeks advice from experts of the EC Member States for the elaboration of its proposals.

(2) When transmitting its proposals to the Council of the European Communities, the EC Commission shall transmit copies thereof to the EFTA States.

At the request of one of the Contracting Parties, a preliminary exchange of views takes place in the EEA Joint Committee.

(3) During the phase preceding the decision of the Council of the European Communities, in a continuous information and consultation process, the Contracting Parties consult each other again in the EEA Joint Committee at the significant moments at the request of one of them.

(4) The Contracting Parties shall cooperate in good faith during the information and consultation phase with a view to facilitating, at the end of the process, the decision-taking in the EEA Joint Committee.

Article 100

The EC Commission shall ensure experts of the EFTA States as wide a participation as possible according to the areas concerned, in a preparatory stage of draft measures to be submitted subsequently to the committees which assist the EC Commission in the exercise of its executive powers. In this regard, when drawing up draft measures the EC Commission shall refer to experts of the EFTA States on the same basis as its refers to experts of the EC Member States.

In the cases where the Council of the European Communities is seised in accordance with the procedure applicable to the type of committee involved, the EC Commission shall transmit to the Council of the European Communities the views of the experts of the EFTA States.

Article 101

(1) In respect of committees which are covered neither by Article 81 nor by Article 100 experts from EFTA States shall be associated with the work when this is called for by the good functioning of this Agreement.

These committees are listed in Protocol 37. The modalities of such an association are set out in the relevant sectoral Protocols and Annexes dealing with the matter concerned.

(2) If it appears to the Contracting Parties that such an association should be extended to other committees which present similar characteristics, the EEA Joint Committee may amend Protocol 37.

Article 102

(1) In order to guarantee the legal security and the homogeneity of the EEA, the EEA Joint Committee shall take a decision concerning an amendment of an Annex to this Agreement as closely as possible to the adoption by the Community of the corresponding new Community legislation with a view to permitting a simultaneous application of the latter as well as of the amendments of the Annexes to the Agreement. To this end, the Community shall, whenever adopting a legislative act on an issue which is governed by this Agreement, as soon as possible inform the other Contracting Parties in the EEA Joint Committee.

(2) The part of an Annex to this Agreement which would be directly affected by the new legislation is assessed in the EEA Joint Committee.

(3) The Contracting Parties shall make all efforts to arrive at an agreement on matters relevant to this Agreement.

The EEA Joint Committee shall, in particular, make every effort to find a mutually acceptable solution where a serious problem arises in any area which, in the EFTA States, falls within the competence of the legislator.

(4) If, notwithstanding the application of the preceding paragraph, an agreement on an amendment of an Annex to this Agreement cannot be reached, the EEA Joint Committee shall examine all further possibilities to maintain the good functioning of this Agreement and take any decision necessary to this effect, including the possibility to take notice of the equivalence of legislation. Such a decision shall be taken at the latest at the expiry of a period of six months from the date of referral to the EEA Joint Committee or, if that date is later, on the date of entry into force of the corresponding Community legislation.

(5) If, at the end of the time-limit set out in paragraph 4, the EEA Joint Committee has not taken a decision on an amendment of an Annex to this Agreement, the affected part thereof, as determined in accordance with paragraph 2, is regarded as provisionally suspended, subject to a decision to the contrary by the EEA Joint Committee. Such a suspension shall take effect six months after the end of the period referred to in paragraph 4, but in no event earlier than the date on which the corresponding EC act is implemented in the Community. The EEA Joint Committee shall pursue its efforts to agree on a mutually acceptable solution in order for the suspension to be terminated as soon as possible.

(6) The practical consequences of the suspension referred to in paragraph 5 shall be discussed in the EEA Joint Committee. The rights and obligations which individuals and economic operators have already acquired under

this Agreement shall remain. The Contracting Parties shall, as appropriate, decide on the adjustments necessary due to the suspension.

Article 103

(1) If a decision of the EEA Joint Committee can be binding on a Contracting Party only after the fulfilment of constitutional requirements, the decision shall, if a date is contained therein, enter into force on that date, provided that the Contracting Party concerned has notified the Contracting Parties by that date that the constitutional requirements have been fulfilled.

In the absence of such a notification by that date, the decision shall enter into force on the first day of the second month following the last notification.

(2) If upon the expiry of a period of six months after the decision of the EEA Joint Committee such a notification has not taken place, the decision of the EEA Joint Committee shall be applied provisionally pending the fulfilment of the constitutional requirements unless a Contracting Party notifies that such a provisional application cannot take place. In the latter case, or if a Contracting Party notifies the non-ratification of a decision of the EEA Joint Committee, the suspension provided for in Article 102(5) shall take effect one month after such a notification but in no event earlier than the date on which the corresponding EC act is implemented in the Community.

Article 104

Decisions taken by the EEA Joint Committee in the cases provided for in this Agreement shall, unless otherwise provided for therein, upon their entry into force be binding on the Contracting Parties which shall take the necessary steps to ensure their implementation and application.

CHAPTER 3

HOMOGENEITY, SURVEILLANCE PROCEDURE AND SETTLEMENT OF DISPUTES

SECTION 1

HOMOGENEITY

Article 105

(1) In order to achieve the objective of the Contracting Parties to arrive at as uniform an interpretation as possible of the provisions of the Agreement and those provisions of Community legislation which are substantially

reproduced in the Agreement, the EEA Joint Committee shall act in accordance with this Article.

(2) The EEA Joint Committee shall keep under constant review the development of the case-law of the Court of Justice of the European Communities and the EFTA Court. To this end judgments of these Courts shall be transmitted to the EEA Joint Committee which shall act so as to preserve the homogeneous interpretation of the Agreement.

(3) If the EEA Joint Committee with two months after a difference in the case-law of the two Courts has been brought before it, has not succeeded to preserve the homogeneous interpretation of the Agreement, the procedures laid down in Article 111 may be applied.

Article 106

In order to ensure as uniform an interpretation as possible of this Agreement, in full deference to the independence of courts, a system of exchange of information concerning judgments by the EFTA Court, the Court of Justice of the European Communities and the Court of First Instance of the European Communities and the Courts of last instance of the EFTA States shall be set up by the EEA Joint Committee. This system shall comprise:

(a) transmission to the Registrar of the Court of Justice of the European Communities of judgments delivered by such courts on the interpretation and application of, on the one hand, this Agreement or, on the other hand, the Treaty establishing the European Economic Community and the Treaty establishing the European Coal and Steel Community, as amended or supplemented, as well as the acts adopted in pursuance thereof in so far as they concern provisions which are identical in substance to those of this Agreement;

(b) classification of these judgments by the Registrar of the Court of Justice of the European Communities including, as far as necessary, the drawing up and publication of translations and abstracts;

(c) communications by the Registrar of the Court of Justice of the European Communities of the relevant documents to the competent national authorities, to be designated by each Contracting Party.

Article 107

Provisions on the possibility for an EFTA State to allow a court or tribunal to ask the Court of Justice of the European Communities to decide on the interpretation of an EEA rule are laid down in Protocol 34.

SECTION 2

SURVEILLANCE PROCEDURE

Article 108

(1) The EFTA States shall establish an independent surveillance authority (EFTA Surveillance Authority) as well as procedures similar to those existing in the Community including procedures for ensuring the fulfilment of obligations under this Agreement and for control of the legality of acts of the EFTA Surveillance Authority regarding competition.

(2) The EFTA States shall establish a court of justice (EFTA Court).

The EFTA Court shall, in accordance with a separate agreement between the EFTA States, with regard to the application of this Agreement be competent, in particular, for:

(a) actions concerning the surveillance procedure regarding the EFTA States;

(b) appeals concerning decisions in the field of competition taken by the EFTA Surveillance Authority;

(c) the settlement of disputes between two or more EFTA States.

Article 109

(1) The fulfilment of the obligations under this Agreement shall be monitored by, on the one hand, the EFTA Surveillance Authority and, on the other, the EC Commission acting in conformity with the Treaty establishing the European Economic Community, the Treaty establishing the European Coal and Steel Community and this Agreement.

(2) In order to ensure a uniform surveillance throughout the EEA, the EFTA Surveillance Authority and the EC Commission shall cooperate, exchange information and consult each other on surveillance policy issues and individual cases.

(3) The EC Commission and the EFTA Surveillance Authority shall receive any complaints concerning the application of this Agreement. They shall inform each other of complaints received.

(4) Each of these bodies shall examine all complaints falling within its competence and shall pass to the other body any complaints which fall within the competence of that body.

(5) In case of disagreement between these two bodies with regard to the action to be taken in relation to a complaint or with regard to the result of

the examination, either of the bodies may refer the matter to the EEA Joint Committee which shall deal with it in accordance with Article 111.

Article 110

Decisions under this Agreement by the EFTA Surveillance Authority and the EC Commission which impose a pecuniary obligation on persons other than States, shall be enforceable. The same shall apply to such judgments under this Agreement by the Court of Justice of the European Communities, the Court of First Instance of the European Communities and the EFTA Court.

Enforcement shall be governed by the rules of civil procedure in force in the State in the territory of which it is carried out. The order for its enforcement shall be appended to the decision, without other formality than verification of the authenticity of the decision, by the authority which each Contracting Party shall designate for this purpose and shall make known to the other Contracting Parties, the EFTA Surveillance Authority, the EC Commission, the Court of Justice of the European Communities, the Court of First Instance of the European Communities and the EFTA Court.

When these formalities have been completed on application by the party concerned, the latter may proceed to enforcement, in accordance with the law of the State in the territory of which enforcement is to be carried out, by bringing the matter directly before the competent authority.

Enforcement may be suspended only by a decision of the Court of Justice of the European Communities, as far as decisions by the EC Commission, the Court of First Instance of the European Communities or the Court of Justice of the European Communities are concerned, or by a decision of the EFTA Court as far as decisions by the EFTA Surveillance Authority or the EFTA Court are concerned. However, the courts of the States concerned shall have jurisdiction over complaints that enforcement is being carried out in an irregular manner.

SECTION 3

SETTLEMENT OF DISPUTES

Article 111

(1) The Community or an EFTA State may bring a matter under dispute which concerns the interpretation or application of this Agreement before the EEA Joint Committee in accordance with the following provisions.

(2) The EEA Joint Committee may settle the dispute. It shall be provided with all information which might be of use in making possible an in-depth examination of the situation, with a view to finding an acceptable solution. To this end, the EEA Joint Committee shall examine all possibilities to maintain the good functioning of the Agreement.

(3) If a dispute concerns the interpretation of provisions of this Agreement, which are identical in substance to corresponding rules of the Treaty establishing the European Economic Community and the Treaty establishing the European Coal and Steel Community and to acts adopted in application of these two Treaties and if the dispute has not been brought before the EEA Joint Committee, the Contracting Parties to the dispute may agree to request the Court of Justice of the European Communities to give a ruling on the interpretation of the relevant rules.

If the EEA Joint Committee in such a dispute has not reached an agreement on a solution within six months from the date on which this procedure was initiated or if, by then, the Contracting Parties to the dispute have not decided to ask for a ruling by the Court of Justice of the European Communities, a Contracting Party may, in order to remedy possible imbalances,

- either take a safeguard measure in accordance with Article 112(2) and following the procedure of Article 113;
- or apply Article 102 mutatis mutandis.

(4) If a dispute concerns the scope or duration of safeguard measures taken in accordance with Article 111(3) or Article 112, or the proportionality of rebalancing measures taken in accordance with Article 114, and if the EEA Joint Committee after three months from the date when the matter has been brought before it has not succeeded to resolve the dispute, any Contracting Party may refer the dispute to arbitration under the procedures laid down in Protocol 33. No question of interpretation of provisions of this Agreement referred to in paragraph 3 may be dealt with in such procedures. The arbitration award shall be binding on the parties to the dispute.

CHAPTER 4

SAFEGUARD MEASURES

Article 112

(1) If serious economic, societal or environmental difficulties of a sectorial or regional nature liable to persist are arising, a Contracting Party may unilaterally take appropriate measures under the conditions and procedures laid down in Article 113.

(2) Such safeguard measures shall be restricted with regard to their scope and duration to what is strictly necessary in order to remedy the situation. Priority shall be given to such measures as will least disturb the functioning of this Agreement.

(3) The safeguard measures shall apply with regard to all Contracting Parties.

Article 113

(1) A Contracting Party which is considering taking safeguard measures under Article 112 shall, without delay, notify the other Contracting Parties through the EEA Joint Committee and shall provide all relevant information.

(2) The Contracting Parties shall immediately enter into consultations in the EEA Joint Committee with a view to finding a commonly acceptable solution.

(3) The Contracting Party concerned may not take safeguard measures until one month has elapsed after the date of notification under paragraph 1, unless the consultation procedure under paragraph 2 has been concluded before the expiration of the stated time-limit. When exceptional circumstances requiring immediate action exclude prior examination, the Contracting Party concerned may apply forthwith the protective measures strictly necessary to remedy the situation.

For the Community, the safeguard measures shall be taken by the EC Commission.

(4) The Contracting Party concerned shall, without delay, notify the measures taken to the EEA Joint Committee and shall provide all relevant information.

(5) The safeguard measures taken shall be the subject of consultations in the EEA Joint Committee every three months from the date of their adoption with a view to their abolition before the date of expiry envisaged, or to the limitation of their scope of application.

Each Contracting Party may at any time request the EEA Joint Committee to review such measures.

Article 114

(1) If a safeguard measure taken by a Contracting Party creates an imbalance between the rights and obligations under this Agreement, any

other Contracting Party may towards that Contracting Party take such proportionate rebalancing measures as are strictly necessary to remedy the imbalance. Priority shall be given to such measures as will least disturb the functioning of the EEA.

(2) The procedure under Article 113 shall apply.

PART VIII

FINANCIAL MECHANISM

Article 115

With a view to promoting a continuous and balanced strengthening of trade and economic relations between the Contracting Parties, as provided for in Article 1, the Contracting Parties agree on the need to reduce the economic and social disparities between their regions. They note in this regard the relevant provisions set out elsewhere in this Agreement and its related Protocols, including certain of the arrangements regarding agriculture and fisheries.

Article 116

A Financial Mechanism shall be established by the EFTA States to contribute, in the context of the EEA and in addition to the efforts already deployed by the Community in this regard, to the objectives laid down in Article 115.

Article 117

Provisions governing the Financial Mechanism are set out in Protocol 38.

PART IX

GENERAL AND FINAL PROVISIONS

Article 118

(1) Where a Contracting Party considers that it would be useful in the interests of all the Contracting Parties to develop the relations established by this Agreement by extending them to fields not covered thereby, it shall submit a reasoned request to the other Contracting Parties within the EEA Council. The latter may instruct the EEA Joint Committee to examine all the aspects of this request and to issue a report.

The EEA Council may, where appropriate, take the political decisions with a view to opening negotiations between the Contracting Parties.

(2) The agreements resulting from the negotiations referred to in paragraph 1 will be subject to ratification or approval by the Contracting Parties in accordance with their own procedures.

Article 119

The Annexes and the acts referred to therein as adapted for the purposes of this Agreement as well as the Protocols shall form an integral part of this Agreement.

Article 120

Unless otherwise provided in this Agreement and in particular in Protocols 41 and 43, the application of the provisions of this Agreement shall prevail over provisions in existing bilateral or multilateral agreements binding the European Economic Community, on the one hand, and one or more EFTA States, on the other, to the extent that the same subject matter is governed by this Agreement.

Article 121

(1) The provisions of this Agreement shall not preclude cooperation:

(a) within the framework of the Nordic cooperation to the extent that such cooperation does not impair the good functioning of this Agreement;

(b) within the framework of the regional union between Switzerland and Liechtenstein to the extent that the objectives of this union are not attained by the application of this Agreement and the good functioning of this Agreement is not impaired;

(c) within the framework of cooperation between Austria and Italy concerning Tyrol, Vorarlberg and Trentino-South Tyrol/Alto Adige, to the extent that such cooperation does not impair the good functioning of this Agreement.

Article 122

The representatives, delegates and experts of the Contracting Parties, as well as officials and other servants acting under this Agreement shall be required, even after their duties have ceased, not to disclose information of the kind covered by the obligation of professional secrecy, in particular information about undertakings, their business relations or their cost components.

Article 123

Nothing in this Agreement shall prevent a Contracting Party from taking any measures:

(a) which it considers necessary to prevent the disclosure of information contrary to its essential security interests;

(b) which relate to the production of, or trade in, arms, munitions and war materials or other products indispensable for defence purposes or to research, development or production indispensable for defence purposes, provided that such measures do not impair the conditions of competition in respect of products not intended for specifically military purposes;

(c) which it considers essential to its own security in the event of serious internal disturbances affecting the maintenance of law and order, in time of war or serious international tension constituting threat of war or in order to carry out obligations it has accepted for the purpose of maintaining peace and international security.

Article 124

The Contracting Parties shall accord nationals of EC Member States and EFTA States the same treatment as their own nationals as regards participation in the capital of companies or firms within the meaning of Article 34, without prejudice to the application of the other provisions of this Agreement.

Article 125

This Agreement shall in no way prejudice the rules of the Contracting Parties governing the system of property ownership.

Article 126

(1) The Agreement shall apply to the territories to which the Treaty establishing the European Economic Community and the Treaty establishing the European Coal and Steel Community is applied and under the conditions laid down in those Treaties, and to the territories of the Republic of Austria, the Republic of Finland, the Republic of Iceland, the

Principality of Liechtenstein, the Kingdom of Norway and the Kingdom of Sweden.

(2) Notwithstanding paragraph 1, this Agreement shall not apply to the Aland Islands. The Government of Finland may, however, give notice, by a declaration deposited when ratifying this Agreement with the Depository, which shall transmit a certified copy thereof to the Contracting Parties, that the Agreement shall apply to those Islands under the same conditions as it applies to other parts of Finland subject to the following provisions:

> (a) The provisions of this Agreement shall not preclude the application of the provisions in force at any given time on the Aland Islands on:
>> (i) restrictions on the right for natural persons who do not enjoy regional citizenship in Aland, and for legal persons, to acquire and hold real property on the Aland Islands without permission by the competent authorities of the Islands;
>>
>> (ii) restrictions on the right of establishment and the right to provide services by natural persons who do not enjoy regional citizenship in Aland, or by any legal person, without permission by the competent authorities of the Aland Islands.
>
> (b) The rights enjoyed by Alanders in Finland shall not be affected by this Agreement .
>
> (c) The authorities of the Aland Islands shall apply the same treatment to all natural and legal persons of the Contracting Parties.

Article 127

Each Contracting Party may withdraw from this Agreement provided it gives at least 12 months' notice in writing to the other Contracting Parties.

Immediately after the notification of the intended withdrawal, the other Contracting Parties shall convene a diplomatic conference in order to envisage the necessary modification to bring to the Agreement.

Article 128

(1) Any European State becoming a member of the Community shall, and the Swiss Confederation or any European State becoming a member of EFTA may, apply to become a party to this Agreement. It shall address its application to the EEA Council.

(2) The terms and conditions for such participation shall be the subject of an agreement between the Contracting Parties and the applicant State. That

agreement shall be submitted for ratification or approval by all Contracting Parties in accordance with their own procedures.

Article 129

(1) This Agreement is drawn up in a single original in the Danish, Dutch, English, Finnish, French, German, Greek, Icelandic, Italian, Norwegian, Portuguese, Spanish and Swedish languages, each of these texts being equally authentic.

The texts of the acts referred to in the Annexes are equally authentic in Danish, Dutch, English, French, German, Greek, Italian, Portuguese and Spanish as published in the *Official Journal of the European Communities* and shall for the authentication thereof be drawn up in the Finnish, Icelandic, Norwegian and Swedish languages.

(2) This Agreement shall be ratified or approved by the Contracting Parties in accordance with their respective constitutional requirements.

It shall be deposited with the General Secretariat of the Council of the European Communities by which certified copies shall be transmitted to all other Contracting Parties.

The instruments of ratification or approval shall be deposited with the General Secretariat of the Council of the European Communities which shall notify all other Contracting Parties.

(3) This Agreement shall enter into force on the date and under the conditions provided for in the Protocol adjusting the Agreement on the European Economic Area.

In witness whereof the undersigned Plenipotentiaries have signed this Agreement ...

As amended by the Protocol adjusting the Agreement on the European Economic Area signed at Brussels on 17 March 1993, arts 2–6.

COUNCIL DECISION CONCERNING THE NAME TO BE GIVEN TO THE COUNCIL FOLLOWING THE ENTRY INTO FORCE OF THE TREATY ON EUROPEAN UNION
(93/591/EU, Euratom, ECSC, EC)
(Brussels, 8 November 1993)

The Council shall henceforth be called the 'Council of the European Union' and shall be so designated, in particular in all the acts which it adopts, including those under Titles V and VI of the Treaty on European Union; political declarations which the Council adopts under the common foreign and security policy will thus be made in the name of 'the European Union'.

As corrected at OJ L285/41 (1993).

DECISION OF THE EUROPEAN PARLIAMENT ON THE REGULATIONS AND GENERAL CONDITIONS GOVERNING THE PERFORMANCE OF THE OMBUDSMAN'S DUTIES
(94/262/ECSC, EC Euratom)
(Strasbourg, 9 March 1994)

The European Parliament,

Having regard to the Treaties establishing the European Communities, and in particular Article 138e(4) of the Treaty establishing the European Community, Article 20d(4) of the Treaty establishing the European Coal and Steel Community, Article 107d(4) of the Treaty establishing the European Atomic Energy Community,

Having regard to the opinion of the Commission,

Having regard to the Council's approval,

Whereas the regulations and general conditions governing the performance of the Ombudsman's duties should be laid down, in compliance with the provisions of the Treaties establishing the European Communities;

Whereas the conditions under which a complaint may be referred to the Ombudsman should be established as well as the relationship between the performance of the duties of Ombudsman and legal or administrative proceedings;

Whereas the Ombudsman, who may also act on his own initiative, must have access to all the elements required for the performance of his duties; whereas to that end Community institutions and bodies are obliged to supply the Ombudsman, at his request, with any information which he requests of them, unless there are duly substantial grounds for secrecy, and without prejudice to the Ombudsman's obligation not to divulge such information; whereas the Member States' authorities are obliged to provide the Ombudsman with all necessary information save where such information is covered by laws or regulations on secrecy or by provisions preventing its being communicated; whereas if the Ombudsman finds that the assistance requested is not forthcoming, he shall inform the European Parliament, which shall make appropriate representations;

Whereas it is necessary to lay down the procedures to be followed where the Ombudsman's enquiries reveal cases of maladministration; whereas provision should also be made for the submission of a comprehensive report by the Ombudsman to the European Parliament at the end of each annual session;

Whereas the Ombudsman and his staff are obliged to treat in confidence any information which they have acquired in the course of their duties; whereas the Ombudsman is, however, obliged to inform the competent authorities of facts which he considers might relate to criminal law and which have come to his attention in the course of his enquiries;

Whereas provision should be made for the possibility of cooperation between the Ombudsman and authorities of the same type in certain Member States, in compliance with the national laws applicable;

Whereas it is for the European Parliament to appoint the Ombudsman at the beginning of its mandate and for the duration thereof, choosing him from among persons who are Union citizens and offer every requisite guarantee of independence and competence;

Whereas conditions should be laid down for the cessation of the Ombudsman's duties;

Whereas the Ombudsman must perform his duties with complete independence and give a solemn undertaking before the Court of Justice of the European Communities that he will do so when taking up his duties; whereas activities incompatible with the duties of Ombudsman should be laid down as should the remuneration, privileges and immunities of the Ombudsman;

Whereas provisions should be laid down regarding the officials and servants of the Ombudsman's secretariat which will assist him and the budget thereof; whereas the seat of the Ombudsman should be that of the European Parliament;

Whereas it is for the Ombudsman to adopt the implementing provisions for this Decision; whereas furthermore certain transitional provisions should be laid down for the first Ombudsman to be appointed after the entry into force of the Treaty on European Union;

HAS DECIDED AS FOLLOWS:

Article 1

1. The regulations and general conditions governing the performance of the Ombudsman's duties shall be as laid down by this Decision in accordance with Article 138e(4) of the Treaty establishing the European Community, Article 20d(4) of the Treaty establishing the European Coal and Steel Community and Article 107d(4) of the Treaty establishing the European Atomic Energy Community.

2. The Ombudsman shall perform his duties in accordance with the powers conferred on the Community institutions and bodies by the Treaties.

3. The Ombudsman may not intervene in cases before courts or question the soundness of a court's ruling.

Article 2

1. Within the framework of the aforementioned Treaties and the conditions laid down therein, the Ombudsman shall help to uncover maladministration in the activities of the Community institutions and bodies, with the exception of the Court of Justice and the Court of First Instance acting in their judicial role, and make recommendations with a view to putting an end to it. No action by any other authority or person may be the subject of a complaint to the Ombudsman.

2. Any citizen of the Union or any natural or legal person residing or having its registered office in a Member State of the Union may, directly or through a Member of the European Parliament, refer a complaint to the Ombudsman in respect of an instance of maladministration in the activities of the Community institutions or bodies, with the exception of the Court of Justice and the Court of First Instance acting in their judicial role. The Ombudsman shall inform the institution or body concerned as soon as a complaint is referred to him.

3. The complaint must allow the person lodging the complaint and the object of the complaint to be identified; the person lodging the complaint may request that his complaint remain confidential.

4. A complaint shall be made within two years of the date on which the facts on which it is based came to the attention of the person lodging the complaint and must be preceded by the appropriate administrative approaches to the institutions and bodies concerned.

5. The Ombudsman may advise the person lodging the complaint to address it to another authority.

6. Complaints submitted to the Ombudsman shall not affect time limits for appeals in administrative or judicial proceedings.

7. When the Ombudsman, because of legal proceedings in progress or concluded concerning the facts which have been put forward, has to declare a complaint inadmissible or terminate consideration of it, the outcome of any enquiries he has carried out up to that point shall be filed without further action.

8. No complaint may be made to the Ombudsman that concerns work relationships between the Community institutions and bodies and their officials and other servants unless all the possibilities for the submission of internal administrative requests and complaints, in particular the procedures referred to in Article 90(1) and (2) of the Staff Regulations, have been exhausted by the person concerned and the time limits for replies by the authority thus petitioned have expired.

9. The Ombudsman shall as soon as possible inform the person lodging the complaint of the action he has taken on it.

Article 3

1. The Ombudsman shall, on his own initiative or following a complaint, conduct all the enquiries which he considers justified to clarify any suspected maladministration in the activities of Community institutions and bodies. He shall inform the institution or body concerned of such action, which may submit any useful comment to him.

2. The Community institutions and bodies shall be obliged to supply the Ombudsman with any information he has requested of them and give him access to the files concerned. They may refuse only on duly substantial grounds of secrecy.

They shall give access to documents originating in a Member State and classed as secret by law or regulation only where that Member State has given its prior agreement.

They shall give access to other documents originating in a Member State after having informed the Member State concerned. In both cases, in accordance with Article 4, the Ombudsman may not divulge the content of such documents.

Officials and other servants of Community institutions and bodies must testify at the request of the Ombudsman; they shall speak on behalf of and in accordance with instructions from their administrations and shall continue to be bound by their duty of professional secrecy.

3. The Member States' authorities shall be obliged to provide the Ombudsman, whenever he may request, via the Permanent Representations of the Member States to the European Communities, with any information that may help to clarify instances of maladministration by Community institutions or bodies unless such information is covered by laws or regulations on secrecy or by provisions preventing its being communicated. Nevertheless, in the latter case, the Member State concerned may allow the Ombudsman to have this information provided that he undertakes not to divulge it.

4. If the assistance which he requests is not forthcoming, the Ombudsman shall inform the European Parliament, which shall make appropriate representations.

5. As far as possible, the Ombudsman shall seek a solution with the institution or body concerned to eliminate the instance of maladministration and satisfy the complaint.

6. If the Ombudsman finds there has been maladministration, he shall inform the institution or body concerned, where appropriate making draft recommendations. The institution or body so informed shall send the Ombudsman a detailed opinion within three months.

7. The Ombudsman shall then send a report to the European Parliament and to the institution or body concerned. He may make recommendations in his report. The person lodging the complaint shall be informed by the Ombudsman of the outcome of the inquiries, of the opinion expressed by the institution or body concerned and of any recommendations made by the Ombudsman.

8. At the end of each annual session the Ombudsman shall submit to the European Parliament a report on the outcome of his inquiries.

Article 4

1. The Ombudsman and his staff, to whom Article 214 of the Treaty establishing the European Community, Article 47(2) of the Treaty establishing the European Coal and Steel Community and Article 194 of the Treaty establishing the European Atomic Energy Community shall apply, shall be required not to divulge information or documents which they obtain in the course of their inquiries. They shall also be required to treat in confidence any information which could harm the person lodging the complaint or any other person involved, without prejudice to paragraph 2.

2. If, in the course of inquiries, he learns of facts which he considers might relate to criminal law, the Ombudsman shall immediately notify the competent national authorities via the Permanent Representations of the Member States to the European Communities and, if appropriate, the Community institution with authority over the official or servant concerned, which may apply the second paragraph of Article 18 of the Protocol on the Privileges and Immunities of the European Communities. The Ombudsman may also inform the Community institution or body concerned of the facts calling into question the conduct of a member of their staff from a disciplinary point of view.

Article 5

Insofar as it may help to make his enquiries more efficient and better safeguard the rights and interests of persons who make complaints to him, the Ombudsman may cooperate with authorities of the same type in certain Member States provided he complies with the national law applicable. The Ombudsman may not by this means demand to see documents to which he would not have access under Article 3.

Article 6

1. The Ombudsman shall be appointed by the European Parliament after each election to the European Parliament for the duration of the parliamentary term. He shall be eligible for reappointment.

2. The Ombudsman shall be chosen from among persons who are Union citizens, have full civil and political rights, offer every guarantee of independence, and meet the conditions required for the exercise of the highest judicial office in their country or have the acknowledgement competence and experience to undertake the duties of Ombudsman

Article 7

1. The Ombudsman shall cease to exercise his duties either at the end of his term of office or on his resignation or dismissal.

2. Save in the event of his dismissal, the Ombudsman shall remain in office until his successor has been appointed.

3. In the event of early cessation of duties, a successor shall be appointed within three months of the office's falling vacant for the remainder of the parliamentary term.

Article 8

An Ombudsman who no longer fulfills the conditions required for the performance of his duties or is guilty of serious misconduct may be dismissed by the Court of Justice of the European Communities at the request of the European Parliament.

Article 9

1. The Ombudsman shall perform his duties with complete independence, in the general interest of the Communities and of the citizens of the Union. In the performance of his duties he shall neither seek nor accept instructions from any government or other body. He shall refrain from any act incompatible with the nature of his duties.

2. When taking up his duties, the Ombudsman shall give a solemn undertaking before the Court of Justice of the European Communities that he will perform his duties with complete independence and impartiality and that during and after his term of office he will respect the obligations arising therefrom, in particular his duty to behave with integrity and discretion as regards the acceptance, after he has ceased to hold office, of certain appointments or benefits.

Article 10

1. During his term of office, the Ombudsman may not engage in any other political or administrative duties, or any other occupation, whether gainful or not.

2. The Ombudsman shall have the same rank in terms of remuneration, allowances and pension as a judge at the Court of Justice of the European Communities.

3. Articles 12 to 15 and Article 18 of the Protocol on the Privileges and Immunities of the European Communities shall apply to the Ombudsman and to the officials and servants of his secretariat.

Article 13

The seat of the Ombudsman shall be that of the European Parliament.

Article 14

The Ombudsman shall adopt the implementing provisions for this Decision.

Article 15

The first Ombudsman to be appointed after the entry into force of the Treaty on European Union shall be appointed for the remainder of the parliamentary term.

Article 17

This Decision shall be published in the *Official Journal of the European Communities*. It shall enter into force on the date of its publication.

COUNCIL DECISION ON THE TAKING OF DECISIONS BY A QUALIFIED MAJORITY OF THE COUNCIL

(Brussels, 29 March 1994)

Article 1

If Member of the Council representing a total of 23 to 25 votes indicate their intention to oppose the adoption by the Council of a Decision by qualified majority, the Council will do all in its power to reach, within a reasonable time and without prejudicing obligatory time limits laid down by the Treaties and by secondary law, such as in Articles 189B and 189C of the Treaty establishing the European Community, a satisfactory solution that could be adopted by at least 65 votes. During this period, and always respecting the Rules of Procedure of the Council, the President undertakes, with the assistance of the Commission, any initiative necessary to facilitate a wider basis of agreement in the Council. The Members of the Council lend him their assistance.

Article 2

The present Decision shall be published in the Official Journal of the European Communities.

As amended by Council Decision 1 January 1995.

COUNCIL DECISION ON THE SYSTEM OF THE EUROPEAN COMMUNITIES' OWN RESOURCES
(94/728 EC, Euratom)
(Luxembourg, 31 October 1994)

The Council of the European Communities,

Having regard to the Treaty establishing the European Community, and in particular Article 201 thereof,

Having regard to the Treaty establishing the European Atomic Energy Community, and in particular Article 173 thereof,

Having regard to the proposal from the Commission,

Having regard to the opinion of the European Parliament,

Having regard to the opinion of the Economic and Social Committee,

Whereas Council Decision 88/376/EEC, Euratom of 24 June 1988 on the system of the Communities' own resources expanded and amended the composition of own resources by capping the VAT resource base at 55% of gross national product ('GNP') for the year at market prices, with the maximum call-in rate being maintained at 1.4%, and by introducing an additional resource based on the total GNP of the Member States;

Whereas the European Council meeting in Edinburgh on 11 and 12 December 1992 reached certain conclusions;

Whereas the Communities must have adequate resources to finance their policies;

Whereas, in accordance with these conclusions, the Communities will, by 1999, be assigned a maximum amount of own resources corresponding to 1.27% of the total of the Member States' GNPs for the year at market prices;

Whereas observance of this ceiling requires that the total amount of own resources at the Communities' disposal for the period 1995 to 1999 does not in any one year exceed a specified percentage of the sum of the Member States' GNPs for the year in question;

Whereas on overall ceiling of 1.335% of the Member States' GNPs is set for commitment appropriations; whereas an orderly progression of commitment appropriations and payment appropriations should be ensured;

Whereas these ceilings should remain applicable until this Decision is amended;

Whereas, in order to make allowance for each Member State's ability to contribute to the system of own resources and to correct the regressive aspects of the current system for the least prosperous Member States, in accordance with the Protocol on economic and social cohesion annexed to the Treaty on European Union, the Communities' financing rules should be further amended:

- by lowering the ceiling for the uniform rate to be applied to the uniform value added tax base of each Member State from 1.4 to 1.0% in equal steps between 1995 and 1999,
- by limiting at 50% of GNP from 1995 onwards the value added tax base of the Member States whose per capita GNP in 1991 was less than 90% of the Community average, ie Greece, Spain, Ireland and Portugal, and by reducing the base from 55 to 50% in equal steps over the period 1995 to 1999 for the other Member States;

Whereas the European Council has examined the correction of budgetary imbalances on numerous occasions, particularly at its meetings on 25 and 26 June 1984;

Whereas the European Council of 11 and 12 December 1992 confirmed the formula for calculating the correction of budgetary imbalances defined in Decision 88/376/EEC, Euratom;

Whereas the budgetary imbalances should be corrected in such a way as not to affect the own resources available for Community policies;

Whereas the monetary reserve, hereinafter referred to as 'the EAGGF monetary reserve', is covered by specific provisions;

Whereas the conclusions of the European Council provided for the creation in the budget of two reserves, one for the financing of the Loan Guarantee Fund, and the other for emergency aid in non-member countries; whereas these reserves should be covered by specific provisions;

Whereas the Commission will by the end of 1999 submit a report on the operation of the system, which will contain a review of the mechanism for correcting budgetary imbalances granted to the United Kingdom; whereas it will also by the end of 1999 present a report containing the results of a study on the feasibility of creating a new own resource, as well as on arrangements for the possible introduction of a fixed uniform rate applicable to the VAT base;

Whereas provisions must be laid down to cover the changeover from the system introduced by Decision 88/376/EEC, Euratom to that arising from this Decision;

Whereas the European Council provided that this Decision should take effect on 1 January 1995,

HAS LAID DOWN THESE PROVISIONS, WHICH IT RE-COMMENDS TO THE MEMBER STATES FOR ADOPTION:

Article 1

The Communities shall be allocated resources of their own in accordance with the detailed rules laid down in the following Articles in order to ensure the financing of their budget.

The budget of the Communities shall, without prejudice to other revenue, be financed wholly from the Communities' own resources.

Article 2

1. Revenue from the following shall constitute own resources entered in the budget of the Communities:

> (a) levies, premiums, additional or compensatory amounts, additional amounts or factors and other duties established or to be established by the institutions of the Communities in respect of trade with non-member countries within the framework of the common agricultural policy, and also contributions and other duties provided for within the framework of the common organisation of the markets in sugar;
>
> (b) Common Customs Tariff duties and other duties established or to be established by the institutions of the Communities in respect of trade with non-member countries and customs duties on products coming under the Treaty establishing the European Coal and Steel Community;
>
> (c) the application of a uniform rate valid for all Member States to the VAT assessment base which is determined in a uniform manner for Member States according to Community rules. However, the assessment base to be taken into account for the purposes of this Decision shall, from 1995, not exceed 50% of GNP in the case of Member States whose per capita GNP, in 1991 was less than 90% of the Community average; for the other Member States the assessment base to be taken into account shall not exceed:

– 54% of their GNP in 1995,
– 53% of their GNP in 1996,
– 52% of their GNP in 1997,
– 51% of their GNP in 1998,
– 50% of their GNP in 1999;

The cap of 50% of their GNP to be introduced for all Member States in 1999 shall remain applicable until such time as this Decision is amended;

(d) the application of a rate – to be determined pursuant to the budgetary procedure in the light of the total of all other revenue – to the sum of all the Member States' GNP established in accordance with the Community rules laid down in Directive 89/130/EEC, Euratom.

2. Revenue deriving from any new charges introduced within the framework of a common policy, in accordance with the Treaty establishing the European Community or the Treaty establishing the European Atomic Energy Community, provided the procedure laid down in Article 201 of the Treaty establishing the European Community or in Article 173 of the Treaty establishing the European Atomic Energy Community has been followed, shall also constitute own resources entered in the budget of the Communities.

3. Member States shall retain, by way of collection costs, 10% of the amounts paid under 1(a) and (b).

4. The uniform rate referred to in paragraph 1(c) shall correspond to the rate resulting from:

(a) the application to the VAT assessment base for the Member States of:
 – 1.32% in 1995,
 – 1.24% in 1996,
 – 1.16% in 1997,
 – 1.08% in 1998,
 – 1.00% in 1999.

The 1.00% rate in 1999 shall remain applicable until such time as this Decision is amended;

(b) the deduction of the gross amount of the reference compensation referred to in Article 4(2). The gross amount shall be the compensation amount adjusted for the fact that the United Kingdom is not participating in the financing of its own compensation and the Federal

Republic of Germany's share is reduced by one-third. It shall be calculated as if the reference compensation amount were financed by Member States according to their VAT assessment bases established in accordance with Article 2(1)(c).

5. The rate fixed under paragraph 1(d) shall apply to the GNP of each Member State.

6. If, at the beginning of the financial year, the budget has not been adopted, the previous uniform VAT rate and rate applicable to Member States' GNPs, without prejudice to the provisions adopted in accordance with Article 8(2) as regards the EAGGF monetary reserve, the reserve for financing the Loan Guarantee Fund and the reserve for emergency aid in third countries, shall remain applicable until the entry into force of the new rates.

7. For the purposes of applying this Decision, GNP shall mean gross national product for the year at market prices.

Article 3

1. The total amount of own resources assigned to the Communities may not exceed 1.27% of the total GNPs of the Member States for payment appropriations.

The total amount of own resources assigned to the Communities may not, for any of the years during the period 1995 to 1999, exceed the following percentages of the GNPs of the Member States for the year in question:

- 1995: 1.21,
- 1996: 1.22,
- 1997: 1.24,
- 1998: 1.26,
- 1999: 1.27.

2. The commitment appropriations entered in the general budget of the Communities over the period 1995 to 1999 must follow an orderly progression resulting in a total amount which does not exceed 1,335% of the total GNPs of the Member States in 1999. An orderly ratio between commitment appropriations and payment appropriations shall be maintained to guarantee their compatibility and to enable the ceilings mentioned in paragraph 1 to be observed in subsequent years.

3. The overall ceilings referred to in paragraphs 1 and 2 shall remain applicable until such time as this Decision is amended.

Article 4

The United Kingdom shall be granted a correction in respect of budgetary imbalances. This correction shall consist of a basic amount and an adjustment. The adjustment shall correct the basic amount to a reference compensation amount.

1. The basic amount shall be established by:

   (a) calculating the difference in the financial year, between:
   - the percentage share of the United Kingdom in the sum total of the payments referred to in Article 2(1)(c) and (d) made during the financial year, including adjustments at the uniform rate in respect of earlier financial years, and
   - the percentage share of the United Kingdom in total allocated expenditure:

   (b) applying the difference thus obtained to total allocated expenditure;

   (c) multiplying the result by 0.66.

2. The reference compensation shall be the correction resulting from application of (a), (b) and (c) of this paragraph, corrected by the effects arising for the United Kingdom from the changeover to capped VAT and the payments referred to in Article 2(1)(d).

It shall be established by:

   (a) calculating the difference, in the preceding financial year, between:
   - the percentage share of the United Kingdom in the sum total of VAT payments which would have been made during that financial year, including adjustments in respect of earlier financial years, for the amounts financed by the resources referred to in Article 2(1)(c) and (d) if the uniform VAT rate had been applied to non-capped bases, and
   - the percentage share of the United Kingdom in total allocated expenditure;

   (b) applying the difference thus obtained to total allocated expenditure:

   (c) multiplying the result by 0.66:

   (d) subtracting the payment by the United Kingdom taken into account in the first indent of point 1(a) from those taken into account in point (a), first indent of this subparagraph;

   (e) subtracting the amount calculated at (d) from the amount calculated at (c).

3. The basic amount shall be adjusted in such a way as to correspond to the reference compensation amount.

Article 5

1. The cost of the correction shall be borne by the other Member States in accordance with the following arrangements.

The distribution of the cost shall first be calculated by reference to each Member State's share of the payments referred to in Article 2(1)(d), the United Kingdom being excluded; it shall then be adjusted in such a way as to restrict the share of the Federal Republic of Germany to two-thirds of the share resulting from this calculation.

2. The correction shall be granted to the United Kingdom by a reduction in its payments resulting from the application of Article 2(1)(c) and (d). The costs borne by the other Member States shall be added to their payments resulting from the application for each Member State of Article 2(1)(c) and (d).

3. The Commission shall perform the calculations required for the application of Article 4 and this Article.

4. If, at the beginning of the financial year, the budget has not been adopted, the correction granted to the United Kingdom and the costs borne by the other Member States as entered in the last budget finally adopted shall remain applicable.

Article 6

The revenue referred to in Article 2 shall be used without distinction to finance all expenditure entered in the budget. However, the revenue needed to cover in full or in part the EAGGF monetary reserve, the reserve for the financing of the Loan Guarantee Fund and the reserve for emergency aid in third countries, entered in the budget shall not be called up from the Member States until the reserves are implemented. Provisions for the operation of those reserves shall be adopted as necessary in accordance with Article 8(2).

The first paragraph shall be without prejudice to the treatment of contributions by certain Member States to supplementary programmes provided for the Article 130l of the Treaty establishing the European Community.

Article 7

Any surplus of the Communities' revenue over total actual expenditure during the financial year shall be carried over to the following financial year.

Any surpluses generated by a transfer from EAGGF Guarantee Section chapters, or surplus from the Guarantee Fund arising from external measures, transferred to the revenue account in the budget, shall be regarded as constituting own resources.

Article 8

1. The Community own resources referred to in Article 2(1)(a) and (b) shall be collected by the Member States in accordance with the national provisions imposed by law, regulation or administrative action, which shall, where appropriate, be adapted to meet the requirements of Community rules. The Commission shall examine at regular intervals the national provisions communicated to it by the Member States, transmit to the Member States the adjustments it deems necessary in order to ensure that they comply with Community rules and report to the budget authority. Member States shall make the resources provided for in Article 2(1)(a) to (d) available to the Commission.

2. Without prejudice to the auditing of the accounts and to checks that they are lawful and regular as laid down in Article 188c of the Treaty establishing the European Community, such auditing and checks being mainly concerned with the reliability and effectiveness of national systems and procedures for determining the base for own resources accruing from VAT and GNP and without prejudice to the inspection arrangements made pursuant to Article 209(c) of that Treaty, the Council shall, acting unanimously on a proposal from the Commission and after consulting the European Parliament, adopt the provisions necessary to apply this Decision and to make possible the inspection of the collection, the making available to the Commission and payment of the revenue referred to in Articles 2 and 5.

Article 9

The mechanism for the graduated refund of own resources accruing from VAT or GNP-based financial contributions introduced for Greece up to 1985 by Article 127 of the 1979 Act of Accession and for Spain and Portugal up to 1991 by Articles 187 and 374 of the 1985 Act of Accession shall apply to the own resources accruing from VAT and the GNP-based resources referred to in Article 2(1)(c) and (d) of this Decision. It shall also apply to payments by the two last-named Member States in accordance with Article 5(2) of this Decision. In the latter case the rate of refund shall be that applicable for the year in respect of which the correction is granted.

Article 10

The Commission shall submit, by the end of 1999, a report on the operation of system, including a re-examination of the correction of budgetary imbalances granted to the United Kingdom, established by this Decision. It shall also by the end of 1999 submit a report on the findings of a study on the feasibility of creating a new own resource, as well as on arrangements for the possible introduction of a fixed uniform rate applicable to the VAT base.

Article 11

1. Member States shall be notified of this Decision by the Secretary-General of the Council and the Decision shall be published in the *Official Journal of the European Communities.*

Member States shall notify the Secretary-General of the Council without delay of the completion of the procedures for the adoption of this Decision in accordance with their respective constitutional requirements.

This Decision shall enter into force on the first day on the month following receipt of the last of the notifications referred to in the second subparagraph. It shall take effect on 1 January 1995.

2. (a) Subject to (b), Decision 88/376/EEC, Euratom shall be repealed as of 1 January 1995. Any references to the Council Decision of 21 April 1970 on the replacement of financial contributions from Member States by the Communities own resources, to Council Decision 85/257/EEC, Euratom of 7 May 1985 on the Communities' System of own resources, or to Decision 88/376/EEC, Euratom shall be construed as references to this Decision.

   (b) Article 3 of Decision 85/257/EEC, Euratom shall continue to apply to the calculation and adjustment of revenue from the application of rates to the uncapped uniform VAT base for 1987 and earlier years.

Articles 2, 4 and 5 of Decision 88/376/EEC, Euratom shall continue to apply to the calculation and adjustment of revenue accruing from application of a uniform rate valid for all Member States to the VAT base determined in a uniform manner and limited to 55% of the GNP of each Member State and to the calculation of the correction of budgetary imbalances granted to the

United Kingdom for the years 1988 to 1994. When Article 2(7) of that Decision has to be applied, the value added tax payments shall be replaced by financial contributions in the calculations referred to in this paragraph for any Member State concerned; this system shall also apply to the payment of adjustments of corrections for earlier years.

COUNCIL DECISION DETERMINING THE ORDER IN WHICH THE OFFICE OF PRESIDENT OF THE COUNCIL SHALL BE HELD

(95/2/EC, Euratom, ECSC)
(Brussels, 1 January 1995)

The Council of the European Union,

Having regard to the Treaty establishing the European Coal and Steel Community, and in particular, the second paragraph of Article 27 thereof,

Having regard to the Treaty establishing the European Community, and in particular the second paragraph of Article 146 thereof,

Having regard to the Treaty establishing the European Atomic Energy Community, and in particular Article 116 thereof,

Whereas Article 12 of the Act annexed to the Treaty concerning the Accession of the Kingdom of Norway, the Republic of Austria, the Republic of Finland and the Kingdom of Sweden to the European Union adjusted the above provisions, laying down that the Council shall determine the order in which the office of President of the Council shall determine the order in which the office of President to the Council shall be held in turn by the Member States,

HAS DECIDED AS FOLLOWS:

Article 1

1. The office of President shall be held:

   - for the first six months of 1995 by France,
   - for the second six months of 1995 by Spain,
   - for the subsequent periods of six months by the following Member States in turn in the following order: Italy, Ireland, Netherlands,

Luxembourg, United Kingdom, Austria, Germany, Finland, Portugal, France, Sweden, Belgium, Spain, Denmark, Greece.

2. The Council, acting unanimously on a proposal from the Member States concerned, may decide that a Member State may hold the Presidency during a period other than that resulting from the above order..

Article 2

This Decision shall be published in the Official Journal of the European Communities.

COMMISSION MEMORANDUM ON APPLYING ARTICLE 171 OF THE EC TREATY
(96/C 242/07)
(5 June 1996)

1. Article 171 of the EC Treaty as amended by the Treaty on European Union stipulates that penalties may be imposed on a Member State which has not complied with a judgment finding that it has failed to fulfil an obligation under the Treaty.

It is for the Court of Justice to take the final decision on the penalties to be imposed. The Commission, however, as the guardian of the Treaties, has a decisive part to play at an earlier stage in the proceedings in that it is responsible for initiating the Article 171 procedure and, where appropriate, bringing a case before the Court of Justice. It also gives its view on the actual amount of the lump sum or penalty payment.

2. As this is a new mechanism which supplements the existing procedure for failure to comply, the Commission, in a spirit of openness, believes that it must publicly state the criteria it means to apply in asking the Court to impose monetary penalties. In so doing, the Commission would stress that both the criteria selected and the way they are applied will be dictated by the need to ensure that Community law is effectively enforced. Once the general criteria set out below have been applied in individual cases and the Court of Justice itself has begun to hand down decisions on the matter, the Commission will be able to gradually refine its views, this Memorandum being only an initial approach to the question.

3. Under Article 171, if a Member State has failed to take the necessary measures to comply with a judgment of the Court of Justice within the time limit laid down in the reasoned opinion addressed to it by the Commission, the latter may bring the case before the Court of Justice. In so doing, the Commission specifies '*the amount of the lump sum or penalty payment to be paid by the Member State concerned which it considers appropriate in the circumstances*'.

Within this procedure, the Commission has *a discretion in deciding* whether to refer the case to the Court but, if it does decide to do so, it is required to *give its view as to the penalty and the amount thereof* when lodging its application.

This does not, however, in the Commission's view, mean that it must ask for a penalty to be imposed in every case. Where circumstances warrant (eg where the infringement is minor or there is no risk of the offence being repeated), the Commission may refrain from asking for a penalty to be imposed; it must nevertheless state its reasons.

4. Article 171 offers a choice between two types of pecuniary sanction, *a lump sum or a penalty payment*. The basic object of the whole infringement procedure is *to secure compliance as rapidly as possible*, and the Commission considers that *a penalty payment* is the most appropriate instrument instrument for achieving it.

This does not, however, mean that it will never ask for a *lump sum* to be imposed.

5. Decisions as to the *amount of the penalty* must be taken with an eye to its actual purpose, which is to ensure that Community law is effectively enforced. The Commission considers that the amount must be calculated on the basis of three fundamental criteria:

- *the seriousness of the infringement,*
- *its duration,*
- *the need to ensure that the penalty itself is a deterrent to further infringements.*

6. As regards *seriousness*, an infringement in the form of failure to comply with a judgment is always quite clearly serious. However, for the specific purpose of fixing the amount of the penalty, the Commission will also take account of two parameters closely linked to the underlying infringement which gave rise to the original judgment, viz *the importance of the Community rules which have been infringed and the effects of the infringement on general and particular interests.*

6.1. In assessing *the importance of the Community provisions which have been infringed,* the Commission will have regard to their nature and scope rather than to their standing in the hierarchy of norms. Thus, for example, an infringement of the principle of non-discrimination must always be regarded as very serious, regardless of whether it has come about through a breach of the principle laid down by the EC Treaty itself or of the principle as set out in a regulation or directive. Generally speaking, for example, attacks on fundamental rights and on the four fundamental freedoms enshrined in the Treaty should be regarded as serious and a penalty appropriate to that degree of seriousness should be imposed in such cases.

6.2. The *effects of the infringement on general or particular interests* will have to be gauged on a case-by-case basis. Examples of such effects would be a loss of own resources resulting from an infringement or the particularly damaging effects of pollution arising from an action in breach of Community law. Where the effects of an infringement on the general interest are concerned, *its impact on the functioning of the Community* must be taken into account. Clearly, an unwarranted prohibition on the marketing in one Member State of goods manufactured in another has an immediate and obvious effect on the functioning of the common market, but other, less drastic measures, or even in some cases a failure by a Member State to act, may have just as much effect on the functioning of the Community.

6.3. More specifically, when taking *the interests of individuals* into account for the purpose of calculating the amount of a penalty, the Commission does not set out to obtain redress for the damage and loss suffered as a result of an infringement, since such redress may be obtained by commencing proceedings before the national courts. The Commission's purpose is rather to take into consideration *the effects of an infringement from the point of view of the individual and the economic operators concerned*; thus, for example, consequences are not the same where the breach concerns, either an individual case of misapplication (non-recognition of a diploma), or the failure to implement a directive on the mutual recognition of diplomas, which would prejudice the interests of an entire profession.

7. The Commission will also take account of the *duration of an infringement* in deciding the amount of a penalty. In proceedings whose object is to establish that a judgment of the Court of Justice has not been complied with the duration will, as a rule, be considerable.

8. From the point of view of the effectiveness of the penalty, it is important to set *amounts* such that the penalty has a *deterrent effect*. To impose purely symbolic penalties would negate the whole purpose of this addition to the infringement procedure and run counter to the ultimate objective of the procedure, which is to ensure that Community law is fully enforced.

A decision as to whether to ask for a penalty to be imposed will depend on the circumstances of the case, as stated at point 3. But, once it has been found that a penalty should be imposed, for it to have a deterrent effect it must be set at a higher figure if there is any *risk of a repetition* (or where there has been a repetition) of the failure to comply, in order to cancel out any economic advantage which the Member State responsible for the infringement might derive in the case in point.

NB As a follow-up to this memorandum, on 8 January 1997 the Commission adopted a method for calculating the penalty payment on the basis of a flat rate applicable to all types of infringement. The flat rate is ECU 500 for each day's delay and it is multiplied by two coefficients, one taking into account the seriousness of the infringement and the second the duration. The first coefficient varies between 1 and a maximum of 20; the second between 1 and 3. A deterrent effect is achieved by applying a special 'factor' based on each Member State's financial capacity, as measured by its GDP. To ensure that the penalty payment is proportional, account is also taken of the number of votes each Member State has in the Council, thereby reflecting the say it had in establishing the Community law which has been infringed. The factor obtained by combining GDP and the weighting of votes is invariable for each Member State.

EUROPEAN COMMUNITIES ACT 1972
(1972 c 68)

PART I

GENERAL PROVISIONS

1   Short title and interpretation

(1) This Act may be cited as the European Communities Act 1972.

(2) In this Act

'the Communities' means the European Economic Community, the European Coal and Steel Community and the European Atomic Energy Community;

'the Treaties' or 'the Community Treaties' means, subject to sub-section (3) below, the pre-accession treaties, that is to say, those described in Part I of Schedule I to this Act, taken with

(a) the treaty relating to the accession of the United Kingdom to the European Economic Community and to the European Atomic Energy Community, signed at Brussels on January 22 1972; and

(b) the decision, of the same date, of the Council of the European Communities relating to the accession of the United Kingdom to the European Coal and Steel Community; and

(c) the treaty relating to the accession of the Hellenic Republic to the European Economic Community and to the European Atomic Energy Community, signed at Athens on 28th May 1979; and

(d) the decision, of 24th May 1979, of the Council relating to the accession of the Hellenic Republic to the European Coal and Steel Community; and

(e) the decisions of the Council of 7th May 1985, 24th June 1988, and 31st October 1994, on the Communities' system of own resources; and

(g) the treaty relating to the accession of the Kingdom of Spain and the Portuguese Republic to the European Economic Community and to the European Atomic Energy Community, signed at Lisbon and Madrid on 12th June 1985; and

(h) the decision, on 11th June 1985, of the Council relating to the accession of the Kingdom of Spain and the Portuguese Republic to the European Coal and Steel Community; and

(j) the following provisions of the Single European Act signed at Luxembourg and The Hague on 17th and 28th February 1986, namely Title II (amendment of the treaties establishing the Communities) and, so far as they relate to any of the Communities or any Community institution, the preamble and Titles I (common provisions) and IV (general and final provisions); and

(k) Titles II, III and IV of the Treaty on European Union signed at Maastricht on 7th February 1992, together with the other provisions of the Treaty so far as they relate to those Titles, and the Protocols adopted at Maastricht on that date and annexed to the Treaty Establishing the European Community with the exception of the Protocol on Social Policy on pay 117 of Cm 1934; and

(l) the decision, of 1st February 1993, of the Council amending the Act concerning the election of the representatives of the European Parliament by direct universal suffrage annexed to Council Decision 76/787/ECSC, EEC, Euratom of 20th September 1976; and

(m) the Agreement on the European Economic Area signed at Oporto on 2nd May 1992 together with the Protocol adjusting that Agreement signed at Brussels on 17th March 1993, and any other treaty entered into by any of the Communities, with or without any of the Member States, or entered into, as a treaty ancillary to any of the Treaties, by the United Kingdom;

(n) the Treaty concerning the accession of the Kingdom of Norway, the Republic of Austria, the Republic of Finland and the Kingdom of Sweden to the European Union, signed at Corfu on 24th June 1994;

and any expression defined in Schedule 1 to this Act has the meaning there given to it.

(3) If Her Majesty by Order in Council declares that a treaty specified in the Order is to be regarded as one of the Community Treaties as herein defined, the Order shall be conclusive that it is to be so regarded; but a treaty entered into by the United Kingdom after 22 January 1972, other than a pre-accession treaty to which the United Kingdom accedes on terms settled on or before that date, shall not be so regarded unless it is so specified, nor be so specified unless a draft of the Order in Council has been approved by resolution of each House of Parliament.

(4) For purposes of subsections (2) and (3) above, 'treaty' includes any international agreement, and any protocol or annex to a treaty or international agreement.

2 General implementation of Treaties

(1) All such rights, powers, liabilities, obligations and restrictions from time to time created or arising by or under the Treaties, and all such remedies and procedures from time to time provided for by or under the Treaties, as in accordance with the Treaties are without further enactment to be given legal effect or used in the United Kingdom shall be recognised and available in law, and be enforced, allowed and followed accordingly; and the expression 'enforceable Community right' and similar expressions shall be read as referring to one to which this subsection applies.

(2) Subject to Schedule 2 to this Act, at any time after its passing Her Majesty may by Order in Council, and any designated Minister or department may by regulations, make provision –

> (a) for the purpose of implementing any Community obligation of the United Kingdom, or enabling any such obligation to be implemented, or of enabling any rights enjoyed or to be enjoyed by the United Kingdom under or by virtue of the Treaties to be exercised;
>
> (b) for the purpose of dealing with matters arising out of or related to any such obligation or rights or the coming into force, or the operation from time to time, of subsection (1) above;

and in the exercise of any statutory power or duty, including any power to give directions or legislate by means of orders, rules, regulations or other subordinate instrument, the person entrusted with the power or duty may have regard to the objects of the Communities and to any such obligation or rights as aforesaid.

In this subsection 'designated Minister or department' means such Minister of the Crown or government department as may from time to time be designated by Order in Council in relation to any matter or for any purpose, but subject to such restrictions or conditions (if any) as may be specified by the Order in Council.

(3) There shall be charged on and issued out of the Consolidated Fund or, if so determined by the Treasury, the National Loans Fund, the amounts required to meet any Community obligation to make payments to any of the Communities or member states, or any Community obligation in respect of contributions to the capital or reserves of the European Investment Bank or in respect of loans to the Bank, or to redeem any notes or obligations issued or created in respect of any such Community obligation; and, in except as other wise provided by or under any enactment,

> (a) any other expenses incurred under or by virtue of the Treaties or this Act by any Minister of the Crown or government department may be paid out of moneys provided by Parliament; and

(b) any sums received under or by virtue of the Treaties or this Act by any Minster of the Crown or government department, save for such sums as may be required for disbursements permitted by any other enactment, shall be paid into the Consolidated Fund or, if so determined by the Treasury, the National Loans Fund.

(4) The provision that may be made under subsection (2) above includes, subject to Schedule 2 to this Act, any such provision (of any such extent) as might be made by Act of Parliament, and any enactment passed or to be passed, other than one contained in this Part of this Act, shall be construed and have effect subject to the foregoing provisions of this section; but, except as may be provided by any Act passed after this Act, Schedule 2 shall have effect in connection with the powers conferred by this and the following sections of this Act to make Orders in Council and regulations.

(5) The references in that subsection to a Minister of the Crown or government department and to a statutory power or duty shall include a Minister or department of the Government of Northern Ireland and a power or duty arising under or by virtue of an Act of the Parliament of Northern Ireland.

(6) A law passed by the legislature of any of the Channel Islands or of the Isle of Man, or a colonial law (within the meaning of the Colonial Laws Validity Act 1865) passed or made for Gibraltar, if expressed to be passed or made in the implementation of the Treaties and of the obligations of the United Kingdom thereunder, shall not be void or inoperative by reason of any inconsistency with or repugnancy to an Act of Parliament, passed or to be passed, that extends to the Island or Gibraltar or any provision having the force and effect of an Act there (but not including this section), nor by reason of its having some operation outside the Island or Gibraltar; and any such Act or provision that extends to the Island or Gibraltar shall be construed and have effect subject to the provisions of any such law.

3   Decisions on, and proof of, Treaties and Community Instruments, etc

(1) For the purposes of all legal proceedings any question as to the meaning or effect of any of the Treaties, or as to the validity, meaning or effect of any Community instrument, shall be treated as a question of law and, if not referred to the European Court, be for determination as such in accordance with the principles laid down by and any relevant decision of the European Court or any court attached thereto.

(2) Judicial notice shall be taken of the Treaties, of the Official Journal of the Communities and of any decision of, or expression of opinion by, the

European Court or any court attached thereto on any such question as aforesaid; and the Official Journal shall be admissible as evidence of any instrument or other act thereby communicated of any of the Communities or of any Community institution.

(3) Evidence of any instrument issued by a Community institution, including any judgment or order of the European Court or any court attached thereto, or of any document in the custody of a Community institution, or any entry in or extract from such a document, may be given in any legal proceedings by production of a copy certified as a true copy by an official of that institution; and any document purporting to be such a copy shall be received in evidence without proof of the official position or handwriting of the person signing the certificate.

(4) Evidence of any Community instrument may also be given in any legal proceedings –

(a) by production of a copy purporting to be printed by the Queen's Printer;

(b) where the instrument is in the custody of a government department (including a department of the Government of Northern Ireland), by production of a copy certified on behalf of the department to be a true copy by an officer of the department generally or specially authorised so to do;

any any document purporting to be such a copy as is mentioned in paragraph (b) above of an instrument in the custody of a department shall be received in evidence without proof of the official position or handwriting of the person signing the certificate, or of his authority to do so, or of the document being in the custody of the department.

(5) In any legal proceedings in Scotland evidence of any matter given in a manner authorised by this section shall be sufficient evidence of it.

PART II

AMENDMENT OF LAW

4 General provision for repeal and amendment

(1) The enactments mentioned in Schedule 3 to this Act (being enactments that are superseded or to be superseded by reason of Community obligations and of the provision made by this Act in relation thereto or are not compatible with Community obligations) are hereby repealed, to the extent specified in column 3 of the Schedule, with effect from the entry date or other date mentioned in the Schedule; and in the enactments mentioned in

Schedule 4 to this Act there shall, subject to any transitional provision there included, be made the amendments provided for by that Schedule.

(2) Where in any Part of Schedule 3 to this Act it is provided that repeals made by that Part are to take effect from a date appointed by order, the orders shall be made by statutory instrument, and an order may appoint different dates for the repeal of different provisions to take effect, or for the repeal of the same provision to take effect for different purposes; and an order appointing a date for a repeal to take effect may include transitional and other supplementary provisions arising out of that repeal, including provisions adapting the operation of other enactments included for repeal but not yet repealed by that Schedule, and may amend or revoke any such provisions included in a previous order.

(3) Where any of the following sections of this Act, or any paragraph of Schedule 4 to this Act, affects or is construed as one with an Act or Part of an Act similar in purpose to provisions having effect only in Northern Ireland, then

(a) unless otherwise provided by Act of the Parliament of Northern Ireland, the Governor of Northern Ireland may by Order in Council make provision corresponding to any made by the section or paragraph, and amend or revoke any provision so made; and

(4) Where Schedule 3 or 4 to this Act provides for the repeal or amendment of an enactment that extends or is capable of being extended to any of the Channel Islands or the Isle of Man, the repeal or amendment shall in like manner extend or be capable of being extended thereto.

5 Customs duties

(1) Subject to subsection (2) below, on and after the relevant date there shall be charged, levied, collected and paid on goods imported into the United Kingdom such Community customs duty, if any, as is for the time being applicable in accordance with the Treaties or, if the goods are not within the common customs tariff of the Economic Community and the duties chargeable are not otherwise fixed by any directly applicable Community provision, such duty of customs, if any, as the Treasury, on the recommendation of the Secretary of State, may by order specify.

For this purpose 'the relevant date', in relation to any goods, is the date on and after which the duties of customs that may be charged thereon are no longer affected under the Treaties by any temporary provision made on or with reference to the accession of the United Kingdom to the Communities.

(2) Where as regards goods imported into the United Kingdom provision

may, in accordance with the Treaties, be made in derogation of the common customs tariff or of the exclusion of customs duties as between member States, the Treasury may by order make such provisions as to the customs duties chargeable on the goods, or as to exempting the goods from any customs duty, as the Treasury may on the recommendation of the Secretary of State determine.

(3) Schedule 2 to this Act shall have effect in connection with the powers to make orders conferred by subsections (1) and (2) above.

6 The Common agricultural policy

(1) There shall be a Board in charge of a government department, which shall be appointed by and responsible to the Ministers, and shall be by the name of the Intervention Board for Agricultural Produce a body corporate (but not subject as a statutory corporation to restrictions on its corporate capacity); and the Board (in addition to any other functions that may be entrusted to it) shall be charged, subject to the direction and control of the Ministers, with such functions as they may from time to time determine in connection with the carrying out of the obligations of the United Kingdom under the common agricultural policy of the Economic Community.

(2) Her Majesty may by Order in Council make further provision as to the constitution and membership of the Board, and the remuneration (including pensions) of members of the Board or any committee thereof, and for regulating or facilitating the discharge of the Board's functions, including provision for the Board to arrange for its functions to be performed by other bodies on its behalf and any such provision as was made by Schedule 1 to the Ministers of the Crown Act 1964 in relation to a Minister to whom that Schedule applied; and the Ministers –

> (a) may, after consultation with any body created by a statutory provision and concerned with agriculture or agricultural produce, by regulations modify or add to the constitution or powers of the body so as to enable it to act for the Board, or by written directions given to the body require it to discontinue or modify any activity appearing to the Ministers to be prejudicial to the proper discharge of the Board's functions; and
>
> (b) may by regulations provide for the charging of fees in connection with the discharge of any functions of the Board.

(3) Sections 5 and 7 of the Agriculture Act 1957 (which make provision for the support of arrangements under section 1 of that Act for providing guaranteed prices or assured markets) shall apply in relation to any Community arrangements for or related to the regulation of the market for

any agricultural produce as if references, in whatever terms, to payments made by virtue of section 1 were references to payments made by virtue of the Community arrangements by or on behalf of the Board and as if in section 5(1)(d) the reference to the Minister included the Board.

(4) Agricultural levies of the Economic Community, so far as they are charged on goods exported from the United Kingdom or shipped as stores, shall be paid to and recoverable by the Board; and the power of the Ministers to make order under section 5 of the Agriculture Act 1957, as extended by this section, shall include power to make such provision supplementary to any directly applicable Community provision as the Ministers consider necessary for securing the payment of any agricultural levies so charged, including provision for the making of declarations or the giving of other information in respect of goods exported, shipped as stores, warehoused or otherwise dealt with.

(5) Except as otherwise provided by or under any enactment, agricultural levies of the Economic Community, so far as they are charged on goods imported into the United Kingdom, shall be levied, collected and paid, and the proceeds shall be dealt with, as if they were Community customs duties, and in relation to those levies the following enactments shall apply as they would apply in relation to Community customs duties, that is to say:

(a) The Customs and Excise Management Act 1979 (as for the time being amended by any later Act) and any other statutory provisions for the time being in force relating generally to customs or excise duties on imported goods; and

(b) sections 1, 3, 4, 5, 6 (including Schedule 1), 7, 8, 9, 12, 13, 15, 17 and 18 of the Customs and Excise Duties (General Reliefs) Act 1979 but so that –

(i) any references in sections 1, 3 and 4 to the Secretary of State shall include the Ministers; and

(ii) the reference in section 15 to an application for an authorisation under regulations made under section 2 of that Act shall be read as a reference to an application for an authorisation under regulations made under section 2(2) of this Act;

and if, in connection with any such Community arrangements as aforesaid, the Commissioners of Customs and Excise are charged with the performance, on behalf of the Board or otherwise, of any duties in relation to the payment of refunds or allowances on goods exported or to be exported from the United Kingdom, then in relation to any such refund or allowance section 133 (except subsection (3) and the reference to that subsection in subsection (2) and section 159 of the Customs and Excise Management Act

1979 shall apply as they apply in relation to a drawback of excise duties, and other provisions of that Act shall have effect accordingly.

(6) The enactments applied by subsection (5)(a) above shall apply subject to such exceptions and modifications, if any, as the Commissioners of Customs and Excise may by regulations prescribe, and shall be taken to include section 10 of the Finance Act 1901 (which relates to changes in customs import duties in their effect on contracts), but shall not include (section 126 of the Customs and Excise Management Act 1979).

(8) Expressions used in this section shall be construed as if contained in Part I of the Agriculture Act 1957; and in this section 'agricultural levy' shall include any tax not being a customs duty, but of equivalent effect, that may be chargeable in accordance with any such Community arrangements as aforesaid, and 'statutory provision' includes any provision having effect by virtue of any enactment and, in subsection (2), any enactment of the Parliament of Northern Ireland or provision having effect by virtue of such an enactment.

11 Community offences

(1) A person who, in sworn evidence before the European Court or any court attached thereto makes any statement which he knows to be false or does not believe to be true shall, whether he is a British subject or not, be guilty of an offence and may be proceeded against and punished –

(a) in England and Wales as for an offence against section 1(1) of the Perjury Act 1911; or

(b) in Scotland as for an offence against section 1 of the False Oaths (Scotland) Act 1933; or

(c) in Northern Ireland as for an offence against Article 3(1) of the Perjury (Northern Ireland) Order 1979.

Where a report is made as to any such offence under the authority of the European Court (or any court attached thereto), then a bill of indictment for the offence may, in England or Wales or in Northern Ireland, be preferred as in a case where a prosecution is ordered under section 9 of the Perjury Act 1911 or Article 13 of the Perjury (Northern Ireland) Order 1979 but the report shall not be given in evidence on a person's trial for the offence.

(2) Where a person (whether a British subject or not) owing either –

(a) to his duties as a member of any Euratom institution or committee, or as an officer or servant of Euratom; or

(b) to his dealings in any capacity (official or unofficial) with any

Euratom institution or installation or with any Euratom joint enterprise;

has occasion to acquire, or obtain cognisance of, any classified information, he shall be guilty of a misdemeanour if, knowing or having reason to believe that it is classified information he communicates it to any unauthorised person or makes any public disclosure of it, whether in the United Kingdom or elsewhere and whether before or after the termination of those duties or dealings; and for the purpose 'classified information' means any facts, information, knowledge, documents or objects that are subject to the security rules of a member State or of any Euratom institution.

This subsection shall be construed, and the Official Secrets Act 1911 to 1939 shall have effect, as if this subsection were contained in the Official Secrets Act 1911, but so that in that Act sections 10 and 11, except section 10(4), shall not apply.

(3) This section shall not come into force until the entry date.

12 Furnishing of information to Communities

Estimates, returns and information that may under section 9 of the Statistics of Trade Act 1947 or section 3 of the Agricultural Statistics Act 1979 be disclosed to a government department or Minster in charge of a government department may in like manner, be disclosed in pursuance of a Community obligation to a Community institution.

SCHEDULE 1

DEFINITIONS RELATING TO COMMUNITIES

PART I

THE PRE-ACCESSION TREATIES

(1) The 'ECSC Treaty', that is to say, the Treaty establishing the European Coal and Steel Community, signed at Paris on the 18th April 1951.

(2) The 'EEC Treaty', that is to say, the Treaty establishing the European Economic Community, signed at Rome on the 25th March 1957.

(3) The 'Euratom Treaty', that is to say, the Treaty establishing the European Atomic Energy Community, signed at Rome on the 25th March 1957.

(4) The Convention on certain Institutions common to the European Communities, signed at Rome on the 25th March 1957.

(5) The Treaty establishing a single Council and a single Commission of the European Communities, signed at Brussels on the 8th April 1965.

(6) The Treaty amending certain Budgetary Provisions of the Treaties establishing the European Communities and of the Treaty establishing a single Council and a single Commission of the European Communities, signed at Luxembourg on the 22nd April 1970.

(7) Any treaty entered into before the 22nd January 1972 by any of the Communities (with or without any of the member States), or as a treaty ancillary to any treaty included in this Part of this Schedule, by the member States (with or without any other country).

PART II

OTHER DEFINITIONS

'Economic Community', 'Coal and Steel Community' and 'Euratom' mean respectively the European Economic Community, the European Coal and Steel Community and the European Atomic Energy Community.

'Community customs duty' means, in relation to any goods, such duty of customs as may from time to time be fixed for those goods by directly applicable Community provision as the duty chargeable on importation into member States.

'Community institution' means any institution of any of the Communities or common to the Communities; and any reference to an institution of a particular Community shall include one common to the Communities when it acts for that Community, and similarly with references to a committee, officer or servant of a particular Community.

'Community instrument' means any instrument issued by a Community institution.

'Community obligation' means any obligation created or arising by or under the Treaties, whether an enforceable Community obligation or not.

'Enforceable Community right' and similar expressions shall be construed in accordance with section 2(1) of this Act.

'Entry date' means the date on which the United Kingdom becomes a member of the Communities.

'European Court' means the Court of Justice of the European Communities.

'Member', in the expression 'member State', refers to membership of the Communities.

SCHEDULE 2

PROVISIONS AS TO SUBORDINATE LEGISLATION

1 – (1) The powers conferred by section 2(2) of this Act to make provision for the purposes mentioned in section 2(2)(a) and (b) shall not include power –

(a) to make any provision imposing or increasing taxation; or

(b) to make any provision taking effect from a date earlier than that of the making of the instrument containing the provision; or

(c) to confer any power to legislate by means of orders, rules, regulations or other subordinate instrument, other than rules of procedure for any court or tribunal; or

(d) to create any new criminal offence punishable with imprisonment for more than two years or punishable on summary conviction with imprisonment for more than three months or with a fine of more than level 5 on the standard scale (if not calculated on a daily basis) or with a fine of more than £100 a day.

(2) Sub-paragraph (1)(c) above shall not be taken to preclude the modification of a power to legislate conferred otherwise than under section 2(2), or the extension of any such power to purposes of the like nature as those for which it was conferred; and a power to give directions as to matters of administration is not to be regarded as a power to legislate within the meaning of sub-paragraph (1)(c).

2 – (1) Subject to paragraph 3 below, where a provision contained in any section of this Act confers power to make regulations (otherwise than by modification or extension of an existing power), the power shall be exercisable by statutory instrument.

(2) Any statutory instrument containing an Order in Council or regulations made in the exercise of a power so conferred, if made without a draft having been approved by resolution of each House of Parliament, shall be subject to annulment in pursuance of a resolution of either House.

3 Nothing in paragraph 2 above shall apply to any Order in Council made by the Governor of Northern Ireland or to any regulations made by a Minister or department of the Government of Northern Ireland; but where a provision contained in any section of this Act confers power to make such an Order in Council or regulations, then any Order in Council or regulations made in the exercise of that power, if made without a draft having been approved by resolution of each House of the Parliament of Northern Ireland, shall be subject to negative resolution within the meaning of section 41(6) of

the Interpretation Act (Northern Ireland) 1954 as if the Order or regulations were a statutory instrument within the meaning of that Act.

As amended by the Northern Ireland Constitution Act 1973, s41(1); Interpretation Act 1978, s25(1), sched 3, European Communities (Greek Accession) Act 1979, s1; Customs and Excise Duties (General Reliefs) Act 1979, s19(1), (2), Scheds 2, 3; Customs and Excise Management Act 1979, s177(1), (3), (4), Scheds 4, 6, 7; Agricultural Statistics Act 1979, s7(1), Sched 1; European Communities (Spanish and Portuguese Accession) Act 1985, s1; European Communities (Amendment) Act 1986, ss1, 2; European Communities (Finance) Act 1988, s1; European Communities (Amendment) Act 1993, s1(1); European Parliamentary Elections Act 1993, s3(2); European Economic Area Act 1993, s1; Criminal Justice Act 1982, ss40, 46; Agriculture Act 1993, s64(1), Sched 5; European Communities (Finance) Act 1994, s1; European Union (Accessions) Act 1994, s1; European Communities (Finance) Act 1995, s1.

EUROPEAN PARLIAMENTARY ELECTIONS ACT 1978
(1978 c 10)

1 Election of representatives to the European Parliament

(1) The representatives of the people of the United Kingdom in the European Parliament shall be elected in accordance with this Act.

2 Number of representatives

The number of representatives to the European Parliament to be elected in the United Kingdom shall be 87; and of those representatives –

(a) 71 shall be elected in England;

(b) 8 shall be elected in Scotland;

(c) 5 shall be elected in Wales; and

(d) 3 shall be elected in Northern Ireland.

3 Method of election

European Parliamentary elections shall be held and conducted in accordance with the provisions of Schedule 1 to this Act (with Schedule 2) under the simple majority system (for Great Britain) and the single transferable vote system (for Northern Ireland).

4 Double voting

(1) Without prejudice to any enactment relating to voting offences as applied by regulations under this Act to elections of representatives to the European Parliament held in the United Kingdom, a person shall be guilty of an offence if, on any occasion when under Article 9 elections to the European Parliament are held in all the member States, he votes otherwise than as a proxy more than once in those elections, whether in the United Kingdom or elsewhere.

(2) The provisions of the Representation of the People Act 1983 as applied by regulations under this Act shall have effect in relation to an offence under this section as they have effect in relation to an offence under section 61(2) of that Act (double voting); and, without prejudice to the generality of the foregoing provision, section 61(7) of that Act (which makes such an offence an illegal practice but allows any incapacity resulting from conviction to be mitigated by the convicting court) and section 178 of that Act (prosecutions for offences committed outside the United Kingdom) shall apply accordingly.

6 Parliamentary approval of treaties increasing European Parliament's powers

(1) No treaty which provides for any increase in the powers of the European Parliament shall be ratified by the United Kingdom unless it has been approved by an Act of Parliament.

(2) In this section 'treaty' includes any international agreement, and any protocol or annex to a treaty or international agreement.

7 Expenses

(1) There shall be charged on, and paid out of, the Consolidated Fund –

(a) such reasonable charges as returning officers are by virtue of this Act entitled to in connection with European Parliamentary elections; and

(b) any increase attributable to this Act in the sums charged on and payable out of that Fund under any other enactment.

(2) There shall be paid out of money provided by Parliament –

(a) any additional sums payable by way of rate support grant because of an increase attributable to this Act in the registration expenses of registration officers in Great Britain;

(b) any increase so attributable in the sums payable out of money so provided under section 54(2) of the Representation of the People Act 1983 on account of the registration expenses of registration officers in Northern Ireland; and

(c) any increase so attributable in the sums payable out of money so provided under the House of Commons (Redistribution of Seats) Act 1949.

8 Interpretation

(1) The provisions of this Act, except section 4, apply only in relation to representatives to the European Parliament who fall to be elected in the United Kingdom; and references in this Act (except section 4) to elections to the European Parliament shall be construed accordingly.

(2) In this Act –

(a) any reference to a numbered Article is a reference to the Article so numbered of the Act concerning the election of the representatives of the European Parliament by direct universal suffrage annexed to the decision of the Council of the European Communities dated the 20th September 1976, and any reference to a numbered subdivision of a numbered Article shall be construed accordingly;

(b) 'enactment' includes an enactment contained in an Act of the Parliament of Northern Ireland or an Order in Council made under the Northern Ireland (Temporary Provisions) Act 1972, or in a Measure of the Northern Ireland Assembly.

(3) Except where the context otherwise requires, any reference in this Act to an enactment is a reference to that enactment as amended, and includes a reference to it as applied, by or under any other enactment, including this Act.

9 Citation, etc

(1) This Act may be cited as the European Parliamentary Elections Act 1978.

(2) Any power to make orders or regulations conferred by this Act shall be exercisable by statutory instrument; and any power to make an order under any provision of this Act includes power to vary or revoke a previous order made under that provision.

SCHEDULE 1

SIMPLE MAJORITY SYSTEM (FOR GREAT BRITAIN) WITH STV (FOR NORTHERN IRELAND)

1 – (1) Representatives to the European Parliament shall be elected in Great Britain for the European Parliamentary constituencies for the time being specified in an Order in Council under Schedule 2 to this Act, and in Northern Ireland for a single European Parliamentary constituency comprising the whole of Northern Ireland; and there shall be –

(a) one representative for each such constituency in Great Britain; and

(b) three representatives for the European Parliamentary constituency of Northern Ireland.

(2) There shall be a total of 85 European Parliamentary constituencies, of which –

(a) 71 shall be in England;

(b) 8 shall be in Scotland;

(c) 5 shall be in Wales;

(d) 1 shall be that of Northern Ireland.

2 – (1) The persons entitled to vote as electors at a European Parliamentary election in any particular European Parliament constituency shall be –

(a) those who, on the day appointed under paragraph 3 below for the election, would be entitled to vote as electors at a parliamentary election in a parliamentary constituency wholly or partly comprised in the European Parliamentary constituency (excluding any person not registered in the register of parliamentary electors at an address within the European Parliamentary constituency); and

(b) peers who, on that day, would be entitled to vote at a local government election in an electoral area wholly or partly comprised in the European Parliamentary constituency (excluding any peer not registered at an address within the European Parliamentary constituency for the purposes of local government elections).

(2) In a European Parliamentary election in the constituency of Northern Ireland each vote shall be a single transferable vote, that is to say a vote –

(a) capable of being given so as to indicate the voter's order of preference for the candidates for election as representatives for the constituency; and

(b) capable of being transferred to the next choice –

(i) when the voter is not required to give a prior choice the necessary quota of votes; or

(ii) when, owing to the deficiency in the number of votes given for a prior choice, that choice is eliminated from the list of candidates.

(3) Subject to the provisions of this and the following paragraph, the Secretary of State may by regulations make provision –

(a) as to the conduct of European Parliamentary elections (including the registration of electors and the elimination of candidates' election expenses); and

(b) as to the questioning of such an election and the consequences of irregularities.

(4) Regulations under this paragraph may –

(a) apply, with such modifications or exceptions as may be specified in the regulations, any provision of the Representation of the People Acts or of any other enactment relating to parliamentary elections or local government elections, and any provision made under any enactment;

(b) amend any form contained in regulations made under the Representation of the People Acts so far as may be necessary to enable it to be used both for the purpose indicated in regulations so made and for the corresponding purpose in relation to European Parliamentary elections;

(c) so far as may be necessary in consequence of any provision made by or under this Act, amend any provision made by or under any enactment relating to the registration of parliamentary electors or local government electors.

(5) Section 26 of the Welsh Language Act 1993 (power to prescribe Welsh version) shall apply in relation to regulations under this paragraph as it applies in relation to Acts of Parliament.

(6) No regulations shall be made under this paragraph unless a draft thereof has been laid before Parliament and approved by a resolution of each House of Parliament.

3 – (1) Each general election of representatives to the European Parliament shall be held on a day appointed by order of the Secretary of State.

(2) Subject to sub-paragraph (4) below, where, a European Parliamentary election having been held in any particular European Parliamentary constituency, the seat of a representative to the European Parliament is or falls vacant, a by-election shall be held to fill the vacancy.

(3) A by-election in pursuance of sub-paragraph (2) above shall be held on a day appointed by order of the Secretary of State, being a day not later than six months after the occurrence of either of the following events, namely –

(a) notification of the vacancy by the European Parliament under Article 12(2); or

(b) declaration of the vacancy by the Secretary of State.

(4) A by-election need not be held if the latest date for holding it would fall on or after the relevant Thursday (that is to say the Thursday with which the next period for holding elections to the European Parliament in all the

member States would begin in accordance with Article 10(2) in the absence of any determination by the Council thereunder).

(5) A statutory instrument made under this paragraph shall be laid before Parliament after being made.

4 – (1) In England and Wales the returning officer for a European Parliamentary election in any European Parliamentary constit-uency shall be the person who is the returning officer for parlia-mentary elections in that European Parliamentary constituency as may be designated in an order made by the Secretary of State ...

(4) The council of a local government area wholly or partly situated in a European Parliamentary constituency in England, Wales or Scotland shall place the services of their officers at the disposal of the returning officer for that European Parliamentary constituency for the purpose of assisting him in the discharge of any functions conferred on him in relation to a European Parliamentary election in that European Parliamentary constituency.

(5) In this paragraph 'local government area' means –

(a) in England, a district or London borough;

(aa) in Wales, a county or county borough ...

5 – (1) Subject to sub-paragraph (3) below, and without prejudice to Article 6(1) (incompatibility of office of representative with certain offices in or connected with Community institutions), a person is disqualified for the office of representative to the European Parliament if –

(a) he is disqualified, whether under the House of Commons Disqualification Act 1975 or otherwise, for membership of the House of Commons; or

(b) he is a Lord of Appeal in Ordinary.

(2) A person is disqualified for the office of representative to the European Parliament for a particular European Parliamentary constituency if he is under section 1(2) of the House of Commons Disqualification Act 1975 disqualified for membership of the House of Commons for any particular parliamentary constituency wholly or partly comprised in that European Parliamentary constituency.

(2A) A citizen of the union, determined in accordance with article 8.1 of the Treaty establishing the European Community (as amended by Title II of the Treaty on European Union), who is not a Commonwealth citizen or citizen of the Republic of Ireland is disqualified under this paragraph for the office of representative to the European Parliament if he is disqualified for that office through a criminal law or civil law decision under the law of the Member State of which he is a national.

(2B) In sub-paragraph (2A) above 'a criminal law or civil law decision' has the same meaning as it has in the directive of the Council of the European Communities No 93/109/EC.

(3) A person is not disqualified for office as a representative to the European Parliament by reason only –

(a) that he is a peer, whether of the United Kingdom, Great Britain, England or Scotland; or

(b) that he has been ordained or is a minister of any religious denomination; or

(c) that he holds an office mentioned in section 4 of the House of Commons Disqualification Act 1975 (stewardship of Chiltern Hundreds etc); or

(d) that he holds any of the offices for the time being described in Part II or Part III of Schedule 1 to the House of Commons Disqualification Act 1975 which are for the time being designated in an order by the Secretary of State as non-disqualifying offices in relation to the European Parliament; or

(e) that he is disqualified under section 3 of the Act of Settlement (disqualification for membership of either House of Parliament of persons born out of the Kingdoms of England, Scotland or Ireland or the dominions thereunto belonging except those who are Commonwealth citizens or citizens of the Republic of Ireland), provided that he is a citizen of the Union, determined in accordance with article 8.1 of the Treaty establishing the European Community (as amended by Title II of the Treaty on European Union), who is resident in the United Kingdom.

(4) If any person disqualified under this paragraph for the office of representative to the European Parliament, or for the office of representative to the European Parliament for a particular European Parliamentary constituency, is elected as a representative to the European Parliament or as a representative for that constituency, as the case may be, his election shall be void.

(5) If a representative to the European Parliament becomes disqualified under this paragraph for the office of representative to the European Parliament or for the office of representative to the European Parliament for the European Parliamentary constituency for which he was elected, his seat shall be vacated.

(6) A statutory instrument made under this paragraph shall be subject to annulment in pursuance of a resolution of either House of Parliament.

6 – (1) Any person who claims that a person purporting to hold office as a representative to the European Parliament is disqualified or was disqualified at the time of, or at any time since, his election may apply to the court for a declaration or, as the case may be, declarator to that effect, and the decision of the court on the application shall be final.

(2) On an application under this paragraph the person in respect of whom the application is made shall be the respondent or, as the case may be, defender; and the applicant shall give such security for the costs or expenses of the proceedings, not exceeding £200, as the court may direct.

(3) No declaration or declarator shall be made under this paragraph in respect of any person on grounds which subsisted at the time of his election if there is pending, or has been tried, an election petition in which his disqualification on those grounds is, or was, in issue.

(4) Any declaration or declarator made by the court on an application under this paragraph shall be certified in writing to the Secretary of State forthwith by the court.

(5) The court for the purposes of this paragraph is the High Court, the Court of Session or the High Court of Justice in Northern Ireland according as the European Parliamentary constituency to which the application relates is in England and Wales, or Scotland, or Northern Ireland; and in this paragraph 'disqualified' means disqualified under paragraph 5 above for the office of representative to the European Parliament (whether generally or in relation to a particular European Parliamentary constituency).

As amended by the European Communities (Amendment) Act 1976; Representation of the People Act 1983, s206, Sched 8, paras 21, 22; European Parliamentary Elections Act 1993, s1(1), (2); Welsh Language Act 1993, s35(3); European Parliamentary Elections (Changes to the Franchise and Qualification of Representatives) Regulations 1994, reg 3(1), (2).

EUROPEAN COMMUNITIES (AMENDMENT) ACT 1986
(1986 c 58)

3 Provisions relating to European Assembly

(1) Subject to subsection (2) below and to the repeals and revocations made by section 4(3) below, any enactment or instrument passed or made before the day on which the Single European Act enters into force shall have effect on and after that day with the substitution –

> (a) of a reference to the (or, as the case may be, a) European Parliament for any reference (however worded) to the (or an) Assembly of the European Communities; and
>
> (b) of the words 'European Parliamentary' for the word 'Assembly' and for the words 'European Assembly' wherever that word or those words are used adjectivally with reference to the European Assembly (together with, where necessary, the consequential substitution of 'a' for 'an').

(2) The provisions on which subsection (1) above operates do not include that subsection itself or subsection (3) below or the long title of this Act but, subject to those exceptions, include –

> (a) the long titles of Acts passed before the day mentioned in subsection (1) above;
>
> (b) any provision of an Act or instrument passed or made before that day specifying how that Act or instrument may be cited; and
>
> (c) so much of any Act or instrument so passed or made as uses a mode of citation authorised by another such Act or instrument to refer to that other Act or instrument.

(3) On and after the day mentioned in subsection (1) above the enactments and instruments amended by this section shall have effect as if the Assembly of the European Communities had always been named the European Parliament.

(4) For the purpose of section 6 of the European [Parliamentary] Elections Act 1978 the Single European Act is hereby approved.

4 Short title, interpretation and repeals

(2) In this Act 'the Single European Act' means the Single European Act signed at Luxembourg and The Hague on 17th and 28th February 1986.

EUROPEAN COMMUNITIES (AMENDMENT) ACT 1993
(1993 c 32)

1 Treaty on European Union

(2) For the purpose of section 6 of the European Parliamentary Elections Act 1978 (approval of treaties increasing the Parliament's powers) the Treaty on European Union signed at Maastricht on 7th February 1992 is approved.

2 Economic and monetary union

No notification shall be given to the Council of the European Communities that the United Kingdom intends to move to the third stage of economic and monetary union (in accordance with the Protocol on certain provisions relating to the United Kingdom adopted at Maastricht on 7th February 1992) unless a draft of the notification has first been approved by Act of Parliament and unless Her Majesty's Government has reported to Parliament on its proposals for the co-ordination of economic policies, its role in the European Council of Finance Ministers (ECOFIN) in pursuit of the objectives of Article 2 of the Treaty establishing the European Community as provided for in Articles 103 and 102a, and the work of the European Monetary Institute in preparation for economic and monetary union.

3 Annual report by Bank of England

In implementing Article 108 of the Treaty establishing the European Community, and ensuring compatibility of the statues of the national central bank, Her Majesty's Government shall, by order, make provision for the Governor of the Bank of England to make an annual report to Parliament, which shall be subject to approval by a Resolution of each House of Parliament.

4 Information for Commission

In implementing the provisions of Article 103(3) of the Treaty establishing the European Community, information shall be submitted to the Commission from the United Kingdom indicating performance on economic growth, industrial investment, employment and balance of trade, together with comparisons with those items of performance from other member States.

5 Convergence criteria: assessment of deficits

Before submitting the information required in implementing Article 103(3) of the Treaty establishing the European Community, Her Majesty's Government shall report to Parliament for its approval an assessment of the medium term economic and budgetary position in relation to public investment expenditure and to the social, economic and environmental goals set out in Article 2, which report shall form the basis of any submission to the Council and Commission in pursuit of their responsibilities under Articles 103 and 104c.

6 Committee of the Regions

A person may be proposed as a member or alternate member for the United Kingdom of the Committee of the Regions constituted under Article 198a of the Treaty establishing the European Community only if, at the time of the proposal, he is an elected member of a local authority.

7 Commencement (Protocol on Social Policy)

This Act shall come into force only when each House of Parliament has come to Resolution on a motion tabled by a Minister of the Crown considering the question of adopting the Protocol on Social Policy.

EUROPEAN PARLIAMENTARY ELECTIONS ACT 1993
(1993 c 41)

2 Initial drawing up of the new constituencies

(1) The provisions of this section have effect for the purpose of determining the European Parliamentary constituencies into which England and Wales shall initially be divided in order to give effect to paragraph 1(2)(a) and (c) of Schedule 1 to the principal Act [ie, the European Parliamentary Elections Act 1978], as amended by section 1 above.

(2) For each of England and Wales there shall be a European Parliamentary Constituencies Committee (in this Act referred to as a 'Committee') appointed (whether before or after the passing of this Act) by the Secretary of State; and the provisions of Part I of the Schedule to this Act shall have effect with respect to each Committee.

(3) Part II of the Schedule to this Act (which is derived, with modifications, from provisions of Part I of Schedule 2 to the principal Act) shall have effect with respect to reports of the Committees and Orders in Council consequent thereon.

(4) Parts II and III of Schedule 2 to the principal Act (criteria for dividing Great Britain into European Parliamentary constituencies) shall have effect in relation to reports of the Committees and Orders in Council consequent thereon as they have effect in relation to reports of Boundary Commissions and Orders in Council under that Schedule, except that for the definition of 'enumeration date' in Part III there shall be substituted –

'enumeration date' means 16th February 1993.

(5) For the purposes of the principal Act, an Order in Council which has been made under Part II of the Schedule to this Act shall have effect as if it had been made under Schedule 2 to the principal Act.

(6) Any appointment made or other things done by or in relation to a Committee at a time before the passing of this Act shall be regarded as

valid if it would have been valid at that time, had this Act then been in force.

SCHEDULE

PART I

THE EUROPEAN PARLIAMENTARY CONSTITUENCIES COMMITTEES

(1) Each Committee shall consist of a Chairman and two other members appointed by the Secretary of State.

(2) Each member of a Committee (including the Chairman) shall hold his appointment for such term and on such conditions as may be (or have been) determined before his appointment by the Secretary of State.

(3) The Secretary of State may, after consultation with a Committee, provide the Committee with such staff as he thinks necessary for the proper discharge of their functions.

(4) The Secretary of State shall pay to the members of a Committee (including the Chairman) such remuneration and allowances as he may, with the approval of the Treasury, determine.

PART II

REPORTS OF COMMITTEES AND ORDERS IN COUNCIL

(5) As soon as practicable after the passing of this Act, each of the Committees shall submit to the Secretary of State a report showing the European Parliamentary constituencies into which they recommend that England or, as the case may be, Wales should be divided.

(6) A report of a Committee under this Part of this Schedule showing the European Parliament constituencies into which they recommend that England or Wales should be divided shall state, as respects each European Parliamentary constituency, the name by which they recommend that it should be known.

(7) As soon as may be after a Committee have submitted a report to the Secretary of State under this Part of this Schedule, he shall lay the report before Parliament together with the draft of an Order in Council for giving effect, whether with or without modifications, to the recommendations contained in the report.

(8) (1) The draft of any Order in Council laid before Parliament by the Secretary of State under this Part of this Schedule for giving effect, whether with or without modifications, to the recommendations contained in a report of a Committee may make provision for any matters which appear to him to be incidental to, or consequential on, the recommendations.

(2) Where any such draft gives effect to any such recommendations with modification, the Secretary of State shall lay before Parliament together with the draft a statement of the reasons for the modifications.

(3) If any such draft is approved by a resolution of each House of Parliament, the Secretary of State shall submit it to Her Majesty in Council.

(4) If a motion for the approval of any such draft is rejected by either House of Parliament or withdrawn by leave of the House, the Secretary of State may amend the draft and lay the amended draft before Parliament, and if the draft as so amended is approved by a resolution of each House of Parliament, the Secretary of State shall submit it to Her Majesty in Council.

(5) Where the draft of an Order in Council is submitted to Her Majesty in Council under this Part of this Schedule, Her Majesty in Council may make an Order in terms of the draft which, subject to paragraph 8 of Schedule 2 to the principal Act, shall come into force on such date as may be specified in or determined under the Order and shall have effect notwithstanding anything in any enactment.

(6) The validity of any Order in Council purporting to be made under this Part of this Schedule and reciting that a draft of the Order has been approved by a resolution of each House of Parliament shall not be called in question in any legal proceedings whatsoever.

(9) Nothing in paragraphs 7 and 8 above shall be taken as enabling the Secretary of State to modify any recommendation or draft Order in Council in a manner conflicting with provisions of Part II of Schedule 2 to the principal Act.

EUROPEAN ECONOMIC AREA ACT 1993
(1993 c 51)

2 Consistent application of law to whole of EEA

(1) Where –

(a) the operation of any relevant enactment is limited (expressly or by implication) by reference to the Communities or by reference to some connection with the Communities, and

(b) the enactment relates to a matter to which the Agreement (as it has effect on the date on which it comes into force) relates,

then, unless the context otherwise requires, the enactment shall have effect on and after that date in relation to that matter with the substitution of a corresponding limitation relating to the European Economic Area (or, where appropriate, to both the Communities and the European Economic Area).

(2) Subsection (1) above shall have effect –

(a) subject to the Schedule to this Act, and

(b) subject to such exceptions and modifications as may be prescribed by regulations made by a Minister of the Crown.

(3) Subsection (1) above shall not be regarded –

(a) as having an effect which is inconsistent with the operation, by virtue of the Agreement, of section 2(1) of the 1972 Act, or

(b) as prejudicing any power to make provision for the purpose of implementing any obligation of the United Kingdom created or arising by or under the Agreement, or for any other purpose mentioned in section 2(2)(a) or (b) of the 1972 Act relating to the Agreement;

and any instrument made for such purpose under section 2(2) of the 1972 Act or under any other enactment may exclude the operation of subsection (1) above.

(4) In relation to matters to which the Agreement (as it has effect on the date on which it comes into force or subsequently) relates, the powers

conferred by section 2(2) of the 1972 Act shall include power to make provision for the elimination or reduction of any difference between –

(a) the application of any relevant enactment in cases having a connection with member States, and

(b) its application in cases having a connection with other States within the European Economic Area;

and paragraph 1(1)(a), (c) and (d) of Schedule 2 to the 1972 Act shall not apply to the powers conferred by section 2(2) of that Act so far as they are exercisable by virtue of this subsection.

(5) In relation to matters to which the Agreement (as it has effect on the date on which it comes into force or subsequently) relates, the powers conferred by section 2(2) of the 1972 Act shall include power to make provision for the avoidance, elimination or reduction of any difference between –

(a) the application of an instrument made under that section on or after the date on which the Agreement comes into force in cases having a connection with member States, and

(b) its application in cases having a connection with other States within the European Economic Area.

(6) The provision that may be made by virtue of subsection (4) above includes provision amending the Schedule to this Act.

(7) In this section (and in the Schedule to this Act) 'relevant enactment' means a provision of an Act passed, or of any subordinate legislation made, before the date on which the Agreement comes into force.

3 General implementation of Agreement

(1) Subject to section 2 above, where by virtue of the Agreement (as it has effect on the date on which it comes into force) it is necessary for a purpose mentioned in section 2(2)(a) or (b) of the 1972 Act that any relevant provision should have effect with modifications which can be ascertained from the Agreement, then on and after that date the provision shall have effect with those modifications.

(2) A Minister of the Crown may by regulations modify or exclude the operation of subsection (1) above in relation to a relevant provision where it appears to him appropriate to do so because of the suspension of any part of the Agreement in accordance with the terms of the Agreement.

(3) Subsection (1) above shall not be regarded –

(a) as providing for modifications the effect of which is achieved through the operation, by virtue of the Agreement, of section 2(1) of the 1972 Act, or

(b) as prejudicing any power to make provision for the purpose of implementing any obligation of the United Kingdom created or arising by or under the Agreement, or for any other purpose mentioned in section 2(2)(a) or (b) of the 1972 Act relating to the Agreement;

and any instrument made for such a purpose under section 2(2) of the 1972 Act or under any other enactment may exclude the operation of subsection (1) above.

(4) Subsection (1) above shall not apply so as to require a modification if that modification, or a corresponding modification limited so as to relate only to the Communities, –

(a) could have been made, by Act passed before the date on which the Agreement comes into force, for a purpose mentioned in section 2(2)(a) or (b) of the 1972 Act, but

(b) was not made (by that or other means).

(5) In this section 'relevant provision' means –

(a) a provision of an Act passed, or of any subordinate legislation made, before the date on which the Agreement comes into force;

(b) a provision of any other instrument made before that date by a person as against whom the effect of a directive issued by a Community institution (if such a directive were relevant) might be relied upon in proceedings to which he was a party.

4 Amendment of 1972 Act s3

Subsections (2) to (5) of section 3 of the 1972 Act (provisions as to judicial notice and evidence) –

(a) shall have effect in relation to the EFTA Court (to be established under Article 108 of the Agreement) as they have effect in relation to the European Court, and

(b) shall have effect in relation to the EFTA Surveillance Authority (also to be established under that Article) as they have effect in relation to a Community institution other than the European Court.

5 Regulations

The power to make regulations under section 2(2) or section 3(2) above shall be exercisable by statutory instrument; and any statutory instrument containing such regulations, if made without a draft having been approved by resolution of each House of Parliament, shall be subject to annulment in pursuance of a resolution of either House.

6   Interpretation

(1) In this Act, except where the context otherwise requires, –

'the 1972 Act' means the European Communities Act 1972;

'Act' includes an Act of the Parliament of Northern Ireland and a Measure of the Northern Ireland Assembly;

'the Agreement' means the Agreement on the European Economic Area signed at Oporto on 2nd May 1992 as adjusted by the Protocol signed at Brussels on 17th March 1993;

'Minister of the Crown' includes the Treasury;

'subordinate legislation' means Orders in Council, orders, rules, regulations, schemes, warrants, byelaws and other instruments made under any Act.

(2) References in this Act to the date on which the Agreement comes into force are references to the date on which (in accordance with the Protocol signed at Brussels on 17th March 1993) it comes into force otherwise than as regards Liechtenstein.

APPENDIX

DRAFT TREATY OF AMSTERDAM

DRAFT TREATY OF AMSTERDAM
(Brussels, 19 June 1997)

SECTION I

FREEDOM, SECURITY AND JUSTICE

CHAPTER 1

FUNDAMENTAL RIGHTS AND NON-DISCRIMINATION

General principles underlying the Union
Amend Article F of the TEU

1. The Union is founded on the principles of liberty, democracy, respect for human rights and fundamental freedoms, and the rule of law, principles which are common to the Member States.

2. The Union shall respect fundamental rights, as guaranteed by the European Convention for the Protection of Human Rights and Fundamental Freedoms signed in Rome on 4 November 1950 and as they result from the constitutional traditions common to the Member States, as general principles of Community law.

3. The Union shall respect the national identities of its Member States.

4. The Union shall provide itself with the means necessary to attain its objectives and carry through its policies.

New fourth paragraph in the Preamble to the TEU

CONFIRMING their attachment to fundamental social rights as defined in the European Social Charter signed at Turin on 18 October 1961 and in the 1989 Community Charter of the Fundamental Social Rights of Workers.

Action in the event of a breach by a Member State of the principles on which the Union is founded

New Article Fa in the TEU

1. The Council, meeting in the composition of the Heads of State or Government and acting by unanimity on a proposal by one third of the Member States or by the Commission and after obtaining the assent of the European Parliament, may determine the existence of a serious and persistent breach by a Member State of principles mentioned in Article F(1), after inviting the government of the Member State concerned to submit its observations.

2. Where such a determination has been made, the Council, acting by a qualified majority, may decide to suspend certain of the rights deriving from the application of this Treaty to the State in question, including the voting rights of the representative of the Government of that Member State in the Council. In doing so, the Council shall take into account the possible consequences of such a suspension on the rights and obligations of natural and legal persons.

The obligations of the Member State concerned under this Treaty shall in any case continue to be binding on that State.

3. The Council, acting by a qualified majority, may decide subsequently to vary or revoke measures taken under paragraph 2 in response to changes in the situation which led to their being imposed.

4. For the purposes of this Article, the Council shall act without taking into account the vote of the representative of the Member State concerned. Abstentions by members present in person or represented shall not prevent the adoption of decisions referred to in paragraph 1. A qualified majority shall be defined as the same proportion of the weighted votes of the members of the Council concerned as laid down in Article 148(2) of the Treaty establishing the European Community.

The provisions of this paragraph shall also apply in the event of voting rights being suspended pursuant to paragraph 2.

5. For the purposes of this Article, the European Parliament shall act by a two thirds majority of the votes cast, representing a majority of its members.

New Article 236 in the TEC

1. Where a decision has been taken to suspend voting rights of a Member State in accordance with Article Fa(2) of the Treaty on European Union, these voting rights shall also be suspended with regard to this Treaty.

2. Moreover, and where the existence of a serious and persistent breach by a Member State of the principles mentioned in Article F(1) has been determined in accordance with Article Fa(1) of the TEU, the Council, acting by a qualified majority, may decide to suspend certain of the rights deriving from the application of this Treaty to the State in question. In doing so, the Council shall take into account the possible consequences of such a suspension on the rights and obligations of natural and legal persons.

The obligations of the Member State concerned under this Treaty shall in any case continue to be binding on that State.

3. The Council, acting by a qualified majority, may decide subsequently to vary or revoke measures taken in accordance with paragraph 2 in response to changes in the situation which led to their being imposed.

4. When taking decisions referred to in paragraphs 2 and 3, the Council shall act without taking into account the votes of the representative of the Member State concerned. By way of derogation from Articles 148 and 189a(1), a qualified majority shall be defined as the same proportion of the weighted votes of the members of the Council concerned as laid down in Article 148(2).

The provisions of this paragraph shall also apply in the event of voting rights being suspended in accordance with paragraph 1. In such cases, a decision requiring unanimity shall be taken without the vote of the representative of the Member State concerned.

Respect by any State applying to join the Union for the fundamental principles on which it is founded

Supplement the first sentence of Article O of the TEU

Any European State which respects the principles set out in Article F(1) may apply to become a member of the Union [remainder unchanged].

Non discrimination

New Article 6a in the TEC

Without prejudice to the other provisions of this Treaty and within the limits of the powers conferred by it upon the Community, the Council, acting unanimously on a proposal from the Commission and after consulting the European Parliament, may take appropriate action to combat discrimination based on sex, racial or ethnic origin, religion or belief, disability, age or sexual orientation.

Equality of men and women

Supplement Article 2 of the TEC

The Community shall ... promote ... a high level of employment and social protection, equality between men and women, the raising of the standard of living and quality of life, and economic and social cohesion and solidarity among Member States.

Supplement Article 3 of the TEC with a new paragraph

In all the activities referred to in this Article, the Community shall aim to eliminate inequalities, and to promote equality, between men and women.

Protection of individuals with regard to the processing and free movement of personal data

New Article 213b in the TEC

1. From 1 January 1999, Community acts on the protection of individuals with regard to the processing of personal data and the free movement of such data shall apply to the institutions and bodies set up by, or on the basis of, this Treaty.

2. Before the date referred to in paragraph 1, the Council, acting in accordance with the procedure referred to in Article 189b, shall establish an independent supervisory body responsible for monitoring the application of such Community acts to Community institutions and bodies and shall adopt any other relevant provisions as appropriate.

CHAPTER 2

PROGRESSIVE ESTABLISHMENT OF AN AREA OF FREEDOM, SECURITY AND JUSTICE

Over-arching objectives of Treaty provisions on freedom, security and justice

Amend Article B, fourth indent, in the TEU

– to maintain and develop the Union as an area of freedom, security and justice, in which the free movement of persons is assured in conjunction with appropriate measures with respect to external borders controls, immigration, asylum and the prevention and combating of crime.

NEW TITLE IN THE TEC

Free movement of persons, asylum and immigration

Article A

In order to establish progressively an area of freedom, security and justice, the Council shall adopt:

(a) within a period of five years after the entry into force of this Treaty, measures aimed at ensuring the free movement of persons in accordance with Article 7a, in conjunction with directly related flanking measures with respect to external borders controls, asylum and immigration, in accordance with the provisions of Article B(2) and (3), C(1)(a) and (2)(a), and measures to prevent and combat crime in accordance with the provisions of Article K3(e) of the Treaty on European Union;

(b) other measures in the fields of asylum, immigration and safeguarding the rights of third country nationals, in accordance with the provisions of Article C;

(c) measures in the field of judicial cooperation in civil matters as provided for in Article E;

(d) appropriate measures to encourage and strengthen administrative cooperation, as provided for in Article F;

(e) measures in the field of police and judicial cooperation in criminal matters aimed at a high level of security by preventing and combating crime within the Union in accordance with the provisions of the Treaty on European Union.

Article B

The Council, acting in accordance with the procedure referred to in Article G, shall, within a period of five years after the entry into force of this Treaty, adopt:

1. Measures with a view to ensuring, in compliance with Article 7a, the absence of any controls on persons, be they citizens of the Union or nationals of third countries, when crossing internal borders.

2. Measures on the crossing of the external borders of the Member States which shall establish:

> (a) standards and procedures to be followed by Member States in carrying out checks on persons at such borders;
>
> (b) rules on visas for intended stays of no more than three months, including:
>
>> (i) the list of third countries whose nationals must be in possession of visas when crossing the external borders and those whose nationals are exempt from that requirement;
>>
>> (ii) the procedures and conditions for issuing visas by Member States;
>>
>> (iii) a uniform format for visas;
>>
>> (iv) rules on a uniform visa.

3. Measures setting out the conditions under which the nationals of third countries shall have the freedom to travel within the territory of the Member States during a period of no more than three months.

NB As a result of this provision, Articles 100c and 100d of the TEC will be repealed.

Protocol on External Relations of the Member States with Regard to the Crossing of External Borders

THE HIGH CONTRACTING PARTIES,

TAKING INTO ACCOUNT the need of the Member States to ensure effective controls at their external borders, in cooperation with third countries where appropriate,

HAVE AGREED upon the following provisions, which shall be annexed to the Treaty establishing the European Community:

The provisions on the measures on the crossing of external borders included in Article B(2)(a) of Title ... shall be without prejudice to the competence of Member States to negotiate or conclude agreements with third countries as long as they respect Community law and other relevant international agreements.

Article C

The Council, acting in accordance with the procedure referred to in Article G, shall, within a period of five years after the entry into force of this Treaty, adopt:

1. Measures on asylum, in accordance with the Convention of 28 July 1951, the Protocol of 31 January 1967 relating to the Status of Refugees and other relevant treaties, within the following areas:

   (a) criteria and mechanisms for determining which Member State is responsible for considering an application for asylum submitted by a third country national in one of the Member States;

   (b) minimum standards on the reception of asylum seekers in Member States;

   (c) minimum standards with respect to the qualification of third country nationals as refugees;

   (d) minimum standards on procedures in Member States for granting or withdrawing refugee status.

2. Measures on refugees and displaced persons within the following areas:

   (a) minimum standards for giving temporary protection to displaced persons from third countries who cannot return to their country of origin and for persons who otherwise need international protection;

   (b) promoting a balance of effort between Member States in receiving and bearing the consequences of receiving refugees and displaced persons.

3. Measures on immigration policy within the following areas:

   (a) conditions of entry and residence, and standards on procedures for the issue by Member States of long term visas and residence permits, including those for the purpose of family reunion;

   (b) illegal immigration and illegal residence, including repatriation of illegal residents.

4. Measures defining the rights and conditions under which nationals of third countries who are legally resident in a Member State may reside in other Member States.

5. Measures adopted by the Council pursuant to paragraphs 3 and 4 shall not prevent any Member State from maintaining or introducing in the areas concerned national provisions which are compatible with this Treaty and with international agreements.

Measures to be adopted pursuant to paragraphs 2(b), 3(a) and 4 shall not be subject to the five year period referred to above.

Article D

1. This Title shall not affect the exercise of the responsibilities incumbent upon Member States with regard to the maintenance of law and order and the safeguarding of internal security.

2. In the event of one or more Member States being confronted with an emergency situation characterised by a sudden inflow of nationals from a third country and without prejudice to paragraph 1, the Council may, acting by qualified majority on a proposal from the Commission, adopt provisional measures of a duration not exceeding six months for the benefit of the Member States concerned.

Article E

Measures in the field of judicial cooperation in civil matters having cross-border implications, to be taken in accordance with Article G and insofar as necessary for the proper functioning of the internal market, shall include:

(a) improving and simplifying:
- the system for cross-border service of judicial and extrajudicial documents;
- cooperation in the taking of evidence;
- the recognition and enforcement of decisions in civil and commercial cases, including extrajudicial cases;

(b) promoting the compatibility of the rules applicable in the Member States concerning the conflict of laws and of jurisdiction;

(c) eliminating obstacles to the good functioning of civil proceedings, if necessary by promoting the compatibility of the rules on civil procedure applicable in the Member States.

Article F

The Council, acting in accordance with the procedure referred to in Article G, shall take measures to ensure cooperation between the relevant departments of the administrations of the Member States in the areas covered by this Title, as well as between those departments and the Commission.

Article G

1. During a transitional period of five years following the entry into force of this Treaty, the Council shall act unanimously on a proposal from the Commission or on an initiative of a Member State and after consulting the European Parliament.

2. After this period of five years:
   - the Council shall act on proposals from the Commission; the Commission shall examine any request made by a Member State that it submit a proposal to the Council;
   - the Council, acting unanimously after consulting the European Parliament, shall take a decision with a view to making all or parts of the areas covered by this Title governed by the procedure referred to in Article 189b and adapting the provisions relating to the powers of the Court of Justice.

3. By derogation from the provisions of paragraphs 1 and 2:
   - measures referred to in Article B(2)(b) (i) and (iii) shall, from the entry into force of this Treaty, be adopted by the Council acting by a qualified majority on a proposal from the Commission and after consulting the European Parliament;
   - measures referred to in Article B(2)(b) (ii) and (iv) shall, after a period of five years following the entry into force of this Treaty, be adopted by the Council acting in accordance with the procedure referred to in Article 189b.

Article H

1. The provisions of Article 177 shall apply to this Title under the following circumstances and conditions: where a question on the interpretation of this Title or on the validity or interpretation of acts of the institutions of the Community based on this Title is raised in a case pending before a court or a tribunal of a Member State against whose decisions there is no judicial remedy under national law, that court or tribunal shall, if it considers that

a decision on the question is necessary to enable it to give judgement, request the Court of Justice to give a ruling thereon.

2. In any event, the Court of Justice shall not have jurisdiction to rule on any measure or decision taken pursuant to Article B(1) relating to the maintenance of law and order and the safeguarding of internal security.

3. The Council, the Commission or a Member State may request the Court of Justice to give a ruling on a question of interpretation of this Title or of acts of the institutions of the Community based on this Title. The ruling given by the Court of Justice in response to such a request shall not apply to judgements of courts or tribunals of the Member States which have become res judicata.

Article I

The application of this Title shall be subject to the provisions of Protocol Y on the position of the United Kingdom and Ireland and to Protocol Z on the position of Denmark, without prejudice to Protocol X on the application of certain aspects of Article 7a to the United Kingdom and to Ireland.

Protocol Y on the Position of the United Kingdom and Ireland

THE HIGH CONTRACTING PARTIES

DESIRING to settle certain questions relating to the United Kingdom and Ireland

HAVING REGARD to Protocol X on the application of certain aspects of Article 7a of the TEC to the United Kingdom and to Ireland

HAVE AGREED upon the following provisions which shall be annexed to the Treaty establishing the European Community and the Treaty on European Union:

Article 1

Subject to Article 3, the United Kingdom and Ireland shall not take part in the adoption by the Council of proposed measures pursuant to Title [ ] of the TEC. By way of derogation from Article 148(2) and 189a(1) of the TEC, a qualified majority shall be defined as the same proportion of the weighted votes of the members of the Council concerned as laid down in Article 148(2). The unanimity of the members of the Council, with the exception of the representative of the governments of the United Kingdom and Ireland, shall be necessary for decisions of the Council which must be adopted unanimously.

Article 2

In consequence of Article 1 and subject to Articles 3, 4 and 6, none of the provisions of Title [ ] of the TEC, no measure adopted pursuant to that Title, no provision of any international agreement concluded by the Community pursuant to that Title, and no decision of the Court of Justice interpreting any such provision or measure shall be binding upon or applicable in the United Kingdom or Ireland; and no such provision, measure or decision shall in any way affect the competences, rights and obligations of those States; and no such provision, measure or decision shall in any way affect the acquis communautaire nor form part of Community law as they apply to the United Kingdom or Ireland.

Article 3

1. The United Kingdom or Ireland may notify the President of the Council in writing, within three months after a proposal or initiative has been presented to the Council pursuant to Title [ ] of the TEC, that it wishes to take part in the adoption and application of any such proposed measure, whereupon that State shall be entitled to do so. By way of derogation from Article 148(2) and 189a(1) of the TEC, a qualified majority shall be defined as the same proportion of the weighted votes of the members of the Council concerned as laid down in Article 148(2).

The unanimity of the members of the Council, with the exception of a member which has not made such a notification, shall be necessary for decisions of the Council which must be adopted unanimously. A measure adopted under this paragraph shall be binding upon all Member States which took part in its adoption.

2. If after a reasonable period of time a measure referred to in paragraph 1 cannot be adopted with the United Kingdom or Ireland taking part, the Council may adopt such measure in accordance with Article 1 without the participation of the United Kingdom or Ireland. In that case Article 2 applies.

Article 4

The United Kingdom or Ireland may at any time after the adoption of a measure by the Council pursuant to Title [ ] of the TEC notify its intention to the Council and to the Commission that it wishes to accept such measure.

In that case, the procedure provided for in Article 5a(3) of the TEC shall apply mutatis mutandis.

Article 5

A Member State which is not bound by a measure adopted pursuant to Title [ ] of the TEC shall bear no financial consequences of that measure other than administrative costs entailed for the institutions.

Article 6

Where, in cases referred to in this Protocol, the United Kingdom or Ireland is bound by a measure adopted by the Council pursuant to Title [ ] of the TEC, the relevant provisions of that Treaty, including Article H, shall apply to that State in relation to that measure.

Article 7

Articles 3 and 4 shall be without prejudice to the Schengen Protocol.

Article 8

Ireland may notify the President of the Council in writing that it no longer wishes to be covered by the terms of this Protocol. In that case, the normal Treaty provisions will apply to Ireland.

Protocol X on the Application of Certain Aspects of Article 7a of the TEC to the United Kingdom and to Ireland

THE HIGH CONTRACTING PARTIES

DESIRING to settle certain questions relating to the United Kingdom and Ireland,

HAVING REGARD to the existence for many years of special travel arrangements between the UK and Ireland,

HAVE AGREED upon the following provisions, which shall be annexed to the Treaty establishing the European Community and to the Treaty on European Union:

Article 1

The United Kingdom shall be entitled, notwithstanding Article 7a of the Treaty establishing the European Community, any other provision of this Treaty or of the Treaty on European Union, any measure adopted under these Treaties, or any international agreement concluded by the Community or by the Community and its Member States with one or more third States, to exercise at its frontiers with other Member States such controls on persons seeking to enter the United Kingdom as it may consider necessary for the purpose:

(a) of verifying the right to enter the United Kingdom of citizens of States which are Contracting Parties to the Agreement on the European Economic Area and of their dependants exercising rights conferred by Community law, as well as citizens of other States on whom such rights have been conferred by an agreement to which the UK is bound; and

(b) of determining whether or not to grant other persons permission to enter the United Kingdom.

Nothing in Article 7a or in any other provision of these Treaties or in any measure adopted under them shall prejudice the right of the United Kingdom to adopt or exercise any such controls. References to the United Kingdom in this Article shall include territories for whose external relations the United Kingdom is responsible.

Article 2

The United Kingdom and Ireland may continue to make arrangements between themselves relating to the movement of persons between their territories ("the Common Travel Area"), while fully respecting the rights of persons referred to in Article 1(a). Accordingly, as long as they maintain such arrangements, the provisions of Article 1 shall apply to Ireland with the same terms and conditions as for the United Kingdom. Nothing in Article 7a, in any other provision of the Treaties referred to above or in any measure adopted under them, shall affect any such arrangements.

Article 3

The other Member States shall be entitled to exercise at their frontiers or at any point of entry into their territory such controls on persons seeking to enter their territory from the United Kingdom or any territories whose external relations are under their responsibility for the same purposes stated in Article 1, or from Ireland as long as the provisions of Article 1 apply to Ireland.

Nothing in Article 7a or in any other provision of these treaties or in any measure adopted under them shall prejudice the right of the other Member States to adopt or exercise any such controls.

Title VI of the TEU

Provisions on police and judicial cooperation in criminal matters

New Article K1 in the TEU

Without prejudice to the powers of the European Community, the Union's objective shall be to provide citizens with a high level of safety within an area of freedom, security and justice by developing common action among the Member States in the fields of police and judicial cooperation in criminal matters and by preventing and combating racism and xenophobia.

That objective shall be achieved by preventing and combating crime, organized or otherwise, in particular terrorism, trafficking in persons and offences against children, illicit drug trafficking and illicit arms trafficking, corruption and fraud, through:

- closer cooperation between police forces, customs authorities and other competent authorities in the Member States, both directly and, through Europol, in accordance with the provisions of Article K2 and K4;
- closer cooperation between judicial and other competent authorities of the Member States in accordance with the provisions of Articles K3(a) to (d) and K4;
- approximation, where necessary, of rules on criminal matters in the Member States, in accordance with the provisions of Article K3(e).

New Article K2 in the TEU

1. Common action in the field of police cooperation shall include:

(a) operational cooperation between the competent authorities, including the police, customs and other specialized law enforcement services of the Member States in relation to the prevention, detection and investigation of criminal offences;

(b) the collection, storage, processing, analysis and exchange of relevant information, including information held by law enforcement agencies of reports on suspicious financial transactions, in particular through

Europol, subject to appropriate provisions on the protection of personal data;

(c) cooperation and joint initiatives in training, the exchange of liaison officers, secondments, the use of equipment, and forensic research;

(d) the common evaluation of particular investigative techniques in relation to the detection of serious forms of organized crime.

2. The Council shall promote cooperation through the European Police Office (Europol) and shall in particular, within a period of five years after the date of entry into force of this Treaty:

(a) enable Europol to facilitate and support the preparation, and to encourage the coordination and carrying out of specific investigative actions by the competent authorities of the Member States, including operational actions of joint teams comprising representatives of Europol in a support capacity;

(b) adopt measures allowing Europol to ask the competent authorities of the Member States to conduct and coordinate their investigations in specific cases and to develop specific expertise which may be put at the disposal of Member States to assist them in investigating cases of organized crime;

(c) promote liaison arrangements between prosecuting/investigating officials specialising in the fight against organised crime in close cooperation with Europol;

(d) establish a research, documentation and statistical network on cross-border crime.

New Article K3 in the TEU

Common action on judicial cooperation in criminal matters shall include:

(a) facilitating and accelerating cooperation between competent ministries and judicial or equivalent authorities of the Member States in relation to proceedings and the enforcement of decisions;

(b) facilitating extradition between Member States;

(c) ensuring compatibility in rules applicable in the Member States, as may be necessary to improve such cooperation;

(d) preventing conflicts of jurisdiction between Member States;

(e) progressively adopting measures establishing minimum rules relating to the constituent elements of criminal acts and to penalties in the fields of organized crime, terrorism and drug trafficking.

Declaration to the Final act on Article K3(e).

The Conference agrees that the provisions of Article K3(e) shall not have as a consequence to oblige a Member State whose legal system does not provide for minimum sentences to adopt them.

New Article K4 in the TEU

The Council shall lay down the conditions and limitations under which the competent authorities referred to in Articles K2 and K3 may operate in the territory of another Member State in liaison and in agreement with the authorities of that State.

Article K5 in the TEU (former Article K2)

This Title shall not affect the exercise of the responsibilities incumbent upon Member States with regard to the maintenance of law and order and the safeguarding of internal security.

Article K6 in the TEU (former Article K3)

1. In the areas referred to under this Title, Member States shall inform and consult one another within the Council with a view to coordinating their action. To that end, they shall establish collaboration between the relevant departments of their administrations.

2. The Council shall take measures and promote cooperation, using the appropriate form and procedures as set out in this Title, contributing to the pursuit of the objectives of the Union. To that end, acting unanimously on an initiative of any Member State or of the Commission, the Council may:

   (a) adopt common positions defining the approach of the Union to a particular matter;

   (b) adopt framework decisions for the purpose of approximation of the laws and regulations of the Member States; framework decisions shall be binding upon the Member States as to the result to be achieved but shall leave to the national authorities the choice of form and methods; they shall not entail direct effect;

   (c) adopt decisions for any other purpose consistent with the objectives of this Title, excluding any approximation of the laws and regulations of the Member States. These decisions shall be binding and shall not entail direct effect; the Council, acting by a qualified majority, shall adopt measures necessary to implement those decisions at the level of the Union;

(d) establish conventions which it shall recommend to the Member States for adoption in accordance with their respective constitutional requirements. Member States shall begin the procedures applicable within a time limit to be set by the Council.

Unless they provide otherwise, conventions shall, once adopted by at least half of the Member States, enter into force for those Member States. Measures implementing conventions shall be adopted within the Council by a majority of two thirds of the High Contracting Parties.

3. Where the Council is required to act by a qualified majority, the votes of its members shall be weighted as laid down in Article 148(2) of the Treaty establishing the European Community, and for their adoption, acts of the Council shall require at least 62 votes in favour, cast by at least 10 members.

4. For procedural questions, the Council shall act by a majority of its members.

New Article K7 of the TEU

1. The Court of Justice of the European Communities shall have jurisdiction, subject to the conditions laid down in this Article, to give preliminarily rulings on the validity and interpretation of framework decisions and decisions, on the interpretation of conventions established under this Title and on the validity and interpretation of the measures implementing them.

2. By a declaration made at the time of the signing of this Treaty or any time thereafter, any Member State shall be able to accept a jurisdiction of the Court of Justice to give preliminary rulings as specified in paragraph 1.

3. Where a Member State has made a declaration pursuant to paragraph 2 of this Article:

(a) any court or tribunal of that State against whose decisions there is no judicial remedy under national law may request the Court of Justice to give a preliminary ruling on a question raised in a case pending before it and concerning the validity or interpretation of an act referred to in paragraph 1 if that court or tribunal considers that a decision on the question is necessary to enable it to give judgement, or

(b) any court or tribunal of that State may request the Court of Justice to give a preliminary ruling on a question raised in a case pending before it and concerning the interpretation or validity of an act referred to in paragraph 1 if that court or tribunal considers that a decision on the question is necessary to enable it to give judgement.

4. Any Member State, whether or not it has made a declaration pursuant to paragraph 2, shall be entitled to submit statements of case or written observations to the Court in cases which arise under paragraph 3.

5. The Court of Justice shall have no jurisdiction to review the validity or proportionality of operations carried out by the police or other law enforcement agencies of a Member State or the exercise of the responsibilities incumbent upon Member States with regard to the maintenance of law and order and the safeguarding of internal security.

6. The Court of Justice shall have jurisdiction to review the legality of framework decisions and decisions in actions brought by a Member State or the Commission on grounds of lack of competence, infringement of an essential procedural requirement, infringement of this Treaty or of any rule of law relating to its application, or misuse of powers. The proceedings provided for in this paragraph shall be instituted within two months of the publication of the measure.

7. The Court of Justice shall have jurisdiction to rule on any dispute between Member States regarding the interpretation or the application of acts adopted under Article K6(2) whenever such dispute cannot be settled by the Council within six months of its being referred to the Council by one of its members. Moreover, the Court shall have jurisdiction to rule on any dispute between Member States and the Commission regarding the interpretation or the application of conventions established under Article K6(2)(d).

Article K8 of the TEU (former Article K4)

1. A Coordinating Committee shall be set up consisting of senior officials. In addition to its coordinating role, it shall be the task of the Committee to:
   - give opinions for the attention of the Council, either at the Council's request or on its own initiative;
   - contribute, without prejudice to Article 151 of the Treaty establishing the European Community, to the preparation of the Council's discussions in the areas referred to in Article K1.

2. The Commission shall be fully associated with the work in the areas referred to in this Title.

Article K9 of the TEU (former Article K5)

Within international organizations and at international conferences in which they take part, Member States shall defend the common positions adopted under the provisions of this Title.

The provisions of Articles J8 and J9 shall apply as appropriate to matters falling under this Title.

New Article K10 in the TEU

Agreements referred to in Article J14 may cover matters falling under this Title.

Article K11 of the TEU (former Article K6)

1. The Council shall consult the European Parliament before adopting any measure referred to in Article K6 (2)(b), (c) and (d). The European Parliament shall deliver its opinion within a time-limit which the Council may lay down, which shall not be less than three months. In the absence of an opinion within that time-limit, the Council may act.

2. The Presidency of the Council and the Commission shall regularly inform the European Parliament of discussions in the areas covered by this Title.

3. The European Parliament may ask questions of the Council or make recommendations to it. Each year, it shall hold a debate on the progress made in the areas referred to in this Title.

Article K12 of the TEU (former Article K7)

1. Member States which intend to establish closer cooperation between themselves may be authorized, subject to Articles [1] and [2] (2), to make use of the institutions, procedures and mechanisms laid down by the Treaties provided that the cooperation proposed:

   (a) respects the powers of the European Community, and the objectives laid down by this Title;

   (b) has the aim of enabling the Union to develop more rapidly into an area of freedom, security and justice.

2. The authorization referred to in paragraph 1 shall be granted by the Council, acting by a qualified majority at the request of the Member States concerned and after inviting the Commission to present its opinion; the request shall also be forwarded to the European Parliament.

If a member of the Council declares that, for important and stated reasons of national policy, it intends to oppose the granting of an authorization by qualified majority, a vote shall not be taken. The Council may, acting by a qualified majority, request that the matter be referred to the European Council for decision by unanimity.

The votes of the members of the Council shall be weighted in accordance with article 148(2) of the Treaty establishing the European Community. For their adoption, decisions shall require at least 62 votes in favour, cast by at least 10 members.

3. Any Member State which wishes to become a party to cooperation set up in accordance with this Article shall notify its intention to the Council and to the Commission, which shall give an opinion to the Council within three months of receipt of that notification, possibly accompanied by a recommendation for specific arrangements as it may deem necessary for that Member State to become a party to the cooperation in question. Within four months of the date of that notification, the Council shall decide on the request and on possible specific arrangements as it may deem necessary. The decision shall be deemed to be taken unless the Council, acting by a qualified majority, decides to hold it in abeyance; in this case, the Council shall state the reasons for its decision and set a deadline for reexamining it. For the purposes of this paragraph, the Council shall act under the conditions set out in Article (2) of the TEU (2).

4. The provisions of Articles K1 to K13 shall apply to the closer cooperation provided for by this Article, save as otherwise provided for in this Article and in Articles (..) and (..).

The provisions of the Treaty establishing the European Community concerning the powers of the Court of Justice of the European Communities and the exercise of those powers shall apply to paragraphs 1, 2 and 3.

5. This Article is without prejudice to the provisions of the Protocol integrating the Schengen acquis into the framework of the Union.

NB The former Article K7 will be repealed.

Article K13 of the TEU (former Article K8)

1. The provisions referred to in Articles 137, 138, 138e, 139 to 142, 146, 147, 148(3), 150 to 153, 157 to 163, 191a and 217 of the Treaty establishing the European Community shall apply to the provisions relating to the areas referred to in this Title.

2. Administrative expenditure which the provisions relating to the areas referred to in this Title entail for the institutions shall be charged to the budget of the European Communities.

3. Operational expenditure to which the implementation of those provisions gives rise shall also be charged to the budget of the European Communities, except where the Council acting unanimously decides otherwise. In cases

where expenditure is not charged to the budget of the European Communities it shall be charged to the Member States in accordance with the GNP scale, unless the Council acting unanimously decides otherwise.

4. The budgetary procedure laid down in the Treaty establishing the European Community shall apply to the expenditure charged to the budget of the European Communities.

Article K14 of the TEU (former Article K9)

The Council, acting unanimously on the initiative of the Commission or a Member State, and after consulting the European Parliament, may decide that action in areas referred to in Article K1 shall fall under Title ... of the Treaty establishing the European Community, and at the same time determine the relevant voting conditions relating to it. It shall recommend the Member States to adopt that decision in accordance with their respective constitutional requirements.

Protocol Integrating the *Schengen acquis* into the Framework of the European Union

THE HIGH CONTRACTING PARTIES TO THE TREATY OF AMSTERDAM

NOTING that the Agreements on the gradual abolition of checks at common borders signed by some Member States of the European Union in Schengen on 14 June 1985 and on 19 June 1990, as well as related agreements and the rules adopted on the basis of these agreements, are aimed at enhancing European integration and, in particular, at enabling the European Union to develop more rapidly into an area of freedom, security and justice

DESIRING to incorporate the above mentioned agreements and rules into the framework of the European Union

CONFIRMING that the provisions of the *Schengen acquis* are applicable only if and as far as they are compatible with the Union and Community law

TAKING INTO ACCOUNT the fact that Ireland and the United Kingdom of Great Britain and Northern Ireland are not parties to and have not signed the above-mentioned agreements; that provision should, however, be made to allow those Member States to accept some or all of the provisions thereof

RECOGNIZING that, as a consequence, it is necessary to make use of the provisions of the Treaty on European Union and of the Treaty establishing the European Community concerning closer cooperation between some

Member States and that those provisions should only be used as a last resort

TAKING INTO ACCOUNT the need to maintain a special relationship with the Republic of Iceland and the Kingdom of Norway, both States which have confirmed their intention to become bound by the provisions mentioned above, on the basis of the Agreement signed in Luxembourg on 19th December 1996

HAVE AGREED upon the following provisions, which shall be annexed to the Treaty of Amsterdam:

Article A

The Kingdom of Belgium, the Kingdom of Denmark, the Federal Republic of Germany, the Hellenic Republic, the Kingdom of Spain, the French Republic, the Italian Republic, the Grand Duchy of Luxembourg, the Kingdom of the Netherlands, the Republic of Austria, the Portuguese Republic, the Republic of Finland and the Kingdom of Sweden, signatories to the Schengen Agreements, are authorized to establish closer cooperation among themselves within the scope of those agreements and related provisions, as they are listed in the annex to this Protocol, hereinafter referred to as the "*Schengen acquis*". This cooperation shall be conducted within the institutional and legal framework of the European Union and with respect for the relevant provisions of the Treaty on European Union and of the Treaty establishing the European Community.

Article B

1. From the date of entry into force of this Protocol, the *Schengen acquis*, including the decisions of the Executive Committee established by the Schengen agreements which have been adopted before this date, shall immediately apply to the thirteen Member States referred to in Article A, without prejudice to the provisions of paragraph 2. From the same date, the Council will substitute itself for the said Executive Committee.

The Council, acting by the unanimity of its Members referred to in Article A, shall take any measure necessary for the implementation of this paragraph. The Council, acting unanimously, shall determine, in conformity with the relevant provisions of the Treaties, the legal basis for each of the provisions or decisions which constitute the *Schengen acquis*.

With regard to such provisions and decisions and in accordance with that determination, the Court of Justice of the European Communities shall exercise the powers conferred upon it by the relevant applicable provisions of the Treaties. In any event, the Court of Justice shall have no jurisdiction on measures or decisions relating to the maintenance of law and order and the safeguarding of internal security.

As long as the measures referred to above have not been taken and without prejudice to Article D, second subparagraph, the provisions or decisions which constitute the *Schengen acquis* shall be regarded as acts based on Title VI of the TEU.

2. The provisions of paragraph 1 shall apply to the Member States which have signed accession Protocols to Schengen from the dates decided by the Council, acting with the unanimity of its Members mentioned in Article A, unless the conditions for the accession of any of those States to the *Schengen acquis* are met before the date of the entry into force of this Protocol.

Article C

Ireland and the United Kingdom of Great Britain and Northern Ireland, which are not bound by the *Schengen acquis*, may at any time request to take part in some or all of the provisions of this acquis.

The Council shall decide on the request with the unanimity if its members referred to in Article A and of the representative of the Government of the State concerned.

Article D

1. Proposals and initiatives to build upon the *Schengen acquis* shall be subject to the relevant provisions of the Treaties.

In this context, where either Ireland or the United Kingdom or both have not notified the President of the Council in writing within a reasonable period that they wish to take part, the authorization referred to in Articles 5a of the TEC or K12 of the TEU shall be deemed to have been granted to the Members States referred to in Article A and to Ireland or the United Kingdom where either of them wishes to take part in the areas of cooperation in question.

2. The relevant provisions of the Treaties referred to in the first subparagraph of paragraph 1 shall apply even if the Council has not adopted the measures referred to in Article B(1), second subparagraph.

Article E

The Republic of Iceland and the Kingdom of Norway shall be associated with the implementation of the *Schengen acquis* and its further development on the basis of the Agreement signed in Luxembourg on 19 December 1996. Appropriate procedures shall be agreed to that effect in an Agreement to be concluded with those States by the Council, acting by the unanimity of its Members mentioned in Article A. Such Agreement shall include provisions on the contribution of Iceland and Norway to any financial consequences resulting from the implementation of this Protocol.

A separate Agreement shall be concluded with the above-mentioned countries by the Council, acting unanimously, for the establishment of rights and obligations between Ireland and the United Kingdom of Great Britain and Northern Ireland on the one hand, and Iceland and Norway on the other, in domains of the *Schengen acquis* which apply to these States.

Article F

The Council shall, acting by a qualified majority, adopt the modalities for the integration of the Schengen Secretariat into the General Secretariat of the Council.

Article G

For the purposes of the negotiations for the admission of new Member States into the European Union, the *Schengen acquis* and further measures taken by the institutions within its scope shall be regarded as an *acquis* which must be accepted in full by all States candidates for admission.

SCHENGEN ACQUIS

1. The Agreement, signed in Schengen on 14 June 1985, between the Governments of the States of the Benelux Economic Union, the Federal Republic of Germany and the French Republic on the gradual abolition of checks at their common borders.

2. The Convention, signed in Schengen on 19 June 1990, between the Kingdom of Belgium, the Federal Republic of Germany, the French Republic, the Grand Duchy of Luxembourg and the Kingdom of Netherlands, implementing the Agreement on the gradual abolition of checks at their common borders, signed in Schengen on 14 June 1985, with related Final Act and common declarations.

3. The Accession Protocols and Agreements to the 1985 Agreement and the

1990 Implementation Convention with Italy (signed in Paris on 27 November 1990), Spain and Portugal (both signed in Bonn on 25 June 1991), Greece (signed in Madrid on 6 November 1992), Austria (signed in Brussels on 28 April 1995) and Denmark, Finland and Sweden (all signed in Luxembourg on 19 December 1996), with related Final Acts and declarations.

4. Decisions and declarations adopted by the Executive Committee established by the 1990 Implementation Convention, as well as acts adopted for the implementation of the Convention by the organs upon which the Executive Committee has conferred decision making powers.

Protocol to the Treaty Establishing the European Community on Asylum for Nationals of EU Member States

THE HIGH CONTRACTING PARTIES

WHEREAS pursuant to the provisions of Article F(2) of the Treaty on European Union (TEU) "the Union shall respect fundamental rights as guaranteed by the European Convention for the Protection of Human Rights and Fundamental Freedoms signed in Rome on November 4 1950";

WHEREAS the Court of Justice of the European Communities has jurisdiction to ensure that in the interpretation and application of Article F(2) of the TEU the law is observed by the European Community;

WHEREAS pursuant to Article O of the TEU any European State, when applying to become a Member of the Union, must respect the principles set out in Article F(1) of the TEU;

BEARING IN MIND that Article 236 of the Treaty establishing the European Community (TEC) establishes a mechanism for the suspension of certain rights in the event of a serious and persistent breach by a Member State of those principles;

RECALLING that each national of a Member State, as a citizen of the Union, enjoys a special status and protection which shall be guaranteed by the Member States in accordance with the provisions of Part Two of the TEC;

BEARING IN MIND that the TEC establishes an area without internal frontiers and grants every citizen of the Union the right to move and reside freely within the territory of the Member States;

RECALLING that the question of extradition of nationals of Member States of the Union is addressed in the European Convention on Extradition of 13 December 1957 and the Convention of 27 September 1996 based on Article

K3 of the TEU concerning extradition between the Member States of the European Union;

WISHING to prevent that the institution of asylum is resorted to for purposes alien to those for which it is intended;

WHEREAS this Protocol respects the finality and the objectives of the Convention relating to the Status of Refugees of 28 July 1951;

HAVE AGREED upon the following provisions which shall be annexed to the TEC:

Sole Article

Given the level of protection of fundamental rights and freedoms by the Member States of the European Union, Member States shall be regarded as constituting safe countries of origin in respect of each other for all legal and practical purposes in relation to asylum matters. Accordingly, any application for asylum made by a national of a Member State may be taken into consideration or declared admissible for processing by another Member State only in the following cases:

(a) if the Member State of which the applicant is a national proceeds after the entry into force of this Treaty, availing itself of the provisions of Article 15 of the Convention for the Protection of Human Rights and Fundamental Freedoms, to take measures derogating in its territory from its obligations under that Convention;

(b) if the procedure referred to Article Fa(1) of the TEU, has been initiated and until the Council takes a decision in respect thereof;

(c) if the Council, acting on the basis of Article Fa(1) of the TEU, has determined, in respect of the Member State of which the applicant is a national, the existence of a serious and persistent breach by that Member State of principles mentioned in Article F(1);

(d) if a Member State should so decide unilaterally in respect of the application of a national of another Member State; in that case the Council shall be immediately informed; the application shall be dealt with on the basis of the presumption that it is manifestly unfounded without affecting in any way, whatever the cases may be, the decision-making power of the Member State.

SECTION II

THE UNION AND THE CITIZEN

CHAPTER 3

EMPLOYMENT

Amend Article B of the TEU

The Union shall set itself the following objectives:

– to promote economic and social progress which is balanced and sustainable and a high level of employment, in particular ...

Amend Article 2 of the TEC

The Community shall have as its task ... to promote throughout the Community a harmonious and balanced development of economic activities, a high level of employment and social protection, sustainable and non-inflationary growth respecting the environment, a high degree of competitiveness and convergence of economic performance, ...

Amend Article 3 of the TEC
Additional indent before (i)

(...) the promotion of coordination between employment policies of the Member States with a view to enhancing their effectiveness by developing a coordinated strategy for employment.

New Title on Employment to be inserted after Title VI of the TEC

Article 1

Member States and the Community shall, according to this Title, work towards developing a coordinated strategy for employment and particularly for promoting a skilled, trained and adaptable workforce and labour markets responsive to economic change with a view to achieving the objectives defined in Article B of the Treaty on European Union and in Article 2 of this Treaty.

Article 2

1. Member States, through their employment policies, shall contribute to the achievement of the objectives referred to in Article [1] in a way consistent with the broad guidelines of the economic policies of the Member States and of the Community adopted pursuant to Article 103(2).

2. Member States, having regard to the national practices related to the responsibilities of management and labour, shall regard promoting employment as a matter of common concern and shall coordinate their action in this respect within the Council, in accordance with the provisions of Article [4].

Article 3

1. The Community shall contribute to a high level of employment by encouraging cooperation between Member States and by supporting and, if necessary, complementing their action. In doing so, the competences of the Member States shall be respected.

2. The objective of a high level of employment shall be taken into consideration in the formulation and implementation of Community policies and activities.

Article 4

1. The European Council shall each year consider the employment situation in the Community and adopt conclusions thereon, on the basis of a joint annual report by the Council and the Commission.

2. On the basis of the conclusions of the European Council, the Council, acting by a qualified majority on a proposal from the Commission and after consulting the European Parliament, the Economic and Social Committee, the Committee of the Regions and the Employment Committee referred to in Article [6], shall each year draw up guidelines which the Member States shall take into account in their employment policies. These guidelines shall be consistent with the broad guidelines adopted pursuant to Article 103(2).

3. Each Member State shall provide the Council and the Commission with an annual report on the principal measures taken to implement its employment policy in the light of the guidelines for employment as referred to in paragraph 2.

4. The Council, on the basis of the reports referred to in paragraph 3 and having received the views of the Employment Committee shall each year carry out an examination of the implementation of the employment policies

of the Member States in the light of the guidelines for employment. The Council, acting by a qualified majority on a recommendation from the Commission, may, if it considers it appropriate in the light of that examination, make recommendations to Member States.

5. On the basis of the results of that examination, the Council and the Commission shall make a joint annual report to the European Council on the employment situation in the Community and on the implementation of the guidelines for employment.

Article 5

The Council, acting in accordance with the procedure referred to in Article 189 b and after consulting the Economic and Social Committee and the Committee of the Regions, may adopt incentive measures designed to encourage cooperation between Member States and to support their action in the field of employment through initiatives aimed at developing exchanges of information and best practices, providing comparative analysis and advice as well as promoting innovative approaches and evaluating experiences, in particular by recourse to pilot projects.

Those measures shall not include harmonization of the laws and regulations of the Member States.

Article 6

The Council, after consulting the European Parliament, shall establish an Employment Committee with advisory status to promote coordination between Member States on employment and labour market policies. The tasks of the Committee shall be:

- to monitor the employment situation and employment policies in the Member States and the Community;
- without prejudice to Article 151, to formulate opinions at the request of either the Council or the Commission or on its own initiative, and to contribute to the preparation of the Council proceedings referred to in Article [4].

In fulfilling its mandate, the Committee shall consult the social partners.

The Member States and the Commission shall each appoint two members of the Committee.

CHAPTER 4

SOCIAL POLICY

Article 117
(see in particular Article 1 Social Agreement)

The Community and the Member States, having in mind fundamental social rights such as those set out in the European Charter signed at Turin on 18 October 1961 and in the 1989 Community Charter of the Fundamental Social Rights of Workers, shall have as their objectives the promotion of employment, improved living and working conditions, so as to make possible their harmonization while the improvement is being maintained, proper social protection, dialogue between management and labour, the development of human resources with a view to lasting high employment and the combating of exclusion.

To this end the Community and the Member States shall implement measures which take account of the diverse forms of national practices, in particular in the field of contractual relations, and the need to maintain the competitiveness of the Community economy.

They believe that such a development will ensue not only from the functioning of the common market, which will favour the harmonization of social systems, but also from the procedures provided for in this Treaty and from the approximation of provisions laid down by law, regulation or administrative action.

NB Protocol (No 14) on social policy annexed to the TEC and the Agreement on social policy attached thereto will be repealed

Article 118
(see Article 2 Social Agreement)

1. With a view to achieving the objectives of Article 117, the Community shall support and complement the activities of the Member States in the following fields:

- improvement in particular of the working environment to protect workers' health and safety;
- working conditions;
- the information and consultation of workers;
- the integration of persons excluded from the labour market, without prejudice to Article 127;

- equality between men and women with regard to labour market opportunities and treatment at work.

2. To this end, the Council may adopt, by means of directives, minimum requirements for gradual implementation, having regard to the conditions and technical rules obtaining in each of the Member States. Such directives shall avoid imposing administrative, financial and legal constraints in a way which would hold back the creation and development of small and medium-sized undertakings.

The Council shall act in accordance with the procedure referred to in Article 189b after consulting the Economic and Social Committee.

The Council, acting in accordance with the same procedure, may adopt measures designed to encourage cooperation between Member States through initiatives aimed at improving knowledge, developing exchanges of information and best practices, promoting innovative approaches and evaluating experiences in order to combat social exclusion.

3. However, the Council shall act unanimously on a proposal from the Commission, after consulting the European Parliament and the Economic and Social Committee, in the following areas:

- social security and social protection of workers;
- protection of workers where their employment contract is terminated;
- representation and collective defence of the interests of workers and employers, including co-determination, subject to paragraph 6;
- conditions of employment for third-country nationals legally residing in Community territory;
- financial contributions for promotion of employment and job-creation, without prejudice to the provisions relating to the Social Fund.

4. A Member State may entrust management and labour, at their joint request, with the implementation of directives adopted pursuant to paragraphs 2 and 3.

In this case, it shall ensure that, no later than the date on which a directive must be transposed in accordance with Article 189, management and labour have introduced the necessary measures by agreement, the Member State concerned being required to take any necessary measure enabling it at any time to be in a position to guarantee the results imposed by that directive.

5. The provisions adopted pursuant to this Article shall not prevent any Member State from maintaining or introducing more stringent protective measures compatible with the Treaty.

6. The provisions of this Article shall not apply to pay, the right of association, the right to strike or the right to impose lock-outs.

Article 118a
(See Article 3 Social Agreement)

1. The Commission shall have the task of promoting the consultation of management and labour at Community level and shall take any relevant measure to facilitate their dialogue by ensuring balanced support for the parties.

2. To this end, before submitting proposals in the social policy field, the Commission shall consult management and labour on the possible direction of Community action.

3. If, after such consultation, the Commission considers Community action advisable, it shall consult management and labour on the content of the envisaged proposal. Management and labour shall forward to the Commission an opinion or, where appropriate, a recommendation.

4. On the occasion of such consultation, management and labour may inform the Commission of their wish to initiate the process provided for in Article 118b. The duration of the procedure shall not exceed nine months, unless the management and labour concerned and the Commission decide jointly to extend it.

Article 118b
(See Article 4 Social Agreement)

1. Should management and labour so desire, the dialogue between them at Community level may lead to contractual relations, including agreements.

2. Agreements concluded at Community level shall be implemented either in accordance with the procedures and practices specific to management and labour and the Member States or, in matters covered by Article 118, at the joint request of the signatory parties, by a Council decision on a proposal from the Commission.

The Council shall act by qualified majority, except where the agreement in question contains one or more provisions relating to one of the areas referred to in Article 118(3), in which case it shall act unanimously.

Article 118c
(See in particular Article 5 Social Agreement)

With a view to achieving the objectives of Article 117 and without prejudice to the other provisions of this Treaty, the Commission shall encourage cooperation between the Member States and facilitate the coordination of their action in all social policy fields under this chapter, particularly in matters relating to:

- employment;
- labour law and working conditions;
- basic and advanced vocational training;
- social security;
- prevention of occupational accidents and diseases;
- occupational hygiene;
- the rights of association and collective bargaining between employers and workers.

To this end, the Commission shall act in close contact with Member States by making studies, delivering opinions and arranging consultations both on problems arising at national level and on those of concern to international organizations.

Before delivering the opinions provided for in this Article, the Commission shall consult the Economic and Social Committee.

Article 119
(See Article 6 Social Agreement)

1. Each Member State shall ensure that the principle of equal pay for male and female workers for equal work or work of equal value is applied.

2. For the purpose of this Article, 'pay' means the ordinary basic or minimum wage or salary and any other consideration, whether in cash or in kind, which the worker receives directly or indirectly, in respect of his employment, from his employer.

Equal pay without discrimination based on sex means:

    (a) that pay for the same work at piece rates shall be calculated on the basis of the same unit of measurement;

    (b) that pay for work at time rates shall be the same for the same job.

3. The Council, acting in accordance with the procedure referred to in Article 189b, and after consulting the Economic and Social Committee, shall adopt

measures to ensure the application of the principle of equal opportunities and equal treatment of men and women in matters of employment and occupation, including the principle of equal pay for equal work or work of equal value.

4. With a view to ensuring full equality in practice between men and women in working life, the principle of equal treatment shall not prevent any Member State from maintaining or adopting measures providing for specific advantages in order to make it easier for the underrepresented sex to pursue a vocational activity or to prevent or compensate for disadvantages in professional careers.

Article 119a
(See Article 120 of TEC)

Member States shall endeavour to maintain the existing equivalence between paid holiday schemes.

Article 120
(See Article 7 Social Agreement)

The Commission shall draw up a report each year on progress in achieving the objectives of Article 117, including the demographic situation in the Community. It shall forward the report to the European Parliament, the Council and the Economic and Social Committee.

The European Parliament may invite the Commission to draw up reports on particular problems concerning the social situation.

CHAPTER 5

ENVIRONMENT

Amend seventh indent of the Preamble to the TEU

Determined to promote economic and social progress for their peoples, taking into account the principle of sustainable development and within the context of the accomplishment of the internal market ... .

Amend Article B of the TEU

The Union shall set itself the following objectives:

– to promote economic and social progress and to achieve balanced and sustainable development, in particular through ...

Amend Article 2 of the TEC

The Community shall have as its task, by establishing a common market and an economic and monetary union and by implementing the common policies or activities referred to in Articles 3 and 3a, to promote throughout the Community a harmonious, balanced and sustainable development of economic activities, sustainable and non inflationary growth, a high degree of convergence of economic performance, a high level of employment and of social protection, a high level of protection and improvement of the quality of the environment, the raising of the standard of living and quality of life, and economic and social cohesion and solidarity among Member States.

Integration of environmental protection into all sectoral policies

New Article 3d in the TEC

Environmental protection requirements must be integrated into the definition and implementation of Community policies and activities referred to in Article 3, in particular with a view to promoting sustainable development.

Replace paragraphs 3 to 5 of Article 100a of the TEC by paragraphs 3 to 9 as follows

3. The Commission, in its proposals envisaged in paragraph 1 concerning health, safety, environmental protection and consumer protection, will take as a base a high level of protection, taking account in particular of any new development based on scientific facts. Within their respective powers, the European Parliament and the Council will also seek to achieve this objective.

4. If, after the adoption by the Council or by the Commission of a harmonization measure, a Member State deems it necessary to maintain national provisions on grounds of major needs referred to in Article 36, or relating to the protection of the environment or the working environment, it shall notify the Commission of these provisions as well as the grounds for maintaining them.

5. Moreover, without prejudice to the previous subparagraph, if, after the adoption by the Council or by the Commission of a harmonization measure, Member State deems it necessary to introduce national provisions based

on new scientific evidence relating to the protection of the environment or the working environment on grounds of a problem specific to that Member State arising after the adoption of the harmonization measure, it shall notify the Commission of the envisaged provisions as well as the grounds for introducing them.

6. The Commission shall, within six months of the notifications as referred to in paragraphs 4 and 5, approve or reject the national provisions involved after having verified that they are not a means of arbitrary discrimination or a disguised restriction on trade between Member States and that they shall not constitute an obstacle to the functioning of the internal market.

In the absence of a decision by the Commission within this period the national provisions referred to in paragraphs 4 and 5 shall be deemed to have been approved.

When justified by the complexity of the matter and in the absence of danger for human health, the Commission may notify the Member State concerned that the period referred to in this paragraph may be extended for a further period of up to six months.

7. When, pursuant to paragraph 6, a Member State is authorized to maintain or introduce national provisions derogating from a harmonization measure, the Commission shall immediately examine whether to propose an adaptation to that measure.

7a. When a Member State raises a specific problem on public health in a field which has been the subject of prior harmonization measures, it shall bring it to the attention of the Commission which shall immediately examine whether to propose appropriate measures to the Council.

8. By way of derogation from the procedure laid down in Articles 169 and 170, the Commission and any Member State may bring the matter directly before the Court of Justice if it considers that another Member State is making improper use of the powers provided for in this Article.

9. The harmonization measures referred to above shall, in appropriate cases, include a safeguard clause authorizing the Member States to take, for one or more of the non-economic reasons referred to in Article 36, provisional measures subject to a Community control procedure.

CHAPTER 6

PUBLIC HEALTH

Amend Article 129 of the TEC

1. A high level of human health protection shall be ensured in the definition and implementation of all Community policies and activities.

Community action, which shall complement national policies, shall be directed towards improving public health, preventing human illness and diseases, and obviating sources of danger to human health. Such action shall cover the fight against the major health scourges, by promoting research into their causes, their transmission and their prevention, as well as health information and education.

The Community shall complement the Member States' action in reducing drugs related health damage, including information and prevention.

2. The Community shall encourage cooperation between the Member States in the areas referred to in this Article and, if necessary, lend support to their action.

Member States shall, in liaison with the Commission, coordinate among themselves their policies and programmes in the areas referred to in paragraph 1. The Commission may, in close contact with the Member States, take any useful initiative to promote such coordination.

3. The Community and the Member States shall foster cooperation with third countries and the competent international organizations in the sphere of public health.

4. The Council, acting in accordance with the procedure referred to in Article 189b, after consulting the Social and Economic Committee and the Committee of the Regions shall contribute to the achievement of the objectives referred to in this Article through adopting:

   (a) measures setting high standards of quality and safety of organs and substances of human origin, blood and blood derivatives; these measures shall not prevent any Member State from maintaining or introducing more stringent protective measures;

   (b) by way of derogation from Article 43, measures in the veterinary and phytosanitary fields which have as their direct objective the protection of public health;

   (c) incentive measures designed to protect and improve human health, excluding any harmonization of the laws and regulations of the Member States.

The Council, acting by a qualified majority on a proposal from the Commission, may also adopt recommendations for the purposes set out in this Article.

5. Community action in the field of public health shall fully respect the responsibilities of the Member States for the organization and delivery of health services and medical care. In particular, measures referred to in paragraph 4(a) shall not affect national provisions on the donation or medical use of organs and blood.

CHAPTER 7

CONSUMER PROTECTION

Amend Article 129a in the TEC

1. In order to promote the interests of consumers and to ensure a high level of consumer protection, the Community shall contribute to protecting the health, safety and economic interests of consumers, as well as to promoting their right to information, education and to organize themselves in order to safeguard their interests.

2. Consumer protection requirements shall be taken into account in defining and implementing other Community policies and activities.

3. The Community shall contribute to the attainment of the objectives referred to in paragraph 1 through:

(a) measures adopted pursuant to article 100a in the context of the completion of the internal market;

(b) measures which support, supplement and monitor the policy pursued by the Member States.

4. The Council, acting in accordance with the procedure referred to in Article 189b and after consulting the Economic and Social Committee, shall adopt the measures referred to in paragraph 3(b).

5. Measures adopted pursuant to paragraph 4 shall not prevent any Member State from maintaining or introducing more stringent protective measures. Such measures must be compatible with this Treaty. The Commission shall be notified of them.

CHAPTER 8

OTHER COMMUNITY POLICIES

(a) Citizenship of the Union

Amend Article 8 of the TEC

1. Citizenship of the Union is hereby established. Every person holding the nationality of a Member State shall be a citizen of the Union. Citizenship of the Union shall complement and not replace national citizenship.

Add a new third subparagraph to Article 8d of the TEC

Every citizen of the Union may write to any of the institutions or bodies referred to in this Article or in Article 4 in one of the languages mentioned in Article 248 and have an answer in the same language.

New paragraph in the Preamble to the TEC

Determined to promote the development of the highest possible level of knowledge for their peoples through a wide access to education and its continuous updating.

(b) Culture

Amend Article 128(4) of the TEC

The Community shall take cultural aspects into account in its action under other provisions of this Treaty, in particular in order to respect and to promote the diversity of its cultures.

(d) Countering fraud affecting the financial interests of the Community

Amend Article 209a of the TEC

1. The Community and the Member States shall counter fraud and any other illegal activities affecting the financial interests of the Community through measures to be taken in accordance with this Article, which shall

act as a deterrent and be such as to afford effective protection in the Member States.

2. Member States shall take the same measures to counter fraud affecting the financial interests of the Community as they take to counter fraud affecting their own financial interests.

3. Without prejudice to other provisions of this Treaty, the Member States shall coordinate their action aimed at protecting the financial interests of the Community against fraud. To this end they shall organize, together with the Commission, close and regular cooperation between the competent authorities.

4. The Council, acting in accordance with the procedure referred to in Article 189b, after consulting the Court of Auditors, shall adopt the necessary measures in the fields of the prevention of and fight against fraud affecting the financial interests of the Community with a view to affording effective and equivalent protection in the Member States. These measures shall not concern the application of national criminal law and the national administration of justice.

5. The Commission, in cooperation with Member States, shall each year submit to the Council and to the European Parliament a report on the measures taken for the implementation of this Article.

(e) Strengthening customs cooperation

New Article in the TEC

Within the scope of application of this Treaty, the Council, acting in accordance with the procedure referred to in Article 189b, shall take measures in order to strengthen customs cooperation between Member States and between the latter and the Commission. These measures shall not concern the application of national criminal law and the national administration of justice.

(f) Outermost regions

Amend Article 227(2)

2. The provisions of the Treaty establishing the European Community shall apply to the French overseas departments, the Azores, Madeira and the Canary Islands.

However, taking account of the structural social and economic situation of the French overseas departments, the Azores, Madeira and the Canary Islands, which is compounded by their remoteness, insularity, small size, difficult topography and climate, economic dependence on a few products, the permanence and combination of which severely restrain their development, the Council, acting by a qualified majority on a proposal from the Commission and after consulting the European Parliament, shall adopt specific measures aimed, in particular, at laying down the conditions of application of the present Treaty to those regions, including common policies.

The Council shall, when adopting the relevant measures referred to in the previous subparagraph, take into account areas such as customs and trade policies, fiscal policy, free zones, agriculture and fisheries policies, conditions for supply of raw materials and essential consumer goods, State aids and conditions of access to structural funds and to horizontal Community programmes.

The Council shall adopt the measures referred to in the second subparagraph taking into account the special characteristics and constraints of the outermost regions without undermining the integrity and the coherence of the Community legal order, including the internal market and common policies.

(g) Island regions

Amend Article 130a, second paragraph

In particular, the Community shall aim at reducing disparities between the levels of development of the various regions and the backwardness of the least favoured regions or islands, including rural areas.

(i) Services of general economic interest

New Article 7d

Without prejudice to Articles 77, 90 and 92, and given the place occupied by services of general economic interest in the shared values of the Union as well as their role in promoting social and territorial cohesion, the Community and the Member States, each within their respective powers and within the scope of application of this Treaty, shall take care that such services operate on the basis of principles and conditions which enable them to fulfil their missions.

(j) Public Service Broadcasting

Protocol to the TEC

THE HIGH CONTRACTING PARTIES

CONSIDERING that the system of public broadcasting in the Member States is directly related to the democratic, social and cultural needs of each society and to the need to preserve media pluralism

HAVE AGREED upon the following interpretative provisions, which shall be annexed to the Treaty establishing the European Community:

The provisions of this Treaty shall be without prejudice to the competence of Member States to provide for the funding of public service broadcasting in so far as such funding is granted to broadcasting organizations for the fulfilment of the public service remit as conferred, defined and organized by each Member State, and that such funding does not affect trading conditions and competition in the Community to an extent which would be contrary to the common interest, while the realization of the remit of that public service shall be taken into account.

(m) Animal welfare

Protocol to the TEC

THE HIGH CONTRACTING PARTIES

DESIRING to ensure improved protection and respect for the welfare of

animals as sentient beings

HAVE AGREED upon the following provision which shall be annexed to the Treaty establishing the European Community:

In formulating and implementing the Community's agriculture, transport, internal market and research policies, the Community and the Member States shall pay full regard to the welfare requirements of animals, while respecting the legislative or administrative provisions and customs of the Member States relating in particular to religious rites, cultural traditions and regional heritage.

(n) Trans-European networks

Amend third indent of Article 129c(1) of the TEC

In order to achieve the objectives referred to in Article 129b, the Community:

....

- may support projects of common interest supported by Member States, which are identified in the framework of guidelines referred to ... (rest unchanged).

(o) Statistics

New Article 213a in the TEC

1. Without prejudice to the provisions of Article 5 of the Protocol on the Statute of the European System of Central Banks and of the European Central Bank, the Council, acting in accordance with Article 189b, shall adopt measures for the production of statistics where necessary for the performance of the activities of the Community.

2. The production of Community statistics shall conform to impartiality, reliability, objectivity, scientific independence, cost-effectiveness and statistical confidentiality; it shall not entail excessive burdens on economic operators.

CHAPTER 9

SUBSIDIARITY

Protocol on the Application of the Principles of Subsidiarity and Proportionality

The HIGH CONTRACTING PARTIES

DETERMINED to establish the conditions for the application of the principles of subsidiarity and proportionality enshrined in Article 3b of the Treaty establishing the European Community with a view to defining more precisely the criteria for applying them and to ensure their strict observance and consistent implementation by all institutions

WISHING to ensure that decisions are taken as closely as possible to the citizens of the Union

TAKING ACCOUNT of the Interinstitutional Agreement of 28 October 1993 between the European Parliament, the Council and the Commission on procedures for implementing the principle of subsidiarity

HAVE CONFIRMED that the conclusions of the Birmingham European Council on 16 October 1992 and the overall approach to the application of the subsidiarity principle agreed by the European Council meeting in Edinburgh on 11–12 December 1992, will continue to guide the action of the Union's institutions as well as the development of the application of the principle of subsidiarity, and, for this purpose, have agreed on the following provisions which shall be annexed to the Treaty establishing the European Community:

1. In exercising the powers conferred on it, each institution shall ensure that the principle of subsidiarity is complied with. It shall also ensure compliance with the principle of proportionality, according to which any action by the Community shall not go beyond what is necessary to achieve the objectives of the Treaty.

2. The application of the principles of subsidiarity and proportionality shall respect the general provisions and the objectives of the Treaty, particularly as regards the maintaining in full of the acquis communautaire and the institutional balance; it shall not affect the principles developed by the Court of Justice regarding the relationship between national and Community law, and it should take into account Article F(3) of the TEU, according to which "the Union shall provide itself with the means necessary to attain its objectives and carry through its policies".

3. The principle of subsidiarity does not call into question the powers conferred on the European Community by the Treaty, as interpreted by the Court of Justice. The criteria referred to in Article 3b(2) shall relate to areas for which the Community does not have exclusive competence. The principle of subsidiarity provides a guide as to how those powers are to be exercised at the Community level. Subsidiarity is a dynamic concept and should be applied in the light of the objectives set out in the Treaty. It allows Community action within the limits of its powers to be expanded where circumstances so require, and conversely, to be restricted or discontinued where it is no longer justified.

4. For any proposed Community legislation, the reasons on which it is based shall be stated with a view to justifying that it complies with the principles of subsidiarity and proportionality; the reasons for concluding that a Community objective can be better achieved by the Community must be substantiated by qualitative or, wherever possible, quantitative indicators.

5. For Community action to be justified, both aspects of the subsidiarity

principle shall be met: the objectives of the proposed action cannot be sufficiently achieved by Member States' action in the framework of their national constitutional system and can therefore be better achieved by action on the part of the Community.

The following guidelines should be used in examining whether the abovementioned condition is fulfilled:

- the issue under consideration has transnational aspects which cannot be satisfactorily regulated by action by Member States;
- actions by Member States alone or lack of Community action would conflict with the requirements of the Treaty (such as the need to correct distortion of competition or avoid disguised restrictions on trade or strengthen economic and social cohesion) or would otherwise significantly damage Member States' interests;
- action at Community level would produce clear benefits by reason of its scale or effects compared with action at the level of the Member States.

6. The form of Community action shall be as simple as possible, consistent with satisfactory achievement of the objective of the measure and the need for effective enforcement. The Community shall legislate only to the extent necessary. Other things being equal, directives should be preferred to regulations and framework directives to detailed measures. Directives as provided for in Article 189, while binding upon each Member State to which they are addressed as to the result to be achieved, shall leave to the national authorities the choice of form and methods.

7. Regarding the nature and the extent of Community action, Community measures should leave as much scope for national decision as possible, consistent with securing the aim of the measure and observing the requirements of the Treaty. While respecting Community law, care should be taken to respect well established national arrangements and the organization and working of Member States legal systems. Where appropriate and subject to the need for proper enforcement, Community measures should provide Member States with alternative ways to achieve the objectives of the measures.

8. Where the application of the principle of subsidiarity leads to no action being taken by the Community, Member States are required in their action to comply with the general rules laid down in Article 5 of the Treaty, by taking all appropriate measures to ensure fulfilment of their obligations under the Treaty and by abstaining from any measure which could jeopardize the attainment of the objectives of the Treaty.

9. Without prejudice to its right of initiative, the Commission should:

- except in cases of particular urgency or confidentiality, consult widely before proposing legislation and, wherever appropriate, publish consultation documents;
- justify the relevance of its proposals with regard to the principle of subsidiarity; whenever necessary, the explanatory memorandum accompanying a proposal will give details in this respect. The financing of Community action in whole or in part from the Community budget shall require an explanation;
- take duly into account the need for any burden, whether financial or administrative, falling upon the Community, national governments, local authorities, economic operators and citizens, to be minimized and proportionate to the objective to be achieved;
- submit an annual report to the European Council, the Council and the European Parliament on the application of Article 3b of the Treaty. This annual report shall also be sent to the Committee of the Regions and to the Economic and Social Committee.

10. The European Council shall take account of the Commission report referred in paragraph 9, fourth indent, within the report on the progress achieved by the Union which it is required to submit to the European Parliament in accordance with Article D of the Treaty on European Union.

11. While fully observing the procedures applicable, the European Parliament and the Council shall, as an integral part of the overall examination of Commission proposals, consider their consistency with Article 3b. This concerns the original Commission proposal as well as amendments which the European Parliament and the Council envisage making to the proposal.

12. In the course of the procedures referred to in Articles 189b and 189c, the European Parliament shall be informed of the Council's position on the application of Article 3b, by way of a statement of the reasons which led the Council to adopt its common position. The Council shall inform the European Parliament of the reasons on the basis of which all or part of a Commission proposal is deemed to be inconsistent with Article 3b of the Treaty.

13. Compliance with the principle of subsidiarity shall be reviewed in accordance with the rules laid down by this Treaty.

CHAPTER 10

TRANSPARENCY

Amend the second paragraph of Article A of the TEU

This Treaty marks a new stage in the process of creating an ever closer Union among the peoples of Europe, in which decisions are taken as openly as possible and as closely as possible to the citizen.

New Article 191a in the TEC

1. Any citizen of the Union, and any natural or legal person residing or having its registered office in a Member State, shall have a right of access to European Parliament, Council and Commission documents, subject to the principles and the conditions to be defined in accordance with paragraphs 2 and 3.

2. General principles and limits on grounds of public or private interest governing this right of access to documents shall be determined by the Council, acting in accordance with the procedure referred to in Article 189b within two years of the entry into force of the Treaty.

3. Each institution referred to above shall elaborate in its own rules of procedure specific provisions regarding access to its documents (1).

SECTION III

AN EFFECTIVE AND COHERENT EXTERNAL POLICY

CHAPTER 12

THE COMMON FOREIGN AND SECURITY POLICY

Amend Article C, second subparagraph, of the TEU

The Union shall in particular ensure the consistency of its external activities as a whole in the context of its external relations, security, economic and development policies. The Council and the Commission shall be responsible for ensuring such consistency and shall cooperate to this end. They shall ensure the implementation of these policies, each in accordance with its respective powers.

TITLE V

Provisions on a common foreign and security policy

Article J1

1. The Union shall define and implement a common foreign and security policy covering all areas of foreign and security policy, the objectives of which shall be:

- to safeguard the common values, fundamental interests, independence and integrity of the Union in conformity with the principles of the United Nations Charter;
- to strengthen the security of the Union in all ways;
- to preserve peace and strengthen international security, in accordance with the principles of the United Nations Charter, as well as the principles of the Helsinki Final Act and the objectives of the Paris Charter, including those on external borders;
- to promote international cooperation;
- to develop and consolidate democracy and the rule of law, and respect for human rights and fundamental freedoms.

2. The Member States shall support the Union's external and security policy actively and unreservedly in a spirit of loyalty and mutual solidarity.

The Member States shall work together to enhance and develop their mutual political solidarity. They shall refrain from any action which is contrary to the interests of the Union or likely to impair its effectiveness as a cohesive force in international relations.

The Council shall ensure that these principles are complied with.

Article J2 (former J1(3))

The Union shall pursue the objectives set out in Article J1 by:

- defining the principles of and general guidelines for the common foreign and security policy;
- deciding on common strategies;
- adopting joint actions;
- adopting common positions;
- and strengthening systematic cooperation between Member States in the conduct of policy.

Article J3 (former J8(1) and (2), first subparagraph)

1. The European Council shall define the principles of and general guidelines for the common foreign and security policy, including for matters with defence implications.

2. The European Council shall decide on common strategies to be implemented by the Union in areas where the Member States have important interests in common.

Common strategies shall set out their objectives, duration and the means to be made available by the Union and the Member States.

3. The Council shall take the decisions necessary for defining and implementing the common foreign and security policy on the basis of the general guidelines defined by the European Council.

The Council shall recommend common strategies to the European Council and shall implement them, in particular by adopting joint actions and common positions.

The Council shall ensure the unity, consistency and effectiveness of action by the Union.

Article J4 (former J3)

1. The Council shall adopt joint actions. Joint actions shall address specific situations where operational action by the Union is deemed to be required. They shall lay down their objectives, scope, the means to be made available to the Union, if necessary their duration, and the conditions for their implementation.

2. If there is a change in circumstances having a substantial effect on a question subject to joint action, the Council shall review the principles and objectives of that action and take the necessary decisions. As long as the Council has not acted, the joint action shall stand.

3. Joint actions shall commit the Member States in the positions they adopt and in the conduct of their activity.

4. The Council may request the Commission to submit to it any appropriate proposals relating to the common foreign and security policy to ensure the implementation of a joint action.

5. Whenever there is any plan to adopt a national position or take national action pursuant to a joint action, information shall be provided in time to allow, if necessary, for prior consultations within the Council. The obligation

to provide prior information shall not apply to measures which are merely a national transposition of Council decisions.

6. In cases of imperative need arising from changes in the situation and failing a Council decision, Member States may take the necessary measures as a matter of urgency having regard to the general objectives of the joint action. The Member State concerned shall inform the Council immediately of any such measures.

7. Should there be any major difficulties in implementing a joint action, a Member State shall refer them to the Council which shall discuss them and seek appropriate solutions. Such solutions shall not run counter to the objectives of the joint action or impair its effectiveness.

Article J5 (former J2(2))

The Council shall adopt common positions. Common positions shall define the approach of the Union to a particular matter of a geographical or thematic nature. Member States shall ensure that their national policies conform to the common positions.

Article J6 (former J2(1))

Member States shall inform and consult one another within the Council on any matter of foreign and security policy of general interest in order to ensure that the Union's influence is exerted as effectively as possible by means of concerted and convergent action.

Article J7 (former J4)

1. The common foreign and security policy shall include all questions relating to the security of the Union, including the progressive framing of a common defence policy, in accordance with the second subparagraph, which might lead to a common defence, should the European Council so decide. It shall in that case recommend to the Member States the adoption of such a decision in accordance with their respective constitutional requirements.

The Western European Union (WEU) is an integral part of the development of the Union providing the Union with access to an operational capability notably in the context of paragraph 2. It supports the Union in framing the defence aspects of the common foreign and security policy as set out in this Article. The Union shall accordingly foster closer institutional relations with the WEU with a view to the possibility of the integration of the WEU into the Union, should the European Council so decide. It shall in that case recommend to the Member States the adoption of such a decision in accordance with their respective constitutional requirements.

The policy of the Union in accordance with this Article shall not prejudice the specific character of the security and defence policy of certain Member States and shall respect the obligations of certain Member States, which see their common defence realized in NATO, under the North Atlantic Treaty and be compatible with the common security and defence policy established within that framework.

The progressive framing of a common defence policy will be supported, as Member States consider appropriate, by cooperation between them in the field of armaments.

2. Questions referred to in this Article shall include humanitarian and rescue tasks, peacekeeping tasks and tasks of combat forces in crisis management, including peacemaking.

3. The Union will avail itself of the WEU to elaborate and implement decisions and actions of the Union which have defence implications.

The competence of the European Council to establish guidelines in accordance with Article J3 shall also obtain in respect of the WEU for those matters for which the Union avails itself of the WEU.

When the Union avails itself of the WEU to elaborate and implement decisions of the Union on the tasks referred to in paragraph 2 all Member States of the Union shall be entitled to participate fully in the tasks in question. The Council, in agreement with the institutions of the WEU, shall adopt the necessary practical arrangements to allow all Member States contributing to the tasks in question to participate fully and on an equal footing in planning and decision-taking in the WEU.

Decisions having defence implications dealt with under this paragraph shall be taken without prejudice to the policies and obligations referred to in paragraph 1, third subparagraph.

4. The provisions of this Article shall not prevent the development of closer cooperation between two or more Member States on a bilateral level, in the framework of the WEU and the Atlantic Alliance, provided such cooperation does not run counter to or impede that provided for in this Title.

5. With a view to furthering the objectives of this Article, the provisions of this Article will be reviewed in accordance with Article N.

Protocol on Article J7 of the Treaty on European Union

THE HIGH CONTRACTING PARTIES

BEARING IN MIND the need to implement fully the provisions of Article J7(1), second subparagraph, and (3) of the TEU

BEARING IN MIND that the policy of the Union in accordance with Article J7 shall not prejudice the specific character of the security and defence policy of certain Member States and shall respect the obligations of certain Member States, which see their common defence realized in NATO, under the North Atlantic Treaty and be compatible with the common security and defence policy established within that framework

HAVE AGREED upon the following provision, which shall be annexed to the Treaty on European Union

The European Union shall draw up, together with the WEU, arrangements for enhanced cooperation between them, within a year from the entry into force of this Protocol.

Article J8 (former J5)

1. The Presidency shall represent the Union in matters coming within the common foreign and security policy.

2. The Presidency shall be responsible for the implementation of common measures; in that capacity it shall in principle express the position of the Union in international organizations and international conferences.

3. The Presidency shall be assisted by the Secretary-General of the Council who shall exercise the function of High Representative for the common foreign and security policy. The Secretary-General, High Representative for the common foreign and security policy, shall be seconded by the deputy Secretary-General of the Council referred to in Article 151 of the TEC who shall be responsible for the running of the General Secretariat.

4. The Commission shall be fully associated in the tasks referred to in paragraphs 1 and 2. The Presidency shall be assisted in those tasks if need be by the next Member State to hold the Presidency.

5. The Council may, whenever it deems it necessary, appoint a special representative with a mandate in relation to particular policy issues.

Article J9 (former J2(3) and J5(4))

1. Member States shall coordinate their action in international

organizations and at international conferences. They shall uphold the common positions in such fora.

In international organizations and at international conferences where not all the Member States participate, those which do take part shall uphold the common positions.

2. Without prejudice to the previous paragraph and Article J4(3), Member States represented in international organizations or international conferences where not all the Member States participate shall keep the latter informed of any matter of common interest.

Member States which are also members of the United Nations Security Council will concert and keep the other Member States fully informed. Member States which are permanent members of the Security Council will, in the execution of their functions, ensure the defence of the positions and the interests of the Union, without prejudice to their responsibilities under the provisions of the United Nations Charter.

Article J10 (former J6)

The diplomatic and consular missions of the Member States and the Commission Delegations in third countries and international conferences, and their representations to international organizations, shall cooperate in ensuring that the common positions and common measures adopted by the Council are complied with and implemented.

They shall step up cooperation by exchanging information, carrying out joint assessments and contributing to the implementation of the provisions referred to in Article 8c of the Treaty establishing the European Community.

Article J11 (former J7)

The Presidency shall consult the European Parliament on the main aspects and the basic choices of the common foreign and security policy and shall ensure that the views of the European Parliament are duly taken into consideration. The European Parliament shall be kept regularly informed by the Presidency and the Commission of the development of the Union's foreign and security policy.

The European Parliament may ask questions of the Council or make recommendations to it. It shall hold an annual debate on progress in implementing the common foreign and security policy.

Article J12 (former J8(3) and (4))

1. Any Member State or the Commission may refer to the Council any question relating to the common foreign and security policy and may submit proposals to the Council.

2. In cases requiring a rapid decision, the Presidency, of its own motion, or at the request of the Commission or a Member State, shall convene an extraordinary Council meeting within forty-eight hours or, in an emergency, within a shorter period.

Article J13

1. Decisions under this Title shall be taken by the Council acting unanimously. Abstentions by members present in person or represented shall not prevent the adoption of such decisions.

When abstaining in a vote, any member of the Council may qualify its abstention by making a formal declaration under the present subparagraph. In that case, it shall not be obliged to apply the decision, but shall accept that the decision commits the Union. In a spirit of mutual solidarity, the Member State concerned shall refrain from any action likely to conflict with or impede Union action based on that decision and the other Member States shall respect its position. If the members of the Council qualifying their abstention in this way represent more than one third of the votes weighted in accordance with Article 148(2) of the TEC, the decision shall not be adopted.

2. By derogation from the provisions of paragraph 1, the Council shall act by qualified majority:

- when adopting joint actions, common positions or taking any other decision on the basis of a common strategy;
- when adopting any decision implementing a joint action or a common position.

If a member of the Council declares that, for important and stated reasons of national policy, it intends to oppose the adoption of a decision to be taken by qualified majority, a vote shall not be taken. The Council may, acting by a qualified majority, request that the matter be referred to the European Council for decision by unanimity.

The votes of the members of the Council shall be weighted in accordance with article 148(2) of the Treaty establishing the European Community. For their adoption, decisions shall require at least 62 votes in favour, cast by at least 10 members.

This paragraph shall not apply to decisions having military or defence implications.

3. For procedural questions, the Council shall act by a majority of its members.

New Article J14

When it is necessary to conclude an agreement with one or more States or international organizations in implementation of this Title, the Council, acting unanimously, may authorize the Presidency, assisted by the Commission as appropriate, to open negotiations to that effect. Such agreements shall be concluded by the Council acting unanimously on a recommendation from the Presidency. No agreement shall be binding on a Member State whose representative in the Council states that it has to comply with the requirements of its own constitutional procedure; the other members of the Council may agree that the agreement shall apply provisionally to them.

The provisions of this Article shall also apply to matters falling under Title VI.

Article J15 (former J8(5))

Without prejudice to Article 151 of the Treaty establishing the European Community, a Political Committee shall monitor the international situation in the areas covered by common foreign and security policy and contribute to the definition of policies by delivering opinions to the Council at the request of the Council or on its own initiative. It shall also monitor the implementation of agreed policies, without prejudice to the responsibility of the Presidency and the Commission.

Article J16

The Secretary-General of the Council, High Representative for the common foreign and security policy, shall assist the Council in matters coming within the scope of the common foreign and security policy, in particular through contributing to the formulation, preparation and implementation of policy decisions, and, when appropriate and acting on behalf of the Council at the request of the Presidency, through conducting political dialogue with third parties.

Article J17 (former J9)

The Commission shall be fully associated with the work carried out in the common foreign and security policy field.

Article J18 (former J11)

1. The provisions referred to in Articles 137, 138, 139 to 142, 146, 147, 150 to 153, 157 to 163, 191a and 217 of the Treaty establishing the European Community shall apply to the provisions relating to the areas referred to in this Title.

2 Administrative expenditure which the provisions relating to the areas referred to in this Title entail for the institutions shall be charged to the budget of the European Communities.

3. Operational expenditure to which the implementation of those provisions gives rise shall also be charged to the budget of the European Communities, except for such expenditure arising from operations having military or defence implications, and cases where the Council acting unanimously decides otherwise.

In cases where expenditure is not charged to the budget of the European Communities it shall be charged to the Member States in accordance with the GNP scale, unless the Council acting unanimously decides otherwise. As for expenditure arising from operations having military or defence implications, Member States which have made a formal declaration under Article J13(1), second subparagraph, shall not be obliged to contribute to the financing thereof.

4. The budgetary procedure laid down in the Treaty establishing the European Community shall apply to the expenditure charged to the budget of the European Communities.

Inter Institutional Agreement between the European Parliament, the Council and the European Commission on provisions regarding financing of the Common Foreign and Security Policy

General Provisions

A. CFSP operational expenditure shall be charged to the budget of the European Communities, unless the Council decides otherwise, in accordance with Article J17 of the treaty.

B. CFSP expenditure shall be treated as expenditure not necessarily resulting from the Treaty. However, the following specific modalities of implementation of the expenditure in question are hereby laid down by common agreement between the European Parliament, the Council and the Commission.

Financial Arrangements

C. On the basis of the preliminary draft budget established by the Commission, the European Parliament and the Council shall annually secure agreement on the amount of the operational CFSP expenditure to be charged to the Communities' budget and on the allocation of this amount among the articles of the CFSP budget chapter (for articles: see suggestions under G).

In the absence of agreement, it is understood that the European Parliament and the Council shall at least agree to enter in the CFSP budget the amount contained in the previous budget, unless the Commission proposes to lower that amount.

D. The total amount of operational CFSP expenditure shall be entirely entered in one (CFSP) budget chapter, under the articles of this chapter (as suggested in G). This amount shall cover the real predictable needs and a reasonable margin for unforeseen actions. No funds will be entered into a reserve. Each article shall cover common strategies or joint actions already adopted, measures which are foreseen but not yet adopted and all future – i.e. unforeseen – actions to be adopted by the Council during the financial year concerned.

E. In conformity with the Financial Regulation, the Commission, on the basis of a Council decision, will have the authority to, autonomously, make credit-transfers between articles within one budget chapter, i.e. the CFSP envelope, the flexibility deemed necessary for a speedy implementation of CFSP actions will be assured.

F. In the event of the amount of the CFSP budget during the financial year being insufficient to cover the necessary expenses, the European Parliament and the Council shall agree to find a solution as a matter of urgency, on a proposal by the Commission.

G. Within the CFSP budget chapter, the articles into which the CFSP actions are to be entered, could read along the following lines:

- observation and organisation of elections/participation in democratic transition processes
- EU-envoys

- Prevention of conflicts/peace and security processes
- Financial assistance to disarmament processes
- Contributions to international conferences
- Urgent actions

The European Parliament, the Council and the Commission agree that the amount for actions entered under the article mentioned in the sixth indent cannot exceed 20 per cent of the global amount of the CFSP budget chapter.

Ad hoc concertation procedure

H. An ad hoc concertation procedure shall be set up, with a view to reaching an agreement between the two arms of the budgetary authority as far as the aforementioned amount of CFSP expenditure and the distribution of this amount over the articles of CFSP budget chapter are concerned.

I. This procedure will be applied at the request of the European Parliament or the Council, notably if either of these institutions intends to depart from the preliminary draft budget of the Commission.

J The ad hoc concertation procedure has to be concluded before the date set by the Council for establishing its draft budget.

K. Each arm of the budgetary authority shall take whatever steps are required to ensure that the results which will be secured in the ad hoc concertation procedure, are respected throughout the budgetary procedure.

Consultation and information of the European Parliament

L. On a yearly basis the Presidency of the Council shall consult the European Parliament on a document established by the Council on the main aspects and basic choices of the CFSP, including the financial implications for the Communities budget. Furthermore, the Presidency shall on a regular basis inform the European Parliament on the development and implementation of CFSP actions.

M. The Council shall, each time it adopts a decision in the field of CFSP entailing expenses, immediately and in each case communicate to the European Parliament an estimate of the costs envisaged ("fiche financiÈre"), in particular those regarding time-frame, staff employed, use of premises and other infrastructure, transport facilities, training requirements and security arrangements.

N. The Commission shall inform the budgetary authority on the execution of CFSP actions and the financial forecasts for the remaining period of the year on a quarterly basis.

CHAPTER 13

EXTERNAL ECONOMIC RELATIONS

New Article 113(5) of the TEC

5. The Council, acting unanimously on a proposal from the Commission and after consulting the European Parliament, may extend the application of paragraphs 1 to 4 to international negotiations and agreements on services and intellectual property insofar as they are not covered by these paragraphs.

Amend Article 228(2) of the TEC

2. Subject to the powers vested in the Commission in this field, the signing, which may be accompanied by a decision on provisional application before entry into force, and the conclusion of the agreements shall be decided on by the Council, acting by a qualified majority on a proposal from the Commission. The Council shall act unanimously when the agreement covers a field for which unanimity is required for the adoption of internal rules and for the agreements referred to in Article 238.

By way of derogation from the rules laid down in paragraph 3, the same procedure shall apply for a decision to suspend the application of an international agreement, and for the purpose of establishing the position to be adopted on behalf of the Community in a body set up by an agreement based on Article 238, when that body is called upon to adopt decisions having legal effects, with the exception of decisions supplementing or amending the institutional framework of the agreement.

The European Parliament shall be immediately and fully informed on any decision under this paragraph concerning the provisional application or the suspension of agreements, or the establishment of the Community position in a body set up by an agreement.

SECTION IV

THE UNION'S INSTITUTIONS

Protocol on the Institutions with the Prospect of Enlargement of the European Union

THE HIGH CONTRACTING PARTIES

HAVE AGREED upon the following provisions, which shall be annexed to the Treaty on European Union and to the Treaties establishing the European Communities:

Article 1

At the date of entry into force of the first enlargement of the Union, notwithstanding Article 157(1) of the TEC, the Commission shall comprise one national of each of the Member States, provided that, by that date, the weighting of the votes in the Council has been modified, whether by reweighting of the votes or by dual majority, in a manner acceptable to all Member States, taking into account all relevant elements, notably compensating those Member States which give up the possibility of nominating a second member of the Commission.

Article 2

At least one year before the membership of the European Union exceeds twenty, a conference of representatives of the governments of Member States shall be convened in order to carry out a comprehensive review of the provisions of the Treaties on the composition and functioning of the institutions.

CHAPTER 14

THE EUROPEAN PARLIAMENT

Legislative procedures

Assent procedure

The assent procedure will apply to the following provisions:

New Treaty provisions

Article Fa	Sanctions in the event of a serious and persistent breach of fundamental rights by a Member State

Existing Treaty provisions

Article O	Accession procedure

Article 130d | Structural and cohesion funds

Article 138(3) | Proposals by the European Parliament for a uniform electoral procedure.

Article 228(3), second subpara. | Conclusion of certain international agreements

Co-decision procedure

The co-decision procedure will apply to the following provisions.

New Treaty provisions

Article (5) | Employment – Incentive measures

Article 119 | Social policy – Equal opportunities and treatment

Article 129 | Public health (former basis Article 43 – consultation)
- minimum requirements regarding quality and safety of organs
- veterinary and phytosanitary measures with the direct objective the protection of public health

Article 191a | General principles for transparency

Article 209a | Countering fraud affecting the financial interests of the Community

New Article | Customs cooperation

Article 213a | Statistics

Article 213b | Establishment of independent advisory authority on data protection

Existing Treaty provisions[1]

Article 6 | Rules to prohibit discrimination on grounds of nationality (cooperation)

Article 8a(2)[2] | Provisions for facilitating the exercise of citizens' right to move and reside freely within the territory of the Member States (assent)

Article 51[(2)] Internal market (consultation)

– rules on social security for Community immigrant workers

Article 56[(2)] Coordination of provisions laid down by law, regulation or administrative action for special treatment for foreign nationals (right of establishment)

Article 57(2)[(2)] Coordination of the provisions laid down by law, regulation or administrative action in Member States concerning the taking up and pursuit of activities as self-employed persons (consultation)

Amendment of existing principles laid down by law governing the professions with respect to training and conditions of access for natural persons (consultation)

Article 75(1) Transport policy (cooperation)

– Common rules applicable to international transport to or from the territory of a Member State or passing across the territory of one or more Member States;

– the conditions under which non-resident carriers may operate transport services within a Member State;

– measures to improve transport safety.

Article 84 Transport policy (cooperation)

– sea and air transport

Social policy Articles resulting from the

	transposition into the Treaty of the agreement on social policy (Article 2(2)), except for aspects of that Agreement which are currently subject to unanimity (Article 2(3)) (see Chapter 4 – Social provisions)(cooperation)
Article 125	Implementing decisions relating to the European Social Fund (cooperation)
Article 127(4)	Vocational training (cooperation) – Measures to contribute to the achievement of the objectives of Article 127
Article 129d 3rd subpara.	Other measures (TENs) (cooperation)
Article 130e	ERDF implementing decisions (cooperation)
Article 130o	Adoption of measures referred in Articles 130k and l – 2nd subpara. research (cooperation)
Article 130s(1)	Environment (cooperation) – Action by the Community in order to achieve the objectives of Article 130r
Article 130w	Development cooperation (cooperation).

NB [1] The procedure currently applicable is indicated between brackets after the content of each Article

[2] The Council shall act unanimously.

Simplification of the co-decision procedure

Amend Article 189b of the TEC

1. Where reference is made in this Treaty to this Article for the adoption of an act, the following procedure shall apply.

2. The Commission shall submit a proposal to the European Parliament and the Council.

The Council, acting by a qualified majority after obtaining the opinion of the European Parliament,

- if it approves all the amendments contained in the European Parliament's opinion, may adopt the proposed act thus amended;
- if the European Parliament does not propose any amendments, may adopt the proposed act;
- shall otherwise adopt a common position and communicate it to the European Parliament. The Council shall inform the European Parliament fully of the reasons which led it to adopt its common position. The Commission shall inform the European Parliament fully of its position.

If, within three months of such communication, the European Parliament:

(a) approves the common position or has not taken a decision, the act in question shall be deemed to have been adopted in accordance with that common position;

(b) rejects, by an absolute majority of its component members, the common position, the proposed act shall be deemed not to have been adopted;

(c) proposes amendments to the common position by an absolute majority of its component members, the amended text shall be forwarded to the Council and to the Commission, which shall deliver an opinion on those amendments.

3. If, within three months of the matter being referred to it, the Council, acting by a qualified majority, approves all the amendments of the European Parliament, the act in question shall be deemed to have been adopted in the form of the common position thus amended; however, the Council shall act unanimously on the amendments on which the Commission has delivered a negative opinion. If the Council does not approve all the amendments, the President of the Council, in agreement with the President of the European Parliament, shall within six weeks convene a meeting of the Conciliation Committee.

4. The Conciliation Committee, which shall be composed of the members of the Council or their representatives and an equal number of representatives of the European Parliament, shall have the task of reaching agreement on a joint text, by a qualified majority of the members of the Council or their representatives and by a majority of the representatives of the European Parliament. The Commission shall take part in the Conciliation Committee's proceedings and shall take all the necessary initiatives with a view to reconciling the positions of the European Parliament and the Council. In fulfilling this task, the Conciliation Committee shall address the

common position on the basis of the amendments proposed by the European Parliament.

5. If, within six weeks of its being convened, the Conciliation Committee approves a joint text, the European Parliament, acting by an absolute majority of the votes cast, and the Council, acting by a qualified majority, shall each have a period of six weeks from that approval in which to adopt the act in question in accordance with the joint text. If either of the two institutions fails to approve the proposed act within that period, it shall be deemed not to have been adopted.

6. Where the Conciliation Committee does not approve a joint text, the proposed act shall be deemed not to have been adopted.

7. The periods of three months and six weeks referred to in this Article shall be extended by a maximum of one month and two weeks respectively at the initiative of the European Parliament or the Council.

Organization and composition of the European Parliament

Amend Article 137 of the TEC

The European Parliament, which shall consist of representatives of the peoples of the States brought together in the Community, shall exercise the powers conferred upon it by this Treaty.

The number of Members of the European Parliament shall not exceed seven hundred.

Add to Article 2 of the Act of 20 September 1976 (Article 138(2) of the TEC)

In the event of amendments to this paragraph, the number of representatives elected in each Member State must ensure appropriate representation of the peoples of the States brought together in the Community.

Amend the first subparagraph of Article 138(3) of the TEC

The European Parliament shall draw up a proposal for elections by direct universal suffrage in accordance with a uniform procedure in all Member States or in accordance with principles common to all Member States.

Add a new paragraph as Article 138(4) of the TEC (2)

The European Parliament shall, after seeking an opinion from the Commission and with the approval of the Council acting by unanimity, lay down the regulations and general conditions governing the performance of the duties of its Members.

NB A corresponding amendment will be made to the Act concerning the election of representatives of the European Parliament

CHAPTER 15

THE COUNCIL

Qualified majority voting

New Treaty provisions

Article 4, new Title on Employment	–	Employment guidelines
Article 5, new Title on Employment	–	Incentive measures
Article 118(2)	–	Social exclusion
Article 119(3)	–	Equality of opportunity and treatment of men and women
Article 129(4)	–	Public health
Article 191a	–	Transparency
Article 209a	–	Countering fraud
Article 213a	–	Statistics
Article 213b	–	Establishment of independent advisory authority on data protection
Article 227(2)	–	Outermost regions
New Article	–	Customs cooperation

Existing Treaty provisions

Article 45(3)	–	Compensatory aid for imports of raw materials
Article 56(2)	–	Coordination of provisions laid down by law, regulation or administrative action for special treatment for foreign nationals (right of establishment)
Article 130i(1)	–	Adoption of the research framework programme
Article 130i(2)	–	Adapting or supplementing the research framework programme
Article 130o	–	Setting up of joint undertakings in R&T development

Amend Article 151 of the TEC

1. A committee consisting of the Permanent Representatives of the Member States shall be responsible for preparing the work of the Council and for carrying out the tasks assigned to it by the Council. The Committee may adopt procedural decisions in cases provided for in the Council's Rules of Procedure.

2. The Council shall be assisted by a General Secretariat, under the responsibility of a Secretary-General seconded by a Deputy Secretary-General who shall be responsible for the running of the General Secretariat. The Secretary-General and the Deputy Secretary-General shall be appointed by the Council acting unanimously.

The Council shall decide on the organization of the General Secretariat.

3. The Council shall adopt its Rules of Procedure.

For the purpose of applying Article 191a(3), the Council shall elaborate in these Rules the conditions under which the public shall have access to Council documents. For the purpose of this paragraph, the Council shall define the cases in which it is to be regarded as acting in its legislative capacity, with a view to allowing greater access to documents in those cases, while at the same time preserving the effectiveness of its decision-making process. In any event, when the Council acts in its legislative capacity, the results of votes and explanations of vote as well as statements in the minutes shall be made public.

CHAPTER 16

THE COMMISSION

Appointment of the Members of the Commission

Amend the first and second subparagraphs of Article 158(2) of the TEC

The governments of the Member States shall nominate by common accord the person they intend to appoint as President of the Commission; the nomination shall be approved by the European Parliament.

The governments of the Member States shall, by common accord with the nominee for President, nominate the other persons whom they intend to appoint as Members of the Commission.

Composition and organization of the Commission

New first subparagraph in Article 163 of the TEC

The Commission shall work under the political guidance of its President.

CHAPTER 17

THE COURT OF JUSTICE

Amend Article L of the TEU

The provisions of the Treaty establishing the European Community, the Treaty establishing the European Coal and Steel Community and the Treaty establishing the European Atomic Energy Community concerning the powers of the Court of Justice of the European Communities and the exercise of those powers shall apply only to the following provisions of this Treaty:

(a) [unchanged];

(b) provisions of Title VI, under the conditions provided for by Articles K7 and K12;

(c) Article F(2) with regard to action of the institutions, insofar as the Court has jurisdiction under the Treaties establishing the European Communities and under this Treaty;

(d) Articles L to S.

CHAPTER 18

OTHER INSTITUTIONAL ISSUES

(a) Court of Auditors

Amend Article E of the TEU

The European Parliament, the Council, the Commission, the Court of Justice and the Court of Auditors shall exercise their powers under the conditions and for the purposes provided for ... (rest unchanged).

Amend the third subparagraph of Article 173 of the TEC

The Court shall have jurisdiction under the same conditions in actions brought by the European Parliament, by the Court of Auditors and by the ECB for the purpose of protecting their prerogatives.

Amend the second subparagraph of Article 188c(1) of the TEC

The Court of Auditors shall provide the European Parliament and the Council with a statement of assurance as to the reliability of the accounts and the legality and regularity of the underlying transactions which shall be published in the Official Journal of the European Communities.

Amend the first subparagraph of Article 188c(2) of the TEC

The Court of Auditors shall examine whether all revenue has been received and all expenditure incurred in a lawful and regular manner and whether the financial management has been sound. In doing so, it shall report in particular on any cases of irregularity.

Amend Article 188c(3) of the TEC

The audit shall be based on records and, if necessary, performed on the spot in the other institutions of the Community, on the premises of any body which manages revenue or expenditure on behalf of the Community and in the Member States, including on the premises of any natural or legal person in receipt of payments from the budget. In the Member States the audit shall be carried out in liaison with national audit bodies or, if these do not have the necessary powers, with the competent national departments. The Court of Auditors and the national audit bodies of the Member States shall cooperate in a spirit of trust while maintaining their independence. These bodies or departments shall inform the Court of Auditors whether they intend to take part in the audit.

The other institutions of the Community, any bodies managing revenue or expenditure on behalf of the Community, any natural or legal person in receipt of payments from the budget, and the national audit bodies or, if these do not have the necessary powers, the competent national departments, shall forward to the Court of Auditors, at its request, any document or information necessary to carry out its task.

In respect of the European Investment Bank's activity in managing Community expenditure and revenue, the Court's rights of access to information held by the Bank shall be governed by an agreement between the Court, the Bank and the Commission. In the absence of an agreement, the Court shall nevertheless have access to information necessary for the audit of Community expenditure and revenue managed by the Bank.

Amend Article 206(1) of the TEC

The European Parliament, acting on a recommendation from the Council which shall act by a qualified majority, shall give a discharge to the Commission in respect of the implementation of the budget. To this end, the Council and the European Parliament in turn shall examine the accounts and the financial statement referred to in Article 205a, the annual report by the Court of Auditors together with the replies of the institutions under audit to the observations of the Court of Auditors, the statement of assurance referred to in Article 188c(1), second subparagraph and any relevant special reports by the Court of Auditors.

(b) Economic and Social Committee

The Economic and Social Committee will be consulted in the following new provisions to be included in the TEC.

Employment

Article 4	Guidelines
Article 5	Incentive measures

Social matters

Article 118(2) and (3)   Legislation on social matters

Article 119(3)   Application of the principle of equal opportunities and equal treatment

Public Health

Article 129(4)   Measures to contribute to the achievement of the objectives of this Article

Add a new fourth subparagraph to Article 198 of the TEC

The Economic and Social Committee may be consulted by the European Parliament.

(c) Committee of the Regions

Protocol No. 16 shall be repealed.

Amend the third subparagraph of Article 198a of the TEC

The members of the Committee and an equal number of alternative members shall be appointed for four years by the Council acting unanimously on proposals from the respective Member States. Their term of office shall be renewable. No member of the Committee shall at the same time be a Member of the European Parliament.

NB Article 6 of the Act of 20 September 1976 will be amended accordingly

Amend the second paragraph of Article 198b of the TEC

It shall adopt its Rules of Procedure.

Amend the first subparagraph of Article 198c of the TEC

The Committee of the Regions shall be consulted by the Council or by the Commission where this Treaty so provides and in all other cases, in particular those which concern cross-border cooperation, in which one of these two institutions considers it appropriate.

Add a new fourth subparagraph to Article 198c of the TEC

The Committee of the Regions may be consulted by the European Parliament.

Scope of consultation

The Committee of the Regions will be consulted under the following provisions in the TEC.

Employment

Article 4	Guidelines
Article 5	Incentive measures

Social matters

Article 118(2) and (3)	Legislation on social matters

Public health

Article 129(4)	Measures to contribute to the achievement of the objectives of this Article

Environment

Article 130s(1)(2)(3)	Environment

Social fund

Article 125	Implementing decisions

Vocational training

Article 127(4)	Measures to contribute to the achievement of the objectives of this Article

Transport

Article 75	Transport

(d) Financial provisions

Amend the first subparagraph of Article 205 of the TEC

The Commission shall implement the budget, in accordance with the provisions of the regulations made pursuant to Article 209, on its own responsibility and within the limits of the appropriations, having regard to the principles of sound financial management. Member States shall cooperate with the Commission to ensure that the budget appropriations are used in accordance with the principles of sound financial management.

(f) Seats

Protocol on the location of the seats of the institutions and of certain bodies and departments of the European Community

THE REPRESENTATIVES OF THE GOVERNMENTS
OF THE MEMBER STATES,

Having regard to Article 216 of the Treaty establishing the European Community, Article 77 of the Treaty establishing the European Coal and Steel Community and Article 189 of the Treaty establishing the European Atomic Energy Community,

Having regard to the Treaty on European Union,

Recalling and confirming the Decision of 8 April 1965, and without prejudice to the decisions concerning the seat of future institutions, bodies and departments,

Have agreed upon the following provisions, which shall be annexed to the Treaty of Amsterdam,

Sole Article

(a) The European Parliament shall have its seat in Strasbourg where the 12 periods of plenary sessions, including the budget session, shall be held.

The periods of additional plenary sessions shall be held in Brussels. The committees of the European Parliament shall meet in Brussels. The General

Secretariat of the European Parliament and its departments shall remain in Luxembourg.

(b) The Council shall have its seat in Brussels. During the months of April, June and October, the Council shall hold its meetings in Luxembourg.

(c) The Commission shall have its seat in Brussels. The departments listed in Articles 7, 8 and 9 of the Decision of 8 April 1965 shall be established in Luxembourg.

(d) The Court of Justice and the Court of First Instance shall have their seats in Luxembourg.

(e) The Court of Auditors shall have its seat in Luxembourg.

(f) The Economic and Social Committee shall have its seat in Brussels.

(g) The Committee of the Regions shall have its seat in Brussels.

(h) The European Investment Bank shall have its seat in Luxembourg.

(i) The European Monetary Institute and the European Central Bank shall have their seat in Frankfurt.

(j) The European Police Office (Europol) shall have its seat in The Hague.

CHAPTER 19

ROLE OF NATIONAL PARLIAMENTS

Draft Protocol on the Role of National Parliaments in the European Union

THE HIGH CONTRACTING PARTIES

RECALLING that scrutiny by individual national parliaments of their own government in relation to the activities of the Union is a matter for the particular constitutional organization and practice of each Member State

DESIRING, however, to encourage greater involvement of national parliaments in the activities of the European Union and to enhance their ability to express their views on matters which may be of particular interest to them

HAVE AGREED upon the following provisions, which shall be annexed to the Treaty on European Union:

I. Information for national Parliaments of Member States

1. All Commission consultation documents (green and white papers and communications) shall be promptly forwarded to national parliaments of the Member States.

2. Commission proposals for legislation as defined by the Council in accordance with Article 151 of the Treaty establishing the European Community, shall be made available in good time so that the Government of each Member State may ensure that its own national parliament receives them as appropriate.

3. A six-week period shall elapse between a legislative proposal or a proposal for a measure to be adopted under Title VI of the Treaty on European Union being made available in all languages to the European Parliament and the Council by the Commission and the date when it is placed on a Council agenda for decision either for the adoption of an act or for adoption of a common position pursuant to article 189b or 189c, subject to exceptions on grounds of urgency, the reasons for which shall be stated in the act or common position.

II. The Conference of European Affairs Committees

4. The Conference of European Affairs Committees, hereinafter referred to as COSAC, established in Paris on 16–17 November 1989, may make any contribution it deems appropriate for the attention of the EU institutions, in particular on the basis of draft legal texts which Representatives of Governments of the Member States may decide by common accord to forward to it, in view of the nature of its subject matter.

5. COSAC may examine any legislative proposal or initiative in relation to the establishment of an area of freedom, security and justice which might have a direct bearing on the rights and freedoms of individuals. The European Parliament, the Council and the Commission shall be informed of any contribution made by COSAC under this paragraph.

6. COSAC may address to the European Parliament, the Council and the Commission any contribution which it deems appropriate on the legislative activities of the Union, notably in relation to the application of the principle of subsidiarity, the area of freedom, security and justice as well as questions regarding fundamental rights.

7. Contributions made by COSAC shall in no way bind national parliaments or prejudge their position.

SECTION V

CLOSER COOPERATION – "FLEXIBILITY"

A. GENERAL CLAUSES TO BE INSERTED AS A NEW TITLE IN THE COMMON PROVISIONS OF THE TEU

Article (1)

1. Member States which intend to establish closer cooperation between them may make use of the institutions, procedures and mechanisms laid down by the Treaties provided that the cooperation:

(a) is aimed at furthering the objectives of the Union and at protecting and serving its interests;

(b) respects the principles of the Treaties and the single institutional framework of the Union;

(c) is only used as a last resort, where the objectives of the Treaties could not be attained by applying the relevant procedures laid down therein;

(d) concerns at least a majority of Member States;

(e) does not affect the "acquis communautaire" and the measures adopted under the other provisions of the Treaties;

(f) does not affect the competences, rights, obligations and interests of those Member States which do not participate therein;

(g) is open to all Member States and allows them to become parties to the cooperation at any time, provided that they comply with the basic decision and with the decisions taken within that framework;

(h) complies with the specific additional criteria laid down in Article 5a of the TEC and Article K12 of this Treaty, depending on the area concerned and is authorized by the Council in accordance with the procedures laid down therein.

2. Member States shall apply, as far as they are concerned, the acts and decisions adopted for the implementation of the cooperation in which they participate. Member States not participating in such cooperation shall not impede the implementation thereof by the participating Member States.

Article (2)

1. For the purposes of the adoption of the acts and decisions necessary for the implementation of the cooperation referred to in Article (1), the relevant institutional provisions of the Treaties shall apply. However, while all

members of the Council shall be able to take part in the deliberations, only those representing participating Member States shall take part in the adoption of decisions; the qualified majority shall be defined as the same proportion of votes of the Council members concerned weighted in accordance with Article 148(2) of the Treaty establishing the European Community; unanimity shall be constituted by only those Council members concerned.

2. Expenditure resulting from implementation of the cooperation, other than administrative costs entailed for the institutions, shall be borne by the participating Member States, unless the Council, acting unanimously, decides otherwise.

Article (3)

The Council and the Commission shall regularly inform the European Parliament of the development of closer cooperation established on the basis of this Title.

B. CLAUSES SPECIFIC TO THE TEC

Article 5a TEC

1. Member States which intend to establish closer cooperation between themselves may be authorized, subject to Articles (1) and (2) of the TEU, to make use of the institutions, procedures and mechanisms laid down by this Treaty, provided that the cooperation proposed:

(a) does not concern areas which fall within the exclusive competence of the Community;

(b) does not affect Community policies, actions or programmes;

(c) does not concern the citizenship of the Union or discriminate between nationals of Member States;

(d) remains within the limits of the powers conferred upon the Community by this Treaty;

(e) and does not constitute a discrimination or a restriction of trade between Member States and does not distort the conditions of competition between the latter.

2. The authorization referred to in paragraph 1 shall be granted by the Council, acting by a qualified majority on a proposal from the Commission and after consulting the European Parliament.

If a member of the Council declares that, for important and stated reasons of national policy, it intends to oppose the granting of an authorization by qualified majority, a vote shall not be taken. The Council may, acting by a qualified majority, request that the matter be referred to the European Council for decision by unanimity.

Member States which intend to establish closer cooperation as referred to in paragraph 1 may address a request to the Commission, which may submit a proposal to the Council to that effect. In the event of the Commission not submitting a proposal, it shall inform the Member States concerned of the reasons for not doing so.

3. Any Member State which wishes to become a party to cooperation set up in accordance with this Article shall notify its intention to the Council and to the Commission, which shall give an opinion to the Council within three months of receipt of that notification. Within four months of the date of that notification, the Commission shall decide on it and on possible specific arrangements as it may deem necessary.

4. The acts and decisions necessary for the implementation of cooperation activities shall be subject to all the relevant provisions of this Treaty, save as otherwise provided for in this Article and in Articles (1) and (2) (1) of the Treaty on European Union.

5. This Article is without prejudice to the provisions of the Protocol integrating the Schengen acquis in the framework of the European Union.

C. SPECIFIC CLAUSES IN TITLE VI TEU (JHA)

See Article K12 in Chapter 2

SECTION VI

SIMPLIFICATION AND CONSOLIDATION OF THE TREATIES

Simplification

Proposed amendments for simplifying the Treaties (cf. CONF/4156/1/97 REV.1) shall form the second Part of the Treaty of Amsterdam.

Consolidation

Declaration to the Final Act

The High Contracting Parties agreed that the technical work begun during the course of this Intergovernmental Conference shall continue as speedily as possible with the aim to draft a consolidation of all the relevant Treaties, including the Treaty on European Union.

They agreed that the final results of this technical work, which shall be made public for illustrative purposes under the responsibility of the Secretary-General of the Council, shall have no legal value.

INDEX

AdvocatesAdvocates-General, 122, 160

Coal and Steel Community,
   commercial policy, 16
   competition, freedom of, 10, 15
   concentration of undertakings, 12
   institutions, 4
   pricing practices, 7 et seq
   task, 2, 3
   Treaty, 1 et seq
      period of, 17
Commission, 118 et seq, 211 et seq, 244, 446
   members, 119–121, 440
   President, 120
   procedures of, 231 et seq
Council. *See* European Council
Council of Europe,
   cooperation with, 156
Court of Auditors, 129 et seq, 441, 446
   members, 130–131
   task, 129, 131–132
Court of First Instance, 123–124, 170 et seq, 236 et seq, 446
   appeal from, 123, 172–173
   jurisdiction, 123, 238, 389, 440, 441
   members, 123, 237
   procedure, 170
Court of Justice, 112 et seq, 160 et seq, 244, 255, 446
   judgment, revision of, 169
   jurisdiction, 122, 255, 389, 440, 441
   members, 122–123, 161
   organisation, 162–164
   penalties, 334–337
   procedure, 164 et seq

European Community,
   activities, 20, 21
   agriculture, 39 et seq
      common policy, 40 et seq, 344
      Guidance and Guarantee Fund, 101, 102

European Community (*contd.*)
   aids, grant of, 62
   borders,
      common, 393
      external, 378
   budget, 142 et seq
   capital, free movement of, 46 et seq, 53 et seq
   Central Bank, 22, 78, 174 et seq
   Central Banks, System of, 22, 174 et seq
   citizenship of Union, 25 et seq, 411
   competition, rules on, 58 et seq
   Conciliation Committee, 134
   convergence criteria, 199–200
   cooperation, 449
   customs,
      cooperation, 412
      duties, 28 et seq, 343
      tariff, 31 et seq
   discrimination, 23, 376
   dumping, 62
   Economic and Social Committee, 137 et seq, 442, 446
   equality, 376, 405
   establishment, right of, 47 et seq
   excessive deficit procedure, 198 et seq
   finance, 142 et seq
   goods, free movement of, 27 et seq
   imports, quantitative restrictions on, 35 et seq
   institutions, 22, 112 et seq, 431 et seq. *See also* Commission; Court of Auditors; Court of First Instance; Court of Justice; European Council; European Parliament
      common provisions, 132 et seq
   offences, 346–347
   seat of, 150, 445–446
   setting up, 158–159
   internal market, 24
   Investment Bank, 22, 101, 141, 446
   liability of, 150

Index

European Community (contd.)
  laws, approximation of,   66 et seq
  Monetary Institute,   82, 446
  own resources,   322 et seq
  networks, trans-European,
    98–100, 415
  Ombudsman,   114, 313 et seq
  overseas countries, association with,
    109 et seq
  payments, restrictions on,   53
  persons, free movement of,   46 et
    seq, 377
  policies,   27 et seq
    agricultural,   40 et seq
    animal welfare,   414
    broadcasting,   414
    commercial,   90 et seq
    consumer protection,   98, 410
    culture,   96–97, 411
    development cooperation,
      108–109, 399
    economic,   69 et seq, 100, 137,
      200, 208, 413, 431
    education,   95
    employment,   399–401
    environment,   105, 399, 406–408
    fraud,   149, 411
    industry,   100
    monetary,   74 et seq, 200
    personal data,   376
    public health,   97–98, 409–410
    social,   91 et seq, 100, 137, 203,
      208, 362, 402–406
    statistics,   415
    vocational training,   95–96
    youth,   95
  proportionality,   415–418
  Regional Development Fund,   101
  Regions, Committee of,   139 et seq,
    362, 443–445, 446
  research and development,   102 et
    seq, 108
  services, free movement of,   46 et
    seq, 51 et seq
  Social Fund,   94, 101, 102, 142
  subsidiarity,   415–418
  task,   20
  taxation,   64 et seq
  transport,   55 et seq, 98
  Treaty,   19 et seq
    amendments,   375 et seq
    exclusions from,   154
    implementation,   340

European Community, Treaty (contd.)
  interpretation of,   127, 341
  United Kingdom, application to,
    201, 204, 382 et seq
European Council,   116–118, 211 et
  seq, 243, 244, 438, 446
  name,   312
  presidency, order of,   116, 332–333
  qualified majority of,   321, 438
European Economic Area,
  agreement on,   264 et seq, 366–369
  agricultural and fishery products,
    270–271
  capital, free movement of,   273,
    277–279
  competition,   281–285
  consumer protection,   289
  cooperation,   271–272, 279, 290 et
    seq, 297, 308
  Council,   295
  disputes, settlement of,   304–305
  environment,   289
  establishment, right of,   275–276
  financial mechanism,   307
  goods, free movement of,   268–270,
    272–273
  homogeneity,   301
  Joint Committee,   296
  Joint Parliamentary Committee,
    297
  objectives and principles,   266–268
  persons, free movement of,   273–274
  procedure, decisionmaking,   298
  surveillance,   303–304
  safeguard measures,   305–307
  services, free movement of,   273,
    276–277
  social policy,   287–289
  state aid,   285–287
  transport,   279–281
European Parliament,   112 et seq,
  244, 359–360, 391, 432, 445
  election of,   225 et seq, 351 et seq,
    363–365
  members,   216–217, 437
    disqualification,   357
    duties,   438
European Union,
  asylum,   262, 377, 397
  citizenship of,   25 et seq, 411
  community law, implementation of,
    258
  Coordinating Committee,   390

European Union (*contd.*)
    enlargement,   431 et seq
    environment,   406–408
    'flexibility',   448
    foreign and security policy,   245 et seq, 258, 419 et seq
    justice and home affairs,   251–254, 386
    member state,
        breach of principles by,   374
        nationality of,   257
    membership,   256, 375
    national parliaments, role of,   257, 446–447
    objectives,   242–243, 373, 399
    police cooperation,   262–263, 386
    Schengen acquis,   393 et seq
    transparency,   419
    Treaty,   241 et seq
        amendments,   373 et seq
        approval,   361
        common provisions,   242

Fundamental rights. *See also* European Community
    joint declaration of,   230

Luxembourg Accords,   222 et seq

Ombudsman,
    appointment,   114, 318

Ombudsman (*contd.*)
    dismissal,   319
    duties,   313 et seq

Organisation for Economic Cooperation and Development,
    cooperation with,   156

Own resources,
    system of,   322 et seq

Treaty. *See also* Coal and Steel Community; European Community; European Union
    Amsterdam (draft),   373 et seq
    European Atomic Energy Community, 157
    European Coal and Steel Community, 1 et seq, 156
    European Community,   19 et seq
        amendments,   375 et seq
    European Union,   241 et seq
        amendments,   373 et seq
    simplification,   450
    Single Council and Single Commission,   211 et seq

United Nations,
    relations with,   156

Western European Union,
    declarations on,   258–262